THE SOCIAL TEACHINGS OF WILHELM EMMANUEL VON KETTELER

Bishop of Mainz (1811-1877)

Translation by
Rupert J. Ederer

UNIVERSITY
PRESS OF
AMERICA

Preface

This book presents the first complete translation from the original German into English of the
major social teachings of Bishop Wilhelm Emmanuel
von Ketteler (1811-1877).[1] It includes all of the
Bishop's social teachings except those which were
addressed to the specific German historic context
of his own time.[2]

A reader may legitimately ask why anyone would
undertake, near the close of the twentieth century,
to present in translation the works of a Catholic
German bishop a century after his death. The principal reason was a feeling that the issues to which
Bishop von Ketteler addressed himself are still un-
resolved in the present era. In fact, some of them
appear to have reached their culmination as the tu-
multous twentieth century draws toward its close.
More specifically, Bishop von Ketteler's teachings
are no less relevant for our times than are those
of his contemporary, Karl Marx. In the last analysis, the Bishop of Mainz addressed himself to
the same problems stemming from liberal capitalism
which offered to Marx the pretext for developing
his pretentious solution. The Roman Catholic
bishop, of course, rejected that solution and offered an ancient but radically different one.

A more personal reason for completing this
translation involves the perception of a need to
make known the solid legacy of the German contribution to Christian social thought, especially
since the whole fabric of German ethnicity was
soiled by the dark night of 1933-1945. The concentration camps and prisons during that period
were populated also by the kinds of people whose
loyalty to the authentic Christian tradition
brought them into conflict with the post-Christian
Nazi leadership. Included among them were the
pre-war Austrian Chancellor Kurt Schuschnigg, who
was also my former professor, and the great post-
war German Chancellor Konrad Adenauer. Both of
these were exemplary Christians who adhered stead-

iii

fastly to the heritage of Catholic Christian social
thought pioneered by Bishop von Ketteler.

Finally, the important English-speaking world
of scholars and readers ought not to be denied
access, because of the language barrier, to works
that have had a decisive formative influence in
developing the social ethical doctrine of the
largest and oldest Christian Church. The influential Pope Leo XIII openly acknowledged his
dependence on Bishop von Ketteler's seminal Catholic social teachings. Anyone who has studied the
social encyclicals by that pope, including the
best known one, On the Condition of Labor (Rerum
Novarum), written in 1891, will immediately recognize that dependency after a careful examination
of the von Ketteler works.

I wish to acknowledge the help and cooperation
of Mr. Harvey J. Johnson of St. Louis, Missouri.
As editor of the Social Justice Review, he first
edited several of these translations for publication
in that monthly periodical in the period between
1974 and 1977. Thanks are owed to him for his
continuing encouragement as well as for his editorial effort and for permission to use translated
portions which appeared in Social Justice Review.
I am also especially grateful to Sister M. Francesca
Schlang, O.S.F., Professor Emeritus of German at
Daemen College in Buffalo, New York. She offered
valuable advice and editorial assistance especially
in the early stages of the translation process.
Thanks are also due to Dr. Franz H. Mueller, Professor Emeritus of Economics at St. Thomas College in
St. Paul, Minnesota, for valuable suggestions based
on his expertise in the area of German Catholic
social thought. I am deeply indebted to Mrs.Gisela
Ederer whose patient and valuable services as a
skilled typist finally put these translations into
publishable form. Finally, I must express my gratitude to the faculty and administration of the
State University of New York College at Buffalo
who, among other things, granted me sabbatical
leave without which the entire project could not
have been accomplished.

Biographical Introduction [1]

Bishop Wilhelm Emmanuel von Ketteler (1811-1877) was the sixth of nine children born to the family of Baron Maximilian and Baroness Clementine von Kettler. The middle name, Emmanuel, commemorates the fact that he was born on Christmas Day in 1811. The place of birth was in Germany at the baronial estate, Harkotten, located in Münster, Westphalia.

Wilhelm's early schooling was tutorial, as was customary among families of the lower aristocracy. At age thirteen he was sent to Switzerland where the Jesuits operated a secondary school at Brig. He completed his preparatory schooling there and went off to Göttingen University which was to be the first of several universities that he would attend. German universities during this period were not hotbeds of religious piety. Prevailing intellectual currents reflected the French Enlightenment and German influences like Hegel, Kant, and Feuerbach. This provided a harsh contrast to the solidly Catholic atmosphere that Wilhelm enjoyed at home and at the secondary school run by Jesuits. That earlier formation saw him safely through the secularist climate of the university. The young von Ketteler himself admitted that although he had done nothing he really had to be ashamed of, he was still a fairly typical university student. It is not surprising, however, that the first serious test of family solidarity came while the young man was immersed in this university ambience.

It seems that young Wilhelm got himself involved in that not uncommon occurrence among German university students, a fencing duel. It cost him the tip of his nose as well as a two week sentence in the student prison, which he was to serve after the rather severe wound was properly healed. Healing was to be a long painful process, one which was not hastened by the spirited young man's impatience. He ripped the noisome bandage off and set the cure back several weeks, requiring medical attention

which could best be secured in Berlin. The whole
affair caused a temporary breach in what were
normally excellent relations between father and
son - a rupture smoothed over by his kind and concerned mother. It was agreed that Wilhelm would
attend a different university; and he continued
his studies at Berlin where, as he wrote to one of
his sisters, he became completely disgusted with
the immoral conditions which prevailed. He ar-
ranged to transfer to Heidelberg, only to find that
university authorities there expected him to serve
the two week sentence imposed at Göttingen. Rather
than subject himself to that indignity, he decided
on Munich. where he completed his legal studies.
He passed the German equivalent of the bar examination in Münster in 1833.

Upon graduation, Wilhelm von Ketteler took a
position with the Prussian government in Münster
where his new legal skills were put to the test.
His superiors reported that he performed most satis-
factorily. After just one year he served his required year of military service with the 11th Hussar
Regiment. Once again, his superiors gave him good
marks; in fact they urged him to follow a military
career as they saw in him what they perceived to
be good officer material. This was not his calling,
however, and he confided to one of his brothers that
peacetime military service in particular did not
appeal to him. After his year of service he returned to his former civilian government post as a
jurist. There he had the opportunity to learn first-
hand of the tenuous Church-State relations between
the Prussian government and the Catholic Church.
Things were not good, and they were to become worse
still. Already unhappy with a profession which in
his words, "....involved too much paper and too
little heart," von Ketteler resigned in protest when
the Prussian government arrested the Archbishop of
Cologne for insisting in the primacy of canon law
over state law in ecclesiastical matters. He remarked that his stomach could not stand the anti-
Catholic pettifogging in which the government was
habitually engaging. His departure from the civil
service led to a brief period of uncertainty. That
was in 1837 when the man was just 26 years old.

The idea of religious life had occurred to
young von Ketteler at various times, but he waved
this aside with a modest suggestion that for him
to become a priest would require a major miracle
equivalent in magnitude to raising the dead to
life. He decided to return to Munich, where the
intellectual climate had been to his liking and
he also found the religious atmosphere more compatible than at the northern universities. After
a year of study and some travel, von Ketteler still
had not found himself, and he decided to return
home. Enroute to Münster he resolved to stop at
the great Marian shrine at Altötting in Bavaria.
Devotion to the Mother of God had been implanted
in his heart by his own pious mother whom he
revered highly. The religious pilgrimage seems
to have been a turning point in the young man's
life. Soon afterwards he became convinced that
for him there was only one Master worth serving.
Talks with his bishop in Münster led to theological
studies which began in Munich and were completed
in Münster. Wilhelm von Ketteler was ordained a
priest on June 1, 1844. If being born on Christmas
Day was in any way auspicious, being ordained a
priest at thirty-three, the age at which the Master
he had chosen to serve died, may be seen as a second
remarkable coincidence in von Ketteler's life.

His priestly service began with routine assign-
ments in the small Westphalian towns of Beckum and
Hopsten, where the young man promptly won the hearts
of his parishioners. In fact, against his wishes,
enthusiastic supporters nominated him to run against
a Protestant candidate for service in the upcoming
Frankfurt Assembly of 1848. The Assembly was supposed to draft a constitution which would guarantee
basic liberties to citizens in the prevailing monarchical framework. 1848 was a stormy year overall.
It was marked by revolutions that had as their aim
to complete what the French Revolution had not succeeded in doing: overthrowing the remaining
monarchies. Since the rights of the Catholic Church
were under continuous attack at the hands of the
Prussian monarcy, Father von Ketteler served his
term in the Assembly, though he was not given the

opportunity to address it even once. However his
strong voice was fated to be heard not only in
Frankfurt, but throughout Germany and beyond. On
September 18, 1848, two members of the Assembly
were assassinated by rival political elements, and
Father von Ketteler was invited to preach the
funeral oration at the grave site. He spoke, and
all were profoundly impressed as he denounced the
barbarism whereby men would kill one another in the
name of liberty and human rights. For the young
priest life would never be the same. Church authorities, among others, noted that this was no ordinary
man, and he was shortly afterwards appointed administrator of St. Hedwig's Church in Berlin. That was
Berlin's only Catholic parish at the time, and it
embraced some 20,000 souls. In the face of the
Prussian capital city's religious climate which was
quite hostile to Catholicism, Father von Ketteler
nevertheless held the first public Corpus Christi
procession through Berlin's streets. It was an
action that greatly worried the public authorities.
During his brief tenure there he also began construction of a large Catholic hospital in the
parish. The Prussian King, Frederick William IV
recognized von Ketteler's popularity among the
Catholics of Berlin by conferring the Order of the
Red Eagle on him. Given the generally hostile
posture of the Prussian government toward Catholicism, the young priest was less than enthusiastic
about the award.

     More importantly, Father von Ketteler's grave-
side oratory won for him an invitation to preach
six sermons in the city of Mainz marking the li-
turgical season of Advent. These were subsequently
published and are since known as: The Great Social
Issues of The Present. They marked the beginning
of the man's social teaching which was to continue
through his lifetime and establish the ground work
for modern Catholic social doctrine. Piux IX confirmed the appointment of Wilhelm von Ketteler as
Bishop of Mainz. The actual consecration took place
on July 25, 1859 in that city's great ancient
cathedral.

The City of Mainz is one of Germany's charming smaller cities. It lies at the confluence of the Main River into the Rhine, on the West bank of the Rhine and west of Frankfurt. The Catholic Church was not in an altogether healthy condition there, and the effects of secularist French influence were in evidence everywhere, particularly in the schools. Shedding the simple religious beliefs of childhood was one of the badges of having achieved the status of a truly educated man. The new bishop set about to put the house in order by first setting the goal of spiritual perfection for himself. He adopted an austere life-style, rising each morning at four, celebrating his Mass at five, eating simple food and living in three simple rooms. One room was to entertain guests, another was his study, and the third was his bedroom. His daily routine included frequent visits to the Blessed Sacrament, reading from Scripture, and praying the Rosary. He often knelt among his people in the Cathedral when he was not himself presiding at religious devotions. He did battle with a naturally fiery temperament and subdued it to become a model of moderation and gentleness. The old fire was reserved for those who attacked the Faith. Among other things, his gentleness earned for him the title, **Kinderfreund** (Friend of Children); and he was seen at his happiest among the orphans in his diocese. Having fortified his own spiritual life, Bishop von Ketteler set about rekindling the spiritual fervor of his diocese.

Methodically he began by restoring the seminary where future priests were trained. It was in sad shape due to the secularist influence brought along with French occupation, and later to Prussian state interference in the life of the Church. Theology students of his diocese were required to study at Giessen under secular professors and in a generally hostile atmosphere. Over the protests of the Hessian government, Bishop von Ketteler brought the seminary back to Mainz, installed his own trusted professors, and he himself always stayed close to the staff and to the seminarians. The Hessian government, of course, denied him any financial support in this venture. Restoration of the major seminary was followed later by establishment of a minor seminary, also in the face of great opposition and difficulty.

It was at this seminary that the Bishop established the custom of serving on tables for his future "apostles" on Holy Thursday.

Having put the first building blocks into place, the Bishop turned his attention to restoring the rest of the educational structure which he considered so important for his diocese. It was a time when so-called "confessional schools" were under fire; and religious instruction, as such, was being challenged outright. Bishop von Ketteler himself prepared a uniform syllabus for use in religious education throughout his diocese, and he started a teachers' training institute for Catholic teachers. Gradually, the so-called confessional schools crowded out the public schools which the state financed. To help in this difficult educational venture, Bishop von Ketteler founded an order of sisters known as the Congregation of the Sisters of Divine Providence in 1851. This Congregation of sisters later spread beyond the borders of Germany and they operate schools and hospitals also in the United States.

Bishop von Ketteler was not content to simply preach social reform. He established two orphanages in his diocese, one for boys, another for girls. The Sisters of Divine Providence added staffing the girls' orphanage to their other activities; and the bishop also founded an order of brothers to operate the St. Joseph's Home for Boys in nearby Kleinzimmern. These men also trained the boys under their care in useful trades like carpentry and tailoring. Beyond that the Bishop founded the Institute of the Good Shepherd to care for young girls who had gotten into difficulty. There was also an Institute for the Support of Ex-Convicts for men who had a hard time getting themselves readmitted to society after serving prison terms. Bishop von Ketteler invited the Poor Clare Sisters from Aachen to visit and care for the poor sick in their own homes; and the Sisters of Mercy were brought in from Strassburg to staff the St. Vincent's Hospital in Mainz.

x

It was Bishop von Ketteler who had encouraged a fellow student while in Munich to carry through that man's plan for a society which would provide a home away from home for journeymen tradesmen. He was Father Adolph Kolping, and his enterprise was to spread throughout Germany and to many other countries including the United States. Eventually, there was also a home for working single women, where they would also be provided for in sickness and old age.

It was, of course, Bishop Wilhelm Emmanuel von Ketteler's remarkable endeavor in the area of social teaching that gained for him his great reputation as the pioneer of what has come to be called modern Catholic social teaching. His pioneering efforts are evident in the social encyclicals of Pope Leo XIII who is widely known especially for the encyclical, On the Condition of Labor (Rerum Novarum) published in 1891. However, the von Ketteler influence is clear in several other important social encyclicals including: On Socialism (1878), On Christian Marriage (1880), On Civil Government (1881), On the Christian Constitution of States (1885) and, On Human Liberty (1888). Anyone who has studied these documents alongside Bishop von Ketteler's social teachings can understand why the learned Pope referred to the Bishop as his "great predecessor," and remarked that, "It is from him that I have learned." 2

Bishop von Ketteler was the contemporary of Karl Marx (1818-1883), and of Ferdinand Lassalle (1825-64) and Friedrich Engels (1820-95). He was not to be outdone by these socialist agitators in pointing out the fallacies and injustices resulting from laissez faire capitalism, and in decrying the pathetic condition to which this economic philosophy had reduced the working classes of Europe. His presence and work could serve to refute the accusation sometimes made against his Church that it was very late in recognizing and speaking out about the abuses of 19th century capitalism. Bishop von Ketteler, at least, was there from the beginning. His cycle of six sermons

in Mainz on the pressing social issues of the day
were delivered in the same year (1848) that Marx
and Engels first published their Communist Manifesto.
Marx was apparently uncomfortable about what the
Bishop was doing. In a letter written to his companion,
Friedrich Engels, in September 1869 he wrote: "The
dogs (clergy) are toying with the labor problem as,
for example, the priests (Pfaffen) of the Düsseldorf
Congress and Bishop Ketteler in Mainz." 3 The Bishop
did not spare the socialists any more than the
capitalists. He referred to the socialist program
as a cure that was worse than the disease it was supposed to remedy.

Bishop von Ketteler's work and reputation brought
him not only honors, but also trials and enmity. He
clashed repeatedly with the hostile Prussian government and even personally with Bismarck. Consequently,
the government prevented his being appointed successor
to the Cardinal Archbishop of Cologne in 1864. This
did not stop him from writing to Emperor Franz Josef
of Austria after the unfortunate War of 1866 between
Austria and Prussia. He expressed his misgivings
about what Prussian ascendancy among the then independent German States would do to Catholicism. The
Austrian Emperor had written personally to express
his thanks to the Bishop for the care which his
soldiers reported they had received when the battle
raged within the boundaries of the Mainz diocese.
The Bishop had sent nursing sisters to the scene to
help where they could. In fact, wounded Austrian
soldiers had reported to their Emperor that the
Bishop of Mainz had personally been on the scene
to help minister to them. Such actions were not to
endear him with the Prussian government.

Subsequently, in 1875, the government blocked
his appointment as co-adjutor and successor to the
Archbishop of Posen (now the Polish city, Poznan).
The Bishop was not broken up over these rejections.
He remarked that Mainz was just the right size for
him. In hindsight one is entitled to wonder whether
he would have had time for the solid scholarship
evident in his teachings if he had been saddled with
the huge administrative burdens of such larger arch-
dioceses.

Despite all such enmity, Bismarck nevertheless admired and respected Bishop von Ketteler and referred to him as, "an outstanding personality." [4] That did not stop the lower bureaucracy from harassing the great man, however; and on two different occasions he was arrested and summoned to appear before the courts. Fines were imposed each time, although the authorities apparently forgot that they were dealing also with a trained lawyer. In each case the Bishop served as his own counsel and succeeded in getting the fines commuted. Nevertheless, the measures imposed during the Kulturkampf proved to be a severe setback to the progress Bishop von Ketteler had made in restoring Catholicism in Mainz.

The affairs of his diocese had to be left in other hands for a time, when Bishop von Ketteler travelled to Rome for the First Vatican Council convoked by Pope Pius IX in 1870. Here the Bishop found himself in the company of a minority of Council Fathers who were opposed to the solemn definition of the doctrine of papal infallibility at that time. They came to be known as the "Inopportunists," because for the most part they agreed with the doctrine but felt the time was not yet right for the declaration. It was a time of real anguish for Bishop von Ketteler, who had always been a staunch defender of papal infallibility. He too, however, felt that the time was not right. Among other things he wanted the doctrine developed more painstakingly than the Council had had time for. His feeling was that, since the Fathers were now talking about a solemn definition which would stand for all ages, this should not be undertaken until the entire matter had been examined and developed to the last detail. The biographer Lenhart felt that it was the Second Vatican Council in 1962-65 which finally accomplished what Bishop von Ketteler was proposing back in 1870 [5] Unable to bring himself to vote with either of the two available options, Placet (meaning, it pleases me), or Non Placet (it does not please me) the Bishop wrote to Pius IX and asked to be permitted to leave the Council and return home. He explained that he did not want to leave the impression that he in any way opposed the doctrine of papal infallibility - a connotation which could be read into a <u>Non Placet</u> vote. At the same time, he was definitely not pleased with the declaration in the form in which it was being proposed for solemn definition. He had the permission to leave Rome and he did so, leaving word beforehand that he concurred with what the Council majority would rule. It is clear that Pius IX never held this action against the Bishop. On the contrary, he always held him in the highest esteem, remarking once to the rector of the Mainz seminary in private audience about von Ketteler: "He is everything that a bishop should be." 6

After returning to Germany and to his diocese the Bishop found himself once more in the middle of the political arena. When the new Reichstag of Bismarck's Second Reich was formed, he was elected to serve as a delegate. Given the opposition which the Church faced at the hands of the Prussian dominated Reich he decided that the gravity of the situation facing Catholics warranted his accepting the political office. He served from March until December of 1871 during the first two sessions of the new Reichstag, after which he returned home and resolved never again to move into the political arena. The Catholic CenterParty had been established and was under the capable leadership of Ludwig Windhorst. Bishop von Ketteler felt, more than ever, that he could be most effective in championing his Church's interest from his pulpit in the Cathedral at Mainz.

Confirming again Pius IX's great personal esteem for Bishop von Ketteler was the invitation to Rome for the celebration of the Pope's fiftieth jubilee as bishop, in May of 1877. It was during a general audience on that occasion when the Pope, having heard that there were Germans from Mainz present, asked, "And Bishop von Ketteler, is he present?" Told that he was, the Pontiff asked the Bishop to come forward, greeted him with great

warmth and engaged in a few minutes of private
conversation with him before the entire assemblage.
He also invited the Bishop to come to him in private audience the following day. It is reported
that the Pope told him on that occasion: "You wield
a great pen, my son. In fact I believe your pen
writes better than my own." 7

That occurred on May 17, 1877, and that visit
was to be the great Bishop's last journey to his
Church's headquarters!

Bishop von Ketteler left Rome supremely happy.
However, he had developed a fever which, since he
had rarely been sick, he ignored. It became worse
as he made his way north, but he insisted on several
planned stops to visit with various friends. He
arrived in Innsbruck, Austria on June 7 and decided
to return home by way of a detour through eastern
Bavaria to visit with a friend who had become a
Capuchin at the Monastery in Burghausen near
Altötting. Here occurred another striking coincidence in his life. It was at the famous Marian
shrine at Altötting where the Bishop's first journey
to the priesthood began that he said his last Mass
as a Catholic priest. He was barely able to make
it through the ceremony, and afterwards he was put
to bed at the Capuchin monastery in Burghausen.
Fever and illness became progressively worse.
The Bishop lay on his death bed for just thirty-
three days before he closed his eyes in death on
July 13, 1877, thirty three years after he was
ordained a priest at the age of thirty-three! He
was buried as had been his wish, in a crypt at the
Marian altar in the Cathedral of Mainz. Thus his
career as a Roman Catholic priest ended as it began
in a chapel dedicated to the Mother of God, to whom
he had a singular devotion throughout his life.

NOTES

[1]
For an excellent recent biography of Bishop von Ketteler in the English language, see: Edward C. Bock, <u>Wilhelm von Ketteler, Bishop of Mainz; His Life, Times and Ideas,</u> (Washington: University Press of America, 1977).

[2]
See: Ludwig Lenhart, <u>Bischof Ketteler</u> (Mainz, 1967), II, 47.

[3]
Translator's Note: This is the translator's version of the original German letter of Marx to Engels referred to in: Fritz Vigener, <u>Ketteler</u> (Munich and Berlin, 1924), p. 549. There is another translation which is probably more available to U.S. readers. See: Karl Marx and Friedrich Engels, <u>Selected Correspondence 1846-1895</u> (Westport, Connecticut: Greenwood Press, 1975), p. 263. This is Volume XXIX of a collection known as <u>Works of Marxism - Leninism.</u>

[4]
Lenhart, I, p. 12.

[5]
Lenhart, II, p. 17.

[6]
Lenhart, I, p. 47.

[7]
Otto Pfülf, S.J., <u>Bischof von Ketteler</u> (Mainz, 1899), III, pp. 310-11.

Table of Contents

The Great Social Issues of the Present

Six Sermons Delivered

by

Wilhelm Emmanuel von Ketteler

In Mainz, Germany

in the Year 1848

Translator's Note

The Great Social Issues of the Present (Die
Grossen socialen Fragen der Gegenwart) was actually
a publication in book form of six sermons delivered
by Wilhelm Emmanuel von Ketteler by invitation, in
Mainz, Germany. At the time, he was still a parish
priest of the Münster Diocese. A stirring funeral
oration delivered at the graveside of two fellow
delegates to the Frankfurt National Assembly, to
which the people of his district had elected to
send him as their delegate, brought him national
recognition. The two men had been murdered by
radicals during rioting associated with the con-
vening of that body. Father von Ketteler received
an invitation to preach a cycle of six sermons relating Christian principles to current social
problems. The first was delivered in St. Peter's
Church in Mainz, on the occasion of the anniversary
celebration of that Church's dedication. Because
of overflow crowds the young priest was asked to
deliver the remaining sermons in the great cathedral of Mainz, where he would be installed two
years later as its Bishop.

The six sermons were first published together
in book form in 1849 by Kirchheim and Schott Verlag
in the City of Mainz. A second edition appeared in
1878 by the same publisher known then as Verlag von
Franz Kirchheim of Mainz, Germany. It is worth
nothing that the sermons were delivered in the same
year in which Karl Marx and Friedrich Engels first
published The Communist Manifesto. Bishop von
Ketteler's teachings thus laid the groundwork for
the social teachings of his Church which were to
stand in opposition to the Marxian solution to the
great social problem until the present; and he began the confrontation in the same year in which
Marx and Engels launched their own endeavor.

The Sermons were entitled: page

I. The Christian Concept of Private Property 7
   Rights (Die christliche Idee vom Rechte
   des Eignethums)

3

4

First Sermon

The Christian Concept of the Private Property Right

Feast of the Dedication of St. Peter's Church
in Mainz, 19 November 1848

"Today, salvation has been brought to this house"
(Luke 19:9)

Today, my Christian brethren, we reflect back over the centuries that have passed since the consecration of the ancient churches in this city as houses of the living God; and we look back over the ranks of your ancestors who with one faith, one hope, and one common love walked through these doors. It was they who passed on to you that greatest legacy of all, the faith in which they lived and died happily. It may also be useful to look into the future and to ask whether you and your children will preserve with equal loyalty these houses of God in the true faith, so that future generations will be able to commemorate the consecration of churches as we are doing today. · The most reassuring thought in this regard, however, is the fact that while church buildings depend on human caprice which can be fickle, the Church which we belong to owes its strength and durability not to man, but to God and His only begotten Son, Jesus Christ, to whom is given all power on heaven and on earth.

The survival of the Catholic Church on earth, therefore, is not jeopardized because the powerful of this earth and entire nations may rise against it; nor is it guaranteed because princes and governments may choose to protect it. The Church goes on existing because of the will of Almighty God who once said, "Let it be," and by His word He created the world out of nothing. It is the same God who then said to a mortal man, "You are Peter, and upon this rock I will build my Church, and the gates of hell will not prevail against it." (Matt. 16:18) And that same God later gave the Church His promise, "Heaven and earth shall pass away, but my word shall not pass away."(Luke 21:33) Therefore, whether the servants of the Church, the Apostles of old and their successors go about, unsupported by earthly power, without staff and shoes, without gold and silver, without a constant abode, with only one cloak, or whether respectful nations build palaces for them and surround them with worldly might and splendor, the Rock on which the Church rests is still no more or no less permanent. Men have no more power over the Church than they have over Christ Himself. They can try to make Him king or they can turn around and persecute Him, mock Him, dress Him in the cloak of a fool, and nail Him to a cross; but they are unable to prevent Him from rising from the tomb of

His own power, nor can they foreclose upon the survival of His Kingship here on earth. And so it is with the Church of Christ. Men can bestow upon it earthly treasures and a seat alongside the thrones of kings as our ancestors did; or they can rob it of its earthly possessions, mock and humiliate it as is the case today. Still athe power of the Almighty which resides in the crucified Christ cannot be taken from the crucified church. The Church will survive by this power until the end of time.

By virtue of this faith and conviction, the Church calls itself Catholic, i.e., the Church for all mankind. It possesses a heritage of unchangeable truth more lofty than any imaginable cultural accomplishments of the human spirit. It enjoys a vitality more dynamic than any conceivable ebb and flow of human life. If there were a single truth in all creation greater than that truth possessed by the Catholic Church, if there were a single virtue nobler than those which the Catholic Church strives to inculcate, if there were a single vice or a corruption which the Church could not overcome, then belief in that Church would be a deception and trust in it would be folly. The Church would not be the work of God but rather of man.

Until now, the Church has stood the test of time true to her Divine origin. All through history, no higher mission and no greater power has appeared that could supplant that of the Church. She has the mandate to spread her message as the universal truth for all mankind. "Go out all over the world, and preach the gospel to the whole of creation." (Mark 16:15) Without benefit of temporal resources, without the benefit of human learning and erudition, relying solely on the overpowering Divine truth of its teaching, the early Church went about fulfilling that mandate. She has conquered time and distance until our own day and proclaimed the Gospel throughout the world. She has sought out all the nations of the earth. She has presented her truth alike to kings and beggars, to the learned and proud as well as to simple children. In the face of the endless diversity and confusion to which the human spirit is subject, the Church has always succeeded in discovering and holding herself fast to those qualities and truths which are common

8

to all mankind. Thus, she has always and everywhere
been in tune with the saying of Tertullian, "Oh human
spirit, you are by your nature Christian!"(Tertullian,
Apolog. c. 17) The Catholic Church has been tested
in the face of all human resourcefulness. A thousand
times her enemies have cried out triumphantly, as they
once taunted the crucified Christ, "If you are the Son
of God, come down from the cross." (Matt. 27:40) "If
you are the work of God, climb out of the abyss into
which we have cast you." But the judgement of history
prevailed and the Church, time and again, arose from
the dead by her own mysterious power while her enemies
disappeared often without leaving a significant trace
in history.

Now, once again, we find ourselves at such a point
in history. The enemies of the Church, more numerous
and powerful than ever, stand around the cross onto
which they have nailed the Church. Lies, injustice,
mockery, and contempt are the nails and ropes by which
these hostile forces wish to make certain that they
will never again be confronted by the Church. Even
the rank and file and the poor have all too often
joined the Church's enemies, and this includes some
of her own sons and daughters who are now shamefull-
numbered among her bitterest antagonists. Will the
Church once again be able to rise from her apparent
death; will she be able to counter the disastrous prevailing unbelief with the ancient faith of our fathers;
will she be able to restore her high moral standards
to stem the flood of moral decadence which now threatens
to drown us; will she know how to dispense good
counsel, help, and confidence in this atmosphere of
moral chaos and desperation? We respond without a
moment's hesitation with our resounding, "Yes." What
is more, we are prepared to bear witness to this belief
with every last drop of blood in our veins. Millions
of loyal Catholics around the earth join with us in
our response to the challenge. How else can one explain
the calm and confidence of all steadfast Catholics
in the face of the raging storms? Even as the tower-
ing waves threaten to engulf us, the loyal Catholic
stands secure on the Rock, bolstered by a confidence
that the gates of hell shall not prevail against it!

9

But this serene faith is not enough in our time! We must bear witness to its truth by works. Precisely now when the Church stands abandoned by all worldly power she must more than ever reveal her inner God-given strength and show the world that she possesses the same power that brought Christ's mission to fulfillment as He hung helpless on the Cross and made Christianity victorious in the first centuries when the overwhelming might of Pagan Rome was arrayed against it. Now the Church must draw on the deposit of her embattled faith to present a truth to the world which will work like a sun to dispel the fog which the Father of Liew is spreading. And now she must draw on that reservoir to offer a source of strength, of love, and of virtue which will heal all wounds and lift the crushing burden under which our world is staggering.

How the Church will accomplish this twofold task which now confronts her, to spread the truth and to restore life to a decadent society, is something none of us can answer. The Holy Spirit who guides her will determine her course. All that I am privileged to do at present is to recall the Church's teaching which is relevant to the most vital social problem of our time, namely the Church's teaching regarding the private property right. I would like to point out how superior this teaching is to contemporary opinions regarding the property right and how the Church, fortified with this doctrine, can heal the evil of our time.

Today the haves and the have-nots confront each other with animosity, and the poverty of the masses grows daily. The right to ownership is, for all practical purposes, viewed with suspicion by those who are deprived of property; and from time to time there are manifestations which leap up like flames from the earth, now here, now there, threatening a general conflagration. On the one side we witness a stubborn, narrow interpretation of the property right, and on the other a determination to abolish that right completely. We look desperately for moderation between these extremes. Amid the turmoil we intend to recall the teaching of the Catholic Church on property as it was developed by St. Thomas Aquinas more than 600 years ago. We may perhaps discover that the human spirit, guided by the

10

Faith, came up with an answer to our problem more than half a millennium ago, which mankind, having abandoned that Faith, is now trying in vain to rediscover.

To express the fundamental Church teaching on property rights, St. Thomas falls back on the relationship between God and His creation. We shall re-examine the Saint's treatment of this basic relationship.

St. Thomas teaches that all creatures and all earthly goods, by virtue of their original nature, can belong only to God. This thesis follows logically from the article of faith which tells us that everything other than God himself was created by God out of nothing. Therefore God is the true and exclusive, ultimate proprietor of all creatures. This ultimate dominion of God over His creatures is part and parcel of the essence of creation and is therefore inalienable. Regardless of how the property right comes to be exercised, how it is shared or delegated, or what customs may appear or who may come into possession of property, the ultimate dominion of God over His creatures remains inviolate. In this sense, God has the absolute right and man does not. However, aside from this ultimate absolute dominion of God, St. Thomas speaks of a <u>right to use</u>, and it is here that man's rights over earthly goods become operative. Thus, when we speak of a natural right to private property, where man is concerned one cannot speak of a full and absolute right - that belongs only to God - but only a right to use. From this it is clear that man's right to property - even his right to possess and use property - is never absolute in the sense that man may use earthly goods as he pleases. Man must use the goods of creation as the Creator has ordained their use. Man must conform to the order which God has determined in the use of the things of creation, and he has no right to use them in any manner which goes counter to God's plan of creation. This plan of the Creator for His earthly goods is expressed in the nature of creation itself and expressed in the words which God spoke after He created the world: "Here are all the herbs, 'God told them,' that seed on earth, and all the trees, that carry in them the seeds of their own life, to be your food..."(Gen. 1:29)

11

The conclusion we draw from St. Thomas' teaching is that God has the ultimate dominion over all things. In His providence, however, He destined certain of those things for sustaining man in his corporal needs, and therefore man has a certain natural right to private property - namely - the right to use the things of creation. From this concept of property we draw two important conclusions.

First, the Catholic Church's concept of property has nothing in common with the prevalent view which regards man as the absolute lord of that which he owns. The Church can in no sense support the notion that man has the right to "wheel and deal" as he pleases with the goods of this world. When she speaks of and defends the property right, she must always preserve the three essential elements of that right:
1) that God and God alone is the ultimate and absolute owner of all things;
2) that man has only a restricted right, in effect, to use created things;
3) that in using created things man must always have regard for the order which God established for the universe.

Second, it is clear that such a notion of the property right as we are speaking of is possible only when there is a living faith in God, which acknowledges that this right is based on His will and on a divinely established order. Only since men, who while calling themselves the friends of humanity at the same time as they work to destroy humanity, along with their spiritual ancestors, have shattered men's faith in God has it been possible for such an unholy concept of private property to gain currency. We refer to a concept of ownership whereby man in effect arrogates to himself the rights which only God possesses over property. Once he divorced himself from his God, man pictured himself as the exclusive lord and master of all that he possessed. Accordingly, he viewed his goods merely as a means to satisfy his growing greed. Divorced from his God, man made pleasure-seeking and the satisfaction of his sensual appetites, the purpose of life; and the goods of this earth were, of course, the means to achieve this goal. Then a gap between rich and poor appeared such as the Christian world had never known.

At the same time that the wealthy indulge themselves
in a lavish and wasteful satisfaction of every sensate
whim, they are indifferent to the plight of their less
fortunate fellow men who must often do without even the
bare necessities of life. Thus the rich man is in fact
depriving his brother of the things which the Creator
meant for him to have. The judgement of God rests
heavily on this serious distortion of both the natural
and supernatural order of things - this monumental
injustice! It is not the Catholic Church which brought
on this sorry situation, but unbelief and Godlessness.
As Godlessness has progressively eroded the will to
work among the poor it has simultaneously deprived
the rich of any spirit of active charity.

The doctrine which we have discussed so far -
based on God's ultimate dominion over created things -
constitutes only the essential foundation of the true
Christian notion of property rights. We must proceed
now to build on this foundation the more complete understanding of the property right. As we noted, man's
right to private property is simply a right delegated
by God to man, authorizing man to use the goods of the
earth according to the prescribed order in creation.
This means that the goods of creation are destined to
serve the needs of all mankind. God's will in this
regard could be accomplished in either of two ways.
Men can exercise their God given right to own - or
rather to use - property in common, as communism
proposes. Thus they would administer the goods of
the earth in common and distribute the benefits. The
other alternative is to distribute the goods of the
earth in such a manner that each person has the right
to the exclusive use of certain things in order to
enjoy the fruits of those things.

St. Thomas comes to grips with the problem as
to which of these two approaches is more appropriate
for mankind in general, and thus he solves a problem
which troubles the world 600 years later! Let us
follow his guidance also in this matter. Regarding
man's right to use property, St. Thomas makes a distinction between the right to care for and administer
on the one hand, and the right to enjoy the benefits
coming from property, on the other. The distinction

is self-explanatory. As they appear in nature, the goods of creation are not, by and large, capable of satisfying human needs. They must first be prepared, that is to say, worked on and processed.

Regarding the care and preparation of the goods of this earth for man's use, St. Thomas states that the right of the individual person to own must be acknowledged. This is so, _first_, because only by private ownership will goods be properly cared for. Everyone takes better care of things which belong to him than of those things which men hold in common. Over and above this, every man avoids work where possible, and where things are held in common a man would just as soon leave tasks to his fellow man - as is the case, for example, wherever there is a large number of servants assigned to a task. It is not difficult to recognize the truth of this thesis. If all things were owned in common or assigned only for a specified period of time, or if the inheritance right were abolished, diligent care of property would disappear. Improvement of such property would be virtually out of the question, and even the incentive to discover and try new things would be uprooted from the human spirit. Every man would rely on everyone else; man's natural laziness would have lost its counter-balance, and this would soon lead to the domination of one by the other as well as the deterioration of available resources of the earth. _Secondly_, St. Thomas wrote, only by the private ownership of property will that order be preserved which is necessary for the efficient exploitation of the goods of this earth. If everyone is in charge of everything, there will be general confusion, if not chaos. This truth is self-evident. There is a general diversity in the division of human labor, and all must conform to a general order if all of the needs of men are to be provided for in the way God makes this possible by His plan of creation. Disturb this order, and you jeopardize the welfare of mankind. But the ownership of property by individual families is conducive to this order inasmuch as it determines to a large extent the occupation of the family members, and prevents a sudden switch from one kind of work and life style to another by large numbers of people. How chaotic the division of labor would become if it

were subjected to a constantly recurring redistribu-
tion of the goods of creation among different people!

Finally, St. Thomas argued that only by acknowledging the right of private property can peace be
preserved among men. Experience teaches how easily
common ownership leads to quarrels and disputes. It
is a truth which is painful to the extent that even
blood relatives cannot agree on how to use what they
hold in common without quarrels arising. What would
happen if mankind as a whole had to share every possession and divide up every task? All humanity would
disintegrate into chaos and conflict!

St. Thomas, by virtue of these irrefutable arguments defends the right of private ownership in the
sense of administering and caring for property; and
thus his position is in complete agreement with the
law of God: "Thou shalt not steel," and with the teaching of the Catholic Church, all of which stand completely
and inalterably opposed to the communism proposed in
our time. Communism - whereby the goods of this earth
must be redistributed periodically - contradicts the
law of nature, because it makes impossible the orderly
administration of these goods. It thereby frustrates
their natural purpose, spreads disorder and enmity
among men, and consequently eliminates the necessary
condition for decent human existence.

With reference to the second thesis, which derives
from the right of man to use the things of the earth,
in other words, the right to enjoy the fruits of those
things of which man is in charge, St. Thomas erects a
corresponding obligation. According to him man should
never regard the fruits of his own stewardship of
property as his exclusive property but rather as the
common property of all.[1] Therefore, he should be prepared to share these fruits with others who are in need.
Thus, the Apostle wrote, "...Warn those who are rich
in this present world..(to be)..always ready to give,
and to share the common burden." (I Tim. 6:17-18)
(S. Thom. Aq. Summa Theol. II, IIq.66a 1 et 2)

15

Just as Christian teaching is opposed to false communism, it is no less opposed to the false teaching of private property rights which it confronts with a kind of true communism. God created nature to nourish all mankind, and that goal must be accomplished. Therefore every man should be prepared to make the fruits of what he owns common property to whatever degree this may be necessary to fulfill the intention of the Creator.

We have now presented, to the best of our ability, the teaching of St. Thomas regarding the private property right - a teaching which is also, in effect, the teaching of the Catholic Church. It is scarcely necessary to emphasize how superior this teaching is to the two irreconcilable opposing views on private ownership which confront each other in our time.

The false doctrine of the absolute right of private property sins against nature inasmuch as it sees nothing wrong with using what God intended for feeding and clothing all mankind to satisfy unbounded greed and the most frivolous sensual cravings. It also undermines the noblest sentiments in the human heart and substitutes instead a harshness and insensitivity toward human misery which are not even worthy of animals. This crude doctrine, in effect, sanctions the right to steal, since, as one father of the Church put it, stealing means not only to take what belongs to others, but also to hold back what rightfully ought to belong to others. The notorious saying, "Private property is theft," is not purely and simply false. Aside from enormous falsehood it contains a grain of uncomfortable truth. One can no longer simply wave this saying aside with contempt and ridicule. We must see to it that we eliminate the unpleasant kernel of truth in it, so that it will once again be totally untrue! So long as there is a spark of truth in it, it is capable of setting the world on fire. As one excess leads to another, so one sin against nature begets another. From the exaggerated concept of property rights - communism was begotten. But communism too is a sin against nature. While masquerading as a humanitarian solution it can only bring misery to mankind since it destroys incentive and order as well as peace among men. It begets a war of all against all and thus eradicates the secure foundation upon which human existence is based.

Like a beacon, the truth of the Catholic Church shines through the fog of both of these distortions. The Catholic Church recognizes the half-truths in each of the opposing viewpoints and integrates them in her teaching while rejecting the untruths in both. She does not recognize an unconditional human right to own the goods of this earth, but only a right to make use of them according to the order ordained by God. The Church defends the property right inasmuch as private ownership is required for the diligent care for and management of property, as well as in the interests of order and peace. She blesses a kind of communism inasmuch as the fruits of private ownership must once again become the common property of all mankind.

I cannot get off this subject without dwelling on the way in which this concept of the ownership right fits into the higher plan of Divine Providence, and how everything harmonizes with the Divine plan. Man, while here on earth, must fulfill the will of God. By the power of his intellect he must grasp God's truth, and with his will he must put that truth into action. The intellect and will of man must fulfill that prayer which says, "Thy Will be done." But in accordance with the dignity of the human being, God granted to man a free will. Therefore man only acts in a truly human way and his actions only possess moral worth when of his own free will he carries out the work of God on earth. God respects the free will of man and does not act to set it aside even when man uses this will to harm himself, i.e., acts contrary to God's will. Apply these important truths to the Catholic teaching on private property. God created the earth and all of its resources so that man could draw his sustenance from them, and God could have accomplished this end by a naturally enforced distribution of the earth's abundance. But that was not in His exalted plan. He preferred rather to afford man

17

the opportunity to exercise self-determination and
free will. He wanted to give man the chance to
share in the fulfillment of His divine plan for
order so that he would become God-like. Therefore
he ordained an unequal distribution of the things of
this earth so far as their management and possession
are concerned, in order that man might have the opportunity to share God's largesse with his fellow man.
Thus man is supposed to be drawn into the life of love
which God makes possible for us. It is in the light
of this charity that he ought to administer the goods
of creation which God ordained for all mankind, thereby
sharing in God's loving plan. If the distribution of
the goods of this earth were all predetermined so that
man had no control over it, in other words, if everything were determined by something like physical laws,
or if this matter were determined somehow by government
regulations, then the finest wellspring of human nobility
would be stifled. That is because, my dear Christian
brethren, a life characterized by self-sacrificing acts
of mercy and charity is the only life worthy of the
children of God. Consider for example the life of
sacrifice lived by some small and frail sister of
charity. And I ask you, does not such a life represent a more noble spectacle of spirit, dignity, beauty,
and love than perhaps the life of an entire city?
If we would only return to this life of charity! If
we would only sublimate all of our needs by this love!
If only we would resolve to conquer the world by the
strength of that love and lead it back to the cross
from which it has strayed. Let the ancient See of
St. Boniface lead the way back to this life of active
Christian love. Then and only then will we preserve
our faith, because the Christian faith can only survive where it is activated by Christian charity. I
repeat, my Christian Brethren, let us conquer the
world by our works of love and thereby bring it back
to the Catholic faith. Amen.

18

Second Sermon

The Obligation of Christian Charity

First Sunday of Advent in the Cathedral at
Mainz, 3 December 1848

"Meanwhile, make no mistake about the age we live in;
already it is high time for us to awake from our sleep;"
(Romans 13:11)

Ever since the Apostle Paul spoke these words
to the Romans, the Church recalls them to the faithful
each year at this time, the beginning of Advent. Down
through the ages, many have been obedient to this call.
They awoke from their sleep, put off the things of
darkness, and armed themselves with the weapons of
light and of Our Lord Jesus Christ. On the other
hand, many others have closed their ears and their
hearts to the call of the Church. They persist in
the ways of darkness, of the flesh and of lust. And
now, we too are numbered among the generations which
are predestined by God to hear this call of the Church,
some of us for the last time. Let us cherish this
call for the well-being of our immortal souls. The
times are becoming steadily more portentuous and
critical. The storm clouds that gather over our
heads become ever more ominous; and as they do, the
call of our Church becomes more and more urgent like
the plea of a mother who sees her children threatened
by great danger. In fact, on this very day, the Church
has delivered a sobering warning through the voices [2]
of the bishops of all of Germany. Now I am privileged
to add my unworthy voice to recall to you the words
of the Apostle: "Meanwhile, make no mistake about the
age we live in; already it is high time for us to
awake out of our sleep.." (Romans 13:11)

In these words, it seems to me, there are two
significant thoughts. First of all, we ought to recognize the problems of the times in which we live;
and secondly, this awareness ought to inspire us to
abandon our attempt to live without Christ and to
begin a new life in Christ. We will concern ourselves
today with these thoughts and consider first where the
attempt to live without Christ has brought humanity
in our day, and then what means Christ has given us
to overcome the evil of the times.

My dear Friends, it is impossible to speak of
and recognize the conditions which confront us without time and again coming back to our social problems.
I refer, of course, to the division between the haves
and the have-nots - the plight of our poor brothers,
and the means to remedy these problems. As much weight

21

as we may be tempted to place on the political question and the structure of our government, still the focus of the problem does not lie there. Whatever the form of government that we may choose to establish, still there will not be enough food, enough work, enough bread, enough clothing, enough shelter for our poor. On the contrary, the more men work out solutions to our political problems, the more apparent it becomes - and many don't want to accept that these only scratch the surface of the matter - that our social problems only become still more critical and their solution becomes ever more urgent. The main reason why the poorer sector of our population becomes involved in political movements is because of desperation and the unnaturalness of their poverty. While political leaders and demagogues alike are mainly interested in arrogating political power to themselves, the poor are concerned mainly with improving their material welfare. Until now, the latter still accord some trust to the proclamations of their leaders. They expect that relief will come from making changes in the form of government. But once they come to realize that neither the freedom of the press, the right of association, the right to vote and to assemble, nor nice speeches, nor popular sovereignty are able to feed the hungry, to clothe the naked, to comfort the afflicted, to heal the sick, then the poor will arise in wrath against those who deceived them. In desperation, they will seek a way out of their need and oppression by reaching out for another kind of solution. This particular time in world history may, in fact, be destined as a proof to all mankind that it is not for one form of government or another to assure the welfare of nations, but that this calls for a different and for a higher power. If our times will only make this abundantly clear, then despite all of the grief which they have brought, they will have served a purpose! If we wish to understand our times, then we have to understand the social problems of our times. He who grasps these, understands our era; and he who does not, for him both the present and the future remain an enigma.

As an aid for understanding our social conditions, I presented, several weeks ago, the teaching of the Church on private property. I stated that this teaching is confronted at present by two opposite viewpoints. I explained how the denial of the Church's teaching would inevitably lead to the precarious condition in which we now find ourselves. Permit me to recall this teaching briefly and to proceed from it to a deeper understanding of our present problem. According to the Church's teaching as developed by St. Thomas Aquinas, God, who created all things out of nothing, has absolute dominion over all of his creatures, human beings as well as the goods of the earth. This absolute dominion of God, being an essential derivative of the nature of creation, cannot be infringed by possession, custom, or any human prerogative. Man has only such rights as God means for him to have. In His wisdom, and providence God has destined certain goods of the earth for man's use; and it is His will that these goods should first and foremost be available to satisfy the material needs of all mankind. Therefore, the so-called property right is in essence nothing more than a right to use! With it comes the natural obligation imposed by God to use the fruits of our property according to His will. We pointed out also that this right to use implies two further rights: the right to manage, whereby the goods of this earth are to be prepared for immediate use, and secondly, the right to enjoy the fruits of our property. We reached the conclusion that if God's intention is for all mankind to have access to the goods of the earth to satisfy its material needs, the right to manage property implies the right of the individual to own such property. If this were not the case, then all prudent management would cease, discord and disorder would result, and the conditions whereby man could satisfy his material wants would disappear. However, we also concluded that insofar as the yield from his property is concerned every man must be prepared to regard his property as common. In other words, he must be prepared to cooperate with the will of the Creator in seeing to it that every man may satisfy his urgent needs from the goods of creation!

23

Before I go further, my dear Christian brethren, I would like to remind you that God has favored us with a twofold revelation so that we could arrive at the truth. There is both a natural and a supernatural revelation. We arrive at natural truths through the natural faculties of our soul, i.e., intelligence and reason; we reach supernatural truths with the aid of these same faculties applied to what God's messengers have revealed to us and the grace which Christ has earned for us. Since both kinds of revelation are from God and since God is the Truth, they cannot contradict each other, but they rather serve to fulfill and support each other. If we apply this to the doctrine of private property which I have called <u>Christian</u>, then we can with equal right refer to it as the natural right of private property. For even if I use certain quotations from supernatural revelation, I have nevertheless relied entirely on natural human reason to develop that doctrine. Whoever accepts that God is the Almighty Creator of Heaven and Earth, and whoever agrees further that nature is destined for the support of all mankind, he would have to agree with the teaching which I have put forth here whether he is Christian or just simply a reasonable person. These two teachings are both products of natural revelation, i.e., they are ascertainable by human reason - since only the fool says in his heart, there is no God!

From this standpoint, the two concepts of private property which we encounter in the world represent transgressions not only against Christianity, but also against the natural law. It is not only unChristian, but also unnatural to regard man as the absolute owner of his possessions so that he is justified in using the fruits of his property to satisfy his most frivolous wants when he ought to be using them to alleviate his fellow man's misery. Likewise it is not only unChristian, but also unnatural to teach that goods ought to be held in common even for purposes of management - an arrangement which leads to the elimination of all good management as well as to disorder and discord - so that the natural function of the goods of the earth is in fact frustrated. It is easy to understand how the unhealthy social conditions and tensions in which we now unhappily find ourselves would originate from such nonsensical doctrines, such distortions of natural truths. Thus we are painfully aware, my Christian brethren, of the sorry social conditions which we now face. They are the inevitable consequence of this unnatural interpretation of the private property right, and that in turn is the result of the rejection of our relationship to God, and the deterioration of our living faith in God. But one more question needs to be answered if we are to truly understand our times.

How is it possible for such teachings to arise and spread far and wide when they are so contrary to nature? How is it possible that we see wealthy people who, in flagrant disregard of the most elementary natural laws and with undisturbed consciences, squander their superabundance at the same time that they permit poor people to starve and poor children to be overcome by neglect? How is it possible for us to still enjoy our affluence while our fellow man is in desperate need? How can we still find enjoyment in drink and recreation, and how is it that the human heart does not break when we think of the indigent sick who reach out from their sick-beds for consolation and find no one to console them? How can we travel blissfully about the streets of our great cities seeing there, as we do everywhere, poor waifs who are, like us, made in the image of God, but whose lot is physical degradation and moral corruption? In birth, in youth, and in old age, they are victims of the most degrading kinds of misery. How is it possible for natural human beings to become so unnaturally inhuman? And on the other hand, how is it possible for the poor and their godless seducers, to be taken in by the false and nonsensical doctrine of communism which contravenes all natural rights and common sense, and to expect salvation from something which will obviously corrupt all humanity?

For these questions we have only one answer. It is contained in that teaching of Christianity about which Pascal wrote (Pensées III,8) that it is at the same time so inaccessible to human reason but also such an inescapable truth, that without it man would remain a total mystery to himself. It is the doctrine

of original sin and its transmission to all of mankind.
Certainly, Pascal continues, nothing is harder for us
to swallow than this teaching; and yet, without this
mystery - among the most incomprehensible of Christian
doctrines - we would all be at a loss to explain ourselves and our plight. Actually, from a purely human
standpoint, original sin is folly. There is no need
to harp on the inability of man to come to grips with
this doctrine. We concede that. But this folly contains more wisdom than is contained in all of human
wisdom. Divine folly has more wisdom than all mankind.
(Cor. 1:25) How else can we explain mankind? Its
entire condition testifies to this mystery. And we
too just now are confronted with the same dilemma as
we face our own particular problem. What Pascal says
applies to the individual human being, I maintain
applies equally to the human condition in each epoch
including our own. He who rejects the doctrine of
original sin because he cannot understand it, for him
human history will remain a puzzle. By wanting to
understand everything, he will end up understanding
nothing. Under the delusion of wanting to be reasonable in all things, he becomes totally unreasonable.
He, however, who accepts the teaching on original
sin in faith and in humility, to him all becomes
clear. He understands himself and also all of human
history. The matter we are dealing with proves this
truth once again. Only the doctrine of original sin
sheds real light on the miserable condition of our
time. According to that doctrine - man revolted
against God and as a consequence his natural powers
were diminished. His intellect was darkened and his
will was inclined to evil. The three-pronged lust
and Satan gained a certain power over man, and only
by the grace which Christ the Redeemer won for him
can regain his original dignity and destiny.

This basic teaching of Christianity alone can
explain to us how even the natural truths become
obscured and man's noblest inclinations can become
warped. As long as Christianity prevailed, it enlightened man's understanding and strengthened his
good will. So long as a Christian sense permeated
man's entire being, such perversions of the private
property doctrine as we witness today and such con-

26

sequent division between rich and poor were inconceivable. As for what becomes of man without Christ and without the grace which the Apostle says is destined to renew all that is in heaven and on earth (Ephesians 1:10), world history in general and our own sorry social condition at present provide the best testimony; for reason does not prevail now in regulating man's social relations. It is passion which prevails. Present-day concepts of private property emanate not from reason but from man's basest passions. Naturally the children of the world will not acknowledge this. They ridicule the doctrine of original sin and its consequences. They deny the source and the power of these base passions and maintain that they are simply the products of ignorance and indiscretion. What we need, they tell us, is reform of education and better schools. By this they have in mind a separation of schools from the Church, and a spread of some kind of general human culture.

Like a flower develops out of itself, so human nature must be guided to its full development. Then passions, hardship, and crime will disappear from the earth and true brotherhood will be restored. That is the teaching that is currently preached from the rooftops and passed off as supreme wisdom. I question this wisdom. It is hard to conceive of a more flagrant, obvious falsehood than this. If it were true, then there would have to be two kinds of people on earth, those who are cultured and therefore free of passion, hardship, and crime, i.e., those who act always in a pre-eminently reasonable manner; second there would be those lacking in cultural formation who are therefore slaves to passion and travail. I must ask, does this condition obtain now, or can one imagine a greater untruth? How can one maintain such nonsense in the face of all available statistics in France and Germany which clearly show that neither the level of education nor of general prosperity has any bearing on the crime rate of a nation? Statistics notwithstanding, daily human experience provides even more eloquent testimony against such preposterous claims. What of the miser who piles up wealth or the young world traveller who goes about the world learning languages and acquiring a knowledge of many lands, spending thousands to satisfy

27

his whims without a thought given to his brother in
need? And what of the young lady who flits about as
a social butterfly turning her body into a kind of
golden calf adorned with gold and diamonds without
the least concern for her poor sister? Are all of
these Christians who are lacking only in cultural upbringing? How does culture and refinement make misers
generous or fill playboys and vain young ladies with
concern for their fellowman? What kind of education
and what kind of textbook can implant the spirit of
Christian resignation and self-denial in human hearts?
Show me the generation with true fraternal charity
which you can produce by worldly wisdom and without
Christianity, and I will join you in throwing that
Christianity overboard. So long as I remain convinced
that all earthly wisdom, all science, all worldly
culture together are unable to ignite a single spark
of Christian charity on earth so as to make the miser
generous, I will persist in my belief that mankind
has fallen from grace and can only be healed by
Christianity. The world has turned from Christ, has
spurned His redemption, has fallen prey to its own
passions. That is the ultimate real cause of our
social disorder. The rich man disregards God's
command that he must share his superabundance with
the poor, not because he is lacking in education or
cultural formation, but rather because he is enslaved
by greed and avarice. And the poor man covets what
belongs to others not because he did not study his
lessons in school, but because he is a slave to sloth
and contemns the law of God: "Thou Shalt Not Steal."
Guided by instinct and passions, men can no longer
recognize simple natural truths when these stand opposed to their passions. The abandonment of Christianity
is the source of our troubles, and so long as we fail
to recognize this there is no solution to our problem.
The individual person can only achieve his full dignity
after he realizes within himself that he cannot reach
his high destiny by his own unaided strength. In the
same manner, the world cannot come to grips with its
present serious problems until it comes to realize that
something besides mere human resources are required
for the task. Failing in this, we will sink into barbarism and decay.

28

Inasmuch as we are aware of our plight, once we recognize that our social conditions are the necessary consequence of the unnatural and false concept of the private property right, and that this fallacy is a consequence of the abandonment of Christ so that passions and animal instincts have come to dominate our reason - it is time now to awaken from our sleep. We have only to seek out the means which can elevate us from our social misery. In general, I have already indicated what the remedy is by pointing out that the abandonment of Christianity caused us to fall into the pit. Therefore, only a return to Christ can lead us back. I would still like to point out how powerless the world is with all of its learning and experience, and how potent Christianity is in doctrine, in experience, and in its means of grace for healing our social ills.

First, let us consider the impotence of the world and the power of Christian teaching for dealing with social conditions.

For some time now I have read about all manner of remedies proposed by men of the world for alleviating poverty among the masses of people. I must confess I have found nothing which promises a real solution. So long as their proponents stick with the generalities in which they clothe their proposals, one is easily deceived that they are great benefactors who have learned the secret of how to multiply bread; but when one examines closely their practical measures, one cannot help but pity them. The one wants to help matters by a more equitable distribution of tax burdens; another proposes a system of savings banks; another wants to organize labor; still another proposes emigration; and still another sees a remedy in protective tariffs; others prefer free trade. Some argue for free enterprise or land reform, and others propose the exact opposite. Some see salvation in a republican form of government. These proposals generally have some merit - some more, some less; but for solving our social problems, they are woefully inadequate. There are those who realize this and propose the ultimate solution - common ownership of all things. Whether it will come to that, only time will tell, but this much is certain: by this means we will not assure

that the poor will become rich, but rather that all
will become poor! Anyone who can still make an impartial judgement can appreciate that all worldly
wisdom is woefully incapable of coming to our rescue.
The more powerless the wisdom of the world is for
providing a remedy, the more vital the Christian
teaching becomes. It is precisely for our social
problems that the Christian message is now especially
relevant. Nothing is more appropriate for demonstrat-
ing to us the variety of means which Christianity
affords us than the episode from the life of Christ
described by Luke, the Evangelist. "One of the multi-
tude said to him, Master, bid my brother give me a
share of our inheritance. And he answered, Why, man,
who has appointed me a judge to make awards between
you?" (Luke 12: 13-14). This occasion gave Christ
the opportunity to warn against greed and to point
out that good living had nothing to do with seeking
an abundance of material goods. He then related the
parable of the man who, after a rich harvest, filled
his barns and reflected in self-satisfaction, "Come,
soul, thou hast goods in plenty laid up for many years
to come; take thy rest now, eat, drink and make merry.
And God said, 'Thou fool, this night thou must render
up thy soul; and who will be master now of all thou
hast laid by?' Thus it is with the man who lays up
treasure for himself, and has no credit with God."
(Luke 12: 19-21)

Take heed, my Christian brethren. That is Christ's
answer to those who expect to become prosperous by
dividing up possessions, or who hope to solve social
problems by some superficial remedies. God wants a
more just distribution of property, but not by external
force, rather through a basic reform of man's attitudes.
That is the essential difference between Christian
teaching and the remedies the world proposes. The
world has only superficial remedies which cannot come
to grips with the source of our troubles - man's basic
philosophy. Surface poverty is not our real problem,
rather the poverty of our attitudes. Correct the latter
and you eliminate the former. The two great evils
which have rent our social fabric are an insatiable
greed and a pleasure cult along with great selfishness.
These have virtually annihilated Christian charity.

It is a sickness which has afflicted rich and poor
alike. What good are tax reforms and savings institutions so long as men remain basically self-centered?
This mortal affliction, the world and all its wisdom
is powerless to remedy, whereas the full force of the
Christian message is directed precisely toward straigh-
tening out man's basic attitude. I would like to try
to present various teachings of Jesus to demonstrate
how He proceeds step by step and by every avenue to
cure the soul of its greed and selfishness.

In the passage cited earlier, Our Lord reminds
us of the fleeting value of earthly goods, the foolishness of men who pile up material goods only to be called
before God before they have a chance to enjoy them.
At another point Christ tells us, "Do not lay up treasure for yourselves on earth, where there is moth and
rust to consume it, where there are thieves to break
in and steal; lay up treasure for yourselves in heaven,
where there is no moth or rust to consume it, no thieves
to break in and steal. Where your treasure-house is,
there your heart is too." (Matt. 6: 19-22) Here again
He offers to eradicate greed and selfishness from the
human heart. He demonstrates the folly of seeking
refuge in worldly goods, but at the same time He clears
the way for revealing the reward for a proper use of
material goods. Our Lord goes further. He knows that
noble ideas can captivate the human soul even more
than material satisfaction, so he holds out to the
soul, stifled by selfish pursuit, the goal of perfection: "Jesus said to him, If thou has a mind to be
perfect, go home, sell all that belongs to thee; give
it to the poor, and so the treasure thou hast shall be
in heaven; then come back and follow me......And every
man that has forsaken home or brothers, or sisters,
or father, or mother, or wife, or children, or lands
for my name's sake, shall receive his reward a hundredfold, and obtain everlasting life." (Matt. 19:21,29)
That is a teaching designed to heal the sickness which
afflicts men's souls. To man, suffocated spiritually
by greed, Christ proposes the total poverty which
emancipates the soul completely. The Catholic Church
has witnessed time and again the consequences of such
total dedication in the lives of countless Saints.

Again we find Christ addressing himself to eradicating greed from our hearts when He says: "Thou shalt love the Lord thy God with thy whole heart and thy whole soul and thy whole mind. This is the greatest of the commandments, and the first. And the second, its like, is this, Thou shalt love thy neighbour as thyself." (Matt. 22:37-39) When we ask who our neighbor is, He leads us to the man lying battered and bleeding by the road from Jerusalem to Jericho and teaches us that every beggar, every sick man in need is our neighbor.

My Christian brethren, if we would all obey these teachings for one single day, all of our social problems would disappear as if by magic. Let us, rich and poor alike, love our neighbor as ourselves for one day and the face of the earth will be renewed. Would that the teaching of Christ could capture our hearts!

Let us add to all of this the stirring message, "And the King will answer them, Believe me, when you did it to one of the least of my brethren here, you did it to me." (Matt. 25:40) "He who gives you welcome, gives me welcome too; and he who gives me welcome gives welcome to Him that sent me." ".....And if a man gives so much as a draught of cold water to one of the least of these here, because he is a disciple of mine, I promise you, he shall not miss his reward." (Matt. 10:40,42)

Who can fail to appreciate the power of this message to wipe out our greed? Who can count the tears dried by these words? With these words Our Blessed Savior has, in a manner of speaking, chained thousands of holy virgins to the beds of the poor sick, in whom they see the image of Christ. All of the love which men owe to God, He has placed at the service of the poor and the sick.

Still, Our Blessed Savior knows the human heart and how deeply greed and selfishness are rooted in it. He knows full well what drastic means are needed to eradicate these evils. Therefore he reminds those, for whom higher motives do not suffice, of judgement and eternal punishment. He gives them a glimpse of that awful day when He will come in great majesty and power, when the sheep and the goats will be separated

32

and when He will say to those on the left side: "Go
far from me, you that are accursed, into that eternal
fire which has been prepared for the devil and his
angels. For I was hungry, and you never gave me food,
I was thirsty, and you never gave me drink; I was a
stranger, and you did not bring me home, I was naked,
and you did not clothe me, I was sick and in prison,
and you did not care for me. Whereupon they, in their
turn will answer, Lord, when was it that we saw thee
hungry, or thirsty, or a stranger, or naked, or sick,
or in prison, and did not minister to thee? And He
will answer them, Believe me, when you refused it to
one of the least of my brethren here, you refused it
to me. And these shall pass on to eternal punishment,
and the just to eternal life." (Matt. 25: 41-46)

Finally, for him who remains deaf even to this
warning, Our Savior resorts to the ultimate threat.
He gives him a glimpse of the place of eternal punishment. He tells about the rich spendthrift, dressed in
fine garments and enjoying sumptuous meals at the same
time that poor Lazarus begs for a crust of bread in
vain, and the dogs lick his sores. We see these two
in eternity,Lazarus in Abraham's bosom and the rich
wastrel buried in Hell. We hear the latter call out,
"....Father Abraham, take pity on me; send Lazarus to
dip the tip of his finger in water, and cool my tongue;
I am tormented in this flame. But Abraham said, My
son, remember that thou didst receive thy good fortune
in thy lifetime, and Lazarus, no less, his ill fortune;
now he is in comfort, thou in torment. And besides
all this, there is a great gulf fixed between us and
you, so that there is no crossing from our side of it
to you, no crossing over to us from yours." (Luke 16:
24-27).

That, my Christian brethren, is a brief synopsis
of the teachings by which Christ wishes to uproot the
sources of all of our social problems, greed and selfishness, from our souls. He leads the greedy and
selfish person to the very gates of hell and shows
him the plight of the rich wastrel who pleads for a
drop of water from his place of torment. He takes
him before the seat of judgement and recites the
terrible words, "Depart from me, you that are accursed,

33

into the eternal fire." He introduces him to the rich
man who has amassed worldly goods and who before he
has a chance to enjoy them hears the awful words,
"Thou fool, this night thou must render up thy soul."
He shows him the treasures of earth consumed by rust
and moths and stolen by thieves. He holds up before
him the way of perfection and teaches him to love his
brother as himself, and that every man is his brother.
He represents himself as the poor man and demands that
the love which men owe to God be extended to the poor.

How powerful Christian teaching is and how powerless the teaching of the world is in counteracting
social ills. But Christianity is still more potent
and the world all the more impotent in practical everyday life when it comes to curing these ills.

To cure social evils, it is not enough to provide
more food and clothing for a few poor or to send a few
dollars more to our favorite charity. That is the
smallest part of our task. What is urgent is that
we heal the enormous division that exists in our society,
a deep-seated resentment between rich and poor. We
must halt the tragic moral decline that has victimized
large numbers of our poor fellow men who have lost
all faith, all hope, and all love for God and their
fellow man. We have to elevate from spiritual poverty
those who suffer material poverty. In rich and poor
alike, the source of social evil is in their attitudes.
Just as greed,selfishness, and pleasure-seeking
alienates the rich from the poor, these same motives
coupled with great want engenders great hate among
the poor toward the rich. Instead of looking for the
cause of the trouble where it really lies, and that
includes in part their own failings, the poor see in
the rich man the sole root of their problem. They
are victims of the temptation which afflicts all of
us. They see the splinter in the rich man's eye without being aware of the beam in their own. Thus we
see among so many of our poor fellow men a frightful
degree of moral degradation, where hatred toward one's
fellow man, greed, and covetousness, and sloth operate
side by side with great poverty. Sound teachings and
counsel are of no more avail here than are occasional
hand-outs. They take such hand-outs and use them with

34

the thought that they have this and much more coming
to them. A new force is needed to heal these decadent
attitudes - the force of example and of love. The
poor must once again come to realize that there is
real love in action before they extend any credulity
to the doctrine of charity. For this reason, we must
seek out the poorest of the poor in their hovels,
study the causes and conditions of their poverty,
share their sufferings and their tears. No depravity,
no misery must repel us. We must be prepared to
counter resentment, rebuff, ingratitude with even
greater love until we finally thaw out the icy crust
which has frozen the hearts of so many of the poor,
and conquer hatred with love. Just as God deals with
sinners - and that includes all of us - according to
the overflowing of his merciful love rather than as
a stern judge so as to overcome our lack of charity
and ingratitude, that is how we must overcome the
coldness of our fellow man with an outpouring of our
love. That, I am convinced, is the only way that we
will once again restore a sound disposition among the
great numbers of our poor.

What can the world do to solve this great problem?
We already know that the welfare state has not succeeded
in doing so by its poor laws. And what have the humanitarians of our time succeeded in doing in the practical
order? I must pass over this in silence, since it
stirs me to indignation, as do so many of those who
regard themselves as humanitarians and friends of the
poor at the same time as they are enemies of Christ
and His Church, a condition which they demonstrate by
their bankrupt life-style! What do these humanists
have to offer in the way of a solution of social evils,
for poverty, for reconciling people to each other? By
their fruits you shall know them. What are the fruits
of their love for their fellow man? Do we find them
in the hovels of the poor, at the bedsides of the sick
and the deprived? Do we see them depriving themselves
of anything to aid the poor? Do they live like the
poor? Not a chance! They give expression to their
humanitarianism by sowing the seeds of hate among people.
They live comfortably, even in grand style. They are
themselves guilty of the excesses of the wealthy, and
still they have the nerve to incite the poor against
the rich who are guilty of the same sins as they themselves.

Empty phrases about their love for the people, illusions about an earthly bliss which is simply unattainable in this world, stern denunciations of all and everyone other than themselves, these are the fruits of their supposed love for the people! That is their prescription for solving social problems, for reconciling man to his fellow man, for elevating the poor from their sorry state!

Such is the bankruptcy of the world's power to reconcile people one to another, to cure moral and physical misery. Neither the welfare state nor our humanitarians are able to pass beyond speech-making into action.

Contrast this with the life of Christ. He put his words into action. What a friend of the poor was the Son of God! Of poor parents, born in poverty, raised in modest circumstances, poor in His flight into Egypt, poor during His life at Nazareth. And during His public life? The foxes have their dens, birds have their nest, but He was poorer than they. He had not a place to rest His head. Those whom He chose as His apostles were poor men. Daily He moved among the poor, the sick, the suffering. They followed Him into the desert places. He sought them out in their homes. He shared with them the contempt of the Pharisees. He wept with them, He comforted them. At the end He hung poor and naked on His cross. It is from the life of the God-man, Jesus Christ, a life lived in poverty, that the power of love in action has poured forth abundantly into Christ's Church - as we have witnessed time and again with wonderment and admiration among the members of the Church. One cannot love Christ without being inflamed by a love of His own poverty and therefore of His poor. That is a truth which comes home to us down to our own time. What are the miracles of love towards neighbor and the poor which we encounter in the lives of the Saints, if not the result of that fire of love which Christ brought from Heaven down to earth and by which He wished to set the world on fire? He whose heart is not set on fire by this flame will never be able to love poverty or the poor. It was the poverty of Jesus that suddenly possessed Elizabeth, the daughter of a king, as she

once caught sight of a picture of Christ crucified
while entering a church and fell to her knees in
total disregard of the amazement of those round
about her. It was this fountain of love which so
intoxicated St. Francis of Assisi that he elected
poverty as his bride. Once while enroute to Rome
he was passing by a church, and he saw a group of
his fellow-men lying before the church door steeped
in poverty and begging for alms. He was so touched
by pity and overwhelmed by the desire to share their
poverty that he traded clothes with the poorest beggar
among them and spent several days as one of them.
This fountain of love is the source from which the
mendicant orders of the Catholic Church sprang. The
world can no longer understand them; it ridicules
them. Yet they represent the noblest and greatest
heights to which the world could reach or has ever
aspired! They have served to make rich men poor in
order to make poor men rich! It is from the same
source that the Sisters of Charity came forth, these
priceless flowers, these hearts in which the love of
Christ has taken refuge. These sisters have left
parents, brothers, sisters, all the pleasures of this
world in order to spend their lives at the bedsides
of the poor, the sick, the dying, administering to
their needs. Such a life represents more true Christian
charity and love of neighbor in one single hour than
the entire lifetimes of a whole host of our modern
"friends of the people" combined. In other words,
it is from this source that the human race will eventually regain its strength, its capacity for love,
its health, once it recognizes that no other cure is
available except that which is in Jesus Christ and in
the holy Catholic Church which He established.

    I could still speak to you about the graces which
Christ has made available to us through His Church to
lift man up again after sin has robbed him of his spiritual health. I could speak of the Sacraments which are
the living channels through which the vitality of Christ
flows into our souls. I could speak especially of the
Holy Eucharist whereby Christ so directly brings His
own heart, aflame with love, in contact with our own
hearts so as to unite us all in true charity and harmony
in order to heal all divisions among men. But my time

and my strength are both exhausted.

My Christian brethren, I do not fear the social evils of our time. I know that the world is powerless to abolish them, whereas, the teaching, the life-example, the grace of Christ is strong enough to help the world out of its straits and to dry all of its tears. I fear only godlessness, the lack of faith and the unChristian spirit of our time.

Now that we recognize our times for what they are, let us listen to the call of our Church this day. Let us awaken from our sleep and put on the armor of light and the life of Jesus Christ!

Pray God that today I may have won over even just one soul, one heart to the love of Christ and for the comfort of His poor. Amen!

38

Third Sermon

The Christian Concept of Human Freedom

Sunday before Christmas in the Cathedral
at Mainz, 17 December 1848

"John answered them, I am baptizing you with water;
but there is one standing in your midst of whom you
know nothing;"

(John 1:26)

In considering our present social conditions,
we have reached the conclusion that the real reason
for our plight - where men are alienated from one
another and a gulf separates rich from poor - does
not actually lie in how wealth is distributed or in
the poverty of some as contrasted with the riches of
others. It is to be found rather in the inner disposition of people which manifests itself outwardly
in these symptoms. The inequality of wealth, the
super-abundance enjoyed by some at the same time that
others are in extreme need, taken by itself, does not
necessarily lead to alienation among people. Given
a solid Christian disposition, such inequality can,
in fact, furnish the most solid and finest bond among
men in that it can activate Christian charity and provide the opportunity for true fraternal concern. He
who surveys the present situation without having pre-
judged it cannot deny this fact. He must admit that
our sickness is an inner one, not an external one,
that we suffer from a spiritual disease. Specifically,
our condition stems from unbounded greed and pleasure-
seeking which expresses itself as crass self-seeking
among both rich and poor. From this naked truth we
reached the simple conclusion that all external remedies,
no matter how praiseworthy and useful in themselves,
cannot offer genuine assistance. Just as the sick
man who suffers a serious internal illness is in need
of internal medicine, whereas mere superficial treatment could even occasion his death, we too are in need
of spiritual aid which will improve our inner disposition, whereas superficial remedies will only prolong
our agony. Since the source of our problem is internal,
our remedy must come from within. Speeches about equality will avail naught. What we need is an inner
strength which will surmount inequality and rise above
selfishness, and which is above and beyond all surface
equalization. Speeches about brotherhood are like
sounding brass. What we need is a genuine brotherly
disposition. More talk about love we don't need. We
need a flaming, living charity which alone can thaw
out our icy selfish hearts. We don't need those friends
of the people who offer no proof of their love of their
fellow man other than hatred of the rich. We need men
who understand how to share what they have with the
poor and deprived, as Christ and those who were filled

41

with His spirit have shown us the way.

However, my Christian brethren, as John the
Apostle of love cried out: "He, through whom the
world was made, was in the world, and the world
did not recognize him." (John I: 10-11). And as
John the Baptist before him had proclaimed:"....
....but there is one standing in your midst of
whom you know nothing," (John I:26), we too can
now call out in our time. We stand as before that
pool which the Angel stirred up from time to time
(John V:4). We have only to step into it to be
cured of our spiritual disease, but we refuse. We
have at our beck and call the fountain of living
water, but we refuse to drink of it. The tree of
life, planted by God on earth has burst forth, and
we refuse to eat of its fruit. The Redeemer has come
into the world to renew the face of the earth, but
His own people disdain His redeeming work. Because
of a falling away from Christ and from the Church
which he founded, another great evil has arisen. I
refer to the wasting away of a true, living faith in
God. If we may sum up the work of Redemption in a
few words, it was meant to teach men to acknowledge
God and to give them the strength to live according
to this Faith. The words of Jesus Christ, ".....none
knows the Son truly except the Father, and none knows
the Father truly except the Son, and those to whom
it is the Son's good pleasure to reveal him." (Matt.
11:27) seem to have come to fulfillment in our time
where men have turned their backs on Christ and His
Church. The most gruesome distortion of the true
teaching of God is the distinguishing characteristic
of our age and the inevitable consequence of our falling away from Christ and His Church.

In our discussion of the right of property, we
saw what a grave distortion the loss of the true Faith
has caused in that area. Without a lively, practiced
Faith in God, two extreme positions resulted: the
wholesale abuse of the property right on the one hand,
and its outright annihilation on the other. Both are
equally destructive of true human society. But this
is only a small part of the sad story of how man's
weakened faith in God has disrupted society. As a

building rests on a foundation, so society rests on certain basic truths without which it cannot exist. Numbered among these truths, aside from the right of private property, are the all-important teachings on human liberty, on the destiny of man, and on marriage and the family. When these foundation stones are in order, when they are based on truth, only then can we expect a healthy and vigorous society. If they are otherwise, then society is threatened by collapse like a house whose foundation is destroyed. Having examined our social conditions and recognized to what extent our loss of the true Faith has undermined one foundation stone, the property right, I think it might be worthwhile to direct our attention now to how this disbelief has affected the other bases of our society. Thus we will gain a better perspective of our times; and the imminent collapse of our social structure can be a more compelling incentive than any mere words to lead us to return to Christ and His Church.

I shall begin with the teaching on human liberty and its relation to God's law. First, I would like to make it clear that I have no intention of discussing political liberty or of defending or opposing one or the other form of government. Since I became a priest, I have made it a solemn rule never again to belong to a political party. I feel I owe this to every person and to every political party, since I must put my strength and my services at the disposal of all of them as a servant of God and preacher of His word for the good of their souls. I have remained true to this principle until now and I intend to remain so.

The teaching regarding the freedom of the human person is essentially connected with the teaching about God. Belief and unbelief reach completely opposite conclusions. Therefore I must first speak about God so that I may then correctly teach about human freedom.

If we reflect for a moment on human history, we will recognize, with reference to man's belief in God, three closely related thoughts. First, we see that the belief in a personal God is so deeply imbedded by nature in man's spiritual life that it is to be found wherever there are people. Man cannot deny the existence of the sun because he lives from its warmth. In the

43

same way, mankind, by and large, cannot deny the existence of God since it derives existence and life from
God; and in its own peculiar fashion, it is bound by
the will of God. Secondly, we see the human spirit
inclined toward evil and the intellect so weakened
and darkened that even this most basic of all truths
did not always survive intact but has been subjected
to a continual distortion. Thirdly, we recognize that
man's passions and rebellion against God's law are
the basic sources of this distortion of the true
teachings about God. Only by considering these three
truths in their relationship to each other are we able
to reach an intelligent understanding of human history.
If there were no personal transcendant God, one could
not explain the universal recognition of the existence
of a God. If the proposition: I think, therefore I am,
is true then the proposition: Mankind thinks that of
necessity there is a God, therefore there is a God, is
no less true. Man may twist and turn all he wants. By
doing so he can no more negate his own existence than
he can destroy the idea of God which is essentially
related to his own existence. It is no less necessary,
however, that we recognize and accept as true the weakening and darkening of man's intellect, which is only
made intelligible to us by the doctrine of original
sin. Without that weakening one could not explain the
perversion of this and so many other basic truths. And
without the doctrine of original sin, one could not
really grasp the prevalence of error. Having grasped
these truths, on the other hand, one can understand the
fate which belief in the true God has suffered among men.
Among the pagans - least touched by the influence of
supernatural revelation - we see the knowledge of God
most severely distorted.

But as unnatural and unreasonable as their notion
of God was, still they held fast to it, since they were
thereby able to satisfy an innate belief in some supreme
being. They preferred even the nonsense of man-made gods
to the vastly greater nonsense of no God at all. Insofar
as the pagans fashioned their gods according to their
own passions, they demonstrated to us that the ultimate source of their errors and of the distortion of
the belief in one true God is to be found in their
passions and in their rebellion against the law which

44

an unperverted concept of God imposed upon them. The history of the Jews drives home to us best of all this important teaching, so necessary for grasping the idea of human liberty. It shows us that all distortions of belief in the one true God do not originate in the speculative intellect, but from practice; not by force of reason, but by the rule of passions, and by the revolt in man's life style against the law of God. The knowledge of the true God and His laws was revealed to the Jews; but they became so lukewarm in their attempts to live up to the laws, that they rebelled against the true God and fell into idolatry to escape from Him. Only through Christ, who opened new sources of grace to strengthen man's will and enlighten his mind, do we see man reconciled in a correct understanding of God. After men once again began to feel strong in their belief and lived according to the faith which dwellt within them, any idea of rebellion against God disappeared. They recognized the truth of the words, "Only the fool says in his heart there is no God." (Psalms, 52:1) Among people who live by God's law, the denial of God is not possible. But since men had once again turned from Christ and His saving graces, the rebellion against God's law and eventually against the new notion of God has begun anew in their hearts. Only now, the combat occurs on a new kind of battle ground. The light which Christianity spread through the world prevents such crude errors as marked the pre-Christian era. Error became far more sophisticated and malicious to the point where it transgresses all reasonable limits. It was reserved for our age to repeat here on earth the rebellion of those Angels who, fully aware of their position as God's creatures, nevertheless dared to revolt against God! We have among us not just individual disbelievers, but an entire generation of them. So old as the stones are of which this Church is built and, so long as the sun shines upon the earth and bears witness to the glory of Him Who created it, so long as the raindrops have fallen from heaven to freshen the flowers of the field, so long as the heavenly dew of God's grace has seeped into men's souls to enliven them and quicken them with holy charity, that is how long we have not experienced on this earth such an icy, frigid, diabolical teaching emanating from the mouths of men.

45

After we understand all of this, my Christian brethren, the teaching of human freedom, as it is interpreted according to a Christian belief in God and the Catholic Church as contrasted with its inter-pretation by unbelievers, is easy to grasp.

The unbeliever has, for practical purposes, nothing left but man himself. He does not recognize any subordination of one man to another according to a higher order of things beyond what is merely human. Therefore, he must logically proclaim the sovereignty of each individual. Every law imposed by God or by his fellowman, in fact any rule which is not fashioned by himself, is no law at all but merely compulsion or an unjust intrusion on his sovereignty. Laws are only restrictions which a man imposes on himself of his own free choice. In such a context, to be free means merely to do as one pleases. Every man is free to contradict everything that anyone else has ever proclaimed as true and good and right until he has proved it to his own satisfaction.

Even this notion of freedom has a kernel of truth in it which we need to isolate in order to make clear the massive, grotesque untruth and folly of such a position. Christianity wishes to guarantee to man his innermost freedom, and it accords moral value only to those actions which stem from the free choice of each person. However, it recognizes an objective truth, goodness, and beauty existing independent of man to which man must conform if he wishes to fulfill himself. The unbelief of our time does not understand self-determination in this way. It does not accept an objective truth, goodness, and beauty; and every in-dividual may contest what all others may regard as good so long as he himself does not recognize it as such.

It is difficult to see how any kind of social living among people is still possible when such a con-cept of human liberty prevails. This kind of liberty cannot be limited in any way according to age, sex, or levels of intellectual development. As a matter of fact, how can one still declare anyone insane, given such freedom? Every child, every woman, every mentally depraved person has the same right. Anyone can call into question the entire existing social order whether

46

in the family, the community, or the state. This order
does not even exist until he himself acknowledges it
and indeed, only so long as he is willing to acknowledge
it. Even a contract between two persons would be inconceivable, since such an agreement would constitute
external force at any time after one of the contracting parties began to feel unhappy about the provisions
of the contract. Thus it would constitute a violation
of his basic human rights.

The Christian notion of human liberty as taught by
the Church stands completely opposed to this ridiculous notion which would in fact make all social relationships impossible. The Christian concept of human
liberty assumes the existence of a personal transcendant God in whom dwells all truth, all goodness, and
all beauty. From all eternity, He had the notion of
our earth in His mind, and He created the earth according to this notion. He alone enjoys the absolute
right of self-determination, absolute sovereignty, and
dominion. Nevertheless, He created man according to
His own image, and therefore He incorporated in human
nature something of His own freedom and self-determination.
Yet, the nature of human freedom is such that it implies
in man the capacity to either use it to pursue God's
goodness, truth, and beauty, or to turn aside from
these. In other words, human freedom means that man
is capable of developing according to God's plan, or
to rebel against it at the peril of his own self-
destruction! Because of original sin, the full
liberty of man was dealt a crippling blow inasmuch
as he was more disposed to rebel against God. It was
by the Redemption that full liberty was restored to
man. Christianity accords to man his full right of
self-determination and recognizes in this right his
fullest dignity and nobility. In fact, Christianity
by its doctrine of eternal damnation recognizes the
ultimate consequence of this right, because this
teaching implies that God will even permit men to
eternally contradict Him rather than violate man's
sacred right to self-determination. The ultimate
cause for eternal damnation is abuse of free will
by setting it in final opposition to God's will.
Christianity sees in such a disposition of the will,
not an exercise of legitimate freedom, but rather a
punishable violation of liberty, a transgression against

47

God and His liberty which, of course, is higher than
our own. According to the Christian conception, man
is a free agent of God, who is entitled to help God
complete His work. As a master builder originates a
construction project in His mind and authorizes his
employees to bring it to fulfillment, so God has conceived in His mind the design for the human race and
trusted us to carry it into fulfillment. Inspired by
the goodness, truth, and beauty of this ideal, we
ought to adopt it freely as sons of God and carry it
into execution. In this way God proposes to make His
work our own and to reward us for our free compliance.

We have set forth briefly the two opposed doctrines
of human liberty, and we have shown how they are related to the notion of God and His laws. It remains
for us to stress the importance and obvious falsehood
of that teaching which holds that to be truly free man
cannot accept any law outside of himself.

We are told that man is the only and highest lawgiver who must follow only his own laws; yet man finds
himself limited by nature which is independent of his
will; in fact he must constantly submit to nature's
laws. What power does man have over nature and the
perpetual laws and order which govern it? We see the
stars in the heavens follow their unchangeable course,
just as does the earth on which we live. We watch the
trees and flowers sprout, grow, bloom, and fade according to unchangeable laws. Only an intelligent
being can promote such order in the universe. But
what intelligent being is it that holds nature on its
course? If our intelligence is a part of this higher
intelligence, then why are we so powerless to change
the laws of nature?

But we are bound even more firmly by a law outside ourselves, despite the protests of those who would
dare to violate any law not of their own making. Man's
physical nature is a part of the natural world whose
prisoner he is and whose laws he must obey unless he
wishes to bring about his physical destruction. How
pathetic a spectacle man is, my Christian brethren,
when he maintains, in his insane arrogance, that he
recognizes no law or lawgiver beyond himself - at the
same time that he is forced day and night to minister
to the need of his physical nature. What power does

48

man have over the laws governing his physical nature?
He has two alternatives. Either he obeys them and
enjoys bodily health; or he violates them and suffers
sickness and eventual destruction. Indeed, the Supreme
Lawgiver could not have made more obvious the lying
pretensions of man to be his own lawgiver than to
saddle him with a body and make him subject to its
basest needs. But a man's soul too is subject to a
law and bound by a necessity from which it cannot
escape, and which forces man to recognize a Lawgiver
outside himself. Thought, the freest of all human
actions, must follow the laws of thought. What power
do we have over the laws of thought? It is either -
or. Either we obey these laws and we are reasonable
people, or we disregard them and destroy reason and
we are adjudged as fools.

With each thought, man is forced to acknowledge
a law and therefore a lawgiver. This is the same as
saying there is a higher personal Will which we must
acknowledge and from which we cannot escape.

Finally, we also recognize that man's will, and
the conduct of his life which reflects his will is
subject to a law - the moral law. This law is no less
demanding and no less independent of man's own will
for determining his conduct than the laws of thought
are in governing his thinking. He is no more able to
alter it than he is able to alter the laws of nature
or of thought. He may act according to it and reach
his full dignity as a human being, or he may act counter
to it and destroy his human worth. It is in the area
of morality that the false notion of liberty comes
into play, and where man tries to shake off the yoke
of an outside lawgiver so as to cater to his passions
according to his own laws. But he is eternally destined to fail in this attempt. The consensus of all
mankind will always condemn the attempt to deny the
objective moral law as it is expressed in the teaching
of Christian virtues. No matter how persistently the
advocates of this doctrine of freedom may insist that,
as they see it, theft, robbery, unchastity, and sloth
are licit, the voice of good moral sense will pass
judgement on them and teach them that there is a
supreme Lawgiver and an objective moral law according
to which every man must order his life if he does not

wish to dehumanize himself in the eyes of his fellow man.

Thus God has instilled a goal in man's very nature by virtue of the law which governs him and by virtue of the sanctions which are inseparable from the breach of those laws. To make man in His own image, God gave him freedom. Thereby man was enabled to reach his full dignity, but it is also within his capacity to sink to a most degraded level. At the outermost limit of this folly, men came up with the strange teaching that there is no lawgiver other than man himself and that man needs only to follow his own impulses. To curb this madness, God erected a barrier which proclaims, in effect, "This far and no further!" He has permitted man to proclaim nonsense, but He will not permit him to carry it through with impunity. God forces man, first, to give the lie to his own proclamation, in that man must constantly and of necessity subject himself to a law of nature, a law of thought, and a law of conduct over which he has no control, and in the face of which he is impotent - as impotent as the lowest worm which creeps along the ground.

In the second instance, God has stigmatized rebellion against His laws in nature, thought, and conduct with the mark of death. Man may insist that he follows his own inner impulses, but if he dares to act against the law of physical nature, thought, and conduct which God has ordained for him, if he dares to rebel against the social order which God wills, then he will begin to live in a manner which leads to the destruction of his body, the annihilation of reason, moral degeneration, and chaos in society. Ironclad necessity in the law of God will weigh heavily on him and lead to his inevitable destruction. In the battle against the law of nature, the fool occasions the death of the body. In fighting against the laws of thought, he brings sickness and eventually death to the intellect; in battling against the moral law, he makes life unbearable; and in attacking social order, he makes normal social relations among people an impossibility. Finally, and thirdly, God has linked to the exercise of this erroneous notion of freedom its exact opposite, a most complete and degrading kind

of slavery. If a man will not serve God and live by
His eternal law - which safeguards true human freedom -
such a man will achieve not freedom, but its opposite,
abject slavery. He will be subject to a domination
which does not preserve freedom, but annihilates it.
Every man is subject to the conflict of which the Apostle
Paul spoke: "Inwardly, I applaud God's disposition,
but I observe another disposition in my lower self,
which raises war against the disposition of my conscience, and so I am handed over as a captive to that
disposition towards sin which my lower self contains."
(Romans 7: 22-23). Those who follow the law of God
take pleasure in His law and achieve true freedom since
truth makes a man free. And as the Apostle said further:
"....and natural wisdom brings only death whereas the
wisdom of the spirit brings life and peace. That is
because natural wisdom is at enmity with God, not sub-
mitting itself to His law; it is impossible that it
should." (Rom. 8: 6-7). Therefore, he who will not
be made free by God's law will become a slave of his
own flesh and lust according to the law of the flesh!
The fate of Nebuchadnezar is a prototype of man's
destiny. Man is too proud to be free under God's law,
but not too proud to be a slave to his own basest
passions. Therefore what befell Nebuchadnezar according to Scripture, will also befall man in the deepest
spiritual sense. "...driven from the haunts of men,
with beasts dwell thou, grass like the cattle eat thou,
till seven seasons have passed thee by, and learned
thou hast that the most High is overlord of all human
kingship, to grant it where he will." (Daniel 4:29)

My Christian brethren, let us come to realize
without having to undergo such bitter experience, that
the All High God rules also among men, and that our
freedom is to be found in freely subjecting ourselves
to His laws. It is impossible to conceal the fact,
however, that this guidepost for social living is already badly obscured and that the quest for a freedom
which recognizes no external law and order is already
widespread. On the basis of such a misconception, the
survival of any kind of sane social relationships among
men, whether in the family circle, or in the community,
or beyond, is becoming impossible. If this viewpoint
becomes prevalent, mankind will suffer the fate of
Nebuchadnezar. We shall live like animals, subject

51

to our basest passions; and the seven ages of this
degradation, destruction, wilderness and barbarism
will last until mankind in its abject misery will
come to realize that the All High God is dominant
also in the kingdom of men. Amen.

Fourth Sermon

The Christian Concept of Human Destiny

Monday before Christmas in the Cathedral
at Mainz, 18 December 1848

"And indeed, Lord, thou knowest all things, new and
old; it is thou that hast fashioned me, thy hand has
been laid upon me."
(Psalms 139:5-6)

My Christian Brethren, yesterday we examined the doctrine of human liberty and its relationship to God's law, and we recognized in it an essential basis for social living. The enormous influence of these doctrines on social conditions is apparent in our times. If we mean by liberty, along with the author of "Social Policy"[3] and his followers, as well as all of those who deny the existence of a personal, transcendant God, the right of each individual to recognize as binding only such laws as he himself finds to his liking and to disregard all others, then social human relations become impossible. If the stars were to free themselves of the course to which each is bound, they would collide and destroy each other. That is what would happen to humanity under similar conditions. The evidence of this theory of freedom is already widespread. It remains to be seen whether we may have to live through the horrible drama of a situation where mankind succeeds in emancipating itself completely from all bonds of order. It is certain, however, that if that time actually does come, it will be more frightful than anything men have ever had to experience. It is just as certain that this is exactly what will come to pass unless we change our ways and acknowledge the dominion of God. If we come to recognize, instead, that freedom is the right of a person to develop and conform himself of his own free will to the Divine plan, the we shall participate in the grand design of God, who is concerned with all of reality, including the life of each and every person, and we will enjoy the order in which each man finds his proper role and shares in the unfolding of God's plan.

Today we will move on to that other principle of social living, the understanding that men have of their destiny here on earth. We shall shortly realize what great influence this vital teaching has on social conditions of our time. It is amazing, in fact, how anyone can go through life without ever seriously asking himself the question why he is on earth! That ought to be the first question that we ask ourselves once we acquire the use of reason, since the direction toward which we expend the resources of our bodies and our souls, as well as our gifts and talents depends entirely upon how we answer this question for ourselves. St. Bernard often asked himself in his cell, "Bernard, why are you here?"

We ought to do likewise, time and time again. Otherwise it is entirely possible that we could make the entire journey through life and discover suddenly on our death bed that we have completely missed the point of our pilgrimage on this earth.

Here again, there are just two conceivable reasons for living which relate back to whether a man believes in a personal, transcendant God or not. Our destination is either outside of this world, in God, in which case our life on earth is merely a preparation for that ultimate goal - or else our destiny is to enjoy what we are able to enjoy here on earth and to terminate our existence afterwards like the animals do. The believer prefers the former view, the unbeliever holds the latter. Let us consider both these viewpoints along with the great impact they have on human social relationships. We begin with the viewpoint of the unbeliever.

Whoever has scuttled his belief in a transcendant, personal God such a person must, to be consistent, also abandon his belief in the immortality of the individual soul along with any hope for eternal personal existence after the death of the body. In fact, he must not entertain any notion that man has a destiny beyond the grave. Indeed, men have abandoned these beliefs in our time with the same brashness as they have denied the existence of God. One cannot, therefore, question whether all such unbelievers have really asked themselves why they are on earth. One of the spokesmen for these atheists has stated clearly that the belief in the immortality of man is just as nonsensical as the belief in God. Man's destiny must be his life on this earth, because he knows nothing about what lies beyond. A much larger group than these consistent atheists, however, follow this line of belief only in a practical sense, i.e., by their actions, while they keep pretending to believe in God and in human immortality. Countless numbers of our contemporaries belong to the latter group. They carry on as though they know of no God or of any life after death and as though this life were their final destiny. They render homage to the flesh, which of necessity leads to the death of the spirit. We have to number

them, therefore, among the professing atheists,
since their practical atheism has the same effect on
our social condition.

The consequences of this concept of man's destiny
are truly catastrophic for our society. There are,
it seems to me, at least four. First, the viewpoint
that man is on earth merely to enjoy worldly pleasures,
of necessity has to lead to a general aversion to work.
All work is to some degree difficult and tiresome and
interferes with the pleasure cult. Perhaps a person
who is enslaved to this cult may wish to work in the
sense that a rich man wants to exercise, so that he
will enjoy a better appetite. But work in the sense
of tedious daily labor in the sweat of one's brow,
the kind of work which is rarely recreative and enjoy-
able, in other words, that work which is the common
lot of most of mankind and which is the real source
of the wealth of nations, the kind of work with which
we could not dispense for one day without general
chaos and deprivation, that work which is necessary
to provide us with our daily bread and which the transcendant, personal God told us about when He said,
"You will earn your bread by the sweat of your brow..."
that manner of work will be shunned by people who are
given over to the hedonistic viewpoint. There are
already ominous portents of such a development. If
this sick attitude captivates the masses of the people,
the horrible consequences of such an aversion to honest
labor will be indescribable.

Just as such an attitude must promote disdain for
labor as juxtaposed to the life of pleasure, it must
also, on the other hand, cause an unbounded increase
in the craving for worldly sense pleasures and for the
means to satisfy them. If it becomes, in fact, our
sole objective to enjoy sense pleasures, then given
the uncertainty of a man's life span, a general competition must ensue where each person strives to get
for himself the greatest possible share of the goods
of this world and the means to acquire them.

Thirdly, this hedonism will necessarily cause
those who own a quantity of worldly goods to strive,
by whatever means, to increase them and to hold on to
them for their own exclusive enjoyment. Avarice, hard-

heartedness, and selfishness of the worst sort will
spread more and more among the wealthy. No philosophy
of life is more calculated to harden the hearts of the
wealthy towards the poor. True charity and benevolence
do not flow from natural sympathy. Human experience
bears constant witness to that fact. These virtues
stem from a firm belief in a higher destiny for man
after death. He who believes in eternal life will
invest his capital so as to earn interest in paradise.
The other viewpoint can only generate greed and hard-
ness of heart.

Finally, what must this worldly philosophy do
to the poor who lack all means of achieving the goal
of worldly pleasures? The immediate consequences will
be hatred, envy, and ill-will toward the rich who have
what they themselves do not have; and one can scarcely
be surprised at these logical consequences given the
lack of belief in God. The ultimate consequences will
be that the poor man will resort to any means other
than honest labor to achieve his worldly goal. Cheating,
robbery, theft, and even murder are the logical consequences of this false philosophy - as we are already
beginning to learn to our great sorrow.

That, my Christian Brethren, is the inevitable
outcome of the loss of belief in a life after death,
so far as human social relations are concerned. Disdain
for honest labor along with insatiable greed and pleasure-seeking will be the lot of every person. Among
the rich there will be, in addition, stinginess and
hard-heartedness toward the poor. Among the poor,
theft and robbery, hatred and envy toward the rich
will come to prevail. Eventually, of course, this
corrupt teaching, which makes the enjoyment of earthly
pleasure the ultimate destiny of mankind would have to
come full circle, as every lie must. It would destroy
all civilized social relationships as well as any
genuine pleasure in life.

We must add that this denial of human immortality is not only godless and destructive of all social
order; it is also unreasonable. It stems not from
reason, but from unreason. It is rooted not in the
spirit; it derives from the flesh which, with all of
its sensuous drives, is at war with the spirit.

When we look into the recesses of our souls, a thousand voices cry out to us that we are immortal, that we are destined for eternal life.

If the belief in immortality and in a life after death is a delusion, how could such a belief have arisen and come to prevail? How come we donot graze contentedly like cattle here on earth, and how come one always finds a craving in the human heart, like the craving for a beloved homeland? How could it happen that precisely the greatest and deepest thinkers of all ages, as well as the noblest and purest spirits, have clung to this belief? What does it signify to us when we observe huge flights of birds overhead each Spring and Fall, drawn to their destinies in the same way we are drawn to another abode? At night, as we lift our eyes heavenward and observe the stars in the vast canopy of the heavens, our hearts also wonder and yearn as if to separate themselves from our bodies in the universal quest for some home across the seas that is without sorrows. It is the proof found in man's soul that we are in exile here, that we are destined for a better world.

If man's belief in immortality and in a life beyond this one is nonsense, if it is man's nature to die and to remain dead - as it is the flower's nature to wilt, the tree's destiny to be cut down, the animal's destiny to decay, then how do we explain the deep, universal dread of death in human hearts? This abhorrence can never be overcome except by a belief in immortality. Man clings to nothing so desperately as to the slender thread of life. From the babe at its mother's breast, to the venerable old man who sees his powers fading, there is universal recognition that death is not natural to them, that they are destined for eternal life.

If belief in a hereafter is nonsense, why are the children of the world so disturbed in their hearts as they see worldly goods come, go, and disappear each day of their lives? Why does the transitory nature of their pleasures frighten them so, and why does the realization that their joys are fleeting make them bitter? Why does the rich man suffer virtual torture, who, even while he greedily con-

templates his houses, goods and money, seems to hear
the words, "Thou fool, this night you will be called
to account. What good will your possessions be to
you then?" Why does the man of the world suffer agony
when he begins to sense that the passion with which
he seeks his pleasure is growing cold? Why does the
vain woman go through torture when she recognizes that
all the cosmetics and adornments can no longer preserve
that by which she seduced others? Why should the
transitory nature of all material things of this earth -
since it is of their nature to be transitory - cast
their shadow over all of the joys of this world? That
is the ultimate proof written deep in man's heart,
that he is destined for a life of everlasting joy and
that passing pleasure cannot be his final destiny.

If the belief in man's immortality and in eternal
life is madness, if the enjoyment of the pleasures of
this world is our final destiny, how is it possible
then that the vast majority of mankind is unable to
achieve this destiny? What is the destiny of the poor
on this earth who suffer untold agonies so as scarcely
ever to know a joyous moment? Indeed, one hears the
reply that poverty is about to be abolished, and everyone will be in a position to enjoy the good things
of this world. I will disregard for the moment whether
it is indeed possible to abolish poverty. Assuming
that it were possible, is poverty the only obstacle
to enjoyment of earthly bliss? What of the countless
numbers of those who are sick in body and soul, some
of whom suffer for years and some of whom are even
confined to their sickbeds an entire lifetime? What
is their destiny and what consolation can we offer
them? Our self-annointed humanitarians of the public
forum never quite make it to the bedsides of the indigent sick. That is our task. With what message of
consolation do they equip us? I have witnessed time
and again with amazement the strength which Christian
teaching affords to those who suffer from horrible
and lengthy illnesses. There is no more convincing
evidence of the truth and Divine power of Christianity
than the joy which it is able to bring to the hearts
of the suffering. I have often marvelled and admired
as I witnessed the calm and patience of those who suffered poverty and misery and unspeakable pain, some-

times over a period of years and without a murmur of complaint. There I witnessed an inner joy such as I have never been able to detect among the children of the world surrounded by all of their pleasures. How many of such patient sufferers besieged by great external tribulation, yet displaying an indescribable inner peace, I have already known and loved in my own life time. Everything that I have heard in the world about courage, strength, and resolution appear to me to be mere shadows of the courage, strength and determination of Christian souls bearing their sufferings with their glance turned toward eternal life! Is a Faith which can produce such enormous, spiritual strength to be written off as nonsense? Should we approach these robust spirits and inform them that they have no goal other than to enjoy the passing pleasures of this world? And since they are unable to attain these pleasures, are we to leave them with no other companion in their suffering but the disconsolate thought that they have no further destiny on earth, that they are no longer in a position to achieve the normal goal of humankind? In keeping with such a philosophy, there is nothing left for a considerable part of the human race but suicide! Put an end to mortal life which has as its only purpose the enjoyment of worldly pleasures and which is no longer in a position to do so! Such a teaching is supposed to represent the ultimate truth? No, never! Nature cannot be so unnatural as to give a man his life with a goal that he cannot reach. So long as there is a sick man or a suffering person on earth who feels in his heart that he is destined for happiness, our innermost souls must accept that we are destined for a better life.

Now let us envision ourselves at the deathbed of someone near and dear to us. Even though it is true that we live in an age which is not marked by great love among persons; scarcely any man is so alone that he does not have a son, a brother, a friend to whom he is not bound by some bond of affection. Now place yourself at the bedside of the one who is dearest to you as this one lies dying. Consider the position of such a person at the moment when he draws his last breath, at the moment the light of life leaves the

61

eyes into which you so often saw your own joy mirrored.
Now he can no longer respond to your farewell greeting
and his hand becomes limp in your grasp. Could you
bear the thought of never again enjoying a reunion
with this soul? Can you find any consolation in the
belief that this person has reached his final destiny -
to become a feast for worms, or to be like a tree that
has been felled and is thrown into the fire? Does
it ease your grief to believe that this soul has
died with the body, or that it has become an indis-
tinguishable part of some vague world spirit? How
can we explain the strong, determined, insuperable
craving to see again and to love and possess this
particular personality in its full integrity? Whence
the consolation which the true Christian finds at the
moment of someone's death because of the belief that
he will see the deceased again? That is proof enough
that there is an immortal soul in the person whom you
love, with which your soul is destined to be reunited
for all eternity.

If the belief in a hereafter and in personal survival after death is nonsense, then what are the prospects for human yearning that justice be done to all
men and that everyone ought to get his just deserts?
The instinct for eventual justice cannot be eradicated
from the human spirit. Even the inmates of prisons
who are paying for their crimes and who are often
hardened beyond the reach of all human sentiments demand
justice and want to be dealt with justly. It is this
universal instinct for justice which gives rise to the
concern for justice in human society. The just society
is an ideal that people dream of. In such a societe-
each will get his just deserts according to his good
and bad deeds, either reward or punishment, honor or
dishonor, love or contempt. Can this ideal be fulfilled
on earth? Who passes judgement on men's thoughts?
Yet it is thoughts that determine what a man will do,
and it is a man's intentions that determine the real
worth of our actions. This whole important area of
human action remains exempt from human courts of law.
But even the actual deeds and transactions of men cannot all be made to conform to the ideal of full justice
here on earth. Here we have an appropriate saying:
"One hangs the petty thieves while the big ones remain

at large." I am not suggesting that one does this
kind of thing on purpose, but the fact remains. The
more clever and crafty people are, the more adept
they are at escaping justice on earth. Whereas the
shrewd scoundrel can turn a fat profit dishonestly,
defrauding widows and orphans, all the while enjoying
esteem and a good life, it is entirely possible that
a widow defrauded by him may end up in jail for having taken a piece of bread for her hungry children.
Who will see to it that justice is done between the
evil rich man and the virtuous poor man, between the
person who goes through life in perfect health and
the poor man whose entire lot in life is ill health,
between the one fellow who by lying, swindling, and
intrigue achieves fame and enjoys the esteem of his
fellow man and the other person who suffers unjust
persecution, contempt and dishonor? My Christian
Brethren, if there is no all-knowing Judge who sees
the secrets in men's hearts, if there is no general
judgement where all thoughts, words, and deeds, all
sorrows and joys are judged and balanced off for all
mankind to see, if there is no hereafter where every
man will get his just deserts, we may as well throw
over our poor, imperfect earthly justice too. Then
injustice reigns supreme and all thought of equity
is madness. But that is not the case. Just as
certainly as there is in man a hankering for justice,
there is also a Lord of heaven and earth who holds
the scales of justice in His hands; and there is a
final Court where sentence will be pronounced and
an eternity where every man will reap what he personally has sown - reward for the just, and punishment for the unjust.

    Finally, my Christian Brethren, if life on earth
and its enjoyment were our final and only destiny, why
is it that all good things which this earth has to
offer cannot satisfy fully the heart of any single
person? There must exist something which can satisfy
the universal yearning of the human heart for happiness.
If temporal goods are our final end, then there must
be joys on earth which are available to every man and
which so satisfy the craving for bliss that the human
heart is completely fulfilled. As food satisfies the
body's hunger, that being the natural destiny of food,
so the pleasures of this world ought to satisfy the

cravings of the soul, if they were indeed the ultimate objects toward which the soul is directed. But here again we come up against the limit which God sets for our folly. We like to insist that life here on earth is our final end, but we are unable to come up with any temporal good which we can say is able to satisfy man's thirst for happiness. God has implanted a craving in man's soul which cannot in all eternity be satisfied except by the possession of God. There is conclusive evidence of the high dignity and noble destiny of man in the fact that all the knowledge and all the beauty on this earth has not been able to satisfy man's deepest yearnings. In fact, God has even attached to the enjoyment of worldly pleasures a certain satiety, even revulsion. Who can measure the anguish of a man who has set his sights on fulfilling himself with worldly pleasures and who, after wallowing in them, is left with the inevitable emptiness, disgust and revulsion? What St. Augustine discovered in his own life is what every man learns for himself. He was favored with all the bounty that nature can lavish on a person. He plunged into the world, full of zeal to satisfy his soul's yearning for truth and his heart's hankering for pleasure. After he had exhausted all the knowledge and pleasure which the world had to offer, he made his great acknowledgement: "Lord, you have created us for Yourself. And our hearts cannot rest until they rest in You." From then on he knew peace and found happiness which he had been pursuing in vain. His only regret was that he had found lasting beauty and came to love it so late. Let us follow Augustine and end the quest after what we cannot find, true happiness without God. Like his, our hearts will chase after inner peace without rest and fail to find it until we come to know and love God.

The teaching of Christianity and of our Faith is in full harmony with the inherent recognition of the soul that it is destined for eternal life. According to the teaching of the Church, God created man to know Him, to love Him and to serve Him, and thus to merit a bliss which no ear has yet heard and no eye has yet seen and which no human heart has yet realized. In this world, however, man has no other final destiny, now that he has fallen from grace, but

64

to prepare himself by the ordering of his free will
for eternal happiness, that is to say for the possession of God whom Christ manifested to us here on earth.
That is why the Church rightfully regards life on earth
as a pilgrimage, a kind of exile. It is true that we
are strangers here, and only God and his domain represent our homeland. We are exiles so long as we are not
united with God and so long as we cannot see love, and
be in possession of His eternal essence. We know,
therefore, my Christian Brethren, whence we came.
No one can answer this basic, all-important question
for us. We are from God who created us out of nothing.
We know Who preserves us from the abyss of nothingness.
It is God with His hand upon us. We know why God created
us - to love and possess Him. We know the reason for
our sojourn here on earth - to prepare ourselves for the
Kingdom of God. We know, finally, what this hunger and
thirst in our hearts is all about: They represent a
craving for that enjoyment of eternal bliss.

From this teaching of reason and our Faith about
the destiny of man, we derive some very important conclusions regarding life in society. These stand opposed
to the consequences of atheism referred to earlier; and
they are designed to support and strengthen life in
society, just as the opposed principles serve to undermine and destroy it.

First of all, only this view of man's destiny is
capable of instilling true diligence and cheerful acceptance of the tedium that goes along with work. True,
there is a kind of ambition for work to which a man will
submit for other motives, for example, the diligence of
the great merchant who is restless in his ambition to
enlarge his enterprise. We refer rather to that tedious,
repetitive work of the day laborer who toils for a
meager wage and but seldom achieves the enjoyment of
the world's pleasures. No man would tolerate such work
if he regarded worldly pleasure as his sole destiny.
Still, we can scarcely do without this kind of labor
since the wealth of a nation arises largely from it.
We must either have a race of men who perform such
work dutifully or, as was true in ancient times, we
will have to experience again a situation where one
part of mankind forcefully subjugates the other part

65

so that it can consign this unpleasant work to slaves. It is one of the mysteries of Christianity, that it is capable of instilling a spirit in man which enables him to perform unavoidable and unpleasant tasks cheerfully and without complaint. It is on this spirit that Christianity erected a social order which could be destroyed by man, but can never be rebuilt without the benefit of Christian spirit.

While Christianity, by its teaching of man's final destiny, can inspire true industry and thereby guarantee genuine well-being, it nevertheless moderates by virtue of that same teaching, uncontrolled striving for the goods and pleasures of the world. For the unbeliever, temporal goods and pleasures are the only goal after which man must seek. For the believer, they are only a means designed to help him in his quest for eternal salvation. The rich man who is aware of his eternal destiny will therefore not regard his possessions as the means for satisfying his earthly cravings, but rather as means whereby, through careful stewardship, he can attain to his eternal salvation. In using his riches he will observe the will of God, share his bounty with his less fortunate fellow man, and fight to keep all inordinate attachment to worldly goods from taking first place in his heart. At the same time, the poor man who depends for his existence on a daily wage will not look upon material goods with undisguised greed and view his more fortunate fellow man with hatred and envy. How great and exalted is the spirit of a truly Christian worker who looks with disdain not on the wealthy, but upon earthly riches with their superficial appeal. Convinced that human dignity is not the product of riches but of virtue, he gladly leaves all superficial finery to the rich and engages rather in the pursuit of virtue. He looks with pity upon those who are completely absorbed in this empty pursuit of material goods, and he rises above it in his quest for the eternal treasures. In the peace and joy of his clear conscience, this man finds in the quiet of his own humble homestead more than adequate compensation for all of his toil and labor. With such an attitude, the simple workingman has attained a level of human dignity that is attainable only with great difficulty in any other state of life. The source of

66

such a disposition is the Christian teaching regarding man's final end. It is on the fertile soil like this that one can build a social order which is capable of withstanding the tempests of the ages.

We have discussed the influence of the teaching of man's final end on social living. This guide post for social order has been shattered to its very foundation. The attitude that the destiny of man lies in the enjoyment of material goods has spread through all classes of society. Those who deny God's existence have been joined by many who, for practical purposes, live as though the pursuit of worldly pleasures were their only goal. Such practical atheism has long been the fate of the rich. Now it prevails as the dominant life style of all classes. Whether it will succeed in completing the destruction of healthy social relationships is a moot question. In league with godless teachings regarding private property and liberty, the unrestrained pursuit of material goods will have frightful consequences. It is true that God can send forth His spirit and renew the face of the earth. But then I think of the words of Peter, the Apostle: "God did not spare the angels who fell into sin; he thrust them down to hell, chained them there in the abyss, to await their sentence in torment. Nor did he spare the world he had first made; he brought a flood on that world of wickedness, preserving only Noe, who had born witness to holiness, and only seven others with him. The cities of Sodom and Gomorrha, too he punished with utter ruin, turning them to ashes, for an example to the godless of a later time." (II Peter 2:4-6) And so I fear that we, who in our godlessness have surpassed Sodom and Gomorrha, will not escape God's punishment. But God does not need to send a flood over the earth or let fire and brimstone rain down from heaven. He only needs to permit the passions, which the godless teachings of our time threaten to set loose, run their course. We will then have to drain to the very dregs the beaker of God's wrath!

Fifth Sermon

The Christian Concept of Marriage and the Family

Tuesday before Christmas in the Cathedral
at Mainz, 19 December 1848

"You who are husbands must show love to your wives,
as Christ shewed love to the Church when he gave
Himself upon its behalf."
(Ephesians 6:25-26)

We shall now pursue further the task which we
have set for ourselves, i.e., to analyze the principles on which the entire social structure rests
and the influence which belief and unbelief have
in either undermining or supporting those principles.

All told, I have proposed four such principles,
the idea of human liberty, the final destiny of man,
the right of private property, and the family.

We have already examined the first three of
these and observed what has happened to them because
of the godlessness of our era. They are infected
with and undermined by secularism, and they threaten
to collapse, bringing society and civilization crashing down with them in ruins.

It remains for us to discuss the last principle
of social order, the family. We shall see in what
condition this final support of the entire social
structure is. The family is of incalculable importance. If we find the basic ingredients for
social life still sound and incorrupt in the family,
then this single pillar is yet capable of supporting
the whole structure. Would that we could find more
comfort in the condition of the family, so that we
could find at least there a foundation that remains
solid. If I had the good fortune to be speaking to
an audience all of whose members enjoyed the blessing
of having grown up in genuine Christian families and
of having themselves experienced the saving grace of
Christian family living, then it would be a simple
matter for me to inspire you with zeal for Christ
and His Church which are the fountainheads of such
good fortune, and with a horror of the teachings
which would rob us of this source of so many blessings. How difficult it is to explain the sun to
one who has never experienced the warmth of its rays
shining on his face. And how difficult it is to put
the value and beauty of Christian family living across
to someone, who has not himself experienced this good
fortune. More than ever, I now require the assistance
of God's grace. Grant me your help, O heavenly
Redeemer, through the intercession of your Holy
Mother Mary!

71

Christian family life receives its noble character exclusively from marriage as it was instituted and sanctified by Christ. Let us therefore consider marriage and the influence which faith in God, on the one hand, and disbelief, on the other, have on it.

In the first man and woman we already see the intention of God regarding marriage and its purpose here on earth clearly expressed. When God the Father, as the Holy Bible relates, introduced Eve to Adam, the father of the entire human race gave expression to God's own design for marriage and its purpose. "That is why a man is destined to leave father and mother, and cling to his wife, so that the two become one flesh." (Gen. 2:24). In this quotation we find the three essential components of Christian marriage: love, since a man will leave father and mother for the sake of his wife; unity, for the two partners become as one; indissolubility, since they become as one flesh.

This lofty concept of marriage disappeared along with the state of innocence here on earth. Reason darkened by original sin scarcely grasped the true idea of marriage, and the will, inclined to evil by that same sin, was unable to make such a pure life into a reality. From the time of Adam until the time of Christ, the ideal of marriage disappeared from the earth. What is more, in no area of human life did corruption become more base and more persistent than in this. The Christian preacher hesitates even to hint at the abominations which paganism brought on in the moral life of the people; we do not find there the faintest recognition of the dignity of Christian marriage and Christian family living. Pagans would have been more ready to believe that one could change the paths of the stars than that one could achieve the ideal of Christian marriage here on earth. The debasement of woman was an inevitable consequence of the degradation of marriage. A woman was no longer a person, but a thing. She had no rights, no independence of her own, and her only destiny was to serve the will and the lusts of men. It is even more noteworthy that revelation among the Jews did not make known God's plan for marriage in its full perfection. Christ told his disciples that Moses allowed a man to leave his wife because of "your hard hearts, but

in the beginning it was not so." (Matt. 19:8). Man
was rendered so incapable of grasping the authentic
idea of marriage after his reason and will were
crippled by original sin that God did not even reveal
it in its fulness to the Jews.

That is how matters still stand, my Christian
Brethren. Marriage is an exclusive treasure of
Christianity; and so that there may be no misunderstanding, let me say that marriage is the sacred
possession of a true, living, full Christianity;
I mean Christianity as it is embodied in the Catholic
Church. Only Christianity in the form where it can
bring the full saving grace of its teachings and
sacraments to bear on man's soul is able to effec-
tuate the high ideal of Christian marriage. It is
with man as it is with the soil from which he wishes
to grow fruit. The better the fruit that one aspires
to produce, the more carefully must the soil be
prepared. So it is with Christian virtues. The
better one would cultivate them, the more they require for their successful cultivation the preparation of the soul by the grace of God, won for us by
Christ. In reverence toward marriage we have the
best index of the level of Christian living that a
people has achieved. By the same token, to the extent that a people becomes separated from God and His
Church, to the same extent Christian marriage will
more and more disappear among them. One may observe
this among those creeds which have separated themselves from Christianity's true tree of life, the
Catholic Church. The twig which is first to shrivel
up when the branch is cut off from the vine is marriage.
Whereas the separated Churches are able for centuries
to draw some nourishment from the reservoir of strength
that is left to them from the true Church, what happens
to marriage provides at once the evidence that the
spring from which life flows has been sealed off.
Even there, however, where the branch is not yet fully
separated from the vine which is the Church, and where
from outward appearances there is still a connection,
we begin to see marriage deteriorate. Everyday experience supports this claim. We live in a time of
pseudo-Christianity. So many people are still externally linked with the Church, who really have

73

separated themselves in their basic beliefs. The consequence is the deterioration of marriage and family life, the destruction of the familial spirit which we so much lament today. We can't be surprised, therefore that secularism, where it runs its full course, even dares to wage war against this Christian institution which brings so much happiness to mankind. The secularist dares to contest along with Christianity's teaching about God, human liberty, human destiny, and private property, also the whole idea of marriage, and to present it as a dispensible institution. With this shameless undertaking the battle against God has returned to its original source, the revolt of the flesh against the law of God.

Let us turn now to a consideration of the essence of Christian marriage so that we may gain an appreciation of its great dignity and its enormous benefits for human society.

As I mentioned before, my Christian Brethren, the essential elements of matrimony are all contained in the words which the father of the human race spoke and which express God's design, namely, love, unity, and indissolubility. It was the work of Jesus Christ, not to alter the plan which the Creator put into nature, but to purify it from sin and the corruption that flowed from sin, and to restore it to its pristine, original purpose. In Christianity we find, therefore, the same essential elements of marriage that were expressed by our first parents. But we must recognize with the Apostle Paul: "Only, the grace which came to us was out of all proportion to the fault." (Rom. 5:15). Christ not only restored love, unity, and indissolubility to marriage, He also elevated it to the level of a sacrament reflecting His relationship to His Church, and He thereby immeasurably strengthened it, sanctified it, and clarified it. A sacrament is an outward sign of inner sanctification, and every sacrament is specially designed to confer those graces which are appropriate to the nature of the occasion. Therefore those three properties of marriage also receive, through its elevation to the status of a sacrament, a higher degree of blessing and sanctification. The sacrament first of all sanctifies the love of Christian marriage partners so that the apostle Paul could say to men: "You who are husbands must show love to your wives, as Christ showed love to the Church when he gave himself up on its behalf." (Eph. 5:25-26). To women, he said: "Wives must obey their husbands as they would obey the Lord." (Eph. 5:22-23). And to both he said: "And as you stand in awe of Christ, submit to each other's rights." (Eph. 5: 21-22). How far such love in Christian marriage is removed from the lowly condition which goes by the same name, but which has to do more with infatuation, self-seeking, passion and lust! The love that is sanctified by Christ and His sacramental grace does not change with every whim, but like the love of Christ it is stable and self-sacrificing unto death. The sacrament also sanctifies the unity of marriage so that Christ could say of it: "You have heard that it was said, 'Thou shalt not commit adultery.' But I tell you that he who casts his eyes on a woman so as to lust after her has already committed adultery with her in his heart." (Matt. 5: 27-28). How sublime this statement, how sacred the kind of relationship to which it applies. Christ did not found a religion based on external decency, but one which is interiorly genuine and honest. That is why mere external decency, outward modesty and respect, are never sufficient for Him. He established a relationship in which he preserves even the intentions and secrets that lie in the innermost caverns of a man's heart from infidelity. Finally, through the dignity of sacramental status, Christ has once and for all established the indissolubility of marriage without which there could be neither the kind of love nor that fidelity which Christ intended for marriage, and without which the purpose of marriage would be, in any case, unattainable. Regarding this, Christ made it perfectly clear, after he alluded to the words of the Creator, "And so they are no longer two, they are one flesh; what God, then has joined, let not man put asunder." (Matt. 19:6)

That is what marriage means according to God's design, as Christ has restored it and brought it to its fullest expression. It is a great sacrament, but only in His Church. (cf. Eph. 5:32). It is a relationship between a man and a woman joined by a love that is as true, as pure, as spiritual, as self-sacrificing as is the very love of Christ for His Church. It is preserved by a fidelity which permeates the whole being of a man and his wife, and it protects them against even the most secret improper desires. It is encompassed by a bond which is as strong as this love and this loyalty, and which lasts until death.

Before I proceed further, my Christian Brethren, I cannot restrain myself from asking you this question. Do not your own inner souls tell you that only such a bond between a man and a woman as the Church of Christ is proposing bespeaks true human dignity? No one can have sunk so low in worldliness, sensuousness, and corruption as not to recognize that only that kind of marriage comes up to the ideal which every man cherishes in his heart. Even the crudest ruffian and the bitterest enemy of the Church must desire to be the product of a union which matches the Catholic Church's idea of marriage. But only a divine institution such as the Catholic Church can still attain to such ideals, given the great moral infirmity of our time. Thanks be to God, experience proves that such unions are not merely ideals; they are even now still attained in reality.

However, if Christ demanded pure, binding, self-sacrificing love and fidelity in marriage, He also had to equip souls with sufficient nobility, dignity, and kindness to be able to measure up to this love. In particular, Christianity had to elevate woman from the fallen condition to which paganism reduced her. If man was to fulfill the command of Paul: "You husbands must show love to your wives, as Christ showed love to the Church," then the female sex had to be substantially reconstructed. Love ought to be not deceitful but honest, and it must have truth for its object. Christianity has accomplished this not only in its teaching that every man is made in the image of Christ, but also by the fact that it bestowed on womanhood a spiritual beauty, a dignity, and a purity which it never enjoyed in pagan times. The dignity of woman is entirely the result of Christianity. The more Christian a woman is, the higher she rises in true esteem; the more unChristian she becomes, the deeper she sinks. Paganism produced men whose manly qualities we are forced to respect; for there were great statesmen, great scholars, great warrior. But it was never able to produce a woman with the dignity which adorns the Christian woman. Some like to ascribe the treatment of woman in non-Christian cultures to some low point of morality, and they infer that as human civilization progresses, the problem would disappear. Not so, my Christian Brethren. The true and natural root of the undignified treatment of women lies in the low state in which womankind finds itself outside of Christianity. That low state among non-Christian societies is the strictly logical consequence of the degeneracy of the woman herself. A man could no longer respect the degenerate woman, and that is how things stood until Christ came.

With the beginning of Christianity we immediately encounter that woman to whom the Church refers in the canticle of praise, "Fair in every part, my true love, no fault in all thy fashioning!" (Song of Songs: 4:7). It is the woman to whom the Angel said, "Hail, thou art full of grace; and the Lord is with thee; blessed art thou among women." (Luke 1:28). The Blessed Virgin Mary possesses all of the beauty and dignity of the female sex, and the lustre which radiates from her to all of womankind is so bright that even vice, when it is exposed to just a single ray of her brightness, shrinks back and hides in shame for its baseness. Down through the Christian centuries, Mary has been the true prototype of all Christian women. Mary, the pure and immaculate virgin, is the fountainhead of that spirit of chastity and purity which adorns the brow of the Christian virgin with greater splendor than gold and precious gems. The Christian woman derives her inspiration for humility from Mary, the humble Virgin. It is that spirit of humility which averts her glance from the blandishments of the outside world and directs it toward the inner life of her family. There it affords her the strength to lead a life of wonderful self-sacrifice and self-denial in this great domestic seclusion, where the woman becomes a true bearer of peace, joy, and blessing within her family circle.

From the day when women again depart from these two virtues, they are once more on the way toward that

77

low esteem and loss of dignity which was the lot of the pagan woman. The dignity of woman is so closely related to these virtues that I don't think there is a man who can truly hold in high regard any woman who lacks them. Here again, the enemies of the Church and of Christianity must bear witness. Ask the most immoral man what kind of a woman he wants his mother or sister to be, and he will choose a woman with characteristic Christian virtues as his mother and a virgin with Christian virtues as his sister. If only all women, all maidens, would recognize this great truth and not be taken in by the false display of esteem and love lavished by the rake. A man can only love and respect the Christian woman of true virtue. In his innermost soul he despises the vain and immoral female.

That, my Christian Brethren, is what Christian womanhood and Christian marriage are all about. These are the elements of Christian family living, that sublime school of humanity, that sacred bond which surrounds us through our entire lives and which brings so much blessing, consolation, and joy into men's hearts. How difficult it is to explain the blessedness of the Christian family to a person who has not himself experienced it. The Christian family is the prime educator of mankind, and in this sacred trust the mother once again takes first place. The greatest benefit which God can lavish on a person in the natural order is, without a doubt, the gift of a true Christian mother. I purposely avoided saying simply a tender and loving mother, because if the mother is filled with the spirit of the world, then her love toward the child is not beneficial, but harmful. A Christian mother, on the other hand, is without a doubt the greatest gift which God can give a man. How my whole inner self revolts when I hear people in the world appraise the good fortune of children on the basis of how much wealth their parents have. That child is immeasurably unhappy, even though bedded down in silk and satin, whose mother is unChristian, without faith, and lacking in virtue. On the other hand, the child who is blessed with a truly Christian mother, even if it is clad in rags from the cradle to the grave, is blessed beyond measure. I concur fully with a great Christian thinker who held that the formation of a person is determined for the most part on the mother's lap during the first six years of its life. What development takes place in later years has already been conditioned to a large degree by what values the mother has implanted in the child's heart during those early years. The influences which the child is subjected to during those earliest, tender, impressionable years, when the child's soul is most receptive to every influence, become so much a part of its second nature that they can no longer be erased. Here we are able to recognize the basic absurdity of that philosophy of education which holds that a man can and must develop fully and exclusively from what is in him. If that were so, we should have to withhold the mother's milk from the child and deprive the child of the warmth and closeness of a mother's heart. We would have to allow the child to grow up alone facing four blank white walls, otherwise such an approach would be ruled out. Yes, my Christian Brethren, men who later became the benefactors or destroying angels for the human race often had the germ for their deeds transplanted from a mother's heart. The word of God, "And if anyone hurts the conscience of one of these little ones, that believe in me, he had better have been drowned in the depths of the sea, with a mill-stone hung about his neck..." (Matt. 18:6) applies with special force to the mother. No scandal can equal in its consequences that which the mother gives to her children through bad first impressions. They are like branches of sin and corruption grafted on to the tender trunk, which then determine the direction in which the tree grows. Whoever has learned about education from experience and not from a textbook will support this view. So long as I have had the duty, while in charge of souls, to supervise children, I have had to work extra hard to counteract the poor example from which children suffered who were brought up by unworthy mothers. Yet I never felt fully confident that such children could wholly overcome such bad influence. Woe to the world because of bad, unChristian mothers. This is the greatest evil from which we are now suffering. In the most accurate sense of the word, the unworthy mother lays the ax to the root of the tree. She in-

culcates into the impressionable soul of her children
the spirit of the world, of unbelief, of self-seeking,
of impurity, and that is why these flowers, implanted
by God and nurtured by the blood of Christ, will suf-
focate and wilt. But as deleterious as the influence
of the unChristian mother is on her children, even
though she may masquerade under the name, Christian,
just so beneficial will that seed be which the good
mother plants in the hearts of her children. Even long
after a mother is in her grave, and her son is tossed
to and fro by life's storms so that he is on the verge
of throwing over his Faith and surrendering to an immoral way of life at the risk of his eternal salvation,
the pious, noble image of his mother comes before him
and gently persuades him back onto the way of faith
and virtue. Whoever has come to know first hand
Christianity and its virtues, its inner truth, its
purity, its boundless and selfless love in the life
of a Christian mother or in her counterpart, the
Christian nun, whoever has enjoyed the peace which
Christ called His own in such a family, the recollec-
tion of all of this will safeguard him from every
snare of corruption which lies in life's path. Whoever has seen virtue in such clear form cannot subsequently regard vice without revulsion and disdain,
even though he may himself be caught up in it.

Just as the Christian mother is the educator of
her children, she and her daughter are also educators
of the father of the family. When the heart of a man
is besieged by the spirit of the world, its unbelief
and its vices, due to his constant exposure to the
world, then happy that man if he can come home to a
pious wife and daughter. Eventually there comes a
time when the world will part company with the man
who was unable to part company with the world. Perhaps
years of suffering will precede this forced separation.
But if such a man is fortunate enough to have a wife
or a daughter standing by him who has the seal of
eternal life on her forehead, who in untiring love
and sacrifice provides him with the living example
of Divine power, such a man will ultimately return
to Christ even though he has been far from Him for
a time.

From what we have discussed thus far, it is clear how essentially this concept of marriage is associated with Christ and His Church. It is also clear what a great influence marriage has on the entire fabric of a nation's society. As the family is the prime educator of the individual person, so it is also the just and most vital cell in the entire social human organism. It is in the family that a man learns to use rather than abuse his personal liberty. It is in the family that he learns to conduct himself as a useful member of society first in the family unit, and eventually in the other organs of society. The regulation of the national economic household is basically the same as the economic activity of the largest and smallest businessmen; and just as none of these is able to ignore certain common principles, in the same manner, the moral foundations on which family life rests are the same as those on which the state rests. And just as Christianity understands how to inculcate its lofty virtues into family living, it is also the one institution which is able to provide the foundation for the highest earthly society.

It remains for us to examine to what extent secularism has already weakened and to some extent destroyed this last and most stable support of social order, which is in a more essential sense the very primary cell of that order. Yet I do not want to undertake this task from a pulpit in the Christian house of God. The reverence which I owe to this holy place forbids me to spell out in detail what havoc unbelief and lukewarmness in belief have wrought in the area of family life. It forbids me also to show how they have begun to destroy the high ideals of Christendom, how the Christian concept of love and fidelity between marriage partners has already begun to founder, how the female sex has already begun to abandon that jewel of Christianity, purity and humility of heart, how family life has become disorganized and Christian joy banished from it. I must turn my glance away from that horrible picture. It is sufficient for me to recall that unbelievers have already dared to call into question the validity of the very institution, marriage; and proceeding from there they have begun to unleash upon society the whole flood of moral corruption which is implicit in atheism. After the teaching of secularists about liberty and man's final destiny began to undermine the very foundations of our society, these unbelievers then proceeded to invade the innermost living organism of the social structure. If they succeed, we can confidently expect that the entire structure of society will be demolished and its wreckage will litter the entire earth.

I have now fulfilled my task, Christian Brethren, to the best of my ability. All of the foundations of social order are under siege and threaten to collapse. No external remedy, no formality, no constitution on earth is able to fortify the structure or firm up its foundations. If God does not build the house, they labor in vain who build it. If Christ, the Lord, does not shore up the foundations, all is in vain. Only in Christ is help to be found. Only if we return to the living Faith in Christ and His Church can we still prevent the collapse of society. It was not my intention to paint a horror picture. So far as I am able to see, I have stuck to the truth. The purpose of our investigations was to discover the ultimate causes of the condition in which our society finds itself. Loss of belief in God appears to me to be the sole and ultimate source of our decay; and the belief in Christ and the Catholic Church is the only remedy. Tomorrow, therefore, my last discourse will deal with Christ and His Church. Like all of the foregoing ones it will have just one purpose - to bind you more firmly and more deeply to Christ and His Church.

Sixth Sermon

On the Authority of the Catholic Church

Wednesday before Christmas in the Cathedral
at Mainz, 20 December 1848

"Blessed are the poor in spirit; the kingdom of heaven
is theirs"
(Matthew 5:3-4)

The inner strength which envigorates us is not immediately perceptible. It becomes apparent in the works to which it gives rise. Thus, two oak trees may look alike while one may be filled with a vitality that will keep the tree alive for centuries, whereas the other may bear a germ which will cause it to die in a short time. In the same manner we may observe two people who are from all appearances pretty much alike; yet one is enlivened by an inner strength which enables him to change the world, while the other cannot keep his own house in order.

With this idea as my starting point, my Christian Brethren, I have pointed out to you the inner constructive force of Christianity and of the Church as opposed to the destructive force of secularism, with regard to the structure of our social order. We find Christianity everywhere to be filled with a living spirit so that it spreads vitality, order, and formative influence, whereas secularism is filled with a death-dealing spirit so that wherever it makes its presence felt, there is evident death, confusion, and destruction. Therein, in particular, we are able to appreciate the inner truth and godliness of Christianity as contrasted with the inherent dishonesty of secularism.

The textbooks are full of proofs for the divinity of Jesus Christ, and still the world has refused to believe in Him. Now we are at the point where the proofs are moving from the textbooks into realization - before our own eyes. God has now taken matters into His own hands. He is about to demonstrate to man that Christ, who appeared in human form here on earth, was indeed the Son of the living God and that the Church which He founded is a divine institution for the salvation and sanctification of mankind. He is about to write this proof into world history with huge capital letters. It looks as though God is about to permit unbelief to take on its true configuration, so that it will at last reveal its destructive power to us. Secularism will be allowed to complete its work of destruction. The noble concept of Christian liberty will be suppressed by its crude caricature of liberty, and those who are liberated from the law of God under the pretext of liberty, having become slaves to the passions, will seethe with hatred and envy of one another. Their unbelief will rob man of the salutory hope for a better life hereafter and fill him instead with a desperate craving for the enjoyment of sensual pleasures. It will first destroy private property and bring on the inevitable impoverishment, confusion, and discord. Finally, it will reduce womankind again to the low estate which was its lot in pagan cultures. It will deprive us of the consolation and blessing which a Christian mother and sister can bestow and replace these with immoral and worldly women. After it has thus destroyed the sanctity of the Christian family, then finally, those who survive in the wreckage of our society will once again reach out desperately for the life-giving grace and strength - to Christ and His Church which they are now foolishly rejecting.

There are, my Christian Brethren, those who do not require this frightful proof in order to cling to Christ and His Church. They have already discovered for themselves the sanctifying and enlivening Divine force of Christianity as well as the death-dealing force of unbelief. Such persons must be aware of an overpowering desire to save one or the other of their wayward fellow men from eternal damnation and to lead them back to God. That is the final purpose which I have for appearing before you today once again. I have the overpowering desire to share with my fellow men what I myself have discovered in and learned from Christ and His Church.

Up to now, we have considered the effects of faith and secularism respectively, on social order in human society, and we have concluded that examination. Now we want to turn our attention to the inner principle on which faith and disbelief rest, to determine the truthfulness of that principle. The innermost principle of both of these positions and their essential differences, I find in their teaching about the authority which man ought to follow with both his intellect and his will. The teaching on authority constitutes the deepest, most basic divergence between the believer and the unbeliever. Therefore, my Christian Brethren, I beg for your attention, and I beseech our

Lord, Jesus Christ, out of the love by which he allowed Himself to be nailed to the cross, to assist us through the intercession of Mary, the Mother of Divine Grace.

The belief of the Catholic Church rests on the principle that man, to be completely reasonable, can reach nowhere else but for the hand of the authority which God established here on earth. Thus, there is no conflict between faith and reason. Faith does not require that we use our belief to stamp out reason. On the contrary, through authority, faith wishes man to attain to the full and true use of his reason. As the dew which penetrates the plant does not suppress the plant but helps it to develop and unfold, so authority does not suppress the proper life of the soul but helps it to true development and fulfillment. Secularism, on the other hand, proceeds from the premise that man should be subject to no authority except the dictates of his own reason. It does not come to grips with the questions whether such a state of affairs is appropriate to the human condition, whether it is natural and sensible for a man to rely only upon himself and no one else for guidance, whether it is not far more natural and sensible for him, in fact even necessary for him to seek guidance on the way to acquiring knowledge. The unbeliever thoughtlessly and arbitrarily accepts what suits him, feeling, as he does, that it is undignified for a man to recognize any authority beyond himself. As he rejects every law outside himself which would restrict his will, so he overthrows every authority, every truth outside himself which would restrict his reason. Man must submit only to that law whichhe himself erects for himself, and he should hold as true only that which he himself has fully grasped.

These propositions sound nice, even sublime. They offer to man such a high destiny and promise, the same thing that the first Tempter promised him: "God knows well that as soon as you eat this fruit your eyes will be opened, and you yourselves will be like gods, knowing good and evil." (Gen. 3:5). Let us have a closer look to see whether there is genuine truth in these promises and especially whether they are in conformity with man's nature, whether, in other words, it is possible for him to determine all things without outside influences, solely from within himself. I am already skeptical about this viewpoint of the unbeliever, because I maintain that among those who claim to follow nothing but their own power of reason, there is often a remarkable diversity of interpretations of the same phenomenon. What is true and reasonable must, after all, remain the same always; and about the same phenomenon there can certainly only be one true and reasonable explanation. Yet we find among the apostles of unbelief those men who assert that they follow no authority save their own reason, displaying an amazing variety of viewpoints. If you pose questions to them which are of an essential nature and to which one would expect them to offer some sensible answers as, e.g., about their own soul, its origin, its relation to the body, its destiny after death, we get from one thousand unbelievers one thousand different answers. Now only one of these positions can be valid. Either there is one truth and one reasonable explanation, in which case only one of these people is being reasonable and the rest, unreasonable, or else there is no universally valid truth in which case all thought is unreasonable, the vaunted celebration of reason is foolishness, and this would be the most disconsolate of all doctrines.

But let us examine more closely the proposition that there are people who follow only their reason, nothing else; and let us consider this especially with relation to the history and nature of mankind. First we see the child in its earliest years in the home of its parents. Does one seriously expect that the child at that early age should develop without benefit of external authority solely from within itself and by its own reason? To expect this is to expect the impossible and the proposition is preposterous. Even if man were destined to follow only his own authority, he could only accomplish this after he had reached the full maturity of his reasoning capacity. In his early years, on the other hand, man is the most dependent creature we can imagine. At that age he is so totally dominated by an authority outside himself, the authority of parents and especially of his mother, that the individuality and personality of the child remains largely latent. The voluntaristic and cognitive faculties of the child

in the earliest years are determined not from within
the child, but by the will and intellect of the mother.
Long before the child has begun to think and decide
for itself, external influence has shaped its thinking and determined it. The influence of this direc-
tive power on the cognitive and voluntaristic faculties
of the child, determined externally, i.e., by authority,
is so great that one is scarcely able to shed it entirely in later years. In particular, there is a
certain kind of love, an inclination of the will, which
the child assimilates in its tenderest years at the
mother's breast, and this is of the most decisive importance in shaping its thinking in later years. At
least at this level of human growth, the principle of
the unbeliever, that man must reject any and all authority, represents a monumental falsehood.

Let us accompany the child in its school years.
The decisive influence of parental authority has already given a certain orientation to the individuality
and personality of the child by the time it enters
school. This influence stemming from the home environment and reinforced by the constant daily relationship with parents already make it impossible for
the child to develop entirely from within itself.
Now we confront a new authority in the person of the
teacher. An authority which also acts from outside
the child in shaping the processes of the child's intellect and will. True, there are those who would
now charge the teacher to help the child develop
itself without exercising a determining influence on
its will or intellect. This postulate of the unbeliever is as impossible as the principle on which
it is based is false, and it will never be fulfilled
in real life. True, the independence of the child
must develop, but always and everywhere under the
decisive influence of the teacher. Complementarity
and help from without are so much a part and parcel
of the child's nature that no teacher can take leave
of any child without his own caste of mind and will
having had some influence on the child's intellectual
and volitional processes. Here too, nature is mightier
than all theories. Even if the teacher can avoid all
external influences, he cannot banish all love from
his heart. He either loves the world or he loves God.
Just as the sun cannot shine on a plant without the

89

plant absorbing the wholesome warmth, the teacher cannot withhold the warmth of his love from the subjects which he presents to the children. He cannot prevent this warmth from penetrating to the heart of the child and thereby influencing the mind and will of the child.

So the child grows continually under the influence of one external authority and then another until the time it takes its place in the adult world. Now, one might say, the time has finally come when a man has reached a stage of independence and enjoys the full power of his reason. Now he can at last disregard all authority and follow his own reason. We will not repeat what we have said about the impressions which the child has brought from home and school into the world with him. Let us continue our investigation by supposing that it is true that a man by virtue of his dignity and calling as a man can only accept as true what he himself can grasp. It would then be required that every single person should be in a position to acquire the highest possible level of intellectual development. We all know from experience that there were things that we could not grasp at an earlier stage of our intellectual formation which we subsequently understand after fuller development. Now, therefore, how could we ever be fully confident that we have grasped the full truth of any matter so long as we are not certain that we have attained the highest possible level of our intellectual formation? For a man to have reached that top level, four prerequisites must be in place: first, the highest natural capacity; second, boundless diligence; third and fourth, sufficient leisure and wealth to command the means necessary to achieve this top level of intellectual development. Where one or the other of these requirements is not fulfilled, that goal is not attainable. Even if it were possible for all to afford the time and expenditure of wealth required to develop themselves fully, still only a small percentage of people have the natural endowment and driving ambition needed for the task. What will become of the preponderant majority of mankind who can only attain to a lower grade of intellectual development? Shall we tell them too, that they should follow only their limited reasoning

90

powers and disregard everything that they cannot
grasp fully, given their limitations? No doubt
there are those who would still affirm this, but
the advice is so unreasonable, so unnatural, that
even those who offer it do not follow it. The
great majority of people sense it in their inner
beings that they need authority, leadership, external support. If man is deprived of authentic
leadership, therefore, he will fall under the influence of bad leadership. Just as the person who
pretends to follow only his own rules ends up being
a slave of his own passions, so the one who dis-
dains all authority so that he may obey only his
own reason ends up being a slave to the whims of the
day. The truth of this is evident from what we see
around us. Men are too proud to permit themselves
to be guided by the hand of some higher authority,
but rather than gain real self-determination from
such blindness, they end up becoming subject to the
worst authority of all. They claim to be following only their own reason, and what do we find?
They have traded a single authority for countless
authorities. Instead of the authority of Holy
Scripture, they follow the authority of that most
pathetic wisdom found in miserable newspapers and
filthy novels. Instead of the authority of the
teaching Church, they follow the authority of
Johnny-come-lately, corrupt human beings. The
authority which God established was contrary to
what they fancied as their human dignity, but to
follow docilely every scandal sheet and every seducer who happens by, this they are somehow able
to reconcile with their human dignity. And so there
seem to remain only a precious few who are in a position to operate without authority, namely, those who
possess the natural endowment, the ambition, the
leisure and the material means to command the heights
of all human achievement and from these heights to
pass judgement on them. But even here, the pretended
self-sufficiency is a sham. The learned person is no
more free from all outside influences and authority
than the simple child. No one, not even the greatest
thinker, can declare truthfully that the construction
of his intellect and will is solely and entirely of
his own making, free of all outside influence. Even

the products of his mind and will are colored by the
impressions of his youth, the culture of his nation,
the spirit of the times in which he lives, the relationships which he shares with others, the beliefs in
which he was brought up, and the love or rejection
which marked his general environment and shaped his
outlook. Why don't all great thinkers come up with
the same conclusions for all of their efforts, even
though they claim to be following their reason? Where
does the deceptive shift of opinion in scientific
thought come from? How come all of these great minds
have not yet been able to come to full agreement in
any branch of science? Simply because what they claim
is not true; because countless extraneous influences,
as well as the darkening of the intellect occasioned
by original sin, have in fact dulled their perception
of things.

When all is said and done, there is really no
greater falsehood than that on which the unbeliever
bases his unbelief. His assertion that man by setting
aside all authority can be his own creature and develop
entirely from within himself contradicts nature and
all of human history. It is idle bluster which can
never be lived up to.

But there is a further question. Where can man
find an authority which he can rely upon and follow
in shaping his outlook and character? It is immediately obvious that man cannot and ought not to rely
upon any mere human authority. Human dignity deserves
at least not to have to subject itself to laws and
truths which stem from merely human sources. One
reasonable person enjoys the same status as another,
and it would be undignified and unreasonable to abrogate this parity. If there were only human authorities on earth, then the teaching of the secularist
would be correct, even while expecting the impossible.
Then the lot of mankind is a pathetic one. Man would
have to abandon his highest aspiration, the quest for
truth. He will never get beyond asking the question,
"What is truth?" He finds himself conditioned from
his earliest childhood in his intellectual and volitional processes by outside forces. He has absorbed
likes and dislikes as well as love and hate, and he
cannot know for certain whether one or the other in-

fluence is valid, whether his love for something is rooted in good or evil, since these are based on human authority which left its mark on him. Only his own inner promptings remain as the rule and measure; and in them he recognizes fickleness and change as well as tunnel-vision, all of which leaves him without certitude and true decisiveness. At this point we are faced with two truths. Man can, by his very nature, not operate without authority; and this authority cannot be merely human. It must be a higher infallible authority. He can submit only to such an authority, none other; and without it he would have to live in despair of ever finding truth or surrender himself blindly to human opinions. Now when we ask where this higher, infallible authority is to be found, we are confronted with the great and remarkable fact that throughout all of human history, and in all of the world, there is just one institution which offers to satisfy this longing in our souls, which dares to lay claim to the essentially divine prerogative of infallibility. That institution is the Roman Catholic Church, our holy mother! The doctrine of infallibility of the Church constitutes her essential principle - the characteristic which sets her apart from all other religious systems. With the doctrine of her infallible teaching authority, the Catholic Church stands or falls. Her whole claim to be the teacher of mankind is based on the higher Divine origin of her teaching authority. The Church has never succumbed to the madness of her opponents, who posed as the teachers of mankind even while overthrowing all higher authority. Whether the Church addresses herself to the minor child to demand adherence to her teaching or to the accomplished scholar, she always does so on the same supposition that she has received the mandate to teach mankind from the Son of God - that is to say - from a super-human authority.

As the Church rests on this foundation, so does our own life. Only if we accept this basic teaching of the Church do we ourselves. become living members of the Catholic Church.

I would go well beyond my assigned task if I tried to treat here of the doctrine of the infallibility of the Church and to adduce all of the proofs

93

whereby the Church can claim that the infallible teaching authority was conferred upon her by God. Is is my task here to demonstrate the need man has for authority, and thereby to lay bare the inherent falsehood of the entire structure of secularism. There is just one piece of evidence of the higher origin of the Catholic Church's teaching authority to which I would like to call attention. This identifying mark shines brighter than the sun at midday. I refer to the catholicity, the all-embracing quality of its teaching. A purely human institution has never been able to be catholic or universal. In fact, such an institution could scarcely transcend the borders of the country in which it originated. The teachings of the philosophers never even became the common patrimony of all in their own native lands. They remained the exclusive property of the learned. And what were the consequences of these proud systems of learning? To them one can with justice say: "Let the dead bury their dead."

The pagan religions were intertwined with given nationalities and were never able to achieve universality. In the same manner, all the sects which broke away from the Catholic Church have either long since gone under, or they find themselves undergoing constant transformation; or else they are in a state of dissolution. Every few years they take a new form, or change the mode of their teaching. What is true today, they scuttle tomorrow. How can the follower of a non-Catholic school of philosophy or of a non-Catholic Christian sect still be enthusiastic about his beliefs when he must be convinced by now from the lessons of history that his viewpoint represents merely an emphemeral opinion which shifts and changes like the weather? How can he seriously hope that his present convictions can escape this general pattern? He might just as well hope to be exempt from the inevitability of the death of the body. Only the Catholic Church is exempt from this law of limitation and change. She has seen her claim that her teaching represents truth itself, and that her teaching authority is Divine and immune from human arbitrariness, borne out by an all-important fact in the history of mankind. There is no more foolproof, tangible way to distinguish the human from the Divine than to

94

observe the universality and constancy of the Church's teaching as contrasted with the impermanence of all other learned opinions. The teaching authority of the Catholic Church is not limited to a period of time, to a decade, or to centuries. It is not confined to the peculiarities of a country or of a nation. She shows herself to be, in fact, what she claims to be - a daughter of eternity. While her teaching is, at the same time that it is Divine and truly reasonable, also truly human, it knows no boundaries in time or place beyond mankind itself. So far as humanity reaches in space and time, that is how far the Church reaches with her teaching. It alone remains unchanging. How could it represent error and falsehood given this great unity and catholicity? Her catholicity proves her Divinity, and therewith her infallibility. How exalted is the consciousness of a Catholic whose faith is anchored to the infallible teaching authority of the Church? Every other person may see around him a tiny band of kindred spirits and at the same time feel certain that what he holds to be true today will soon be rejected as false. The Catholic, on the other hand, stands in the company of that large band of martyrs who bore witness to the depth and firmness of their faith by their deaths. He stands in league with that host of holy bishops and confessors who, having abandoned themselves totally to their Faith, studied and developed true knowledge in their lands and in their times. He shares the vast company of the holy hermits and monks who, by the austerity and self-denial of their lives, testified as to the strength of their religious beliefs. He is in the company of that immeasurable band of pious believing men in all ages and in all places, men from all classes and walks of life, who put the one true Faith to the test under all conceivable conditions and found it to be true and sound.

And so, my Christian Brethren, we have come to the end of our assignment. We have examined the basic assumptions, the ultimate principles, on which the Catholic Church, on the one hand, and secularism, on the other, rest. In the effects that we considered earlier, secularism is the vehicle of death, destruction, and confusion, while our Faith is a life-giving force, a source of order. The principle which we considered today, a secularism which rejects all authority outside the person himself, is an idle boast, a bare-faced lie, a gross exaggeration of human capacity. Our Faith, on the other hand, since it reconciles the independence of man with the existence of a higher authority, is in full harmony with the nature of man.

I cannot leave this subject, my Christian Brethren, without adding a few observations based on what has already been said.

The attack of secularism against all law and all truth which comes to a man from outside himself contains the important truth that is rooted in man's universal nature, in his personality, namely: that he cannot accept any merely human authority. Throughout the course of world history, it has occurred over and over again that one segment of the human race has tried to prescribe laws and to regulate the thought and actions of another segment. That is happening today still, even among the apostles of unbelief. In the same breath they condemn all authority and set themselves up as the authority. This "service to mankind" was and continues to be a degradation of it. Since the great break from higher authority - the so-called Reformation - it has become practically universal. In city life, in particular, it has reached its crest, and ultimately it had to lead to a general rebellion.

At the same time, however, there is implicit in the revolt of secularism against all law and truth that is outside of man a great godlessness, an untruth to the effect that man does not want to subject himself to any higher law or truth with or without God, that he does not wish to acknowledge a divine authority, and that he, in fact, wants to be like God.

That part of the truth which it contains gives to secularism its strength, and that part of it which is a lie will defeat it. That is because Christ has already conquered falsehood. What is true with reference to his fellow man is not true with reference to God. Secularism is entitled to overthrow all authority with the single exception of the teaching authority of the Catholic Church. Only the Church claims to be endowed with a God-given infallible authority, and only it can demand to have ultimate authority over men. Secularism must conquer all systems of belief, but it will shatter in pieces against the rock of the Church.

The Catholic Church embraces within her whatever truth there is in the basic principle of secularism, at the same time that she rejects what is untrue about it. She accepts the profound truth that man need not obey any mere man or believe him, and it therefore overthrows all merely human authority. She further acknowledges that any authority from whatever source it may come must justify itself in man's conscience, in his soul, before he needs to obey it. However, she satisfied the natural need of men for a higher authority. She regards herself as endowed with authority by God Himself, and it is only for that reason that the Church feels justified in demanding that men subject themselves to her teaching authority. Just as the Church elevates the service of the lowliest servant girl from the low estate of mere service to another human being to the dignity of service to God, so she also frees the soul of man, who by his very nature cannot develop fully without being influenced by his fellow man, from enslavement to fickle human opinions. She elevates the subjection of the human spirit to an authority to the dignified acknowledgement of a truth revealed by God. Thus, my Christian Brethren, the principles of secularism and of the Church confront us and compel us to make a choice. What secularism promises, it can no more deliver than the first Serpent could keep its promise to change man into God.

Secularism promises to free us from all external authority. It cannot because it did not design human nature and therefore cannot re-design it. Our choice is not whether we wish to submit to authority or not, but rather to which authority we wish to subject ourselves. The question is whether in the all-important question of our eternal salvation we wish to submit to shifting, ephemeral human opinions, or to the authority of the Catholic Church which manifests to

us by its doctrine, which has not changed from its
earliest beginnings, the eternal Kingdom. During the
time of the Reformation, our ancestors heard a similar
cry. They were told to overthrow the teaching authority of the Catholic Church and to burst the bonds
which held reason in check. And what did those who
yielded to this siren song gain? Instead of the mild
yoke and light burden of Jesus Christ, they were loaded
down with the iron yoke of human authority. Our own
ancestors, on the other hand, stood their ground, and
we are grateful to them that we too did not fall prey
to the dominion of shifting, ephemeral opinions, as
the children of the Reformation did. Do not we, my
Christian Brethren, wish to remain as steadfast as
they and refuse to yield to the approaching Tempter
by turning godless and rejecting the world of God
as embodied in the authority of the Church? Our
decision will determine whether later generations,
as well as God Himself, will declare us blessed or
cursed when sentence is passed on us. Amen.

1

A friend of the author, in preparing these sermons
for publication, noted how what he said here gave
rise to certain unwarranted objections and misunder-
standings; so he is taking the liberty of adding this
comment. In the entire sermon, the man who delivered
the sermon was basing all of what he said on the
moral rather than on the legalistic point of view.
Thus, he is teaching- according to the teaching of
the Catholic Church - that everyone has an obligation to use the returns from what he owns for the
general good and not simply for his own good. This
obligation, however, is a moral one - an obligation
in charity - and not one that is to be imposed by
force. If it were the latter kind of obligation,
then the great merit of charity would become mean-
ingless. God has established the world on the
basis of love which gives life, while the mere
letter of the law destroys.

2

On this day the Pastoral message of the bishops
gathered in Würzburg was being delivered to all of
the faithful.

3

Translator's Note: Apparently von Ketteler felt
that the "author of 'Social Policy'" to whom he
refers here was widely enough known so that the
published edition of the sermon did not offer an
explanatory footnote. Thanks to the patient efforts
of a German scholar, Dr. Adolf Geck of Remagen, and
through the good offices of Prof. Dr. Franz H. Mueller
of St. Paul, Minnesota, the translator was able to
determine who this "author" probably was. One Julius
Froebel served in the same Frankfurt Assembly as von
Ketteler in 1848. Froebel was a socialist, and he
wrote a book published in Mannheim in 1847 with the
title: System der Socialen Politik. It was also
referred to at the time by those familiar with it
simply as, der Socialen Politik.

Freedom, Authority and the Church

by

Wilhelm Emmanuel von Ketteler

Bishop of Mainz

1862

Translator's Note

<u>Freedom, Authority and the Church</u> (<u>Freiheit, Autorität und Kirche</u>) was first published in 1862. It went through seven editions and also appeared in translations throughout Europe. Beneath the title it bore the explicatory subtitle: <u>Discussions About Important Current Issues</u>.

This work was originally a written one, unlike Bishop von Ketteler's first work which was a publication of sermons. It was addressed mainly to the problems which Catholics were facing because of the secularization of modern political states in the period following the French Revolution. <u>Freedom, Authority and the Church</u> presents Catholic teaching as it applies, in particular, to the political order. Essentially it centers on what Bishop von Ketteler regarded as a perversion of the principles of liberty, equality, and fraternity which he regarded as originally Christian principles. From there he ranged over such related issues as religious liberty, the so-called separation of church and state, the abuses of authority by governments, whether monarchical or representing majority rule, the indissolubility of marriage, the prior rights of parents in the education of their children, and Freemasonry.

Much of what Bishop von Ketteler wrote in this work is remarkably parallel to what is contained in the <u>Syllabus of Modern Errors</u> promulgated by Pope Pius IX in 1864. Since the Bishop's work preceded the <u>Syllabus</u> by two years, it quite probably influenced the formation of that Pope's teaching, as his work would later also influence that of Pope Leo XIII. Indeed, Pius IX told the rector of the seminary in Mainz, Christopher Moufang, in private audience, that his bishop was everything that a bishop ought to be. That was just one of various occasions when the Pontiff expressed his respect for the Bishop and his work.

103

Foreword

There have been recurrent discussions of the Catholic press here in Germany concerning its present situation, its purpose, and various proposals for rectifying its shortcomings. This is a topic which is of the greatest importance and which merits the earnest attention of anyone who has some concern for the welfare of the Catholic Faith.

The influence which the daily press has in shaping the events of our time by the way in which it molds opinions and the whole mode of thinking is enormous, and it looms larger day by day. What appears in the newspapers is for a great segment of the public its sole source of information and the yardstick by which people make their judgements. In addition, the press possesses a decisive influence over what transpires in our public life and in our legislatures, which likewise play a major role in shaping our everyday lives. The secular press plays a critical role in all of these areas. It leads and guides our politicians. To be praised in the daily press is the highest badge of honor which most popular representatives and political leaders may earn. Its disapproval is their downfall. All too often the actions of our legislatures are not the expressions of what the nation needs but rather of what the press dictates.

In the face of these undeniable realities, it is all the more regretable that the opinions of Catholics, as well as their interests and rights, find only infinitesimally small expression in the pages of the daily press. Although more than half of the population of Germany is Catholic, specifically Catholic viewpoints are not aired beyond the narrow circle of persons who get to read a few Catholic news-sheets. The Catholic Church according to prevailing sentiment as expressed in the daily press would appear to be irrelevant'. In fact, it even seems to be held in downright contempt. From what appears in the newspapers one gets the impression that there are actually no Catholics left in Germany with solid Catholic convictions.

There is no mention of Catholic men or Catholic actions, nor is there any recognition of injustices committed against Catholics. The only time the Catholic Church is acknowledged at all, as a rule, is when some scandal occurs, or when there is disagreement among Catholics. It is this press, with its following, which sets the tone wherever papers are sold and read in Germany. As a result one can travel the length and breadth of Germany without encountering any sign of life in the mainstream of Catholicism. It would seem to be worth our while, therefore, to look into this sorry situation.

To restore some vitality and unity to the Catholic press, it is necessary above all else, in my opinion, to stress a sense of clarity. I am talking about clarity regarding our situation, clarity about the dangers that face us, clarity of purpose, clarity regarding the truths and falsehoods which abound in the ambience which surrounds us; and finally, there must be clarity regarding the principle issues on which the Catholic press and all those Catholics who participate in public life ought to bring their influence to bear, with insistence and with tenacity. Such clarity is of greater importance than anything else in elevating the status of the Catholic press. In order to give adequate representation to the great spiritual force that is undoubtedly present among Catholics in Germany, it is necessary above all to know what we stand for. In this regard, our enemies, without question, have the upper hand. The Catholic presence is, to an unfortunate degree, a timid and a fragile one, and so long as it is not properly oriented regarding what is right and good, it does not dare obtrude into public life. There are many dormant energies in persons who stand and watch with great sorrow while the secular press, by and large, drags in the dirt everything which they hold dear while, at the same time, it boosts everything that is mean and contemptible. Such energies could be released if such persons were properly instructed so that they are sure of their ground and know what the issues are. We are living at a time when all of the ancient structures which our forefathers erected have been torn down; and we

106

Catholics are not yet certain just what kind of structure we are required to rebuild to fulfill our role in the new order of things.

In discussing the great issues that confront us in our time, there is no greater handicap than the ambivalence and ambiguous character of terms which are commonly employed. The Holy Father,[1] in one of his recent allocutions, drew attention to this ongoing adulteration of the real meaning of words. The lie can take the form of equivocation, and thus it can take in the unwary. Those who are in the service of Truth on the other hand, must shun ambiguity and equivocation. A program which employs terms that mean different things to different people would represent merely a false unity. That is why I have resolved to try to render this one service to the Truth in the great cause which we are forced to engage in at the present time, when everything which we regard as good and holy is fighting for its life. I intend to examine the leading slogans of our time to see whether by clarifying their meaning it is possible to dissolve some of the fog which is handicapping us Catholics. This seems to me to be the first necessary step if we are ever going to rally our forces so that we can bring a proper influence to bear in the area of public life. That is what inspired me to undertake this work. I do so in the spirit of St. Augustine who wrote: Quae vera esse perspexeris, tene et Ecclesiae catholicae tribue; quae falsa, respue et mihi, qui homo sum ignosce. (De vera relig. 20)[2]

I   Progress, Enlightenment, Liberty, Equality, and Fraternity

All of these terms are being used and abused in our time, time and again. That is why they have come to be regarded with suspicion by many. Yet, they have a kernel of truth in them, something Godly, regardless of how men have hidden this kernel inside a shell of falsehood and madness. They represent principles which bespeak the highest task of mankind and which represent the noblest truths of Christianity. It would be improper therefore to reject something which is true and just in itself. Rather we ought to strive to combat the falsehood by a correct interpretation of them.

That is why I spoke the following words when I delivered the funeral address in Frankfurt, at the graveside of the victims of those horrible murders which occurred during the uprising of September 18,1848:

"As we stand here at the graveside, I am haunted by a thought which comes to mind, and which I would like to share with you, my Christian Brethren. I see in our world, on the one hand, a violent movement in the direction of the highest ideals of which man is capable, and on the other I see a burgeoning of the basest passions. In the face of the animal savagery which manifested itself in the slaughter of Prince Lichnowsky and General von Auerswald, I find myself more than ever justified in speaking out. I hear the cries for peace on all sides - and who would not sympathize with such a yearning? Yet, I see men more and more divided into factions, torn by disagreements between father and son, brother and sister, friend and friend. On the one hand, I hear the clamor for equality, something which the message of Christianity has offered to us for nearly two thousand years; on the other hand, I see all around me an insane craving to outdo and outstrip one's fellow man. I hear eloquent pleas for fraternity and love - qualities which God Himself obliges us to cultivate. Yet, on every side, I see hatred, calumny, and dishonesty spreading among men like a cancer. I hear cries for help from among our poor, suffering brethren; yet who, that is not purblind,

cannot see how they languish in their need, and who,
that is not heartless, is not in full sympathy with
this cry for help? I see greed and miserliness on
the increase; I see the pursuit of pleasure taking
over. I see men, who call themselves national leaders
do nothing to prevent the growing need. Instead they
make matters worse by undermining people's will to
work and by instigating envy of what someone else
possesses. It never occurs to them to open their own
pocketbooks to help the poor. Instead they work to
destroy the Christian teaching which requires that
a man begin by opening his own heart to share with
his fellow man what he has in superabundance. 'Do you
wish to be perfect, then go sell what you have and
give it to the poor.' I hear the call for freedom,
and I see lying before us here men who were murdered
because they dared to speak their minds freely. I
hear men declare in favor of unity at the same time
that the nation is rent by discord. I hear talk of
humanity even while we stand here as eyewitnesses to
the crassest kind of brutality.

"Oh, yes, I believe in the truth contained in
all of these noble principles which stir mankind at
present. I belittle none of them, and I reaffirm
that they are worthy of man's highest aspirations.
I am impressed with the men of our time who seem to
strive so earnestly toward their fulfillment at the
same time that we appear to be further than ever removed from achieving them. However, and that is the
message which cries out to us from these graves of
our friends as from so many other disturbing developments in our time, there is just one correct way to
achieve these noble principles. Namely, men have
once again to return to Him who brought them into
the world, to the Son of God, Jesus Christ. It was
Jesus Christ who first announced these high ideals
to mankind, ideals which the very men who have parted
company with Him and who deride Him now propose to us
as their new-found truths. There is a difference,
though. Christ not only taught them, He also lived
them! He is the way, the Truth, and the Life. Without Him there is only folly, dishonesty, and death.
Through Him humanity is capable of attaining the
highest ideals. Without Him, it is capable of
nothing. With Him, by the truths which He brought

110

to us, on the way which He laid out for us, we can
turn the earth into a paradise - a paradise where we
will dry the tears of our poor suffering brethren,
where we can establish the rule of love, unity,
fraternity, and true humanity in their perfected form.
Yes, it is my deepest conviction that we could even
bring about common ownership of the goods of this
world as well as eternal peace along with maximum
freedom in our social and political institutions.
But without Him we are destined for shame, disgrace
and destruction, and we are doomed to be regarded
with derision and contempt by the men who will come
after us. That is the truth which cries out to us
from these graves, which the passage of time will
substantiate. Let us take it to heart!"

I presume to reiterate these thoughts, since I
am as convinced of them now as I was then.

The words, progress, enlightenment, liberty,
equality, and fraternity have a noble, exalted, divine
ring to them. They contain great truth, a great challenge by God to men. That is precisely why they infuse such great force into men's hearts for good or
ill, leading them on, either to great accomplishment
or to great misfortune. Men can only be led astray
under the pretense that they are serving the cause
of truth and goodness. That is a fact which, on the
one hand, gives us great consolation. We have here
the best kind of testimony that man, in his deepest
inner cravings, is destined for what is true and
what is good. On the other hand, it gives us cause
for great concern as we view what transpires around
us, because if we are not constantly on our guard we
risk perverting the truth and pressing it into the
service of the Master of deception, who does not
hesitate to use any means at all.

Only Christianity maintains these ideals intact;
and it is necessary to remind the world time and again
that the true dignity of man, the nobility of his calling, the proper ordering of his relationships to his
fellow man were never expressed more fully or more
truly than as they are expressed by Christ and by His
Church. It is Christ and it is His Church which teach
us that God created man in His own image and likeness.

111

God has impressed upon man's nature inextinguishably the imprint of His own Divine essence, His Divine truth, and His Divine love. That is why each and every human being is worthy of our greatest respect. But having created man out of His own love, He did not abandon man to his own resources. Being a loving God, He remains with his creatures; indeed He remains in intimate contact with him, and He continues to shower him in his Divine bounty with new gifts, gifts which go well beyond the mere capacity of the limitations which man's created nature imposes. In this way, God wishes to sustain mankind as a perpetual monument of His love and of the riches of His boundless goodness, and to elevate him to actually share in His divinity. In this continuing expenditure of God's largesse on mankind we catch a glimpse of what is meant by the Christian teaching about supernatural graces.

But man abused his freedom and turned against God by sin. In doing so he broke the supernatural bond which tied him to the Godhead; and what is more, he even blurred the image of God which was imprinted on his nature. That is to say, man damaged his ability to recognize truth and to choose what is good.

This fractured relationship with God could not be repaired without man's free cooperation, since God had created man free; and his freedom requires that man is to serve God of his own free will. On the other hand, the restoration of man's relationship to God could not be accomplished by man's efforts alone, since sinful mankind had forfeited every right to a share in God's divinity. Actually, man had merited only punishment at the hands of a just God. At this point God performed a new supreme act of mercy. As our Savior has said, "God so loved the world, that He gave us His only begotten Son, so that those who would believe in Him may not perish, but have eternal life." (John 3: 16). God Himself became man to save fallen mankind, to reunite man with God; and, as St. Peter expressed it so perfectly, man was once again to share the divine nature. (2 Peter 1:4)

Therein is the entire mission of Christianity. There lies the goal of all true progress for which God has destined mankind. It is Christ, however, who is the sole mediator and guide in bringing mankind back from his misery to full union with God. The restoration and elevation of man is, on the one hand, the continuing action of God become man, who in His mercy restores an undeserving mankind to God. On the other hand, it is something which requires the free consent of man responding to this heavenly invitation. This truth is expressed in the Christian doctrine about the necessity of grace, without which man could not hope to be reunited with God. The acknowledgement of the need for grace lies at the very core of Christian humility.

However, if God wishes to exalt man and restore His disfigured image in mankind, and even to lift man above what his own nature makes him capable of, He can do this only by impressing His divinity, which subsists on truth and love, ever more on man. That is the specific function and purpose of the teachings and of the sacraments of Christianity. They are the instruments of God whereby divine life, divine truth, and divine love are infused into a man's soul, so that he conforms ever more perfectly to God's image and becomes one with God. What binds man to God is the same holy bond which unites men, one to another, into one great family whose members are the beloved children of the same, one, heavenly Father. That is what progress, fraternity, and enlightenment mean in the Christian sense. By this teaching, Christianity relates to all, high and low, rich and poor, down to the humblest slave who is sold like merchandise. All are destined to be children of God, heirs of heaven. All are temples of the Holy Spirit. All are redeemed by the blood of Christ. All have as their intended destiny to possess God one day, to live in His Presence so that all can enjoy the source of eternal truth and love and happiness. It is this final end which Christians have in mind when they celebrate the Christian mysteries during their pilgrimage here on earth. While looking heavenward they pray: "O God, grant that we may one day be fulfilled in the enjoyment of your Divinity, whose image we now honor in the reception of your Flesh and Blood." (From the Missa de Sanctissimo Sacramento)

113

To make ourselves worthy of these truths, the following steps seem to me to be necessary:

First: We Catholics have to avoid conveying the impression - and the Catholic press ought to be especially alert to this - that we are satisfied with things as they once were, that we regard the social and political institutions of a bygone era as beyond improvement, and that our only ambition is to praise them whenever the opportunity presents itself as the only and best design for the future. The truths we have expressed are certainly relevant to the moral well-being and progress of mankind. However, the manner. in which these come to bear in the area of social and political well-being cannot be predicted in advance, just as we cannot tell beforehand what civil and social institutions the spirit of Christianity may give rise to when it has again permeated all of humanity.

Secondly: We have to distinguish between those currents of our time which are justified and those which are not. We have to seek the solution to the great problems of the present era in the truths of Christianity and to oppose these to the false remedies which the spirit of the age holds up for us, so that we may develop a true and worthy sense of direction. Then, so that we may not go astray in this endeavor, we must dedicate ourselves loyally and humbly to the truths of our Catholic Faith so that we may get on with the task of bringing the Catholic viewpoint to bear on our times with joy and with vigor. The truths contained in revelation, as the magisterium of the Church prescribes them, are for us what the fundamental axioms are for the mathematician, and what the rules of logic are for correct thought, and what the moral law is for correct conduct. All of those first principles and laws are in themselves unchangeable. Only their application is remarkably adaptable in many different ways. The same basic laws by which the small child does his multiplication tables govern the great astronomer as he plots the course of the stars. The same is true of the great dogmas of the Church. They are for us the truths which God, who is Eternal Truth, has made known to us. As with all other truths,

114

they too are unchangeable. What is true, is true
eternally. But they are merely principles, foundations upon which man must style his own life and his
social course in harmony with Providence as it unfolds
itself during the course of history. It is our appointed task to erect the entire pattern of human relationships on the basis of these truths. The more
zealously we wish to participate in the task of doing
God's work here on earth, the more it is required of
us that we ourselves stay close to God and to His ways.

II Liberty in General

No word is more used these days, and no word is
more misused than the word, "freedom." It has a remarkable power to inflame human hearts, no matter
whether a person is highly educated or not. Where
there is a human heartbeat, the word, freedom, exercises its magic. Its power does not come from without, but from the most deep-seated cravings within a
man's soul. It is a word which gives expression to
the most exalted dignity of the human being, to the
noblest plan of Divine Providence. However, the
Father of Lies has made it into a horrible perversion,
and it is in this perverted form that the world promotes the idea of freedom. It is only the Truth that
can overcome this monstrous lie. Nothing would be
more dangerous than to try to deny the very idea of
liberty - a truly divine concept - because of the
way it has become perverted. The more the secular
press propagates the false notion of freedom, therefore, the more those who are in the service of truth
ought to stress its true meaning and hold it up in
opposition to the falsehood. It is enough simply
to develop the Christian principles which we hear
expressed time and again in our churches in order to
come to a realization of the true meaning of freedom.
Freedom in the Christian sense, when contrasted with
the nonsensical freedom that is constantly paraded
before the general public to lead it astray, stands
out like bright sunlight next to some dim flickering
torch!

One can only speak of freedom when dealing with
human beings. Everything else on this planet is unfree. Christianity makes this clear to us. Human
freedom is a direct consequence of the fact that man
is made in God's image. Therefore it follows that
human freedom is like the very freedom that God enjoys, though there is still an essential difference.

The freedom of God is, like God's essence, unlimited and unconditional. He alone possesses this
supreme sovereignty. His being, His will, His acts
are determined by Him alone. His freedom in dealing
with anything outside Himself is without limit. It

is this freedom which man enjoys, to a degree, and only to the degree which his human nature permits.

The freedom of man can only be a conditional freedom. It is restricted by obligation - the obligation to submit itself freely to the Divine Will. God subjects human freedom to certain well-defined limits which man cannot transgress, because if he did so, he would be frustrating the Divine plan.

Human freedom does not apply to every aspect of man's existence. In some matters man is only partly free, and in others he is even totally unfree. Man has no control at all over the fact of his birth and over the fact that one day he must die. Nor can he control certain of his most basic needs. He does not have anything to say about what his proper destiny is. The same necessity which determines his existence also compels him to strive for happiness. Here he is limited in his freedom to the choice of means for seeking his proper end, not in his choice of the end, itself.

Now, after having considered freedom in general, let us turn to the notion of freedom in its more specific applications.

III <u>Moral Freedom</u>

According to the teaching of the Catholic Church, moral freedom here on earth is the power of a man freely to seek the good - a power of choice which brings with it also the capacity to choose evil. The concept rules out all <u>external</u> compulsion which would appear to lead a man to do good, but which does not move a man <u>internally</u> to what is good. It also rules out any kind of inner necessity, the kind that compels the will, not by external force, but by some inner pre-determination to choose one or the other option, without the real possibility of rejecting it. In other words, moral freedom would become something other than "voluntary." Finally, moral freedom implies the existence of the possibility of evil, all through our life here on earth. Our merits are conditioned by the existence of this possibility, as is the attainment of our reward, the fulfillment of the purpose for which we are here on earth. That is the achievement of our final destiny, heaven.

It is on this exalted concept of freedom which gives to man his true dignity that the Catholic Church has erected its entire body of doctrine for leading a Christian life. Teachers of the Church who deal with moral doctrine preface their discussion by distinguishing between specifically human acts, those which are free actions in the sense we have mentioned, and those actions of man which are unfree. Only such free actions, according to universal traditions of Catholic moral theology, are then treated as specifically human actions,e.g,,actions in which the full dignity of human nature comes to bear. Christian moral theologians distinguish these from the unfree acts which man has in common with unreasoning beings and indicate that Christian moral teaching deals only with the former, not with the latter. The three essential components of a moral action which they propose for us are: first, a judgement regarding the worth of an action which is made before the action is taken; second, a free inner decision to taken or not to take an action, which becomes the source of the action; and third, the existence of the possibility to decide otherwise.

Closely related to this doctrine is the other important teaching having to do with human conscience. It is especially apparent in the matter of conscience what high regard the Church has for the special dignity of man which he has by virtue of his inner freedom. It is conscience, according to Catholic teaching, which represents that inner judgement that man makes after mature deliberation as to the truth and correctness of an action, that he applies to his life's actions and all of his dealings, and on the basis of which he then takes action. We have here a remarkable inner activity whereby a man sits in judgement of his own actions and of the whole world around him; and does so in an incomparably higher and more universal manner than human courts do since they act in a far more restricted fashion in that limited range of activities over which they have special competence. The Church assigns a degree of sovereignty to conscience which is so sublime that it teaches even the little child that no matter what, one must not go against one's conscience. The Church recognizes, of course, that a conscience can be wrong. That is why she teaches unfailingly what great harm can come from an erroneous conscience and what a great responsibility we have before God, who will one day measure the judgements of this personal court of ours against those of His eternal court, according to whose laws he will eventually be judged.

IV Freedom of Conviction

Just as the Catholic Church holds with reference
to moral freedom that what goes against a man's conscience is sinful, so she also teaches as the Apostle
Paul did about freedom of conviction, the necessity
of following one's convictions - rationabile obsequium -
in the area of religious beliefs. That too is a freedom of the human spirit at the second level of man's
spiritual nature, namely, in the recognition of truth.
As the Catholic Church makes a moral good the object
of inner free choice, so too she requires that the
acceptance of any truth which is worthy of man's recognition must be the object of free inner conviction
in human reason. The motivations for accepting what
is good and what is true must not be merely external,
but they must stem from an interior disposition as is
worthy of man's proper dignity. A man cannot build
his house on someone else's foundation. This means
that he cannot establish true moral behavior on some-
else's will, or genuine conviction of what is true on
someone else's intellectual grasp of the truth. No
matter how proper another person's will may be and
no matter how correct another person's grasp of the
truth may be, a man has to reconcile his own free will
and his own intellect, in other words - his own soul -
to what is good and what is true, before his own
judgements and actions become morally valid. God instilled this truly frightening freedom as an essential
quality of human dignity; and perilous though it may
be, He expects us to use it not only in our relationship to other men but even in our relationship to God
Himself.

The Church applies the self-same principle to
man's religious beliefs. St. Thomas Aquinas, who
gives us the authentic Catholic position on this
matter, said: "For Faith two things are necessary:
first, a credible object for one's belief, and second,
an acceptance of such an object of faith. This acceptance cannot be fully accomplished by mere external motivation, e.g., by miracles which we witness,
or by the conviction of the person who presents the
object for our acceptance. There must be, even more
importantly, an inner motivation which disposes a

121

person to accept an article of faith. Such inner motivation represents the principal and proper basis of faith.

"This inner basis, the Pelagians insist, is nothing more than free will of man. Here they are in error.

"The Faith does, in fact, rest on man's free will acceptance, but his will must first be predisposed for such acceptance by God's grace. Thus, insofar as acceptance is concerned - and that is the principal act of faith - God is the source of our faith inasmuch as, by His grace, He provides us with the all important inner motivation." (<u>Summa</u> IIa IIae q.VI. art. I). 3

We may, therefore, define Christian Faith as the concurrence of free will and intellect in the truths revealed by God, under the influence of Divine grace. The Faith is a gift of God, in other words, inasmuch as the objects of Faith are truths which were made known to us by God through the prophets of the Old Testament and ultimately through His Son; and it is a gift of God, furthermore, inasmuch as the acceptance of these truths can only occur under the influence of God's providence which furnishes us with the necessary grace to move us, enlighten us, and strengthen us for their acceptance. As the physician cures and strengthens a man's weak eyes, so God, in His love, strengthens and brings light to the weak eyes of the human intellect so that it can recognize and grasp the Divine truths of revelation. That is one side of the act of faith. It is an act of God. There is another side too which is necessary to complete it. That is the free will of man, joyfully and wholeheartedly cooperating with all of his heart and soul in surrendering to God's loving revelation, and at the same time endlessly thanking and praising God for having rescued him from his spiritual blindness and impotence. These two actions together - the act of God and the act of man - constitute that great miracle in history, that great, firm faith, that holy conviction which far surpasses all merely human conviction, and which has produced countless numbers of martyrs for the Faith.

It is in this twofold freedom, the freedom of will and intellect, that you have the real essence of human freedom. He who has such freedom has true human dignity, even if he is deprived of other freedoms. He who lacks it, lacks human dignity even if he enjoys all other human freedoms and worldly esteem. The abuse of basic human freedom consists in the choice of evil by the will, and in the choice of untruth by the intellect. Such abuse then leads to the ultimate debasement of man, as when a man uses the· will which is meant for freely accepting the highest Good to, instead, become a slave of evil passions, or as when a man uses that intellect, which is intended for recognizing the eternal Light to become the slave of untruth and of darkness.

It is this double freedom that is encountered in Sacred Scripture when Our Lord was speaking with the Jews who, among all of the nations of the world, took a special pride in their God-given freedom. Christ told them: "If you continue faithful to my word, you are my disciples in earnest; so you will come to know the truth, and the truth will set you free. They answered him, We are of Abraham's breed, nobody every enslaved us yet; what doest thou mean by saying, You shall become free? And Jesus answered them, Believe me when I tell you this; everyone who acts sinfully, is the slave of sin.....Why then, if it is the Son who makes you free men, you will have freedom in earnest." (John 8:31-37).

In the same vein, we have the other teaching which occurs so often in the Epistles of St. Paul, i.e., that true freedom consists in freely becoming the servant of God. Thus, St. Paul says: "If a slave is called to enter Christ's service, he is Christ's freed man, just as the free man, when he is called, becomes the slave of Christ." (ICor.7:22).

Sacred Scripture is very emphatic about the foolishness of those who clamor for the other freedoms while they lack true moral freedom. There is a remarkably apt description of such persons in the

123

second epistle of Peter which fits to the letter so many of the men of our time. The Apostle Peter speaks of those who disdain all authority, who in their foolhardiness and complacency are not fearful of causing division; and he speaks also of those who defame what they do not understand, who are monsters of debauchery, adulterers, who do all in their power to corrupt others by carnal seduction. He remarks about them with these significant words: "What do they offer them? Liberty. And all the time they themselves are enslaved to worldly corruption...(2 Peter 2:19).

It is in this freedom of will and of intellect that we have the basic foundation for all other freedoms as well as for a proper understanding of such other freedoms, as we shall see later.

V Faith and Freedom of Inquiry

Before we begin to discuss political freedom,
we have to come to grips with a certain fallacy. We
are being told constantly that freedom of intellect
and inquiry are not possible for Catholics. This
point of view is expressed time and again among our
enemies and their spokesmen in the daily press as
axiomatic, as requiring no proof and being beyond
question. Twice recently, our attention was drawn
to this nonsensical claim. A few months ago the
newspapers reported how the issue came up among
professors at the university in Königsberg (East
Prussia) whether Catholic and Jewish professors
might be appointed to this hitherto exclusively
Protestant institution. A certain professor who
is highly regarded for his generally liberal disposition proclaimed that there was no problem at
all so far as the appointment of Jews was concerned,
but that Catholics were another matter, since freedom of inquiry was not possible for Catholics.
One cannot conceive of a greater lie or of a greater
insult against us Catholics. Something even worse
took place, however at the University of Tuebingen.
It seems a certain Article IX was inserted in the
Articles of Agreement concluded on April 8, 1857,
according to which the Catholic theological faculty
was to be subject to the ecclesial magisterium of
the Church under the supervision of the bishop. By
virtue of this arrangement, the bishop had the power
to appoint or remove professors of theology and to
pass judgement on their publications and textbooks.
Subsequently, the faculty senate established a committee to determine whether the Catholic faculty
could, under such conditions, continue to be a part
of the university. On the recommendation of a
certain Professor of Botany, Hugo Mohl, the Senate
decided that the Catholic faculty of theology would
no longer be regarded as having freedom of inquiry
and its members were therefore ineligible to remain
on the faculty senate!

What they were saying, in effect, was that since
a Catholic or a Catholic priest was submissive to the
authority of his Church, specifically to his bishop,

125

he thereby loses the right to be regarded as a scientist and as a professor in the full academic sense of the word. The people responsible for this are no longer even capable of an awareness of what an affront such a posture represents to Catholic sensitivities. They are going so far now as to try to persuade the world that the difference between Protestantism and Catholicism is basically a difference between those who espouse science and reasonableness, the Protestants, and the Catholics who oppose them - as though this was the underlying cause of the religious Revolt.

How different things look if we refer back to history and consider the facts. Luther made it a fundamental postulate of his religion, as opposed to Catholicism, that human nature was stripped of all of its higher faculties by the fact of original sin. From that he deduced that man, merely by virtue of his natural capacities, couldn't accomplish anything meritorious; in fact he could not even achieve mere natural virtue. All of his actions were sinful. But if human nature is totally corrupt, this has to include man's natural reasoning capacity. If a man's every action is sinful, then each of his thoughts has to be false. That is precisely Luther's thinking and that is why he abhorred scientific knowledge. It is that thinking which brought him to the notion, Sola Fides - Faith alone. Since he regarded man as totally corrupt, justification could not come from within a man. It had to be a totally external action whereby the merits of Christ covered over man's wickedness. According to such a conception, there can be no healing of man's natural spiritual faculties by the grace gained for us by Jesus Christ. The truth and justice of Christ stands juxta-posed in an exterior relationship to man's totally corrupt nature with its blinded reasoning powers. With such a premise, one has to conclude that there is an irreconcilable contradiction between man's natural reasoning powers and Revelation. If reason, the essence of which lies in its capacity to ascertain truth, is totally corrupt, this can only mean that such capacity has been lost! Therefore independent scientific thought and any reconciliation of the process of reasoning with revealed truth is out of

126

the question. The plight of a person who is so constructed entails a permanent horrible conflict between human intelligence and his religious beliefs. Following this position one flagrant flaw, of course, comes to the surface. How can such a corrupt human nature even attain to this conception of <u>Sola Fides</u>, in other words, to an appreciation of the potency of the justifying merits of Christ, or even to the great sense of its own helplessness of which Luther spoke?

Against this teaching of the total corruption of human nature and the loss of free will which it entails, the Catholic Church took a most decisive stand. It became the focal point of the whole controversy between the old Church and the reformers.[4] Luther's position appeared to exalt the merits of Jesus Christ - hence, the many barbs directed against the self-righteousness of the Catholic position. In truth, what Luther did was to denigrate human reason and human liberty so that a <u>rationabile obsequium</u> - a rational worship of God, a reasonable faith - became an impossibility. The Church, on the other hand, not only attributed every bit as much importance to the merits gained for us by Jesus Christ, but she also salvaged the recognition of human reasoning capacity and human freedom. What would have become of humanity if Luther's teaching that human nature is totally corrupt, together with an all-powerful state, had gained full acceptance everywhere for even just one century? The first reformers had not yet died when the humanists, who greeted the Reformation with enthusiasm even though they had derived their potent scientific urges from Catholicism, in the twilight of their lives were bemoaning the death of all human science. [5]

The teaching of the Catholic Church on this matter can be summed up briefly. Man lost all supernatural grace through original sin. He did not, however, lose his natural capacities which mark him as a rational human being. In other words, he did not lose his free will nor his reasoning intellect. These were simply weakened and impaired. As a consequence of his condition, man can no longer perform any supernaturally meritorious works. He can, however, even without the supernatural assistance of Jesus Christ perform certain virtuous acts and come to recognize

127

certain natural truths. That is why we find much natural goodness and recognition of various truths also among pagans. That is why, furthermore, the Redemption is not to be regarded merely as an imputation of all guilt onto the shoulders of Jesus Christ, who then covers our guilt over in purely exterior fashion as with a great mantle. It is rather a restoration, a healing of our nature. Therefore, finally, revealed truth is not to be regarded as an indictment against fallen human nature, but rather as a mysterious, blessed healing and an elevation of man's spiritual nature. It is bequeathed to man as a saving grace to restore his wounded nature and to strengthen and lift him up to the very presence of God.

The Church has taught these propositions from its very beginning, as she has forcefully rejected any notion that Christianity requires that we must accept what is contrary to reason. It is axiomatic in all Catholic schools that what is unreasonable can and must not be accepted. It is remarkable therefore that our enemies have always tried to saddle us Catholics with this charge that we insist on unreasonable doctrines. Thus far, over the centuries, they have never yet been successful. Therefore, it is a falsehood and an insult when professors at German universities try to slander us Catholics by inferring that because of our beliefs we are somehow reduced to an academically inferior position where our reasoning powers have to be suppressed. The contrary is true. The Church waged bitter battles with the old orthodox Protestant reformers precisely over this issue, because the latter rejected free will and the free cooperation of human reason with the grace of God.[6]

How does one expalin this remarkable turnabout, where modern rationalistic Protestantism attacks the Catholic Church as the enemy of human reason and freedom, inasmuch as it was the Catholic Church which defended these against the attacks of the original reformers? The answer is to be found only partly in the enormous residue of bigotry. More important, it lies in the fact that Protestant rationalism is a reaction and, to a degree, a justifiable one against the

128

old Protestant orthodoxy. But now it has gone to the other extreme and declared the absolute independence of human reason and of the will - a position which rejects all authority and is irreconcilable with human nature that is dependent on God and subject to His Divine plan. That is how rationalism has lost sight of any basic relationship between authority and freedom as well as between any reasonable and free acceptance of legitimate authority. We shall discuss this matter in greater detail in another context later on.

VI   The Two Basic Tendencies of the State

Now we come to a discussion of how the Catholic
viewpoint and, above all, how a Catholic political
press has to stand its ground and do battle.

In all societies we are able to detect two basic
tendencies. The one serves to cement the social body
and hold it together; the other is the one whereby
the members of society stress their own individuality
and their differences and thereby make their own
specific contributions. Both of these tendencies
are, in themselves, justifiable, inasmuch as they
spring from the very nature of a society. A society
must have unity and at the same time safeguard the
individuality of its individual members. If either
the one or the other basic tendency is missing or
destroyed, one cannot begin to speak of society.

A proper balance between these two tendencies
is of vital importance for all human societies,
whether one is speaking of Church or of State, or
of the countless organizations which spring up because of the social nature of man. It is critical
for the well-being and for the achievement of any
society's objectives. The more dignified the members of a society, the tighter the bond which holds
them together and the more successful that society
will be. The reverse is also true.

The most exalted and most perfect version of
such a society is the Catholic Church as God intends
it to be. In the Church one finds the two basic tendencies of society attaining their highest fulfillment. On the one hand one finds the individual human
person with his own specific capacities, developing
these to their utmost perfection. On the other hand,
one finds in the Church a bond of unity which transcends human understanding, because all of the members
are also bound together eternally with God. This
bond is so intimate that Holy Scripture describes it
as a bond which unites its members into one Body!

131

Even though other societies have neither so high a purpose as the Church nor such exalted means to a-chieve their purpose, they too must embrace the two-fold characteristic tendencies of every society. This is especially urgent for that society which we call the State. It will be the more nearly perfect, the nobler the individuality and personality of its members remain, and the more solid the bond which holds the members together.

Selfishness is the deadly enemy of both of these tendencies in civil life. To whatever degree it en-nervates either of them, the state will either see its members degraded or its bond of unity disinte-grated. It is well for us, therefore, to trace the two tendencies to their real source and at the same time to investigate that degradation of them which occurs when egotism moves in to render them ineffec-tive. In the process we will come to appreciate the true meaning of the terms, <u>freedom</u> and <u>revolution</u> on the one hand, and <u>authority</u> and <u>absolutism</u> on the other.

VII Civil and Social Liberty

The social freedom of citizens, civil liberty, is implicit in the first of the two basic tendencies in society, i.e., the right to maintain one's own individuality and personality. Its egotistical abuse carried to the extreme culminates in revolution.

The dignity of the state hinges first and foremost on the personal worth of its members. A body whose members are in poor health cannot be a healthy body, taken as a whole. A house built of defective materials will not end up being a sound structure. Likewise, a community made up of individual members lacking in human dignity cannot end up being a dignified society of high moral worth. The high moral worth which Christianity instills in humanity is precisely what makes the Christian state so superior to any non-Christian state. The blessing which Christendom imparts to civil authority becomes of secondary importance in such a state. The sublime force of Christianity still manifests itself even where only remnants of Christian life survive. Even when only feeble rays of that heavenly light filter into the life of a nation, they provide a mighty impulse to keep it from sinking back into paganism. It is well to remember, therefore, that the Christian composition of a state implies that it is made up of Christian members who strive for Christian perfection. It matters less that the state designates itself as Christian and holds on to a few external Christian customs and practices.

The personal worth of a person depends, as we have suggested, especially on freedom. It is when this freedom finds its true and proper expression in moral freedom that political and social freedoms have real meaning. Let us examine this matter more closely.

VIII   Self-Determination

The essence of liberty, whatever the context, lies in free self-determination stemming from inner conviction rather than from external force. Such free self-determination and free choice are the necessary prerequisities for social and political freedom. What it all means is that a man, in his personal, social, and political life, to the extent that he is able to take care of his own needs without violating the rights of others, enjoys the widest possible latitude in managing his own affairs. This liberty is therefore aptly designated as self-determination or individual autonomy.

If this liberty is to have true meaning, however, it must extend beyond the most immediate personal affairs also to those social concerns which are a part of everyday human existence. Man is by nature utterly social to the extent that he cannot survive in isolation. He is scarcely born when he finds himself in need of his first social contact in the family, so that he can preserve his fragile existence. Gradually his circle of social relations widens much in the same way as ripples in a pond spread outward after a stone has been thrown into it. Human life carries on within a structure of manifold social arrangements some of which are quite universal, like the family, the local community, the state, and others of which are established for achieving more specialized purposes. The right of a man to guide his own destiny in all such societies, whether one is speaking of the family, the community, the province, or other corporate bodies which men establish, is what social and political liberty are all about. Where this is missing, liberty is missing.

We will have frequent occasion to discuss the great value of this social, civil, and political liberty. For the moment it is sufficient to point out that this freedom determines the character of a man in his relationship with his fellow man, whether we are speaking of his grass-roots social contacts or his activities in the higher levels of civil society. It represents a great school for developing true and healthy and realistic perspectives in the life of the state and at the same time it instills strength and dignity in the state itself.

It is self-evident, however, that such individual automony is not unlimited and unconditional. It does not imply total independence. Rather it brings with it the obligation of self-control, the need to submit to the law of God and to the order which God has established in the universe. It implies also the need to respect the rights of all other men with whom one comes in contact. Freedom does not absolve from obedience. Rather it is intimately related to it. It is from obedience that freedom receives its true dignity. In the mind of God all of the various creatures on which He bestowed life have their proper relationship to each other. The more these creatures conform to their respective roles, the more nearly will that harmony be realized which God envisions, where all creatures will achieve their highest destiny and their greatest happiness. The true meaning of that liberty which man, a rational creature of God, enjoys lies in his ability to cooperate freely with God in the fulfillment of the Divine plan, and in that he freely seeks out the role which God has destined for him and which he then carries out according to God's will. That applies in all of his human activities whether in the family or in the state. Therefore his liberty is always conditioned by obedience!

136

IX Revolution

If one member of a body tried to enrich itself at the expense of the other members, the harmony in the body would be destroyed, and the body would begin to disintegrate. Such egotism in the members who make up civil society, we call revolution. Egotism or self-seeking exists, as Christian moral teaching tells us, when a man prefers his own honor and will to the honor and will of God, and when, in the process of seeking his own supposed good, he runs roughshod over the rights of his fellow men.

We have only to apply this concept to civil society to recognize what the essence of revolution is all about. Liberty, when it is kept in harmony with the law of God, when it is guided by a spirit of justice toward all,. and when it contains itself and remains in conformity with the role which God has destined for us is truly something noble and wonderful. Christianity produces people who are capable of using their freedom in that manner. But liberty which is guided by selfishness, which gives in to every craven impulse and becomes an unbridled passion - the self-centered will that is motivated and propelled by pride, sensuousness, and greed - is like a devastating fire which destroys all that it encounters. Such egotism, when it comes into confrontation with civil order which it proposes to destroy and then restructure for its own purposes and to the detriment of all others, is what revolution is all about. It is the revolutionary spirit which we see erupting all around us in our time.

It is clear from our present plight how political liberty is so intimately related to moral liberty. The more moral a man is and the more free he is of selfishness and of domination by unruly passions, the more free he is in the true sense of the word. Whoever learns self-control does not require that any external bonds be placed upon him. A truly Christian nation could operate with a maximum of self-government. On the other hand, revolution and the spirit of· revolt are the enemies of all freedom. The brutal person,

referred to in Sacred Scripture, abuses all freedom
and brings on absolutism!

X State Authority, Political Authority, and Sovereignty

The exercise of power by the state, its sovereign authority in other words, is what the other basic tendency in society, as applied to the state, is all about. It is the tendency that binds together and unifies the citizenry. Its egotistical abuse represents absolutism and improper centralization of authority.

For the political life of a state to prosper depends also upon the proper use of force in keeping with the dignity of a state's authority. Just as Christendom gives to the individual members of the body politic, who represent the building stones of which the state edifice is constructed, their highest purpose, so it also affords to the binding force, which the state possesses, its highest expression, its true and proper guidelines, its fullest sanction and solid foundation. It safeguards state authority from slipping into its egotistical extremes, absolutism and undue centralization of authority. Exercised in conformity with the true Christian spirit, state authority could achieve the fullest perfection that is possible in the secular order. Even when secular authorities have drifted from Christianity, as has so often been the case in recent centuries, civil authority is still in a far better condition than it is in non-Christian states.

The dignity, solidity, and vitality of civil authority does not hinge on its unbounded extension, so that it thinks for all, guides all, determines everything, and rules over all. On the contrary, these are reflected in how well the authorities can steer clear of egotistical abuse of their power, how well they are able to confine their activities to the area which is proper to the state and reasonable for it, and how effectively they operate within this proper sphere of activity.

No fallacy is more nefarious or more widespread than the tendency to look for the strength of the state in the degree of power which it wields. It is like judging the health of the human body by the size

139

of its waistline. A godlike principle for all human affairs, full of beauty and full of delicacy and refinement, is to be found in the correct balance between authority and freedom. Every use of authority - that includes the use of paternal authority which is the first authority we as children encountered in our lives, and it includes also the authority which Christ established in his Church - if it is exercised without regard for the dignity of the human soul and for the God-given freedom and self-determination of each individual, becomes a detrimental thing. In the state there are countless individual entities. There is the individual human person himself, and then there are what the language of jurisprudence terms, moral persons - those numerous social bodies in which men organize up to and including the state itself, which has the ultimate task of uniting all of those individuals and lower organs of society. If this highest social body, the state, oversteps its bounds and usurps and swallows up all of the lower organs of society, then the social organism continues to live, but only on borrowed time. It is as with disease which, when it is present, continues to indicate the presence of life; but life is in the process of being snuffed out. The more the authority of the state moves in this unhealthy direction, the more certain it is that the state will become neglectful of its own proper duties and fail to do what it ought to be doing, to the detriment of all concerned.

The proper sphere of activity for the sovereign authority of the state includes three principal areas. The first, and I would call this the outstanding jewel in the crown of worldly sovereignty, is the safeguarding of justice. What a boon it would be to humanity if closer attention were paid to this function! A brief comment will suffice.

First and foremost, we are talking here about the safeguarding of basic human rights, and that means prompt and expeditious justice. How much remains to be done in this all-important area. It is especially urgent that every person who finds any of his rights violated must have access to a court of law. The Catholic press ought to champion this cause most vigorously. The safe-guarding of rights that are

being violated has always been considered one of the
supreme moral virtues in all of Christendom.

Secondly, the law-making power is an essential
part of the preservation of human rights; therefore
it is one of the loftiest of the state's functions.
In this area too the government of our contemporary
secular state is riddled with abuses. Legislation
should be not merely just, but also simple. What a
contrast between now and former times! Prior to the
old <u>Sachsen-Spiegel</u>,[8] there was not even a written
code of laws in Germany. Our German forefathers
loved the law. They had a deep-seated sense of justice and also workable norms for seeing that justice
was done. But the law was alive within them, and it
came to bear in their deliberations, their customs,
their whole way of thinking. Because of their grasp
of what law was, self-determination was operative and
men still acted as judges of their own actions.
How nice it must have been to see German men sitting
in court each having a full appreciation of the law,
and, as jurors, capable of hearing both sides of a
case and passing intelligent judgement. How different things are now that the pagan Roman law has
invaded the German juridical structure. It is remarkable, isn't it, how modern men protest against
Christian Rome at the same time that they revert
to idolizing pagan Rome. They insult us Roman
Catholics as ultramontan because we follow the
Bishop of Rome as the head of our Church; and at
the same time they indulge in the cult of <u>pagan
ultramontanism</u> trying by every means to poison the
old German spirit of our nation with paganism.

We live in an age of fabrication, and the
modern state has become a law factory in the real
sense of the word. Laws issue forth in a constant
stream; and countless commissions which are established and perpetuate themselves, grind out new
edicts ceaselessly, at the same time as endless
government memoranda promulgate new regulations.
The present-day commission member comes to regard
this activity as his prime duty; and what is more,
he begins to consider that he is the greater benefactor of mankind the more laws he makes. With

inestimable pride he looks upon himself as the center of the whole legislative process. The ideal of the modern age seems to be to provide each year, as the Enlightenment process progresses and we become more intelligent, a whole new set of government ministers, new officials, new parliamentary majorities, and a whole new body of laws. What damage this spirit does to proper respect for the very notion of law! Besides, that is why the majority of people lose contact with laws and their real meaning. Law becomes the exclusive domain of a caste made up of judges and lawyers, who make it their life's work. Anyone who is not in a position to complete legal studies at the university, and to spend years poring over books of laws and regulations, and finally to read through the conflicting decisions of the high courts becomes incapable of grasping what the law of the land is. One German in a thousand today can have any real understanding of the laws which regulate his life. Most of us, where the law is concerned, are like foreigners travelling in a country where we do not know the language. We have to choose a leader and follow him blindly, and we learn only too often that we have been deceived. Hence the great uncertainty today in legal proceedings. It is impossible to predict with any degree of accuracy how a particular court judgement will go. The average citizen, involved in litigation, is pretty much in the position of a man playing a game of chance in a gambling casino. That is why so much premium is placed among litigants on landing a clever attorney. One gets the impression that cleverness in the court room rather than justice becomes the prime consideration. The real tragedy of the whole process lies in the fact that the notion of right disappears more and more from the public consciousness. It becomes less a question of conscientious judgements regarding what is moral or immoral, and more a matter of what one can "win" in the courts, even though one's own conscience might be uneasy about the outcome. That is how the notion of law - a leading guidepost for civil society - gradually deteriorates. What a great boon it would be to simplify the law and eliminate the endless ambiguities!

142

The second principal area of activity by the state is the support of all that deserves support - again, a broad area of beneficent intervention. Man is so constituted that he cannot reach his fulfillment or the full development of his capacities without help from others. If we only think about it, we come to realize how both our spiritual and our temporal needs require the cooperation of countless people, day in and day out. That is why the state ought to pay scrupulous attention to not only safeguarding the rights of every citizen, but also to offering whatever help is necessary so that the citizenry can work out its temporal well-being. In the process, the state ought to cultivate what is moral and good to whatever degree it can without interfering with the individual's right of self-determination.

The third area of competence for state authority, finally, is representing the nation in its dealings with other nations. What a boon it would be if the simplest Christian principles could be brought to bear in this area! Foreign relations in our time all too often follow the promptings of egotism and a "might-makes-right" principle hypocritically disguised as exalted and subtle worldly wisdom. If international relations were conducted in a truthful and upright manner according to the same principles of justice and charity which each Christian tries to apply in his dealings with his neighbor in order not to be regarded as a swindler and a liar, how different things would be today!

Bringing the elementary principles of truth and justice to bear in the area of political life, is, in fact, the loftiest mission which the Catholic press could champion.

143

"By the grace of God" is an expression much abused by both those who favor it and those who oppose it. How few ever really take the time to think what this expression actually means! Instead, bitter debates occur over the justification of the notion, while the first prerequisite for coming to any kind of understanding of the matter - a consensus as to what the term means - is still missing. Instead, the arbitrary prejudices which one side or the other nurtures regarding it continue to dominate the discussion. I maintain that the "Monarchy, by the grace of God" concept, as it has come to be understood since the Reformation by both Catholics and non-Catholic princes and royalty, has become nothing more than a destructive idolatry. At the same time I cherish the notion, when it is understood in the proper sense of the word, as an overriding truth that is deeply rooted in common sense and in Christian doctrine. In fact, I respect it as representing the only valid foundation for temporal authority. Here again, the Catholic press has its work cut out for it. It ought to make every effort to clarify the meaning of "Monarchy by the grace of God" in the true sense of the word, while fighting against the falsification of it by both those who oppose it and by some of those who favor it.

"By the grace of God," above all, does not mean that God has directly conferred temporal power upon some particular person. There have been many princes who gained power by the unjust use of force even though their heirs, quite legitimately, come to regard themselves as rulers "by the grace of God." It is as with private property. The right is God-given, even though the way property is acquired does not always conform to His will. In the same sense, power in the state originates in God, even though it is often appropriated at the outset by improper means.

The other thing that "by the grace of God" does not mean is that every action of the sovereign authority comes from God and must be viewed and accepted as such. The Apostles encouraged the early Christians

145

to obey the pagan rulers, for God's sake, though they themselves defied those rulers when they overstepped the bounds of their legitimate authority.

Authority comes from God, but not the exercise of that authority. The latter, like all capacities and powers which God has conferred on man, are subject to man's free use of them. In the same sense, parental authority is God-given, though it may be abused often enough.

Finally, "by the grace of God" does not infer unconditional and unlimited power. It is precisely from his misinterpretation of it that the absolutism of some monarchs originated. Actually, the term,"by the grace of God," implies the strictest limitations. That is because a ruler who views his authority as coming from God will recognize that he must always exercise that power in obedience to God's will as expressed in His commandments, in His moral laws, in His Divine plan, and in the rights which He has conferred upon all men.

"By the grace of God" means, above all, that temporal order is not a human artifact, but first and foremost, the work of God. Therefore, the power that is part of it is not something that man devised, but rather something that is essentially a divine institution which is totally independent of what human beings want or do not want. Just as God originated the Divine plan for order in the universe without human assistance, so also He has ordained by His almighty power that wherever men live in an ordered relationship with each other, there must be a supreme authority, the exercise of which will be the means whereby the working out of Divine Providence occurs through history. Mankind has the option to recognize this authority or to destroy it, while accepting the inevitable consequences of cutting itself off from all civilization and real human progress, and thereby sinking into barbarism. That is what the expression, "by the grace of God," is all about, as good common sense and also Revelation make it clear.

It is this authority that the Apostle Paul writes about in his Epistle to the Romans.

"Every soul must be submissive to its lawful superiors; authority comes from God only, and all authorities that hold sway are of His ordinance. Thus the man who opposes authority is a rebel against the ordinance of God, and rebels secure their own condemnation. A good conscience has no need to go in fear of the magistrate, as a bad conscience does. If thou wouldst be free from the fear of authority, do right, and thou shalt win its approval; the magistrate is God's minister, working for thy good. Only if thou doest wrong, needst thou be afraid; it is not for nothing that he bears the sword; he is God's minister still, to inflict punishment on the wrong-doer. Thou must needs, then, be submissive, not only for fear of punishment, but in conscience. It is for this same reason that you pay taxes; magistrates are in God's service, and must give all their time to it. Pay every man, then his due; taxes, if it be taxes; customs, if it be customs; respect and honour, if it be respect and honour. Do not let anybody have a claim upon you except the claim which binds us to love one another. The man who loves his neighbour has done all that the law demands." (Rom. 13:1-8).

How beautifully Paul expresses the idea that all authority originates with God and that all of those who possess authority are really servants of God. It is for that reason that we ought to obey them and respect them.

St. Peter expresses substantially the same thought in his first epistle.

"For the love of the Lord, then, bow to every kind of human authority; to the king, who enjoys the chief power, and to the magistrates who hold his commission to punish criminals and encourage honest men. To silence, by honest living, the ignorant chatter of fools; that is what God expects of you. Free men, but the liberty you enjoy is not to be made a pretext for wrong-doing; it is to be used in God's service. Give all men their due; to the brethren, your love; to God, your reverence; to the king, due honor.

"You who are slaves must be submissive to your masters, and shew all respect, not only to those who

147

are kind and considerate, but to those who are hard
to please. It does a man credit when he bears undeserved ill-treatment with the thought of God in
his heart." (I Peter 2:13-19)

We find the same beautiful expression here. The
Christian ought to recognize in the existence of authority a part of the Divine plan for order. He ought to
obey authority and honor it conscientiously for God's
sake, because that is God's will. He ought to shun
those who, under the mantle of Christian freedom, try
to deter him from obeying authority. Remember that
such obedience does not rob us of that freedom which
we enjoy as Christians, since we are not obeying a
human being for the sake of that human being, but as
servants of God.

We have to emphasize, however, that it is not
only the temporal rulers that operate "by the grace
of God." Everything which God has ordained in the
universe operates "by the grace of God." All legitimate power and each genuine right is just as much
"by the grace of God" as the right of kings and
princes.

XII   The Crowning of Christian Kings

These ideas have found noble expression in the
manner in which kings were crowned and anointed since
the Christian era began more than a thousand years
ago. The rite is carefully prescribed by the Church
in the same _Pontificale_ in which the rites for the
consecration of bishops is found. These rites provide the most solemn testimony of what Christianity
thinks about monarchy "by the grace of God." Permit
me to draw certain lessons from this.

The king was required to prepare for the ceremony by several days of prayer and fasting. The
whole thing is all the more solemn in that it occurs
within the framework of the Sacrifice of the Mass
whereby the king receives, under the appearance of
bread and wine, the Lord himself in whose name he
is to exercise sovereignty, and in the service of
Whom he receives his royal dignity, as all of his
subjects will observe in the course of the ceremony.
The coronation itself had to take place, when at
all possible, on a Sunday; and the church was to be
decorated as for a major feast. A throne was erected in the sanctuary alongside one for the queen.
At the same time, the steps ascending to the royal
throne were not to reach as high as the top step ascending to the altar - a reminder to the king that
he should not lift himself above the heavenly King.
On the altar was placed the royal sword, the scepter,
and the holy ointment. All of the bishops of the
realm were to be present for the ceremony. As the
king appeared, dressed in his knightly armor, the
Bishop or Metropolitan presiding at the ceremony
called out to him:

"Noble Prince! As you are about to receive the
holy ointment and the insignia of the realm today at
our hands, who - unworthy though we are - act as representatives of Christ our Savior, it is well that I
should first remind you of the great burden which you
are about to undertake. You are about to receive the
dignity of kingship along with responsibility for all
of your devoted subjects. This is an exalted status
among mortals, but it is also full of peril, responsi-

149

bility, and anxiety. If you will now recall that all power by which kings and lawmakers rule and regulate is from God, Our Lord, so know also that you will have to give an account before God for the subjects who are entrusted to your care.

"Above all, you should take care always to serve the Lord, your God, with your whole spirit and with a pure heart. Preserve to the end, and protect from all of its enemies, the Christian religion and the Catholic faith which has been yours since your infancy. Accord the proper respect to those who govern the Church and to all of its priests, and be careful never to tread underfoot the freedom of the Church. That justice without which no society can long endure, you are sworn to uphold by assuring the good what is their due and the evil-doers their deserved punishment. Protect from oppression the widows and orphans, and all of the poor and the weak. Be gentle and kind to all who approach you as befits your royal dignity. Conduct yourself so that every man is reassured that you rule not for your own benefit, but for the benefit of your entire realm; and be ever mindful that the reward for your good works is to be sought in Heaven and not in this world. May He who lives and reigns eternally grant this. Amen."

Thereupon, the king kneels down and swears the following oath in the presence of the Archbishop:

"I_____,by the grace of God about to be king of_____, acknowledge and promise before God and his angels that I will uphold law, justice, and peace for the Church of God and for the nation entrusted to me, to the extent that, trusting in God's mercy and with the advice of my faithful counsellors, I am able to do this. I also promise to extend to the bishops of God's Church the full honor to which the law entitles them, just as I will preserve what kings and emperors have donated and bequeathed to the Church. I will also accord the requisite honor to abbots, counts, and all of my vassals according to the good advice of my faithful counsellors. So help me God and this holy Book."

150

Then the archbishop together with the assembled
bishops say the following prayer:

"Almighty God, Creator of the universe, sovereign
over all of the angels, King of kings and Ruler of all
rulers, who didst enable Abraham, your faithful servant,
to triumph over all of his enemies, who didst vouchsafe
to Moses and Joshua, the leaders of your people, many
victories, who didst elevate your humble son David to
become the highest king of your nation, and who didst
fill Solomon with great wisdom and love of peaceful-
naess, listen, we beseech you, O Lord, to the prayers
of your humble supplicants, and bestow upon your
servant_____the graces of your blessing; safeguard
him with the power of your righteousness always and
everywhere, so that, strengthened by Abraham's faith,
supported by Moses gentle spirit, and fortified by
Joshua's courage, graced by David's humility and
Solomon's wisdom, he may be pleasing to you in all
of his actions and remain ever in the path of justice
without wavering, guided by your Hand and protected
by the insuperable shield and sword of the heavenly
hosts. Grant that he may gain victory over the enemies of Christ's holy cross, and make them shrink
back in fear of his might, and that he may bring
blessed peace to those who glory in your name through
Christ our Lord, who by the merits of His holy cross
vanquished the power of darkness and who, after con-
quering the rule of Satan, ascended victorious into
Heaven, in whom all power and victory resides, For
He is the glorification of the humble, the life and
salvation of all mankind, who lives and reigns with
You in the unity of the Holy Spirit, as God, forever
and ever. Amen."

While he is anointing the monarch, the archbishop says:

"May the Lord, Jesus Christ, God and Son of God,
who was singled out by the Father to be anointed with
the oil of sanctity, pour forth through this anointment with oil the blessings of the Holy Spirit upon
your head, and let them permeate your whole spirit,
so that by this visible sign you may be deemed worthy
to receive the invisible graces, and that after you
have ruled over your temporal domain in justice, you

151

may enjoy the heavenly reign of Him who is alone without sin, and who lives and reigns with God the Father in union with the Holy Spirit, for all eternity. Amen."

Thereupon, the king takes off his armour and dressed in his royal garments ascends to the throne, accompanied by prelates and by his royal retinue, to participate in celebration of the Holy Mass during which he receives the insignia of the realm.

The coronation itself is performed by all of the bishops present who escort the crown from the altar and place it on the head of the king whereupon the archbishop says:

"Receive the crown of the kingdom, placed upon your head by unworthy but nevertheless episcopal hands, in the name of the Father, and of the Son, and of the Holy Spirit. Know that it symbolizes the glory of sanctity and the honor and works of virile steadfastness. Forget not that by virtue of this crown you share to an extent our own high office inasmuch as we are regarded as shepherds and spiritual providers within the Church, and you are a valiant defender of the Church of Christ against all enemies. You represent the devoted administrator and gracious ruler of the nation which has been entrusted to your care by the blessing of us who stand in the place of the Apostles and of all of the Saints. May you enjoy eternal life along with all of the glorious fighters for justice. May virtues adorn you as precious jewels and may you be crowned with the prize of eternal bliss, with our Savior and Redeemer, Jesus Christ, whose name you bear and whom you represent, now and forever."

When he is conferring the scepter, the archbishop says these words:

"Accept the staff signifying strength and truth, and recognize your grave obligation to encourage the good, deter the evildoer, to give direction to those who go astray, to assist those who are in need, to humble the proud, and to lift up the humble. May Jesus Christ, our Lord, open up the door for you, for it was He who said: 'I am the gate. Who enters

through me will be sanctified.' He who is the key
of the house of David, and the scepter of the house
of Israel, who opens so that no one can close, and
who closes so that no one can open, may He be your
leader, who releases from bondage the prisoners who
sit in darkness and in the shadow of death; so make
yourself worthy to follow in all things Him of whom
the prophet, David, said: 'Your throne, O God, remains
always and forever, the scepter of justice is the
scepter of your kingdom.' Love justice and hate injustice as He hated it. That is why God, your God,
has anointed you as he anointed before all ages, with
precious ointment, Jesus Christ, Our Lord, who lives
and reigns with Him for all eternity. Amen."

After the king is crowned, the blessing and
anointment of the queen begins. The king rises on
his throne, and with the crown upon his head, and
the scepter in his hand, he walks to the altar and
says to the archbishop: "Honorable Father, we beseech you to now place the crown of queen upon the
head of her who is, by God, bound to us for life,
for the praise and glory of our Savior, Jesus Christ."

Later, the archbishop, together with all of the
assembled bishops prays: "Almighty, eternal God,
sanctify with our heavenly blessing your servant,
_____, whom we now see raised to the dignity of
queen, for the well-being of the realm. Bestow of
your wisdom upon her and strengthen her. May she
always acknowledge your Church as a loyal servant.
Through Christ, Our Lord."

In the interests of brevity, we shall pass over
many of the other parts of the ceremony. But we
would still recall the words which the archbishop
says as he hands the scepter to the queen. They sum
up in a few words the true image of a Christian
queen.

"Accept the staff of virtue and of truth. Be
merciful and affable toward the poor. Show care and
concern for widows, the helpless, and the orphans, so
that Almighty God may bestow His many graces upon you,
who lives and reigns forever. Amen."

153

Thus, the queen is installed as the mother of the poor, of widows, and of orphans, actually as the first sister of mercy in the land!

This entire dignified ceremony needs no further explanation. It establishes a priesthood by the grace of God alongside a kingship, by the grace of God. The bishop acts here, as he states, as a representative of Jesus Christ, as a successor of the Apostles. He recognizes the dignity of the monarchy in the name of Jesus Christ, as something that originates with Almighty God. Such recognition of the high status of temporal rule by the Church before the whole nation is one part of the significance of the coronation rite. But that is not all. The Church prays for the king according to the mission which Christ conferred upon it, and it blesses him as Christ empowered her to do. The Church cannot do this, however, without being ever mindful of the great and grave duties of a king. That is why all of the prayers and supplications contain such earnest, simple and plainspoken warnings, as befits true honesty.

XIII The State by the Grace of Mankind
      Two Bases of Statehood: The Will
      of God; The Will of Man

This world order and concept of the state, which
is based upon God and upon His will, and which is oriented toward the service and honor of God, stands opposed to the one which is based solely upon man and
upon human will and which recognizes only service to
mankind and the glorification of so-called humanity.
The state, "by the grace of God," is juxta-posed to
the state, by the grace of mankind. That is the
proper characterization and essence of the so-called
modern state which is a purely human fabrication and
only wishes to be such, even though this state also
has its court theologians at certain German universities; and they lend a certain evangelical lustre to
it.

Let us investigate this notion of the state more
carefully. Thank God, it does not yet have wide acceptance among the German people, at large. Among
those circles which derive their culture from the
daily press, it has practically taken over, however;
and from there, the circle of acceptance threatens
to widen. Such a conception of the state and of the
state's power is the inevitable consequence of godlessness and agnosticism and that unholy philosophy which
rejects any notion of a supernatural order. As opposed to the words of Sacred Scripture, the credo of
this faction reads: There is no power from above.
Whatever power exists comes from the people; whoever
thwarts that power, thwarts the will of the people
and invites the displeasure of the people. We have
to experience all of the necessary, frightful consequences of such a system of political thought and lay
it bare for what it is!

All men are by their nature essentially equal.
Even though one person has greater natural capacities
than another, that does not add up to an essential
difference, merely an accidental one which is of a
fleeting nature. Capacities and knowledge can be
developed. A man, as a man, is totally independent

155

of another man and, in this respect, truly sovereign. The awareness of this sovereignty can remain dormant in a man's soul because of some external circumstances; but if these circumstances change, it will inevitably come to the fore again, since it is a truth buried deeply in our inner consciousness.

Now if a man believes in God, the God from whom he and all of his fellow men derived life, if he recognizes God as eternal Truth, as the true and greatest Lord of all creation, he will also find in such belief the basis for authority. And he will therefore recognize it as his duty to submit to this authority in all of his relations toward God as well as toward his fellow man. Such a person will appreciate the commandment: Thou shalt love the Lord thy God with thy whole heart, with thy whole soul, and with all thy strength! And from this first and greatest commandment correct order with subordination to legitimate authority will develop.

If, on the other hand, a man acknowledges nothing higher than, let us say, Nature, and if he perceives no higher will or intelligence than human will and human reason, his blindness will bring him to the point where, before long, he will come to regard his own will and his own reasoning power as the ultimate criteria of all things. He will then reject all of the past and all of the present, opposing his reason and will to that of the entire race of men, and regarding himself only ⋅ as their equal but even as independent of them. Everything that men have thought becomes merely the thinking of other human beings. Whatever they have decreed in the state, in all civil as well as religious societies, become merely so many human actions which he need not accept as authoritative, or as binding criteria. He is therefore not only the victim of the freest kind of subjectivism, but he is fully justified in following such a course. No other mere human being would have the right to instruct him, to order him, to judge him, or to punish him. The intelligence and will of any other mere human person will stand at the same level as his own intelligence and will. There is nothing higher. The only binding force in human society then is the contract. But even this does not suffice to place limits on people in such

156

a system, and to provide order. That is because everything is regarded as in progress toward some unknown goal. It remains a moot question whether there is anything that is true, good, and just in itself. Chances are that progress will reveal that what he declared his allegiance to today will no longer appear to be true, good, and just tomorrow. What will he do then? Everything will have to remain up in the air, and there remains nothing to impose order except sheer force. The war of all of these absolutely sovereign individualities against all others is an inevitable consequence of such a system. The ultimate question facing every man then becomes no longer, what ought I to do, what may I do, but what am I capable of doing!

That is the spirit that is now forming and stirring in the bosom of mankind; and it already manifests itself, now here, now there, like a destructive sea of flames licking at the foundations of human society. It will gnaw away at society as a hidden worm gradually eats away the roots of a mighty tree. We cannot come to terms with falsehood. If we do, it will eventually devour us. Man has been toying for some time now with godlessness and with the denial that there is a God. Monarchs who spoke of themselves as rulers "by the grace of God" have felt free to mock out religion and the fear of God and to propagate their unbelief. Hardly anything is regarded more lightly today than godlessness. No one seems to worry any more about offending God. The denial of God is regarded virtually as a postulate for appearing learned. No one is concerned about the criminality of hiring people, who flaunt their godlessness, to teach our youth. It is even fashionable now to pervert the very meaning of words by referring to societies which make godlessness their cult, as religious sects. God will not long tolerate such sport. One cannot undermine and destroy the foundation of a house and expect to go on living in it as if it were suspended in the air. Nor can we stand by while the foundations of world order are destroyed without eventually being buried underneath its rubble. If there is no supernatural order, then truth, law and justice, as well as morality and the virtues are all enigmas, and every man is left to his own resources to interpret them.

XIV Absolutism, Centralization

The egotistical abuse of government power, regardless of whether it claims to stem from the "grace of God" or from the "grace of the people," whether it is supposedly based on the will of God or the will of man, culminates in absolutism and in limitless centralization of power.

Absolutism is self-seeking gone wild on the part of those who hold the reins of state power, just as revolution is self-seeking gone wild on the part of the members of society. Both lead to the dissolution of civil society; the former in that it destroys the freedom and individuality of the separate members of society, the latter in that it severs the bond of unity required for any society. One obliterates differences, the other, unity. Both variety as well as unity are requisites of any society, in particular, that society which we call the state.

Absolutism, therefore, represents the quest by state authority for omnipotence, omnicompetence, and the removal of all limitations on the exercise of its authority at the expense of the personal and corporate individual members of society. It is a quest that finds expression especially in the undue centralization of powers. Absolutism is domination without bounds, and it is insanely jealous of all such power. It wants to think for all, provide for all, manage for all, instruct all, and provide happiness for all. It allows others only the privilege of working, paying and, in its liberal form, voting. No independence is tolerated since it views any independent person as a state within the state. It wants to stand alone, and all others must bow to its authority. That is precisely its great weakness, needless to say; and it comes to the fore whenever such a state collapses. Nothing falls apart more suddenly, more unexpectedly, more totally, than such an absolute state. That is because everything rests on one slender base, and when that base goes, everything goes down with it.

In ancient pagan times, this state absolutism reached a high level of development in the days of the Roman empire. That empire developed a kind of idolatry where the emperor himself came to be regarded as a demi-god and as the supreme high priest. Hence, came the rule of law: "Quod principi placuit, legis habet vigorem.."(What pleases the ruler is the law of the land...)9 Since the emperor was not, in fact, God, but had often enough strayed far from God's ways, the vices of the emperor, in effect, became the laws of the land. In such a situation, human dignity and the rights of the individual person had scant chance for survival. Fortunately the modern-day techniques for centralization of authority were not available to Roman emperors, so that there remained a relatively wide area of individual autonomy free from central authority. This turned out to be a real boon for Christianity.

Christianity confronted this ancient Roman absolutism, which had made the weaknesses of its emperors the laws of the land, in the name of the true Lord of the world. The Christian teachings about the one true God, the Redemption of all of mankind, the call to all men to become children of God, the obligation of obeying God before the emperor, the sacredness of man's conscience, the division between spiritual and temporal authority, finally brought about the collapse of the pagan gods.

The medieval era was a period of genuine personal and corporate freedom. Such freedom arose in all of its varied manifestations out of the strong, unspoiled culture of the Germanic tribes, who were especially receptive to Christian liberty, what with their great stress on personal freedom. Unlimited authority in the hands of a human being was unknown to them. What they did accept, so far as authority exercised both by the Church and the state was concerned, was the notion of an order established by God; a power, therefore, which so long as it stayed within bounds set by God, deserved obedience lest God's own order was transgressed. The idea permeated medieval society that any human arbitrariness represented an abuse of proper order, an injustice, a violation of the law. Therefore, anyone called to represent God in a position of authority whether for the Church or for the State was expected to submit to God's plan for order, just like everyone else. Pope and emperor, bishop and prince, priest or layman, all without exception possessed an awareness that when they gave or obeyed orders they merely fulfilled the Divine plan for order which obliged everyone to stay within limits set forth in God's law as expressed in reason and revelation. It goes without saying that, even in such a context, various and sometimes great controversies arose; nevertheless the principle was never called into question. That explains the great freedom of spirit which we have come to associate with the Middle Ages. The kind of abjectness which we now associate with the condition of servitude was simply unknown then. Even at the time when papal authority was at the highest point that it had ever reached, there was a certain generosity of spirit in censuring human abuses and personal weaknesses which we are incapable of understanding in our own time.

Ever since the 15th century, we have come to abandon these ancient principles of Christian-Germanic liberty, and we have reverted to paganism. The absolutism that reigned supreme in ancient pagan times became again the model for the exercise of state authority. As men began to view with disdain the great medieval works of art and to seek out the classical forms of the ancient pagans, as modern philosophy began to view with contempt the spiritual treasures of the medieval era only to exhume the pantheism and materialism of pagans, and as old Germanic legal traditions were put aside in favor of the Roman law taught in Italian schools of law, which we then proceeded to strait-jacket our German nation with, so it came to pass that we borrowed again the conception of the power of civil authority that was at large in the corrupt ancient Roman empire. And we did all of this at precisely the same time that mocking out the Middle Ages became a common sport. That is the route whereby the absolutism of temporal rulers moved in on us and entrenched itself, almost without opposition, on the thrones of Europe.

It is a direction which was nurtured particularly in the Protestant nations where men put aside the ancient Christian distinction between the men who held spiritual authority and those who held temporal authority. There, all authority was combined in the hands of temporal rulers. We can see how rapidly this pagan absolutism progressed when we recognize how suddenly the principle, "cujus regio, ejus religio," gained widespread acceptance. This meant that subjects had to take on the same religion as their prince. Christianity had toppled pagan absolutism through the force of conscience. The martyrs had appeared before the Roman emperors and told them: "We cannot do what you command because our consciences, which are attuned to God's will, do not permit it." With that that kind of action, began the restoration of human dignity. The neo-pagan absolutism attacked this conscience, which had once been its downfall and declared, in effect, that subjects are not entitled to a conscience. They must believe what their prince believes. It happened, therefore, that the subjects in certain Protestant principalities were forced to change their religion several times in short order. For example, in the Palatinate, they were forced to change three or four times and in the city of Oppenheim, ten times prior to the Peace of Westphalia.[10] Thus people had to choose from among even the most vital Christian teachings, now one, now the other position. That may, in fact, be the greatest horror story in the history of the world. Even the ancient Roman emperors, who insisted that the wish of the emperor was the law of the empire, did not attempt to dominate the consciences of their subjects in so crass a manner. Yet, Protestanism adopted this principle with scarcely a murmur.

A temporal authority which was prepared to go to such lengths would, of course, not hesitate to violate other liberties; and so it happened that one freedom after another fell by the wayside.[11] German princes exercised their sovereign power, which according to the ancient Roman pattern had to be unlimited, at the expense of the Church, at the expense of the nation, and at the expense of the freedoms of their subjects. They were supported by their subjects. They were supported also, however, by the actions of the Catholic

House of Bourbon which reached its zenith under
Louis XIV. As a Catholic, Louis XIV could not accept the "cujus regio, ejus religio" principle of
the Protestant princes. Instead, he said, "L'Etat
c'est moi." (I am the state.) And he applied the
principle with such thoroughness that even in France
no trace of the ancient Frankish-Germanic liberty
remained. The absolutism of Louis XIV became the
pattern for all who exercised state authority from
that time on. The absolutism of state authority
became incarnate throughout Europe - with England
excepted, albeit only partially - and it thoroughly
poisoned the entire political system. Even those
parties who have flown the banner of Revolution
in Europe these past 80 years differ only nominally,
but not in essence. Tocqueville made that abundantly clear when he pointed out that what is
called the ancien regime, namely the aggregate of
principles which European princes without exception adopted in recent centuries do not differ essentially from the principles of the Revolution. [12]
Essentially, they are alike. The Roman emperor
says, "Whatever pleases me is the law which governs
the world." The Protestant prince says, "Cujus regio,
ejus religio" - "Everyone must believe what I believe;
every conscience must be guided by my own conscience."
A so-called legitimate ruler says, L'Etat c'est moi," -
"My will is the will of the state." Robespierre
says, "Liberty is the despotism of reason, and reason is what I and the Committee of Public Safety
decree; and you had all better obey its decrees unless you wish to go to the guillotine." Finally,
the great prophet of modern liberalism, Casimir
Perrier, says: "Liberty is the despotism of law, the
law which I and the majority in parliament will prescribe for you." What's the difference? They are
all merely different expressions of the same basic
absolutism on the part of some form of temporal
authority.

That brings us to the most modern form of absolutism, absolutism parading as liberty! Since this form
of absolutism is the least understood and at the same
time the kind that most threatens to destroy all true

163

freedom in our own time, we had better take a careful look at it. First, however, I want to insert certain other fragments which will help us to understand this important problem and shed more light on it.

XV The Letter of Fenelon on Absolutism

Fenelon must be ranked among the most lovable and gentle spirits that Christianity has ever produced. Even non-Catholics recognize his superior qualities. As a contemporary of Louis XIV, he saw first hand how absolutism was taking over. It is of the greatest interest, therefore, to note this man's reaction. We are fortunate enough to have a letter written by him in which he clearly expressed his views on the absolutist state. The authenticity of the letter has been questioned. However, according to the latest research into the matter, there is no doubt that he wrote it.[13]The letter was directed to Louis XIV himself, but it is not certain whether the latter ever received it. We consider it to be the more worthwhile to draw attention to it, because until the present day, even such outstanding men in France as Bossuet have allowed themselves to be taken in by the external glitter of Louis' regime. Thus, many have failed to note the untold harm which this totally rotten system has done to the Church and to all of Christendom, from both a religious and a political standpoint. We are reproducing here, Fenelon's remarkable letter.

"Sire!

"The person who takes the liberty to address this letter to you is not motivated to write to you because of any worldly interests. Neither latent animosity, wounded pride, nor any ignoble ambition to meddle in political affairs could have driven me to do so. This person loves the King, though he is unknown to the King; and he honors the monarch as representing God who, indeed, conferred authority upon him.

"For all of your power and worldly possessions, there is nothing you have that I want. What is more, I would endure any suffering that would be necessary to make you aware of these truths, because unless a king is aware of them, he cannot be either great or good. Do not be surprised at the words expressed by a courageous free man. This is the proper mode of speech for

165

expressing the truth, and your wonder is simply evidence that your ear is not accustomed to hearing plain, unadulterated truth.

"People who like flattery are inclined, when they are told the naked truth, to perceive ulterior motives, exaggerations, and the work of cranks. To tell a king anything but the whole truth is, in itself, a kind of high treason.

"As God is my witness, the person who is addressing you does so with a heart filled with zeal, respect, and every loving good intention for your welfare.

"You were born, Sire, with good straightforward common sense. But those who raised you, trained you in an art of government which is mistrustful, jealous, remote from virtue, distant from what is truly meritorious, at home with devious and obsequious persons, filled with arrogant bearing, and inclined toward what is likely to make you great and glorious.

"For some thirty years, your most distinguished ministers undermined and then destroyed all of the foundations of the state in order to concentrate all power in the hands of the King, which power actually becomes the plaything of the King's ministers.

"The language of court has undergone change. One speaks no more of the state and of the law of the state. Instead, there is always talk about the King and the will of the King.

"Your revenues and expenditures have multiplied phenomenally. You have been exalted like some divinity at the same time that the accomplishments of your predecessors are minimized. The result is that all of France has become impoverished.

"To introduce a reckless and unwholesome luxury into your court, your trusted advisors thought that they could build up the crown on the wreckage of all the classes in the kingdom, as though you could become great at their expense, by reducing your subjects to nothingness. As a matter of fact, the greatness of a king rises and falls with the greatness of his subjects.

166

"True, you have watched jealously over your royal prerogative, perhaps too jealously, especially in those areas that are most obvious. Yet, each minister was, in fact, the unchallenged lord of that branch of government of which he was in charge.

You feel that you are in complete command because you have carefully delineated the area of competence of those to whom power was delegated. And these ministers to whom power is delegated have made their power obvious, in fact, painfully obvious. They have been proud, hard, unjust, and crude. Cunning has dispelled honesty. They have, whether in internal or external affairs recognized no law but the use of threats, heavy-handed tactics, and destruction, against all opposition. They never confided in you when they undertook actions which you might have taken exception to, and which might have alienated them from their King. These regents have gotten the King's ear accustomed to hearing nothing but exaggerated praise which sometimes approached deification, something which you should have put a stop to in your own best interests.

"The King's name has come to be regarded with contempt, and the whole French nation has become an affront to neighbor nations. No citizen could survive this, because only slaves were acceptable. Bloody wars were launched, like the unfortunate war with Holland which your ministers persuaded you to undertake in 1672. This war was started to affirm your royal reputation and to punish the Dutch for a few unfortunate remarks which we practically brought on ourselves because the trade laws promulgated by Richelieu were arbitrarily violated.

"I refer to this war in particular, because it was the one which gave rise to all of the others, and because there was no real reason for it, aside from reputation and revenge which are never legitimate causes for a war. The result was that all of the territorial aggrandizement which resulted from that war must be regarded as unjust seizure.

"I am aware that the consequent peace pacts seem to have righted the injustice because they conceded the captured cities to you. But a war which was started for an unjust cause does not become just

167

merely because the outcome is fortunate. The peace treaties signed by the defeated party are not signed freely. One signs with a knife at one's throat - against one's will - merely to avoid greater harm. One signs as one hands over one's purse to the thief who says, 'Hand it over or die.'

"Therefore, if you wish to look at your conquests as God sees them, you will have to go back to where they all began, to the war with Holland.

"It is nonsense to claim that conquests are necessary for your state. What belongs to another can never be necessary for me. Only one thing is necessary for me, that is - to do what is right.

"It is not even legitimate to justify such conquests on the grounds that they are necessary to safeguard one's boundaries. Boundaries are to be safeguarded by discreet negotiations, moderation of one's demands, and wise fortification of present territory. The need to secure your boundaries does not, by itself give you the right to take over your neighbor's land.

"Ask some upright, knowledgeable men about these matters, and they will testify that what I say here is valid. I would hope that what I have said is enough to bring you to realize that your whole life style has transgressed the bounds of justice and truth, not to mention the spirit of the Gospels. The many terrible shocks that have plagued all of Europe for more than 20 years, the torrents of bloodshed, so much horror perpetrated, so many provinces laid waste, so many cities and towns reduced to ashes are all just the consequences of the unholy war of 1672, which you launched simply because of vain-glory and to punish a few newspaper writers and sensation seeking sloganeers.

"Take a close look, without self-deceit and together with a few upright men, to see whether you have a right to keep all of your possessions - possessions acquired by the peace treaties which you wrung from your enemies by a war which was totally unjustified.

"It is precisely that same war which was the source of all of the evils from which France is still now suffering. Ever since that war, you have tried

168

to impose peace terms not in a spirit of moderation
and equity, but like a demanding dictator of the world.
This arbitrariness in forcing peace terms is the reason
why peace does not last. Your enemies, humiliated
and disgraced, are simply biding their time and looking toward the day when they can rise up again and unite
themselves. That is to be expected, since you yourself
have violated the terms of the peace treaty which you
so arrogantly imposed upon the defeated. You violated
the peace by starting the war again to make enormous
new conquests. You set up the notorious Council for
Reunion where you sat as judge and jury. That means
adding the injustice of insult and mockery to usur-
pation by force. In the Westphalian Peace you played
both ends against the middle to seize Strassburg.
Not a single one of your ministers over all of these
years has dared to refer to these articles to see
whether he could somehow conjure up a justification
for your taking Strassburg.

　　"That arbitrariness has served to unite all of
Europe against you. Even those who have never dared
to openly oppose France look forward eagerly to the
day when you will be weakened and Your Majesty will
be humiliated. They now see in your humiliation the
only salvation for freedom and for the peace of all
Christian nations.

　　"Oh Sire! You had it within your grasp to become a father to your subjects, and a mediator among
our neighbor nations. Instead you are now the hated
enemy of our neighbor nations and run the risk of
being feared as the terrible tyrant among your own
people.

　　"The most unhoped for effect of the bad advise
you have received is the solidarity of the alliance
which the allied powers have formed against you. They
would rather continue to wage war against you than to
make peace with you. Experience has taught them that
such a peace is no peace at all, since they feel that
you would no more live up to any treaty than you have
lived up to previous treaties. In fact, they fear
that you would use any new peace treaty to launch
new agressions as soon as the alliance had disbanded,
so that you could conquer each one of them separately
without difficulty.

"The more successful you are in employing force
of arms, the more your neighbors will fear you, and
the more they will feel compelled to unite to fight
off the enslavement with which they fear they are
threatened by you. And even if they cannot win outright, they nevertheless hope to carry on the campaign
long enough to debilitate Your Majesty. In other words,
your enemies will not feel secure until they have reduced France to a position where it can no longer
threaten its neighbors.

"Sire! Place yourself for a moment in the position of the allied powers. Consider what the outcome
will be if we continue to put our immediate gain ahead
of any consideration for justice and public trust.
In the process, your subjects, whom you ought to love
like your own children, and who until now have been
loyally devoted to their king, will die of starvation.

"Scarcely any hands are left to cultivate our
fields, and cities as well as the country areas are
depopulating more and more. Arts and crafts are no
longer thriving as they are no longer able to provide
proper support for those who engage in them. The
spirit of enterprise has been destroyed. Eventually
you have sacrificed the soundness of our domestic
economy to make and secure ever larger conquests
abroad. Instead of exacting more revenue from the
poor nation, you ought to offer it alms and support.
All of France is nothing more now than a huge hospital - and one without means of support. Government personnel have been demoralized, the nobility
has been bled of its wealth through wartime expenditures, until they now live solely off the income
from government bonds. The ordinary people are on
the verge of mutiny. They demand bread and complain!

"You and you alone, Sire, have brought this
situation about. Now that this vast kingdom has
been reduced to penury, everything rests in your
hands. No one can survive except by your leave.

"Such is the condition of a kingdom which experienced such a promising future. At fault is a
King who was falsely presented as a great blessing
for his people - and he could have been if his fawning

170

counsellors had not led him astray. Thus, a nation -
I have to be frank - which was full of love for you
and confident, has begun to turn against you; and it
has lost what confidence and respect it once had. Your
triumphs and conquests no longer thrill your people.
They cannot celebrate with you since they are embit-
tered and at the point of despair. Instead, unrest
grows throughout your realm, and there is the frightful feeling that the King no longer really cares
what happens to us. He is only worried about his
reputation and his glory. If the King, so it is
said - and no longer secretly - had the interest of
his people at heart, he would then see to it that
they have enough to eat and relieve them of the many
oppressive burdens which grind them down, so that
they may breathe freely again. That would do more
for his reputation than the seizure of a few more
disputed border territories, which only leads to
more wars.

"Sire! What is your response to my judgement?
The movements that stir up the people, a phenomenon
which was long unknown in France, are portentuous,
and they are spreading more and more! Paris itself,
so close to your person, is not immune. Officials
are forced to look the other way when these agitators
commit their outrages; in fact they bribe them so
that they will be still. As a result, malefactors
who ought to be arrested end up being rewarded by
payoffs. Your ministers are reduced to the preposterous and pathetic position where they have to
either permit the unrest to go unpunished and thereby
even to encourage it, or to inflict an inhuman car-
nage on your people - people, whom you yourself have
brought to the point of despair by robbing them of
the bread which they earned by the sweat of their brows,
to support your extravagant wars.

"Not only is the nation short of bread, the King
is short of money! And still you will not recognize
the fate to which you are being driven inevitably.
Since you were fortunate until now, you cannot bear
the thought of misfortune. You are afraid to look up,
and you are even more fearful that someone else will
make known your plight. You shy away from the prospect that your glory might lose some of its lustre.

Alas, it is this idle vanity which engulfs your heart.
That has become more important to you than the need
for justice, than your own inner peace, than the safeguarding of your subjects. Meanwhile these subjects
nurture the vices which stem from their need, to the
neglect of their eternal salvation - something they
cannot reconcile with your sinful vanity.

"Sire! That is your present plight. It is a
plight which you will not recognize, because you are
like a man with blinders. You preoccupy yourself with
little daily trivialities which are of no importance,
while you never dare to survey the total situation to
allow yourself perspective. And it is the overall
situation which is deteriorating imperceptibly, but
before long it will be beyond repair.

"While you seize new land and conquer enemy can-
nons in the heat of battle, while you storm fortifi-
cations, you are scarcely aware that the very ground
on which you are waging war is sinking beneath your
feet. Before long, it will all be for naught! The
whole world sees this and no one dares to make you
aware of it. The time is coming when you will have
to realize what is happening, but perhaps then it will
be too late!

"True valor lies in refusing to deceive oneself
and in recognizing and coming to grips with unpleasant
realities as they arise. But you, Oh Sire, lend your
ear only to those who flatter you with false hopes.
Those men whom you ought to listen to and take seriously
are precisely the ones you go out of your way to avoid.

"You ought to seek the truth above all else,
because you are our King! You ought to demand that
your counsellors lay the unvarnished truth before you
at all times, and encourage those who lack the backbone
to do so.

"Instead, you do just the opposite. You do all in
your power to avoid unpleasantness. But God will one
day remove the camouflage by which you try to conceal
what you will not see, and the whole naked truth will
lay before you.

172

"The arm of justice has been suspended over your royal head for many years, and it is only because the Judge is also a loving Father that you have been spared. He pities a prince who has been surrounded by flatterers most of his life, and He knows well that many of your enemies are just as much His enemies! The All-High knows how to bring to justice those who do injustice and to bring them low so that they will find their way back to Him. For you will never be worthy of the name, Christian, unless you humble yourself before the Almighty."

We shall pass over a part of Fenelon's letter dealing with the deleterious influence which Louis XIV's despotic regime and his patronizing court spirituality had upon the condition of the Church. That will come up in another context. Let us turn to the conclusion of his letter.

"France is in her final agony. Will your confidants wait and remain silent until all is lost? Are these people afraid to·fall out of your good graces? Do they have no love for you? One must have the backbone to risk the displeasure of those whom one loves by telling them the truth, rather than to lull them to sleep with a false sense of security.

"What good are such counsellors, in the last analysis, if they do not make you realize that the lands which are not yours must be given back to their rightful owners, that you are making your own glory more important than the well-being of your people, that you must make amends for the evils which the Church has suffered on your account, that you must make every effort to become a true Christian before death overtakes you?

"I know that those who speak such words of Christian freedom risk falling from the King's good graces, but what is more important, the King's good graces or the true well-being of the King?

"I know that one must comfort, sympathize with, do what is possible to lighten your burden; that one must speak reverently, with reserve, and respect for the king. But I also know that, whatever else, one

173

must eventually speak the truth. Woe to those who
dare not tell you the truth. Woe to you if you do
not have the dignity to hear the truth! It is a
pity that such flatterers continue to enjoy your
confidence when nothing good has yet come of their
presence. It's high time for them to withdraw if the
King cannot master his fear of the unpleasant truth,
so that he surrounds himself with sycophants.

"Perhaps you would ask Oh, Sire, what exactly
should your counsellors have told you. Let it be
recorded here what they should have told you:

"They should have told you: 'King, you must
humble yourself and submit to the almighty hand of
God, unless you want to force His hand to humble you
by His might. You must first merit peace of soul and
swear off all of the false glory which you have come
to idolize. You must reject the false counsel of the
sycophants around you. To save France, you must restore all of the ill-gotten territories to our enemies,
territories which, incidentally, you could not hold
on to without perpetrating still further injustice.
Oh King, is it not your great good fortune that God
will put an end to the success you have enjoyed and
which has blinded you? Is it not good that He will
eventually force you to make the reparations which
are vital for your salvation, and which in your hour
of triumph and glory you never got around to making?'

"Sire! The person who tells you these truths
has only the best interests of the king at heart.
He would gladly give his life to see you as God
would have you be, and he will never, never stop
praying for you!"

174

XVI The Results of Absolutism and Centralization
     by the State

The results of absolutism are pretty well indicated in the foregoing letter of Fenelon. The great
St. Thomas Aquinas recognized them four hundred years
before when he spoke of pagan absolutism. He indicated
especially that it gives rise to, "a servile petty
spirit, which makes men incapable of performing great,
worthwhile works."[14] Since the full implications and
ramifications of absolutism still do not seem to be
fully appreciated, we ought to, perhaps, sum them up
once again.

First of all, absolutist centralization deprives
the vast majority of citizens of any real grasp of the
public affairs that affect their every day lives. Self-
government is an excellent school for all classes of
people to become aware of what their duties and responsibilities as citizens are. Whatever disadvantages
may appear to attach to such self-government, even
these are often valuable means to gain important experience, and they are often self-corrective. Where
this school of experience is lacking, all manner of
twisted and irresponsible viewpoints gain a foothold
and eventually reign supreme in the governance of
society. That is precisely one of the great ailments
that afflicts present-day society. The loudest spokesmen in the press are party spokesmen who see every
issue in a partisan light and who are out of touch
with reality. That is true also of our political
conventions. Only the smallest number of those who
participate in such rallies live face to face with
the conditions which are discussed at such gatherings.
As a result we get all of the superficial palaver with
which the world is filled to satiety.

Secondly, absolute centralization of functions suppresses the civil virtues in public life which were prevalent in earlier times, in particular the willingness
to sacrifice. When there is self-government, it goes
without saying that a large number of the tasks in all
areas of public life are performed by volunteers so
that the best people from all classes have an opportunity to offer services for the public good. Every

175

field of endeavor which depends on voluntary sacrifice immediately lends a higher dignity to those who serve. Centralized power, on the other hand, consigns all activities to the care of salaried officials. However worthy salaried officialdom may be in itself, it is inevitable that many get into salaried positions who work merely for the paycheck and not for the good of their country.

Thirdly, the centralization of government powers robs those classes which depend upon material gain of every opportunity to get involved in any more ennobling activities, and it serves to make them venal and concerned exclusively with pleasure and money. Aside from religious values, participation in public affairs is certainly one of the best means of elevating men above base, material concerns toward loftier interests.

Fourth, centralization tears apart the fabric of those many social organizations which men are accustomed to forming to fulfill their various objectives. It isolates man and atomizes society, thereby bringing about great social distress.

A Frenchman asked how it happened that, after our fathers exerted themselves so mightily to bring about equality among us in the hope that equality would beget true brotherhood, it developed instead that with the reign of this universal quality an ever-widening hatred arose between the various classes of society. Odilon Barrot, himself a veteran liberal, responded promptly, "The evil stems from the fact that our society is totally individualized, and the state remains as the only solid and vital organization; it is this exaggerated centralization which lies at the root of the problem. We have to restore the word, freedom, to the innovations of 1789. It has been lost sight of, and without it the other two words, equality and fraternity, are empty phrases." He commented further about Paris: "Paris is a giant ant hill which labors, consumes, enjoys itself, but lacks completely any social bond. People live in the same neighborhood, even in the same house, but they are strangers to each other. There is nothing that unites these people. Social institutions are lacking. The phenomenon has been compared to a pile of dust which is blown into the air by a gust of wind, without leadership, without cohesion. It smothers all that comes in its path and has no other law but the law of chance. [15]

For this reason centralization of power is also the chief origin of revolution. Since the French have more than their share of experience, let us listen to what the same authority had to say on the matter:

"Those who assert that we Frenchmen were swept into Revolution because we are a frivolous people serve notice that they are themselves rather shallow and lacking in historical insight. To refute this claim, it is enough to go back to 1789. Prior to that year we lived for 800 years without revolution. Could it be possible that prior to 1789 we were more serious and serene and less frivolous than now? I think the opposite is true. Our national character has been altered by the difficult and tragic events which have transpired so that we are less light-hearted and happy now than we used to be. That is a result of the breach of our political and social constitution through the exaggerated expansion of government authority, through the total disorganization and destruction of our social fabric, through the imbalance in the activity of government and the requisite development of individual capacities; in other words, through the centralization of state powers."

He then discussed in detail three reasons why centralization necessarily leads to revolution. The first is because the government takes on staggering responsibilities which it cannot possibly do justice to, while everyone else is stripped of all responsibility. The result is that a spirit of animosity and pessimism develops among the people. The second reason is the distortion which occurs between the metropolitan areas and the province; and the third is the difficulty which stands in the way of any worthwhile reform. [16]

Let us see what he has to say about the first point:

177

"It is a first rule of politics that along with power, there must be corresponding responsibility. At the same moment that power grows, there must be a growth of either legal or moral responsibility. Thus, as state authority grows without bounds, its responsibility also grows without limits. On the other hand, it has to follow inevitably that as individuals are deprived of all participation in public affairs, they not only feel themselves stripped of all responsibility, but they even lose any awareness of it. They must then reach the point where they will attribute any harm that befalls them and each frustration of their wishes, to the state. It is from such exaggerated responsibility and from the corresponding release from personal responsibility of all members of society that all of our revolutions originate."

Centralization of all functions becomes especially damaging in a state which has a constitutional structure. Again, let us see what Barrat says:

"State authority, armed with all of the might of centralized power, exerts its influence upon the chambers of deputies to gain a majority, whatever the cost. Centralized power, therefore becomes the goal of the state, and it enables the state to corrupt the free institutions while at the same time corrupting itself. State power then is no longer a means to distribute discreetly and justly the various functions of the state, but rather it is used exclusively to win over the majority in parliament. All other interests become secondary. Since the state possesses all of the weapons in this battle and is opposed only by impotent and isolated individuals who lack all cohesion and are constantly subject to the centralized powers, the result cannot long remain in doubt."

Little comment is required about this appraisal of the effect of centralized state authority on constitutional government. We see the sorry development before our eyes in the present-day political scene. An omnipotent state authority in league with a political party sets up boards by all manner of methods, some of them devious. Boards, thus constituted, serve to enlarge once again the omnipotence of state authority. That is then called popular government.

All such unhappy products of centralized power
manifest themselves in all European nations to the
extent that centralized power encroaches. They
would be even more destructive, however, wherever
phoney liberalism succeeded in robbing the Church
of its independence and making it subservient to the
state. That is the unmistakeable trend today, as we
have already indicated. May the Catholic press,
therefore, never tire of hurling the stone at the
forehead of this Goliath.

179

XVII The Two Opposing Viewpoints in Politics; the
      Two Rival Political Camps Which Contend at
      the Present Time

We are now able to determine with certainty what
the basic positions are which mold the political parties of our time into two rival camps. In distinguishing political parties, it is their fundamental principles that are important, naturally, and not their external appearances. Unfortunately this is often lost
sight of so that large numbers of careless people base
their political preferences on labels and externalities
without a clear idea of what the real issues are. These
they often enough do not even grasp. Nevertheless, it
is the solemn duty of every man who is involved in
public affairs, and above all of everyone who publishes
a Catholic paper, to be fully aware of the political
principles that are in contention at the present time.
The much used terms, "conservative" and "liberal" have,
in our opinion, become so ambivalent that only those
who revel in ambiguity are content to use them to describe their political viewpoint as a cover-up for their
ideological poverty. They are not acceptable to those
who conscientiously try to operate according to solid
principles in all of their dealings.

The ultimate reality in all things is always God,
and therefore all principles eventually stem from our
relationship to God. For that reason political parties
too, ultimately, differ on the basis of their conception of the world order and its relation to God. We
could settle for the most general kind of distinction
which separates the two parties, with the one holding
that there is a supernatural order of things and the
other denying it. At this point, however, we are not
concerned only with the basic religious differences -
we have already discussed this earlier - but we wish
to examine the underlying political principles which
distinguish political parties in our time.

These clearly stem from the differences that we
have been talking about. On the one side we have the
devotees of the centralization of power in the state,
and on the other, we find those who favor self-government.
The former want all things accomplished by government

181

authority, the latter want maximum autonomy for individuals, communities, families, and corporate
bodies, to provide for their own needs. The former
defend absolutism, the latter support true and genuine
liberty.

That ultimately sums up the opposing political
principles in our time. Both can appear in the same
exterior structure. The principle of omnipotent absolutism as well as that of self-governing societies
and individuals can come dressed up as monarchy or in
constitutional and democratic form. He, therefore,
who is taken in by mere party labels, has lost sight
of the essentials and is likely to be duped by mere
externalities. Those who operate on the principle
of absolute centralized authority, whether in monarchical form or in the form of a bureaucracy or a
constitutional democracy, are all brothers under
the skin and have to be lumped together. The same
spirit motivates all of them, whatever external form
they choose to clothe themselves in, and one is as
bad as the other. Likewise, all of those societies
which operate on the basis of maximum self-determination belong together whether they happen to be called monarchies or republics. Those are the ultimate political principles which divide political
parties.

XVIII   Modern Liberalism, Absolutism in the Guise of Liberty

Contemporary liberalism belongs basically in the camp of those who favor the omnipotent state. It is the intellectual offspring and inheritance of absolute monarchy and bureaucracy of recent centuries. It differs from the latter only in its externals, in its slogans, which suggest something quite different, and in the instruments of power. In reality, and this reality manages to reveal itself from time to time, modern liberalism represents intolerant, relentless centralization and the omnipotent state as opposed to individual and corporate autonomy. One may change the hand which holds the reins, but the reins themselves are held ever tighter. Formerly, princes used to wield absolute power in a manner which laid waste all German freedom. And they declared that they held such power "By the Grace of God." Now the other faction which declares that it holds power by the "Grace of the People" exercises the same absolute power and proposes among other things to complete the demolition of the Church. The lash that was wielded by the absolute monarch is now in the hands of the absolute representative, so-called, of the people; and he is, if anything, even more determined.

That is the current of our time, and it finds expression in the countless voices which keep telling the German people monstrous falsehoods calculated to deceive them. Every trace of individual autonomy and self-determination, every home, every Church, every higher human quality is in jeopardy. It is urgent therefore that we lay the ax to the root of this phoney liberalism and rip away the disguise of liberty, and the will of the people, etc., by which it leads the gullible astray. We have to expose it as the grasping, self-seeking thing that it is. Let us investigate the mendacious character of the principles which underly modern liberalism.

Its first characteristic is the way in which false modern liberalism speaks of liberty and gives the impression that it alone is the guardian of freedom, and that it alone has the mission of promoting liberty on earth. This ruse deceives many people. Those who fall for the deception are labelled as champions of liberty and as great humanitarians. Those who oppose it are characterized as reactionary, self-seeking, lacking in character, as obsequious serfs, as enemies of the people. All pure poppycock! Modern liberalism does not even know what the meaning of liberty is. In fact it is, in principle, the opposite of liberty and leads inevitably to the debasement of people and their eventual enslavement.

This slight of the hand is accomplished by perversion of the words "freedom" and "equality." Phoney liberalism knows only equality and calls it freedom - a grave deception! There is a vital fundamental difference between freedom and equality. Equality exists among slaves and among prisoners, in other words, among those who are without rights. The nation is not free simply because all are equally unfree. Therein lies the great deception in that liberal article of faith: "Freedom is the despotism of law." Suppose that the law is despotic; then the despotism of such despotic laws adds up to a wretched condition of serfdom. That is actually the ideal of modern liberalism, to regulate everything by law, to meddle in everything by legislation, to provide for all by legislation, to restrict every person by a stifling straight-jacket of regulations, and then to order everyone under threat of punishment to accept this situation as blessed freedom. The spokesmen of modern liberalism who prattle interminably about freedom do not fail to stress certain rights, especially the ones which serve their particular purposes, e.g., the freedom of the press, and the freedom of assembly. They cannot help but revert to true form, however, by trampling underfoot the most basic freedom of all: the freedom of conscience. In recent times liberalism has gone so far as to invade the very jurisdiction of the Church by legislation.

That is the phenomenon which came to Germany from France. Mainz was the city where in 1792-93 liberalism first made its unwholesome presence felt. Anyone who wishes to gain an understanding of the

hypocrisy of modern liberalism which, in the guise
of liberty, imposed the worst kind of despotism by
whatever means possible, and which trampled all
personal freedom underfoot, let him read the docu-
mented presentation of the history of Mainz during
those years. [17] That story safeguards the good name
Mainz, since we are often led to believe that the
population of old Mainz yielded abjectly to the
wishes of the Jacobins. The facts show instead how
the vast majority of Mainz citizens bravely and loyally stuck by their Christian and Germanic traditions
and heroically withstood the horrible terrorism which
the Jacobins and the French exercised against them in
εthe name of liberty. Since then, things have changed,
and the citizens of Mainz have forgotten the four
gallows by which liberty was brought to their forefathers.

The second characteristic of modern liberalism
is that it speaks without surcease of "the people."
The state is supposed to represent, in the liberal
view, the majority of the people; laws are supposed
to represent the will of the people, and state authority is supposed to give expression to the popular
will. One gets the impression that liberalism alone
on this planet expresses any real love of the people
and cares about them and defends their interests!
But that is a sham and a deception. In reality,
liberalism exploits the basest passions of the people
as a means to subjugate them. Under the pretext of
popular sovereignty, liberalism reduces the people
to the status of masses without any direction of their
own, and such masses can then be led like sheep and
exploited for one's own purposes. The means by which
this fraudulent system is imposed are popular elections. The people are permitted to vote occasionally,
and they are then given the impression that whatever
happens, occurs because they willed it. Let us take
a closer look at this system.

If modern liberalism were at all honest and consistent, it would have to recognize the principle of
self-determination and individual autonomy despite
its erroneous principles. Then one could at least
coexist with it on a reasonably peaceful basis. In
other words, if all power in the state comes from the

185

people, wouldn't it have to follow that all of the individual persons who comprise the state are the actual personal possessors and bearers of authority in such a state? The state both in its legislative and executive organs, would have to derive all of its authority from the people. But then, reason and honesty dictate that the people would have the right to delegate a limited authority, so that the people could, by the same token, reserve for themselves the right to do what they are able to do in their homes, and in their communities, so as to provide for themselves and fulfill themselves as human beings. Such a condition is in no way compatible with the principle of centralization of authority, and the state would only be permitted the limited, narrow, sphere of activity which is natural to it. Modern liberalism does not see it that way. That would put an end to the busybody government and the incessant grinding out of laws and regulations. Supposedly the people are the source of all rights, but only in the sense that they are able to exercise as few of these rights as possible. The principle right which the people retain is the right to vote. That means going to a voting booth every couple of years for a few minutes to scratch a name on a ballot, in other words, to elect one's own task-master. Thereafter the task-master acts in the name of the people, and whatever he decrees in the exercise of his authority has to be regarded as the will of the people, as popular sovereignty, and as popular liberty. What a mockery of all truth and reality!

That is why it never occurs to spokesmen of liberalism to represent the actual people. They represent their party and disregard completely whatever is not in the interest of their party. We are able to observe this each day in governments where phoney liberalism predominates. For that reason, it is a vital task of the Catholic press to remind the liberal constantly of his original principles and to force him to uphold not only what pleases newspaper writers or what serves his own party interests or those of his colleagues, but rather the interests of the people themselves - out in the towns and in the countryside, at the grass roots. Their viewpoints, their wishes, their needs have to be carefully and conscientiously taken into account.

The third characteristic of modern false liberalism is its godlessness, its contempt in particular for positive Christianity, namely for the Catholic Church and those who are loyal to it. The liberal is fascinated by anything and everything which smacks of the irreligious currents of our time, and at the same time he is contemptuous of anything that is genuinely and truly Christian. In the assemblies where modern liberalism prevails, one does not dare to ever express a positive Christian sentiment. I know of a country where a good, true, solid, Christian people inhabit every valley and every village, where if one were to take an honest poll, these people would turn out ninety true Christians for every ten unbelievers. Yet, whenever anyone takes a Christian position in the legislative assemblies of that land, he is greeted by universal scorn. That is what modern liberalism regards as popular representation.

Catholic men ought to combat tirelessly and without hesitation this absolutism which parades as liberty, this phoney liberalism. It is a breed of absolutism that is more dangerous and more relentless than any previous absolutism. In France, thank God, opposition to it is arising among both Catholics and Protestants in various parties. In Germany, it is mainly the "historico-political papers" which have been opposing it for a long time. And in North Germany, it has formidable and spirited opponents. In central Germany, on the other hand, there is thus far little opposition; and in Prussia it threatens to take over. Pray God that it will fail, and that instead, the German Christian spirit will vanquish this spurious, alien liberalism and establish anew the true German freedom.

187

XIX The Government of Laws

False liberalism has so contorted the meaning of words that even this perfectly good term is no longer free from the taint of excessive centralization of state authority. We have to be careful to distinguish now between an absolutist government of laws and one based on freedom and self-government. The former recognizes only one part of the government of laws - a concept which is genuinely sound only in its entirety.

A government of laws, first of all, requires that there is protection for every right, a court to decide about any violation of rights, whether the violation is perpetrated by state authority or by a private person. Its opposite is the police state. The absolutism of previous centuries violated such a government of laws very severely. The Bourbons established royal courts to nullify the actions brought in the popular courts of law. [18] Frederick the Great ignored the emissaries of the national court. In this respect contemporary liberal absolutism is more tolerant than the absolute monarchies were. The Catholic press ought to push this demand with all of its power and support the establishment of popular courts. Only in this way can rights in Germany be guaranteed the way they ought to be. And only this will force those who administer our laws, who have grown accustomed while the old bureaucratism held sway, to decide everything on the basis of what was expedient for them, to judge each issue according to what the law requires. To have a government of laws, it is necessary also to have an independent, fair-minded judge. Only then will judicial decrees have any value. Such decrees should, in a manner of speaking, be accepted by people as virtually infallible. A judgeship is an exalted, dignified, noble position. It represents a kind of high priesthood where law is concerned. So much the worse where lackey, partisan, unscrupulous judges occupy the bench. Just conduct is impossible without morality, and morality is impossible without fear of the Lord. Independence and non-partisanship is impossible if one person is himself a party unto himself.

189

A government of laws requires also a correct
yardstick against which violations of rights can be
measured, in other words, a just body of laws. Courts,
after all, are only here to decide how a law applies
in a given case. It is futile to talk about a government of laws if the laws themselves no longer express
what is right. Here modern liberalism falls woefully
short, because liberalism grinds its laws out of its
own "law-making factories" and decrees that whatever
it does is just! It knows no false measure or yardstick, no unjust law, because whatever liberalism says
is right. It is inconceivable to me how one can make
so much fuss about the grandeur of legislation and
the primacy of laws if these are nothing more than
the outcome of the efforts of a few human beings who
sat down somewhere and made decisions. It is even
more inconceivable why a nation of people has to pay
any attention to such laws. A government of laws
made by unbelievers is a mere bugaboo. We have an
entirely different story when men believe in an eternal, unchangeable norm for all law as representing
God's will, and when laws made by men give expression
to that Divine law to the extent that men are able to
determine what the will of God is. Then law has God
as its basis, and observance of the law becomes a matter of conscience while contempt for law is tantamount
to contempt for truth and for God's will. Note once
again now how rejection of the supernatural order casts
doubt upon everything else that men do.

How superior and noble the position of the Catholic
Church regarding the origin of laws and their dignity
is, becomes even more clear when we read what St. Thomas
has to say about law.

"I. The community of all men on this earth is
guided and steered by Divine intelligence. Therefore,
the Divine Plan which exists in the mind of God, the
Lord of the universe constitutes a law which, since
God thinks in eternal, not time-bound terms, is there-
fore the eternal law. (<u>Summa</u> <u>Theol</u>. <u>Prima</u> <u>Secunda</u>, q.91,
Art. 1)

"Everything in creation is subject to the eternal
law, be it accidental or necessary. What pertains to

190

the Divine nature and essence, on the other hand, is not subject to Divine law because, it is itself the eternal law." (Ibid. q. 93, Art. 4)

"God imprints in all of nature the principles which govern nature in all of its manifold manifestations. It is in this sense that one says that God commands all of nature. In the words of the Psalmist: 'He has made a law and that law will remain forever!' For this reason every action and phenomenon is subject to the eternal law. (q. 93, Art. 5)

"No one can know the eternal law as it is, in itself, except God and those blessed creatures who are able to perceive God in His essence. Yet, every rational creature recognizes the eternal law and can perceive its reflection more or less, since every recognition of eternal truth is a kind of sharing and radiation of the eternal law. (q. 93, Art. 2)

"II. The light of natural reason whereby we distinguish good and bad - the natural law - is nothing more than the infusion of God's light in us. Therefore, the natural law is obviously nothing but the abiding participation by rational creatures in the eternal law. (q. 91, Art. 2)

"The first commandment of the natural law is: One must do good and avoid evil; all other commands of the natural law stem from this one. (q. 94, Art. 2)

"In its general principles, the natural law has the same validity and meaning for all men. (q. 94, Art. 4)

"In its highest principles, the natural law is always and everywhere unchangeable. (q. 94, Art. 5)

"So far as its universal principles are concerned, the natural law can never be uprooted from the hearts of men. (q. 94, Art. 6)

"III. Law is a command of practical reason. Just as speculative reason derives conclusions in the various sciences from the fundamental unprovable principles in nature, which are not already known to

191

us from nature, but which become known to us by the action of our reason, so has practical reason to proceed from the universal and self-evident principles of the natural law to its more specific applications. These laws, derived from the application of reason to the principles of the natural law, are then called human laws. (q. 91, Art. 3)

"A law is valid inasmuch as it is just. In human affairs, one regards as just what conforms with reason. The ordinary measure of reason however is the natural law. Therefore, human laws are valid only if they are derived from the natural law. If a human law in any way contradicts the natural law, it is no longer a law but a violation of the law. (q. 95, Art. 2)

"All laws, inasmuch as they conform to reason, are derived from the eternal law. Therefore Augustine says: 'In temporal law-giving, nothing is right and legitimate except what men have derived from the natural law.' (q. 93, Art. 3)

"Law must correspond with morality, justice, nature, and it must be enforceable, in conformity with national customs, geared to time and place, necessary, useful, clear, not serving private interests but for the common utility and well-being of all citizens. (Ex. Isadori, lib. 5, Etym. C. 21 Ibid. q. 95, Art. 3)

"Human laws are meant for the whole nation, and the majority of people are not perfected in virtue. Therefore, human laws are not meant to outlaw all vices, only the worst ones which it is possible for most people to avoid. Thus, human law cannot forbid everything that is forbidden by the natural law.

"If laws are changed frequently, they lose their potency, since the preservation of habit is involved here. Habit is a most powerful force for abiding by the law. Therefore laws should never be changed unless the advantage that is to be gained for the common good is as great as the disadvantage involved. That can

192

happen either if a very significant and evident benefit is to be derived from the new statute, or if the greatest need arises, or because the existing law contains an obvious flaw, or if its observance produces results that are mostly disadvantageous (q. 97, Art. 2)

"Habit can establish laws, abrogate and interpret laws (q. 97, Art. 3) He who rules a community has full authority to dispense from human laws which are dependent upon his authority. (q. 97, Art. 4)"

XX The Two Basic Structures of All Political
    Constitutions: The Corporate Order and
    Constitutionalism

As we have seen, the difference between constitutionalism and the corporate order is largely a
formal one rather than a basic one. We have to regard it as superficial for the supporters of one or
the other to base their partisan differences on this
distinction. There is, as a matter of fact, one kind
of constitutionalism which must be rejected out of
hand by every Christian, namely that which holds for
a kind of popular sovereignty that regards the will
of the people rather than the will of God as the sole
source of all authority and of all rights. We are
also aware that constitutionalism has its roots mainly
in this kind of false conception, and of how that is
what has attracted most of its supporters to its
ranks. This conception of constitutionalism is in
no way essential to it; and there is no question but
that a Christian can support proper constitutionalism
whole-heartedly without compromising his Christian
principles.

I believe, therefore, that the Catholic press in
our time has a responsibility to present both positions,
the one favoring constitutionalism and the one favoring
the corporate type of structure and it ought to promote
a peaceable discussion of the two viewpoints. At the
same time, I wish to make it clear that there is an
important difference between the two which ought not
to be overlooked especially in political commentaries.
I myself prefer the corporate order over constitutionalism, and I shall give reasons for my preference.

In general, there are two basic forms according to
which states can be structured. One is mechanical; the
other is organic. We find the pattern for each in nature
where the most important truths are so often mirrored
before our eyes in beautiful imagery.

The first basic form in which we see individual
units bound together in nature is the mechanical one.
Here, the unifying force is merely external. It does
not restructure the units which it embraces into a real

195

inner unity, but rather they are bound together merely on a transitory utilitarian basis. The individual members are bound by an external bond, not by any vital inner principle. Both bureaucracy and constitutionalism have structured themselves according to this pattern. Many individuals who are otherwise united by only the most general bonds, as by the fact that they live in the same area, or by that most unimportant similarity of all, an equality in what they possess, come together to vote; and then they go their separate ways again. There cannot be a real bond of unity even between those who vote and those who are elected. The ones who are elected can only represent one party while those who vote represent every imaginable party in existence. A real basic, living bond of unity between the people and those who are elected to represent them is not possible. The people all too often are out of touch with their representatives especially when the latter do not speak the language of demagogery, or appeal to their baser instincts, or even offer them bribes. Herein is constitutionalism's most vulnerable point, the electioneering process, where principle and actuality stand in blatant contrast to each other. The whole merit of constitutionalism is supposed to be in the idea of popular representation, but true popular representation exists only where elections occur in an atmosphere of calm, level-headed deliberation. In reality, elections are marked by exciting popular passions, by the use of immoral tactics, by the abuse of authority and by self-serving actions.

The second basic form in which we observe unity in nature is the unity in living organisms. In nature, organic unity is on a higher plane than mere mechanical unity. Therefore a political structure which is patterned according to organic unity stands on a higher plane than a machine-like structure. Natural organisms possess an inner unifying force which is alive and which provides a living community among the various parts, a bond of unity. Parts that are thus organically united link up with other higher organisms up to the highest organic form which then binds all of the parts into one overriding individuum. Thus everything in it is alive and operates according to an inner vital principle. Everything about it is marked by a free

196

self-determination and a free self-government whereby
the individual members serve the whole organism. The
activity of the individual member is limited only at
that point where, for its fulfillment, it requires
the intervention of the higher organism.

It appears to me that a political structure that
is based on corporate organization corresponds more
to that pattern and makes possible more genuine self-
government and representation. Corporate bodies seem
to me to be like living bodies and like organisms that
are structured according to the natural order of things.
Their bond is not merely external, transient and accidental, but internal and natural. I believe, therefore, that the old corporate structure embodied a true
representation of common interests, i.e., a representation of the actual, general interests of the people;
whereas the constitutional structure brought about a
mere representation of partisan interests or sometimes
even mere personal interests. Absolutism came along,
however, some 300 years ago. Aided by the egotism of
the corporate bodies themselves - for that is the real
danger inherent in them - it made an end to the corporate mode of organizing society. Today, of course,
the corporate structure would have to take on entirely
different forms than during the Middle Ages. How much
better the crafts, the merchant class, the academi-
cians, the nobility, the religious, the public officials could be represented than they are now, if they
were organized as corporate bodies which represent
their own interest, where every elected representative has to be all things to all people!

197

XXI   Germanism and Romanism

The press is having a field day with these terms at the present time, and it behooves the Catholic press to take on the task of shedding some real light on what this is all about.

Some try to equate the difference between "Germanic" and "Roman" with the difference between "freedom" and "authority." This is obviously arbitrary. Freedom and true authority are in no sense incompatible, so that true freedom is inconceivable without the presence of authority. If a definite proclivity for freedom was an outstanding trait among the German people, that urge for freedom could only have found its full expression because there existed also a solid framework of authority in morals as well as in the German legal tradition.

Others like to make the juxta-position between Germanism and Romanism correspond to one between Protestantism and Catholicism. This fallacy is related to the former one and stands in the most blatant contradiction to historical reality. Traditionally, our German ancestors were devoted with all of their hearts to the Catholic Church, not to Protestantism. It is only in the past few centuries that a portion of the German nation has broken off from the Mother Church. Until then, it never occurred to anyone to propose that there was a tension between the Catholic Church and the true Germanic sense. Such unhistoric viewpoints can only be attributed to the narrowest partisan bias.

Others regard as "Germanic" an unbounded subjectivism which in its exuberance sweeps aside and destroys everything that mankind has ever regarded as good and holy.

Still others do not hesitate to designate as "Germanic" everything which serves their purposes. Whenever they establish a society or start an enterprise of any kind, down to and including a gymnastic or choral group, they go out of their way to present these as being somehow outgrowths of primitive Germanic traditions. In such hands, the term "Germanic" is a seductive device especially for our youngsters, who are deceived into believing that by engaging in such frivolous activities they are imitating their ancestors. This conception of the term does not derive from the German national tradition but from the poverty-stricken imaginations of such people. They themselves are the primitive originators of that kind of Germanism.

No less reprehensible is that exaggerated nationalism, that narrow-minded pan-Germanism which looks down with disdain upon the Romance nations and denies their accomplishments because it is ignorant of them, being unaware that our whole Western culture and history rests on Christianity and on the mixture of Germanic and Romance elements. Nevertheless, there is a certain valid distinction in the discussion of social and political differences between what can be characterized as "Roman" and "Germanic." If we analyze the ancient Roman state, in particular as it developed under the emperors, and compare it with the Christian-Germanic conception of the state during the Middle Ages, we find certain differences.

First, there is the difference between self-government and centralized authority. All Germanic peoples were impregnated with the idea of self-government, and they structured their political systems accordingly. One can find no Germanic institution where this influence was absent. Absolutism with its centralizing trend appeared in German history, if we except the Hohenstaufens who nevertheless derived their inspiration from the same source, when the Roman system, Roman institutions, and the pagan Roman concept of the state began to spread among us.

Secondly, there is the contrast which we discussed in the previous chapter, between the organic and the mechanical composition of the state. The basic pattern for all social and political structures according to the Germanic tradition has always been the family, blood relationship, the clan, and then -

patterned after these - the guild and the estate.
The Roman conception leaned more toward what was
formal and mechanical. In this sense, the corporate
order follows more closely in the Germanic spirit,
and mechanical constitutionalism is more Roman in
its origins.

May we take the liberty of recalling here the
beautiful representation of our German ancestors which
the Roman writer Tacitus made? Even though it may
appear somewhat biased, since it attempted to present
a contrast to the corrupt Romans, it is nevertheless
true and accurate. Tacitus especially extolled certain virtues in the Germans.

They were a God-fearing people. All punishment
was decided by their priests, because they felt that
they were thereby making themselves submissive to the
will of God. Also, they fell into a reverential silence
during their assemblies only under the leadership of
their priests. We see in the cultural makeup of our
ancestors an awareness that obedience and authority
have their basis in God. Even though they were obeying pagan priests, in Tacitus' words - velut Deo
imperante. - (as if God were persuading them) it must
have been far easier for them to grasp the obedience
of which Christianity spoke, "sicut Christo," "ut servi
Christi, "propter Deum," "sicut servi Dei:"Like Christ,
"as servants of Christ," (Ephesians 6:5-6), and "because
of God," "as servants of God." (1 Peter 2: 13 and 16)
The unhappy conception of obedience as servility before
mere human authority was alien to them.

They were also more concerned with good morals
than with laws - again, in marked contrast to what is
true in our times. The great importance of legislative
mills grinding out laws without pause was not yet known
to them.

To mislead others, and to allow oneself to be misled was not yet excused by them as in keeping with
popular morality. No one made light of vices. What
a fine testament to our ancestors. At a time when
so many papers have become mere scandal sheets, one
cannot shed the conviction that most of the people who
engage in this filthy business are not of German blood.

201

Rather they are contaminating our people with an
alien ideology.

Chastity was a leading characteristic among the
early Germans. They lived their lives within bounds
that were carefully marked by moral conduct. They
tolerated no obscene spectacles or festive orgies,
nor did they engage in any secret exchange of dishonorable letters.

Young girls of easy virtue were held in general
contempt, so that they were unable to find a husband
regardless of their youth, their beauty, or their
riches. Young men were chaste and avoided ennervat-
ing debauchery. Young maidens were in no great haste
to marry, all of the while preserving their innocence.
It was in this condition that they eventually married,
and their virtuous conduct was carried over and reflected in the healthfulness and wholesomeness of
their children.

The marriage bond was held to be especially
sacred. Adultery was most exceptional. Adulteresses
had their hair cut short and the rod was used on them
to expel them from the household and from the community.
In some areas, it was customary for women to marry only
once, and widows did not remarry. They selected a man
as if they were to become a part of him in one body.
To limit the number of children or to destroy children
after they were born was regarded as a disgraceful crime.

Family ties were held to be especially sacred
among them. The uncle loved his sister's children as
their own father loved them. The more children there
were, the more diligently the aged were cared for. In
battle, men did not stand side by side at random, but
families and relatives rallied together with their
women and children nearby. The latter served as the
most cherished witnesses of the battle. It was their
praise which the men treasured most of all. They bared
their wounds to mothers and wives, and these did not
blanch at the sight of them. They shared friendship
and animosities of their parents and relatives, but
they did not persist in their animosities.

These people are not insidious or crafty, but open and frank, so that secrets are shared in congenial company.

They do not believe in lavish funerals and they disdain costly monuments. They do not weep or mourn for long, but continue to bear the pain and sorrow over their deceased loved ones all the more sincerely in their hearts. 19

When we reflect on the basic qualities in the character of the early Germans as Tacitus described them, we begin to appreciate why God selected such a virtuous, fine people to become the bearers of Christianity. All of the natural virtues in the Germanic character were fortified and sanctified by the Christian religion to produce what we have to honor and respect as the true Germanic manner. We still find it today wherever Germans retain their fear of the Lord and their Christian belief. Such Germanism was confronted in Tacitus' time by a decadent Romanism, and we see traces of the same in our time in the afterbirth of a degenerate civilization. It is this decadent morality and this rampant unbelief which now pretends to represent the Germanic folk way. We have to protest with all of our might against such blatant misrepresentation of all that is good and worthy of our respect in the German tradition.

Materialism and unbelief, brazen immorality, the rebellion against everything that is sacred and against all authority, the rejection of any notion of a supernatural order, the wholesale perversion and seduction of our youth, the immoral press of our time whose superficial filth finds its way into every home, the pervasive latitudinarionism which wants to elevate all manner of shallow base currents of unbelief to the status of a religious belief, all of these have so little in common with what is genuinely German as the croaking of a frog in a swamp has with the melody of the human voice. All of it merely represents a revival of the basest moral and intellectual decadence into which the ancient paganism of Rome once plunged its people.

203

XXII   Freedom of Religion

What is understood today to be freedom of religion, can best be determined from reading Guizot, who[20]
explains it in his newest and very worthwhile book.

"Religious freedom is the freedom of thought,
conscience, and conduct in matters pertaining to
religion. It is the freedom to believe or not to
believe, for the educated and the priests, as well
as for the faithful. The state offers all of them
the same measure of protection in the exercise of
their right."

He then deals with the question of which particular rights are contained in this basic religious
freedom, and remarks:

"I. The right of individuals to confess their
faith, to worship as they please, to belong to whatever religious body they choose, to remain a member
or to depart as they please.

"II. The right of the various churches to organize, to manage their own internal affairs according to their beliefs, convictions, and traditions.

"III. The right of the faithful and the ministers
of the various churches to teach and to propagate their
faith and their manner of worship by spiritual and
moral means."

After Guizot indicated that this right, like all
others, is capable of abuse, he suggested that the
state is therefore entitled to exercise the necessary
vigilance and control over any such abuse. Then he
concluded:

"In intself, however, barring the most unusual,
occasional circumstances, there is no contesting that
the principle of religious freedom involves essentially
the individual's freedom of conscience and of worship,
and the freedom of churches to regulate their internal
affairs as they see fit, as well as the freedom of

204

religions to organize and to instruct. Furthermore,
it is a fact that the principle of religious freedom
will be either genuine or hypocritical, fruitful or
not, to the extent that it corresponds in practice
to what we have described."

    We believe that this concept corresponds basic-
ally to what is meant in our time when there is talk
of religious freedom and freedom of conscience. It
therefore reflects accurately the spirit of our
times.

XXIII Religious Freedom and the Catholic Church

We come now to the all important question whether religious freedom in the sense just described is opposed to the principles of the Catholic Church. May Catholics who wish to remain true to the principles of their church concede to those of other religions such a position in the State? May Catholic rulers legally permit to their subjects such freedom of conscience without violating their own consciences? Can there be situations in which rulers are even bound in conscience to grant such freedom? Would not such a position be completely opposed to the way the Church operated during the Middle Ages?

Before we proceed to answer these questions, we have to come to grips with an ambiguity that exists here and make clear precisely what is meant. Moral freedom is not a right to do evil, but simply the free and inner self-determination toward what is good; it involves free choice which includes the possibility of choosing what is evil without external compulsion. The freedom to make up one's own mind is, in itself, no right to choose error and to lie. It is the free inner self-determination toward what is truth without external compulsion. The choice of what is good and what is true is at the same time our bounden duty, in fact, the highest obligation that a man has. The choice of what is evil and untrue, on the other hand, is the wanton abuse of our legitimate liberty. Only in this sense can we speak of freedom of religion. The right to adopt a false religion, to organize it, to propagate it does not exist, as such. On the contrary man's first and highest obligation is to seek out the true religion and to give all of his devotion to it. For that reason, the Catholic Church cannot cease to regard the existence of all false religions as the gravest abuse of freedom that it must fight against with all of its might. As opposed to this we are faced with the question whether the Catholic Church can remain loyal to her principles and waive the exercise of external force in the area of religious freedom, or in the area of moral freedom; whether she may leave to the individual freedom of choice in this matter of choice of a religion, as she does regarding his freedom to choose between good and evil;and finally, whether, since she possesses no means of external compulsion, she must demand the exercise of such compulsion by public authorities or at the very least by Catholic rulers? That is the real nub of the problem.

We intend to consider this matter in three parts: First, the position of the Catholic Church towards the unbaptized unbelievers; Secondly, the position of the Catholic Church and the secular authorities in earlier ages toward those who were baptized but who fell into erroneous beliefs; Thirdly, the conclusion which we have to draw from these positions for pertinent situations in our own time.

I

We regard St. Thomas, as certainly the most reliable exponent of Catholic teachings, and he lived in the very times (d. 1274) when it is maintained nowadays, albeit wrongly, that the Catholic Church exercised limitless power. He answered the questions: whether the unbelievers may be forced to accept the true religion as follows:

"The non-believers who, like the pagans and the Jews, have never accepted the true Faith may in no way - nullo modo - be forced to accept it, since Faith is a matter of free consent by the will. (Summa Theol. Sec. Sec. Q. 10 Art.)

The noted and learned Jesuit Suarez addressed himself to the same question 400 years later when he was discussing the power of the Catholic Church and Christian rulers. He said: "It is the universal opinion of theologians that non-believers, whether they are one's subjects or not, may not be forced to accept the Faith even if they have attained sufficient knowledge of it." [21] He then enumerated a long list of the most reputable theologians who supported this position and came to the conclusion that: "This opinion is therefore completely true and certain." To make it the more conclusive, he added: "We regard it, first of all as intrinsically evil - intrinsice malum - to wish to force non-believers

208

who are not one's subjects to accept the Faith, because
such force, to be applied, presupposes the existence of
legitimate authority, as must be obvious. The Church,
however, does not possess legitimate authority over
such persons.[22] He continues: "Secondly, the Church cannot compel even non-believers who are subject to her
temporal authority to accept the Faith. That is because
the direct use of force presupposes full authority and
jurisdiction, and it is clear from what has been said
that the Church has not gotten such full power over her
temporal subjects by any specific commission from Christ."[23]

Until now we have spoken only of non-believers as
individuals. St. Thomas went further now and asked
whether the religious practices of non-believers must
also be tolerated. In other words, we are face to face
now with the issues which Guizot regarded as integral
to religious freedom. St. Thomas first mentioned the
possible objections to his position in his accustomed
manner: "It appears as though the religious practices
of unbelievers must not be tolerated inasmuch as it is
obvious that by their observance of these practices they
are sinning; and we must conclude that he who does not
prevent such a sin when he is able, himself shares in
its guilt." The Saint answered: "Temporal government
has its origin in divine government, and it must, therefore to the extent that it can, imitate it. God,
however, though He is almighty and infinite, permits
certain evils to occur on earth, even though He could
prevent them from occurring. He does this because,
first of all, by presenting evil in this manner He
would deprive man of greater benefits. and secondly,
because therefore greater evils would result." (Sec.
Sec. Q. 10 Art. 11) The greater benefits which
St. Thomas had in mind here are not hard to determine.
God would have to deprive a man of his liberty which
is the highest endowment that man has, if He were to
deny a man every possibility of abusing that liberty.
Applying that principle to temporal governments,
St. Thomas concluded that they too must tolerate certain evils, and he stated finally: "Even though the
non-believers sin because of their religious practices,
these must nevertheless be tolerated, either because
of the good that they still have in them, or because
of the greater evil that would result." Among such

evils, he listed the scandal and discord which might result from forceful interference or, even more important, the hindrance that such interference could prove to be to the true conversion of the unbelievers.

We see here with what great circumspection the great teachers of the Catholic Church opposed that much abused viewpoint according to which anyone who holds authority is obliged to promote as much good as lies within his power. To avoid evil by the use of force involves a whole lot more than simply the possession of physical force, but also legitimate authority. Secondly, it involves the employment of means which do not promote more evil in the process of avoiding evil. It is madness to deprive a neighbor of both of his eyes in an effort to save a hand which may be endangered. Thus every authority - where the liberty and self-determination of the human being is involved - must pause to analyze not only the scope of its legitimate authority, but also the correctness of the means which it wishes to employ.

Since this question has such overriding importance, we shall also see what Suarez, the great interpreter of St. Thomas, had to say about it. Suarez not only confirmed St. Thomas' opinion regarding the toleration of the religious practices of unbelievers, he went further and sets the precise limits to which such toleration can go. His determination is of the greatest practical significance in dealing with the question of how far the limits of religious freedom can extend in our own time and remain in conformity with the Church's principles. In his commentary on St. Thomas, Suarez begins much in the style of the latter. "It appears as though the religious practices of the unbelievers, notably all of the unbaptized as, e.g., pagans and Mohammedans, may not be tolerated in Christian nations since they involve superstition and injury to the honor that is owed to the true God, whose honor Christian rulers have an obligation to uphold. St. Thomas, however, rightly distinguishes two kinds of religious practices: there are those which go against reason and against God insofar as he can be recognized through nature and through the natural powers of the soul, e.g., the worship of idols, etc. Others are contrary to the Christian religion and to its commands

210

not because they are evil in themselves or contrary
to reason as, for example, the practices of Jews and
even many of the customs of Mohammedans and such unbelievers who believe in one true God.

"Regarding the first, the Church may not tolerate
them on the part of her own unbelieving subjects. But
that is merely the general principle. It may happen
often that Christian rulers cannot prevent even such
practices without causing greater harm to the nation
and to the Christian inhabitants. In that case, the
ruler may tolerate such evil with a clear conscience
on the basis of what Christ said to the servant who
asked the master whether they should remove the weeds
from the field. He replied, 'No, or perhaps while you
are gathering the tares you will root up the wheat
with them.' (Matt. 13:29) [24]

"As regards the other religious practices of unbelievers which go contrary to Christian beliefs but
not counter to natural reason, there is no doubt but
that the unbelievers, even though they are subjects,
may not be forced to abandon them. Rather the Church
has to tolerate them. St.Gregory addressed himself
clearly to this problem regarding Jews, and he forbade
anyone to deprive them of their synagogues or to prevent them from observing their religious practices
therein. (Lib. I Epistol. 34). Elsewhere he reaffirmed
that no one should prevent Jews from participating in
their religious observances. (Lib. II. Ep. 15). The
reason is that such observances do not in themselves
violate the natural law, and therefore, the temporal
power of even a Christian ruler does not confer a
right to forbid them. Such action would be based on
the fact that what is being done goes contrary to the
Christian Faith, but that is not enough to compel those
who are not subject to the spiritual authority of the
Church. This opinion is also supported by the fact
that such a ban would involve, to some extent, forcing
people to accept the Faith; and that is never permitted." [25]

From all of what these authorities have said, we
are able to derive certain important principles regarding how the Catholic Church and Christian rulers must
conduct themselves in the matter of religious freedom

of the unbaptized:

1. The acceptance of the Christian Faith, which
is before God the greatest obligation facing any human
being, must be an act of the free will and free self-
determination of each individual, and no one may in
any way - ullo modo, as St. Thomas said - be compelled
to do so by the use of external force.

2. The spiritual authority of the Church, like
that of any temporal authority, is limited. Those who
exercise that authority may not do all that they·would
be capable of doing, or what they regard as useful, nor
may they use any force at their disposal to accomplish
such ends. The application of external force can only
be justified to the extent that the nature of authority
indicates. Thus, every absolutism is unthinkable, and
the implications contained here are of the greatest
significance. It is a basic fallacy of our times,
and many of the best and well-intentioned fall prey
to it - a fallacy, incidentally, which we have grown
accustomed to because of absolutism - to look for
remedies by the use of external force especially as
applied by some great and powerful ruler. Far be it
from us to deny the great blessing that a true Christian ruler would be, but such a ruler would be the
more blessed, the more he operated within the bounds
of what he could legitimately do. When a ruler, with
the best of intentions, goes beyond his authority to
do good, such good turns out to be spurious, and he
can end up doing grave harm to both Church and state. 26
If only the Bourbon rulers, instead of being taken in
by the dazzling glitter of their own omnipotence and
operating under the pretext of being the first sons of
the Church and meddling in every concern of the home,
the Church, and the state, had stayed within the bounds
of their legitimate authority, what great evil the
Church would have been spared. All power has its
limits, and whenever those limits are transgressed, no
matter how good the intentions may be, God's will is opposed; and what was intended as a blessing ends up
being a curse.

3. The spiritual authority of the Church which
was conferred upon it by Christ extends only over her
members, and even then only to the extent that Christ

212

has given her authority. The unbaptized and the non-Christians are not subject to the Church's authority. [27] Thus, she has only the right to preach the gospel to all men and to urge them for the salvation of their souls to join the Church. She does not have proper authority to use external force directly or indirectly to compel anyone to become a member of the Church, or to order anyone else to use such force.

4. The temporal power exercised in the state, whether by Christian rulers or by others, concerns itself only with a part of the temporal well-being of the subjects, not with the supernatural truths of revelation. The scope of temporal power and the authority which is proper to it and not conferred upon it by others derives from the natural order of things and the unchangeable laws which God has implanted in that order. The scope of that authority can be extended if the Church chooses to confer more powers, as the Church did grant additional rights to the ancient Christian rulers - powers which they then exercised in the name of the Church. Likewise, certain historical situations may develop which add to the state's power. Yet, the basic limitation of its authority derives from laws of God who, in laying down His plan for order in the universe, also included a proper sphere for the temporal community. No one, either the Church or the people, has a right to transgress these limits. Christ acknowledged the natural order and sanctified it. In doing so, He imparted to those who were vested with temporal authority as well as to their subjects a purity and nobility of purpose, as well as a loyal devotion to duty which the world had not known hitherto. The temporal order was blessed and ennobled by Him, but He did not enlarge the scope of temporal authority. The new powers which He brought to humanity were conferred upon His Apostles and their successors. Temporal rulers, therefore, do not have the authority to compel non-Christians to convert to the Christian Faith, since that is a purely supernatural concern; nor can the Church grant that authority to temporal rulers, because the Church itself does not have it.

5. On the other hand, religious freedom has its own natural limits as dictated by reason, by natural morality, and by the natural order of things. No reasonable moral freedom can go so far as to destroy

moral order to which everyone has a right. Therefore, Christians as well as non-Christian rulers and those who hold temporal authority are obliged to oppose religious teachings and practices which are in latent violation of the laws of reason and morality. For this reason, Christian rulers may not tolerate, for example, the worship of idols by their subjects, if they are able to prevent it. As Suarez said, "Reason and the natural law demand of human society that it worships the true God. Therefore it must possess the power to require people to honor the true God and to prevent the honoring of false gods. Aside from this, it is the goal of temporal authority to preserve peace and justice in society, but it cannot accomplish this without requiring virtuous conduct among its subjects. But the latter cannot live according to natural morality and virtue unless they have religion and serve the one, true God. Thus, temporal authority is justified and obligated to tolerate only the worship of the true God and to suppress the worship of false gods as unreasonable and immoral." [28]

The same rule applies for all other religious practices which transgress against the natural moral law, but only so far as one's own subjects are concerned. [29]

On the basis of these principles, the Church fully protects the religious freedom of unbelievers in the sense that Guizot required. We have purposely taken pains to discuss this matter at length to show that we are not dealing with a casual opinion, but a matter which has been subject to painful scrutiny and one which rests on important principles. The Church places so high a value on freedom of conscience and freedom of religion that she rejects as immoral and illegitimate any use of external force against those who are not her members. At the same time, she recognizes definite limits beyond which religious freedom would constitute a wrong that would jeopardize the moral well-being of society. Even in the area of morality, freedom reaches its limits when it constitutes a wrong which poses a threat to society. Therefore, religious freedom too must have its limits, not only where it is a threat to the state, but also if it threatens the rights of others to the higher moral benefits of society. That becomes the case, when, as at present, sects are founded which under the guise of religion add up to a denial of Almighty God, foster crass materialism, and thereby lay the groundwork for destroying the entire moral foundations of human society. Such religious liberty is in fact an immoral and unreasonable abomination which God is bound to curse; and states which tolerate it are doomed.

II

These principles which suggest that no manner of compulsion may be employed against unbelievers to force them to believe, and that even their form of worship, so long as it is not immoral in itself and does not reject worship of the one, true God, must be tolerated, seems at first glance to contradict the conduct of the Church and of temporal rulers toward heretics during the Middle Ages. If we take a closer look at the basis for their actions we shall see that there was in fact, no contradiction. By the same token, that basis for action no longer exists in our time, so that the use of external compulsion in matters of faith are no longer an issue at present.

Before we demonstrate that, we have to examine the legal nature of the kind of heresy which alone, according to the principles of the Church, justified punishment because it was an offense against the Faith. Heresy in this sense involved two factors. First, there was a stiff-necked persistence and perseverence by a baptized Christian in error as determined by prior, thorough investigation. Secondly, implicit in this stiff-necked posture, there was active rebellion against the authority of the Church. [30] It is apparent that there is a great difference between one who was in error in the matter of Christian dogmas and a heretic who was subject to punishment. Innocent error is not only no punishable heresy; it is not even an infinitesmal moral violation. Punishable heresy entailed a clear perception of the Christian truth that was in controversy, stiff-necked rejection of it, and at the same time a rejection of the authority of the Church. In the Church's view the real malice

215

of heresy lay actually in rejection of the Church's teaching authority, because the whole body of Christian teaching rests on that authority, and that authority is the arbiter of all disputes and the very essence of the Magisterium. Therefore, where there is no insight into the nature of the Church's authority, where only prejudices prevail, and where the Church's authority is considered to be tantamount to arbitrary human judgements and the judgements of priests, there can be no question of punishable heresy. It is clear that the concept of punishable heresy does not apply when we are dealing with persons who did not themselves choose to leave the bosom of the Church, but who are the descendants of those who centuries ago made that decision. Whether and to what extent their false beliefs constitute sin, only God who sees into the human heart can judge. Externally, it is impossible to pass judgement. Even though the Church regards all those who are validly baptized as members of the one, holy, Catholic Church and therefore as basically and before God subject to ecclesiastical authority, there has never been any intention to exercise external force to punish them. Toward them, the Church can only adopt the position which it takes toward all unbelievers. It is left to their completely free self-determination whether they wish to return to the Faith.

On the basis of this conception of punishable heresy by temporal authorities in earlier times, such authorities regarded it as a civil matter and therefore felt justified in inflicting severe external punishment up to the death penalty itself. Even in Roman law, after the conversion of the emperors to Christendom, heresy came to be regarded as a civil offense. The same view was taken over into German common law, and from there it eventually found its way into laws promulgated by German emperors. It is a conception which developed spontaneously because of the unity of belief that was deeply and universally imbedded in the whole culture, without the Church having had to demand compulsion and the pain of punishment even though she later accepted that as justified. A diversity of various Christion confessions - or if one prefers, churches - was totally unknown to people in those times. People all lived with the conviction that

there was just one, holy, Christian Church which was
spread over the whole world and which alone was the
true Church. This Christian Church was regarded as
a gift from Heaven which was the great common benefit
and possession of all Christians everywhere and the
repository and custodian of all of their greatest
treasures. How could it have happened otherwise
then that men came to regard as a crime, also in the
temporal order, an attack upon this great spiritual
temple of God here on earth, which was also rightly
regarded as the bastion of all social order, especially since the attacks came from its own children
and members. Would it be surprising that men came
to regard the adulteration of the common Faith as a
more serious punishable offense than the counter-
feiting of currency, as St. Thomas pointed out?
The unbaptized retained their full freedom. Baptized Christians, however, were regarded as bound
by their baptismal vows to be loyal to the Church.
They were, therefore, considered the more as criminals when they fell into heresy, the more highly
one came to regard the great benefit of which these
heretics were trying to deprive everyone. Even
though people recognized and accepted unconditionally
the truth that the Faith is basically a matter for
free self-determination, they saw the situation as
essentially different for those who by baptism into
the Church had taken on the sworn responsibility to
remain true to their Faith until death. Aside from
that, the right of all the faithful to be secure in
their beliefs and not to have them jeopardized took
precedence over the religious freedom of the individual. If ever any law emanated from the general consensus of all men in those times, the civil laws
against heretics would have to be regarded as such
laws. One may rightfully regard them as natural laws
in the proper sense of the word, because whenever men
have lived together in civil society, even among the
pagans, they have regarded it as their right to protect from attack by individuals the religious conviction which they all shared. If it is at all legitimate to question this practice, the attack ought to
be launched not against the Church, but against the
legal and national consciousness of all peoples who
have enjoyed unity in religious beliefs.

We must also draw attention to the fact that the actions by temporal authorities against heresy were not exclusively, and often not even chiefly, directed against denial of the Faith. Many other kinds of misconduct were included in the proceedings as, for example, crimes of immorality. The heretic trials of the Middle Ages were far more frequently penal actions against abominable crimes of immorality than against actual sins against the Faith. Later Inquisitorial proceedings in Spain, the horrors of which incidentally have been too much exaggerated, have nothing immediately to do with the Church and with its principles. [32] They were simply the outcome of an ever more prevalent state absolutism which, here too, pretended to be acting in the interests of the Church so as to gain limitless power and, eventually, under this mantle, to acquire total power.

From what we have said, it is clear that treating heresy as a civil matter is no longer legitimate once the unity of the Faith has been shattered. Disunity destroys the essential prerequisites, and in Germany this began with the Religious Revolt. By order of the Capital Court of Charles VI in 1532, heresy already appears to have been removed from the area of civil proceedings. The unity of the Faith was lost to Christendom because of men's fault, something which God rightfully permitted to happen. As it was originally won not by force, but simply by the power of the word of God and by God's grace, and by the virtues of Christians, and the blood of martyrs, so, without a doubt, it will be restored once again. Until that happy day comes, we will have to bear with each other as best we can, and the State will have the obligation, above all, to preserve the religous freedom of all.

It is an absurdity therefore to want to assert that the Catholic Church finds it necessary, or at least nurtures the intention, to secure the services of some ruler who will use temporal power to punish those who abandon the Catholic Faith. The fact is, if we except the period of the Reformation and the Peasant Wars, that Catholics have in recent centuries used no force against others; and least of all have there been such actions on the part of the Church or of the popes. In England, Sweden, and other countries, on the other hand, the most gruesome criminal legal proceedings were taking place not only against those who fell away from religion but against those who remained loyal to the Faith of their fathers. These horrors were perpetrated under laws which prevail practically until our own time. The least one could do would be to not ignore historic facts so stubbornly!

As regards the use of spiritual compulsion against heretics in the context that we have been discussing, the Church has always affirmed the authority to use such force on those who are by belief and by baptism her own members. Such force consists in spiritual and ecclesiastical penalties which have as their special purpose to bring about their spiritual improvement. The most severe of these punishments is excommunication. The Faith is the foundation of the Church. Therefore, as every organization which wishes to survive has the right to protect by expulsion those members who are at odds with its basic constitution, so the Church too must have the right to expel members who make an assault against her foundations. Even when the Church used external means of compulsion, this too was done for improvement and enlightenment purposes, not in the sense that the Faith has to be forced on people or that it is something other than an act of inner conviction. The family as well as the State uses external means of punishment also to bring about inner moral betterment. In any case, the possibility of employing such external means of compulsion was contingent on the state's making such power available, and it comes to an end once the state withdraws its external assistance.

III

If now, after our discussion of the question, to what extent the Church must use external compulsion against the abuse of religious freedom, and whether Catholics may regard religious freedom as essential, we wish to answer the questions as they apply to our own times, we have to present the following conclusions:

219

1) In general, the Church regards the acceptance of religion as a matter for inner self-determination, and would contest the right to use external force by either the state or by ecclesiastical authority.

2) The punishment of heretics by the Church in relatively few instances was not undertaken to effect conversion by external force, but rather in the sense that a Christian accepted certain responsibilities when he was baptized and that he ought to be held accountable for them. Such external punishment, however, only took place in special circumstances and in the case of proclaimed formal heretics in the sense which we discussed above. Validly baptized Protestants are still by virtue of baptism in a certain union with the Church. However, even aside from all other reasons which ought to make it abundantly clear that the Catholic Church has not the remotest inclination to wish to use force against them, the very notion of formal and punishable heresy cannot be applied to them. Any suggestion to the contrary is therefore an irresponsible scare tactic.

3) Heresy as a violation of civil law presupposed unity in Faith, and with the disappearance of that unity it too has become a dead letter.

4) Where other religious organizations exist legally, a Catholic ruler is required to give them the full protection which the law affords. If he were to use external force against them he would violate the principles of his Church. 33

5) In this sense, there exist in Germany along with the Catholic Church also the Lutheran and the Reformed Church. A Catholic ruler, without question, owes them full legal protection as well as love and concern for their well-being.

6) To what extent civil authorities wish to afford to other religious groups the free legal right to operate, the Church leaves this up to their own free self-determination. There is no ecclesiastical principle which would prevent a Catholic from upholding the principle that under given conditions, the civil authorities would best afford full religious freedom

to all, subject to the conditions we have now to mention.

7) We have to insist upon the limits of religious freedom referred to earlier, whereby it is an abuse of that freedom if the state, under the guise of religious freedom, tolerates sects which deny the existence of a personal God, or which jeopardize morality. Such conduct stands in open contradiction to the obligations of civil authority, first of all by virtue of the origin of civil authority. Ultimately, all authority comes from God, and therefore, there can be no more flagrant abuse of that authority than to tolerate the denial of God. Secondly, the ultimate goal of civil authority sets certain limits. That goal is to preserve peace and justice on earth, and neither of these is possible without morality; and morality is impossible without fear of the Lord.

8) The Church will not cease, however, to use that force upon its own members which Christ Himself has entitled her to use, namely, to expel from her midst those members who deny their Faith.

XXIV The Freedom of the Church

Our age has inherited a poor legacy from the past because of the confusion of all principles having to do with the relationship of the Church and the State. The religious divisions were, in the final analysis, merely a means whereby many rulers sought to obtain absolute sovereignty by usurping power from above as held by the Pope and the emperor, and from below by depriving the estates and guilds of their autonomy. From these divisions moreover, the principle evolved that the temporal authority of princes empowered them even to control the consciences of their subjects, to tell them what they had to believe. Thus the entire Protestant population of Germany, which broke away from the Catholic Church in order to be free, had to subject its conscience to the arbitrary will of a temporal ruler. The more this principle came to bear in the temporal order, supported by the absolutist and egotistical spirit of the age, the more any valid concepts dealing with the relationship of Church and State had to become muddled. The same currents naturally affected also Catholic rulers. A single thought prevailed everywhere, which a Prussian king later expressed in these words: "I rest upon my sovereignty as on a rock of iron (rocher de fer). The Bourbon courts were unable to appear as the bearers of ecclesiastical authority because of the religious convictions of their Catholic subjects; nevertheless they surreptitiously usurped such authority, sometimes under the pretext of ancient privileges which popes had once conferred, and sometimes under the pretext of old national freedoms, and at yet other times by the exercise of scheming diplomacy. They thereby usurped, in particular, the right of appointment to high ecclesiastical positions. Servile cardinals, bishops, and canons often enough acted as the pliant tools for this rank undertaking.

The Revolution toppled a part of the royal structure, but it permitted the old systems to survive. In Germany, the Catholic Church as we once knew it was destroyed at the beginning of this century.

223

Ancient dioceses were deprived of their shepherds and divided like the Lord's garments to be distributed in pieces,without the least thought being given to the Church's legal rights. Therefore, one had to expect that officialdom around the Protestant rulers, which had grown up in the tradition of Cujus regio, ejus religio, was not about to treat the Catholic Church any differently. The Protestant Church had lost all semblance of independence, and the Catholic Church was to be regarded in the same manner. The excuse for their conduct they found in the conduct of those courtier canon lawyers who had betrayed the Catholic Church into the hands of Catholic rulers.

This confusion of true principles regarding the relationship between Church and state, to the great detriment of the Catholic Church, has now reached a new level in recent times. Until now one dealt with princes who, even if they operated in systems that were faulty, still had a personal conscience; and they still saw their authority as coming from God. In other words, one could at least continue to talk with them in theistic terms. Today, the Church stands face to face with that false liberal absolutism which we discussed earlier. In the present framework, therefore, political parties battle for victory, after which they exercise limitless power in the false guise of representing the will of the people. It is a new absolutism which acknowledges no God, no history, no traditional rights, no piety, no conscience; and it is filled with a deep hatred of the Catholic Church. The position which this liberalism takes toward the Catholic Church can be summed up as follows: It wishes to claim all of those powers as belonging to the state, which once were usurped from the Catholic Church by absolute rulers and by police states by means of sharp diplomacy and betrayal. On the other hand, it advocates full liberty for all such new societies which crop up posing as religions. It arrogates to state authority the right to regulate by legislation the inner affairs of the Church, as for example, appointment to ecclesiastical positions, the training of priests, etc. This practice has already come to fulfillment in some of the smaller German states. In the meantime, the press in Southwest Germany and

in Central Germany is almost universally in favor of
it with poorly disguised animosity toward the Catholic
Church.

No issue is more critical and deserving of a proper
solution than this one. How it is resolved will determine our whole future. If the efforts of godless liberalism are successful, we will be faced with some of the
bitterest battles imaginable. They will erupt first
when the attempt is made to ram the program through in
the larger states. That liberals have every intention
of doing so, is painfully clear. That is why it is
most urgent that Catholics tirelessly present and defend the correct principles regarding the relationship
between church and state. Only if those correct principles prevail will we have any guarantee that there
will be peace in Germany. Let us examine these principles more closely.

Freedom of the Church means the right of the church
to manage her own affairs according to her own principles and to be subject only to the general laws of
the state.

We distinguish between freedom of the Church and
privileges. In earlier times, the Church enjoyed various
privileges which developed spontaneously because unity
of Faith prevailed. Those are virtually extinct in our
time, but the Church is able to survive without them.
Nevertheless, let us not confuse privileges with legitimate rights, as often happens nowadays. The Church is
entitled to the protection of her legitimate rights,
just as any other legal personality.

We distinguish furthermore between freedom and
the independence of the Church from the state. The
Church does not ask to be independent of the state insofar as the state has certain responsibilities which
are inherent in temporal authority. She considers
obedience and homage to the state and to its laws as
not merely an external matter but as a matter of conscience; and she demands this of her members. She
lives up to all of her civic duties and pays her taxes.
She insists only that the state will not overstep its
bounds and interfere in church affairs in a hostile
and forceful manner.

The Church lays claim to her freedom in this sense
for four reasons. The Christian Church has, from its
origin, a Divine commission. The mandate of the Apostles
was contained in the words of Christ: "I came upon an
errand from my Father, and now I am sending you out in
my turn." (John 20:21) "Go out all over the world, and
preach the gospel to the whole of creation." (Mark 16:15)
That is and will remain the objective of the Church.
Whether or not men will listen to her, she will persist
in her mission and continue to propagate her teaching
among men in the name of God. In the process the Church
will, where it becomes necessary, defy those who can
only kill the body. (Matt. 10:28)

The second reason, why the Church demands her
freedom is the general legal framework of Europe.
So long as our traditional body of positive law sur-
vives, the right of the Church in Germany must be recognized. In German national law and in all constitutions, the right of the Catholic Church is recognized.
It was subject to the strict observance and recognition
of this right and parts of ancient German dioceses
were assigned to the various princes as a kind of recompense. Now if the Catholic Church has the right to
exist, we are not dealing with some fictitious entity,
which legislative majorities can impose an arbitrary
set of restraints on. We are talking about the Catholic
Church as she exists in history, having those same principles and purposes which are recognized as parts of
her basic constitution throughout the world. It is an
essential part of this constitution that ecclesiastical
authority is to be exercised by the successors of the
apostles as Christ has commissioned them. It is precisely here that we find a fundamental difference between Protestantism and the Catholic Church; and every
page of church history will bear this out. A violation of this right is an unwarranted incursion against
the universal historical and positive law.

It is certainly one of the very unique characteristics of our time that there can be legislative bodies
which totally ignore that right and carry on as though
it no longer even exists. The only consolation we
have is the certain knowledge that history will inevitably pass its own severe judgement on these vain
efforts.

The third reason why we insist on freedom of the
Church is the right of autonomy that derives from nature
and reason. It is the bounden duty of the Catholic
press to draw attention of one and all to the blatant
hypocrisy whereby liberalism busies itself, securing
the right of every unChristian and destructive endeavor
to exist in our time while denying this same right to
the Christian Church.   It is hypocritical for liberals
to proclaim freedom of the press and at the same time to
require censorship and special authorization for the
bishops' pastoral letters and to insert penalties into
the state penal codes. It is hypocritical on the part
of modern liberalism when it defends the right of private organizations to examine and appoint their own officials, while at the same time it supports laws which
deny the Catholic Church the right to appoint her officials. It is hypocrisy on the part of liberals to
prattle about freedom of association, while at the same
time opposing the association of persons in cloisters
for pious purposes, accusing them of all sorts of preposterous horrors dreamt up by fiction writers. While
liberals may not suppress these religious establishments with fire and sword, they nevertheless move in
with police measures which serve notice to the public
that what is going on here is on the same level as cold-
blooded murder. 34

If we are unable to appeal to modern liberals on
the basis of the Divine commission, the fear of the
Lord, or positive legislation, and on the basis of
what is right and equitable, then we at least have
to urge them to allow the Church her freedom on the
basis of common decency.

Fourth, we insist on the freedom of the Church
in the name of individual Catholics who live in this
land. It is a favorite trick of the modern secularists
to portray every encounter between Church and state
as a narrow conflict involving a small clique of
priests. For this purpose, the term clerical has been
invented. The freedom of the Church, however, involves the interest of every individual Catholic
Christian. It is the proper wish of every single
Catholic that the Church is to be ruled not by state
appointed officials but by successors of the apostles.

At a time when there is so much talk of the popular will the least one could do would be to pay some attention also to the popular will of the Catholics, who are people too. Furthermore, Catholics have to be brought to realize that a real, basic, genuine Catholic interest is at stake here and now.

The formula for regulating the relationship of the state is so simple, so inherently persuasive, so justifiable, that one really has to marvel why one and all do not rally joyously to its support; namely, <u>The Church has a right to administer her internal ecclesiastical affairs independently, but under the general laws of the state</u>." There can be no inherent conflict between Church and state. Both are institutions which belong to God's divine plan for order, and that plan contains no contradictions. If that viewpoint could once be gotten across, then all controversy between the Church and state would doubtless be eliminated. There exists a party, however, which does not want this peace. It fears a free Church because of the moral force which such a Church represents. It is that party which we have to oppose with all of our resources.

228

XXV The Meaning and Value of the Church's Freedom. Reform

I have to stress again the importance of the idea
that the freedom of the Church is not merely something
which concerns the special interests of some priestly
caste. Rather, the Church's freedom is a vital and
holy concern of all Catholic Christians.

Freedom of the Catholic Church and the quest of
priests for more power are considered to be one and
the same by enemies of the Church. It is supposed
to be merely a question of whether a certain range
of powers will be exercised by secular officials or
by ecclesiastical ones. In other words, it is solely
a matter of ambition and striving for power. Catholics
who know their Church do not share this view at all;
they are convinced that their Church has certain
rights. Yet, they too do not appreciate fully the
significant implications of this question, and they
fail to sense what is the real heart of the matter.
It is urgent for us to convince our opponents that
we are not seeking freedom for the Church out of a
mere lust for power; but it is just as important that
we explain to Catholics how that freedom is in their
own best and most sacred interests. If our Catholics
once appreciate that, then they will not be so apathetic when the men, whom they themselves elect, abuse
their Church and make its life difficult. I shall
try to shed some light on what I am saying here.

One principle objective of the Church is the
filling of ecclesiastical positions according to the
teaching of the Church. Authority in the Church
passed from Christ to His Apostles and from there to
their successors and on to the priests who are ordained
and installed by them. That sums up pretty much the
whole origin and tradition of Church authority and,
as a matter of fact, the very constitution of the
Church. Subsequently it becomes the duty of any
bishop, who does not wish to be a traitor, to assert
that it is his bounden duty to exercise this right.
He is bound in conscience to do so. Accordingly, he
has to fight off any attempt by secular authorities

to make ecclesiastical appointments. Even if just
one ruler usurped the right to exercise the authority
which comes from Christ, by appointing one of his own
royal favorites to just one parish, the entire order
of the Church would be seriously undermined. Therefore, whenever a bishop defends this right, he does it
not because he thirsts for power, but because it is
his duty.

But there is another reason for his defending
the right. The whole well-being of the Church hinges
on the kind of men who are assigned to church positions.
It is true of any organization that it cannot survive
unless good men are appointed to office. What good
is a militia without good leaders; and what kind of
royal court can survive if it is populated by untrust-
worthy officials? The more dutifully a bishop wishes
to fulfill his duties before God and the Christian
people, the more diligent he must be in filling posts
in his diocese in a manner that is pleasing to God.
The exalted office of bishop is undermined and crippled if he does not have the right kind of priests
in the parishes under his jurisdiction. How enormously
important it is for the entire Catholic populace to
have the right priests in their parishes! What a
blow it is for a parish, what a danger to its vital
spiritual interests when a lukewarm priest, filled
with a worldly spirit, is at the head of it. There
is no absolutely foolproof means for assuring that
each position will be filled by only the worthiest
and best priest - something that the Church ardently
wishes. Often enough the bishop is capable of making mistakes in this area. Yet, the greatest possibility for doing the right thing exists if the
bishop is free to make appointments according to
rules and principles set down by the Church. The
prospects are worst when appointments depend upon
worldly opportunism and the caprice of shifting
political parties. Nothing has hurt the Church and
shaken her to her very foundations more than worldly
influence exercised in filling ecclesiastical positions from the top to the very bottom. If the state
has too much influence in this area, such influence,
as a practical matter, rests in the hands of public
officials, ministers, cabinets, privy councils, etc.

Even with the best of intentions these are not likely
to come up with the right man. If they are not favor-
ably disposed toward the Church, then their influence
in making appointments will work as a disease in the
very heart of the Church. Personal worthiness will
no longer be a criterion. Instead, all sorts of ulterior
considerations, craftiness, personal favoritism, political motivations, or even downright hostile motives
designed to damage the Church will become decisive.
What a blow to the real interest of the Catholic communities and of the Church! Has it not become simply
a question in some places whether the bishop or the
Freemasons will fill positions in most of the parishes,
and thus control the Church? What is to become of the
Church if her enemies are able to fill most of the important positions in the Church with men who are sympathetic to their own views, and if such men in such positions are then able to exercise a corrosive influence
upon the priesthood itself? None of the other liberties
which the Church might enjoy would be of any value so
long as the most important benefices are occupied not
by the worthiest priest but by false hirelings.

In this regard, the whole patronage system as it
has evolved over time, contrary to the real spirit of
the Church, represents a great calamity for the Church
and needs to be revised. Benefices as such will not
weaken the Church, but we had better take note of and
rectify the abuses in certain countries where these
are abused and become nothing more than objects of
patronage. In making appointments to benefice-parishes,
four rights have to be taken into account in the proper
order. The first is the right of Jesus Christ as the
originator and source of all authority, in the matter
of ecclesiastical offices; and this right requires that
every position is to be filled as Christ wishes it to
be filled. The second right is the right and the
obligation which the Church has to see to it that every
ecclesiastical position is filled in accordance with
the mandate which Christ gave. The third right is
the right of every parish community to have at its
head a pastor according to Christ's own heart, and
not a hireling. Finally, there is the right of the
patron to cooperate in this appointive process in such
a way as to recommend a priest for the Church who is
Christ-like. The right of patronage is filled with the

gravest responsibility in conscience. To see the patronage right merely as just another property right which one has at his disposal, and then to use it in a manner whereby the rights of Christ and the Faithful are gravely violated represents a horrible abuse. It then becomes the mere shadow of a right, and in fact a frightful injustice.

What great reforms are required in this area to bring the whole matter in line with what the Church stands for! What a boon it would be for the Church; what a blessing would spread throughout the Church if all of its servants from the Pope on down, including all bishops, all canons, all representatives of the bishops, all deans, and the all-important parish priests could be appointed freely as the spirit of the Church requires it, without any undue outside influence and in conformity with the wise and just laws which she has so painstakingly drawn up! That is the real issue summed up in one parcel. That is the reason why we have to battle tirelessly for this right. That is how critical the entire question is for every individual Catholic.

I could go on now and discuss in great detail all of the problems that are involved in the conflict between Church and state. I could point out how urgent and essential the right to train priests is for assuring the Church and the faithful genuine worthy and zealous priests. I could show how religious freedom is related to bolstering the entire Christian community in the pursuit of knowledge and in the way people conduct themselves in ordinary everyday living. But to attempt to develop these points would require time and space that we cannot afford here.

I simply have to conclude that if we battle for the freedom of the Church, we do so because we wish to emancipate the life of the Church from outside interference as much as this is possible. We wish to do so because only in this manner can we present this divine institution to the world in its true form, as Christ founded it and wished it to be. There can be no question of reform in the Church in the sense that we wish to change what Christ established. On the

232

other hand, it is our continuing responsibility to see
to it that the members of the Church, who are mere human
beings, become ever more holy. The more the enemies of
the Church exert themselves to assault the Church of
God, the more we have to see to it that we amend our
ways, do away with abuses in the Church, and overcome
apathy and selfishness. We have to conquer our own
weaknesses and become more Christ-like in an ardent
spirit of self-sacrifice. Then those enemies of the
Church who are well-intentioned will come to understand
that whatever evil they perceive does not represent
the Church, but the spiritual poverty of us who are
its members. They will come to realize that other
evils which they attributed to the Church were not,
in fact, the fault of the Church, but that the Church
itself, in her teachings and in her commandments, is
all-beautiful, all-glorious, all-true, all-God-like
and worthy of their highest respect.

XXVI <u>Freedom, in the Church. Church and Authority</u>

Two objections are likely to be made regarding the issues we have raised thus far. One might say: "You talk about freedom of thought, the right to make up one's own mind, free pursuit of truth. You Catholics are in no position to speak about such freedoms. You have to believe what the Church orders you to believe; in fact, you have to accept what bishops and priests tell you. Whether your reason concurs with what is told to you or not, you have to believe it. You are bound by the authority of your Church as by a chain. While science progresses rapidly from one discovery to the next, you Catholics remain standing still, unable to move with the current. You may not think. You may only obey. Whatever the priests may yet come up with, you will simply have to accept."

The second objection that could be raised would sound like this: "You speak of autonomy, but you have no right to exercise autonomy. That is our demand, not yours. We urge autonomous action by our people, and we demand it for everyone; you require it only for priests. That is not autonomy and self-determination, but rather tutelage and domination by priests."

To grasp the basic untruth of such claims and to be able to refute them intelligently, we have to understand the nature of ecclesiastical authority and also what the thinking is of people who raise such objections.

1) There is a twofold authority in the Church. There is the teaching authority and also the governing authority. The latter we call pastoral authority. The Church's authority comes to bear on the two basic faculties of the soul. The magisterium comes to bear on the reasoning faculty; and the governing authority has to do with the will, in that it involves the practice of Christian virtues.

2) Both kinds of authority are held within strict limits. The teaching authority of the Church is limited to the teaching of Christ and His Apostles. Christ did

235

not speak out about all areas of human knowledge and
learning. He confined Himself to a definite range of
basic truths regarding especially man's relationship
to God, and His teaching was meant to offer guidance
for all aspects of man's journey through time. The
Apostles carried the gospel to the whole world, and
the basic truths of Christianity are summed up in
their essence in the twelve articles of the Apostles'
Creed. It is these twelve articles which still represent, according to all Catholic catechisms, the essence of what the Christian, in obedience to the
magisterium, has to believe. Everything else in
whatever area of human knowledge is left to him to
research as freely as he wishes.

The same holds true for the governing authority
of the Church. It has its definite purpose and limits
contained\in the directions given by Jesus Christ.
It has to do mainly with upholding the structure of
the Church itself as Christ established it, with dis-
pensing the Sacraments, and with seeing to it that its
members fulfill the obligations which a Christian life
calls for. The whole natural order of things is independent of the Church's governing authority; and so
far as every scientific effort in this area is concerned, the principle which obtains in the Church is
that no ecclesiastical authority, no matter how high
up, can dispense from the restrictions imposed by
natural and Divine law. 35

3) The essence of this authority is of such a
nature that it operates through spiritual means. It
directs itself to man's reason and to his free will
and persuades these two faculties of the soul to submit willingly to it, thus giving honor to God who has
endowed man with reason and will.

4) The recognition of any authority by man, as
we noted earlier, presupposes the existence of a supernatural order, a truth and a law, which transcends the
human spirit and the human will. This means that there
exists a personal God in whose very essence eternal
truth and the eternal law abide.

The recognition of authority presupposes in particular: 1. The Divinity of Jesus Christ; 2. The establishment of a church by Christ; 3. The existence

236

of authority in that church as it was placed there by Christ, enabling it to teach and to govern with the promise that the Church could not err in the exercise of its teaching authority.

If these prerequisites are in order, then the submission of the intellect and the will constitutes the first prompting of reason and of a sense of duty; and it is the proper and most noble action of which man, the free spirit, is capable. Indeed, it is his foremost obligation. The rejection of such authority then constitutes irrational human behavior, and it is deserving of punishment because it is an affront to the Lord of Heaven and Earth, an affront which is more unreasonable and deranged than if the dust of the earth were to rise up and try to demolish the order of the universe.

5) These prerequisities form a vital part of the deepest inner conviction of us Catholics. It is on them that we base our Faith and our obedience to the authority of the Church. [36]

We believe in the divinity of Jesus Christ and invoke Him as the Apostle Thomas did: "My Lord and my God! " (John 20:28) We believe that He who established the order of the universe also established an order in the Church; we believe that He entrusted His teachings and authority to this Church; we believe that He gave to her the command to propagate His teaching to all mankind, and to administer His Sacraments and require that His faithful live up to His commandments. Even though human beings, the Apostles and their successors, exercise that authority, we Catholics do not regard them as possessing some kind of arbitrary power with regard to that authority. They merely bear the Ark of the Covenant on their shoulders, but that does not mean that the Ark is the work of their hands. It is the work of God. Neither are the commandments of God in the Ark their word or their law. The word that they bear is something which they too have to accept and believe. The law which they promulgate is the same law to which they also have to render complete obedience. It is because we think as we do and because we are so totally convinced of these truths

237

that we submit to the teaching and governing authority of the Church with the deepest inner joy and in complete freedom. But we do not stop there. The Church which teaches us that the authority which She exercises is reasonable also urges us to constantly use our reason and develop it to the utmost. Thereby the depth and joy of our inner conviction continues to grow, because the more we probe into history, into nature, and into the recesses of our souls, the more we recognize how really Divine our Faith is. If truth, the highest good of mankind in so many ways, remains a locked temple, then the teachings of their Church are for Catholics the real keys which gain for them access to that temple which contains all true knowledge and, therefore, real peace and the greatest happiness for their soul. It is in those teachings that they eventually find God for whom their souls were created - the same God who remains for the world, as St. Paul said, the unknown God (Acts 17:23). [37]

6) The body of the Catholic truth provides irrefutable proof for such conviction and for its position, to the satisfaction of anyone who does not deliberately shut his eyes to it. It is a body of truth that is unique in world history, and there is nothing that can be compared to it. It is not the product of some specific school of thought, of one nation, of one epoch, or of one class of mankind. It is in the true sense a universal body of truth as the Church is a universal Church. It has already spanned 1800 years and penetrated all parts of the world. It has gained the adherence, over all of these centuries and in all of these nations and places, of an unnumbered host of the holiest and worthiest men who were equipped with all kinds of human knowledge and with the wisdom of the ages. These men all agreed as with one voice and with joyous confiction that there was no contradiction between their own intellects and wills and the twofold authority of the Church. On the contrary, they all testify that the more joyfully they submitted to the eternal truths and laws entrusted to the Church, the more sure they were as they proceeded to go on discovering other truths one after the other. [38]

7) The merits of our point of view as presented here may very well be contested by our enemies. All of

the weapons in the arsenal of modern science can be brought to bear against the foundations of our Faith. Men exert themselves to find secrets in the bosom of nature, in the darkest recesses of the human soul, and in the course of world history, which will refute the utter reasonableness of our religious position. The Church is battle-hardened and accustomed to such combat. She does not shy away from any conflict, least of all is She afraid of those brazen scoffers who began their work under the cross where they derided the Lord of our Church. Nor does the Church fear their successors in our own time who are just as brazen in their mockery of the Church. The former assaulted the Head; the latter assault the Body!

Accordingly, it is preposterous for certain of our enemies to spread the word in our time that the Catholics are barred from free, scientific research as if our Faith stood opposed to reason. That is irresponsible, nonsensical, vicious prattle which can only be prompted by blind prejudice and which defies all reason as well as history. Such nonsense is broadcast now not only by the bulk of the German press, but even in the assemblies of various corporate groups; for example, we witnessed it recently in the chamber proceedings in Wuerttemberg. Such conduct represents gross injustice and an insult to the Catholic Church.

8) The viewpoint which gives rise to such affronts is the simple denial of any supernatural order and consequently of any kind of legitimate authority. Such a position is not one which proceeds from reason. It is totally unreasonable in its premises. Its notion of reason stems naturally from an absolutely unlimited subjectivism. The notion of self-government is seen only in the sense of an absolute popular sovereignty, so that free recognition of a higher order or of a higher law appears as the absence of liberty. It is an opinion which stands contradicted in all areas of human knowledge. One note must fall in line with another or else there can be no harmony. One star must follow its course among the other stars or else there will be chaos in outer space. Each member of the body

239

must perform its own proper function or else the body
cannot remain sound. Only the human intellect and
will are somehow supposed to be able to ignore the
need to submit freely to an order established by God,
without destroying real freedom of thought and action!
Thus, any conception of reasonable authority has been
lost on many persons, and freedom to them means simply
the abuse of freedom - a kind of reasoning and use of
the will that have gone beserk because of insane subjectivism.

    9) In any case, this viewpoint carries with it
its own destruction. Man is totally dependent upon
God for his existence and therefore subject to authority. He cannot for long deny God and authority without penalty. The son mentioned in the gospels, who
will not remain subject to his father, does not thereby
gain his freedom. Instead he falls into slavery and
ends up tending swine. That is the grim alternative
which God has proposed to man. Either we serve God
and recognize the authority which He has set up, in
which case we enjoy the freedom of the children of
God, or else we will become subject to ephemeral,
constantly shifting human authority and eventually
to lies and wickedness.

XXVII Church and State: Union and Separation

The quest for the freedom of the Church is often referred to as separation of church and state. Used in one sense, this concept gives no cause for concern, since it comes to grips with and puts to an end some of the practices which have obscured the real difference in the functions of church and state. So far as a separation in the essential relationship between church and state is concerned, the Catholic cannot even consider it. Predictably, our enemies have seized upon the ambiguity in this term. They have made wrong use of it the only use; and they have drawn conclusions which are not only totally unjustified but even completely detrimental to both Church and state. To the Church's demands for its freedom, these people answer: Good, we'll separate Church from the state as you demand and give the Church its freedom. But then the state must divorce itself completely from the Church and leave the Church completely to its own resources. This requires, among other things, that the schools too will have to be separated from the Church and made entirely into state institutions. Such proposals are then activated as though they had to follow as logical consequences of the separation of Church and state. Regretably, Catholics too have allowed themselves to be misled by such tactics. A brief examination of the matter will clarify it and show how untrue and deceptive these supposedly "logical" consequences are.

The relationship of Church and state does not have to do with whether state rather than Church officials will manage ecclesiastical affairs. There is an entirely different and deeper meaning. Autonomy of the Church has nothing at all to do with separation of Church and state. If we demand of the absolutist state authority that it restore certain rights to the family, the community, the corporation, so that these are able to operate in their proper spheres without interference, it doesn't occur to anyone to call that a separation of the family, of the community, of the corporation from the state, and to conclude that the state has divorced itself completely from these institutions. Church and state because of their essence

cannot be completely separated, because in God's overall plan for order, they belong together. They are
necessary supports for each other, and they ought
therefore to cooperate in serving God's purposes to
promote the salvation of mankind. It is a totally
superficial way of looking at the relationship between
Church and state to regard as separation of Church and
state the consignment of a few minor rights to the
Church, which of their very nature belong to her in
any case. That is a hollow play on words used to deceive people and as a front for actions which are
bound to harm both the Church and the state. As a
marriage is not separated because the husband does
what a man ought to do and the wife does what she
ought to do, so Church and state are not separated
when Church and state tend to their own proper functions. If the preservation of the liberties which
the Church seeks is separation, then it is a separation which necessarily leads to unity. It is our
deepest conviction that by the safeguarding of their
proper autonomies, Church and state are not separated;
rather they are truly and firmly united.

The Church can and may not separate itself from
the state, because the Church cannot separate itself
from anything which comes from God. She has to respect the state as a Divine arrangement for helping
mankind reach its proper destiny. She has to require
of her members that they conform to the demands of
the state insofar as these conform to the Divine plan.
She must use all of the spiritual resources at her
command to foster the welfare of the state, rejoice
in the orderly conduct of the state's business, and
griev when the state's essential processes are somehow
disrupted. Finally, she must serve notice to one and
all that whoever opposes temporal authority opposes
God and merits condemnation. (Romans 13:2)

At the same time, the state authority cannot
separate itself from the Church without failing in
its own essential duties. The state must safeguard
the rights of the Church just as it has to protect
the right of all who are in its care. The preservation of justice is the God-given mission of the state,
and justice must be preserved for all concerned. The

state has an obligation to look upon the Church with
benevolent concern and support her in accomplishing
her tasks. This is a part of the state's responsibilities.
These responsibilities come from God and therefore
they stem from the very nature of the state's authority.

The state must see to it that the Church's rights
are safeguarded not merely because God demands this,
but because the state's own well-being requires it.
If it separates itself from the Church and from the
religious convictions of its subjects, it separates
itself from God and thereby destroys its own foundation.

Finally, the state is obligated to protect these
rights and to support the Church on behalf of its own
citizens. They have a right to expect that the state
will respect their religious convictions, and to the
protection and support of their ecclesiastical society.
The state is not some arbitrary abstraction which floats
on clouds but rather a reality determined according to
the needs of the people who make it up. Therefore, to
separate it from their highest interests represents
delinquency to duty on the part of state authority.

What I have said here regarding the obligation of
the state to protect the rights of the Church and to
support it, is meant to apply not only to the Catholic
Church. It applies to any religious society once it is
recognized as such by the state, provided only that such
a society upholds the requirements of natural morality
and honors the one true God, as we discussed earlier.

That opinion regarding the relationship of church
and state, which goes contrary to all sound thinking
by suggesting that the state could separate itself
from the Church, and have the latter go completely on
its own without protection of its rights and without
any assistance, is one that is widely propagated by
a part of the press and by certain popular spokesmen.
It is therefore urgent that we rise up in opposition
to it and remind the public authorities of their responsibilities toward religion and to their constituents.

In the eighth chapter of his work, referred to
earlier, Guizot had some pertinent things to say which
deserve our careful attention.

243

XXVIII   Freedom of the Home and the Family

The social nature of man is rooted ultimately in man's relation to God. It is from that basic relationship that other human relationships originate. Since man is totally dependent on God, God has also made his life and his full development dependent in various ways upon his relationship to other men and to the rest of God's creation. Man cannot exist entirely on his own, because he does not derive his life from himself; and the many kinds of social intercourse he has with others ought to make him ever mindful that the origin of his existence lies elsewhere than in himself. He is constantly and everywhere dependent upon others because he is totally and ultimately dependent upon God.

The highest form of social relationship, however implies a well-ordered and proper love. That is why our Savior says: "Thou shalt love the Lord thy God with thy whole heart and with thy whole soul and thy whole mind. This is the greatest of the commandments, and the first. And the second, its like, is this, Thou shalt love thy neighbor as thyself. On these commandments, all the law and the prophets depend." (Matt. 22: 37-41). Love ought to be the bond which unites God and men - that love that is founded on truth, as Christ has taught it in its fullness. And that love ought to reflect itself in all relationships and unions that men form among themselves. All other relationships ought to be merely the reflection of that one highest relationship and bear this Divine imprint.

The first relationship which a man becomes involved in is the one from which he derives his very life, the family. It represents the first and most necessary link in the chain of those remarkable organisms which condition a man's life. The family is therefore an especially reliable copy of the relation which man has to God. God uses one and the same word to express his relationship to man and as the name for the head of the family. God wishes to be the Father of all mankind; and as His representative in the family, He intends that the head of the family shall bear His own name. That ought to convince us of the high dignity and meaning of the family.

We have already seen what importance our German ancestors placed on the family. The condition in which the family found itself, reflected best of all the contrast between the kind of paganism which was hurtled to its own destruction by moral corruption, and that paganism which was responsive to the light of Christianity and was destined to absorb all of its many blessings. Besides, the family is the first and most important training institute. It represents the school that was founded by God Himself, and it is therefore infinitely more important than all other schools founded by men. The good and the bad seeds which family life inculcates in the souls of its children sprout eventually and bear good or bad fruit accordingly. It is in the family that the child grows up in both body and soul, and that is why the good and bad influence which it derives from the family grows up with it. Once the period of growth has ended, all further influences are of a more superficial nature.

Finally, the family too exists "by the grace of God," and it contains an authority which comes from God. Scripture refers to the family frequently, and God placed the obligation toward parents first among His commandments dealing with man's relations to men. Thus the family along with Church and state is the third society which has an order and an authority that were established by God Himself.

The freedom of the home and the family consists, according to the basic principle which we established for all freedom, in the family's right to carry on its affairs and to guide and order itself without outside interference. In particular, the family implies the right that paternal authority may operate freely according to its own proper nature. Here again, it is understood that such authority must not be regarded as unlimited. It may not transgress other rights, whether we are talking about the rights of the Church or of the state or of the children themselves. In its own proper sphere, however, paternal authority is sacred and inviolable and any incursion against it is a grave violation of the order intended by God.

Absolutism, as a matter of fact, did not spare the family either. As it naturally seeks to guide and rule everything, it has also made incursions into the home where the rights of parents and paternal authority have suffered. We refer especially to those requirements of state authority regarding the raising of children, and to mixed marriages, where the wishes of parents are overridden even when the parents are in full agreement. Above all, the rights of parents are deeply injured and impeded where public schools are established which violate the conscience and religious convictions of parents, especially where compulsory schooling goes along with the arrangement. Since we are going to deal in some detail with this problem later on, we will leave the matter be for now.

It is all the more important for us to make it our task to speak on behalf of the freedom of the home and paternal authority, with determination and perseverance, the more hostile the spirit of the age shows itself to be against home and family. That is the direction in which our age is heading. The spirit of our time is contemptuous of all organic society and therefore of the family. It does not want true society, it wants a mechanism. It dissolves all natural relationships so that it will be confronted only by a mass of isolated individuals. When we rise to the defense of the home and the family, we are representing right reason, the most hallowed traditions of our German nation, the kinds of society that have received all of Christianity's blessings, and one of the most cherished treasures of all of humanity.

247

XXIX Marriage: Its Indissolubility - Civil Marriage

As the family is the natural foundation of the Church and the state, so marriage is the foundation of the family. Everything which strengthens and fortifies the marriage also fortifies and strengthens the family and the home. Everything which weakens and disrupts marriage, weakens and disrupts the home and the family.

Among the ancient Germanic tribes, their solid family life rested upon their lofty conception of marriage. They held marriage and the family in basically the same high respect which God originally intended. Polygamy was practically unknown among them, and they held the indissolubility of marriage in such high regard that a woman did not contract a second marriage even after the death of her husband.

It was left to Christianity, however, to restore marriage to the full dignity which God had intended for it, and to safeguard it against all evil tendencies and passions of which the human heart is capable. Nothing is conceivable which is more noble than marriage as the Church regards it, and there is nothing on earth more salutary for mankind than a family based on the Church's conception of marriage. If all marriages were sealed in the true Christian spirit and as the Church wishes, and if Christian principles informed them and prevailed in marriages, by that fact alone much of the misery which afflicts mankind in this world could be avoided. The formation and perfection of society must take place from below, not from above. To build a house, one must begin with the foundation, and the foundation of the child begins with the first principles of its spiritual development. The foundation of order in the world is Christian marriage, something that is being so much denied at present. People are forgetting the very basis of true welfare in the mistaken belief that some kind of world politics can substitute for it. Thus we have people who are trying to run the state and the world even while they look with disdain on marriage and contemn the laws of correct family living!

The two principal bases on which Christian marriage rests are the unity of man and wife and the indissolubility of the marriage bond. How indissolubility in particular is essential to the fulfillment of the natural function of marriage is clear from the purpose of marriage, to provide a means for the greatest possible fulfillment of the needs which man encounters in his youth. It can only accomplish that purpose properly if it is indissoluble. It is not only in his later life that man is not only threatened by the failings of his fellow man. Then the police and the courts offer him some protection. He is far more vulnerable to the horrible passions and vices in the earliest years of his youth before he reaches the point where he is ready to leave his family and be on his own. What terrible influences he is subject to at that time of his life! If I remain silent about the most unspeakable abuses - even though God will judge them all - how much evil befalls countless numbers of children at the hands of parents who cannot keep their vices in check. Only when marriage is held to be sacred with all evil passions kept under control, and where the parents themselves cultivate a proper disposition and hold to the indissolubility of marriage will a family life be possible which conforms to what God intended. And here I would like to point out that although Protestant teaching permits divorce, all truly Christian Protestant marriage partners still lean toward the notion of indissolubility, and they conduct their lives as though marriage for them is permanent.

As soon as divorce becomes easier, marriage becomes a battleground for evil passions at the expense of sound family living and especially at the expense of the poor children. There is talk of how inhumane it is to force two people to stay together once love between them is gone. What is forgotten is the terrible inhumanity that is practiced toward the children when we think only of the caprices of their parents, and how we imperil this best of all institutions by surrendering our high aspirations for it because of the unfortunate few exceptions who have only themselves to blame. God has made the raising of children part and parcel of marriage. Therefore those parents

250

who do not wish to thwart the natural purpose of marriage are bound by nature, if nothing else, to observe certain conditions as prerequisite to marriage, if they intend to do what is right by their children.

The dissolubility of marriage and civil marriage do not add up to the same thing. In France where dissolubility was abolished in 1829, civil marriage exists side by side with indissolubility. Protestant Germany has no civil marriage, but it has dissolubility. Nevertheless, the two phenomena are closely related. The clamor for civil marriages has as its objective to make it possible for frivolous and otherwise weak Catholics to divorce, and to attempt new marriages in contravention to the laws of their Church and the teachings of their Faith. Beyond that it also serves to de-Christianize marriage and therefore the family by regarding these as mere civil institutions. I am well aware that an appeal is made to freedom of conscience to support this demand. Nevertheless, there is obviously no better way for the state to observe freedom of conscience than by allowing every man to act according to the laws of his religion and his Church in matters relating to marriage - the property rights of marriage partners excepted, and these are not an issue here. So long as a person belongs to a Church, he cannot complain if he is judged according to the principles of the creed which he himself professes. To support the irresponsible in gross violation of the most sacred laws of their Church cannot be regarded as the function of the state.

What we would also like to call special attention to is the fact that the call for civil marriage stands opposed to the spirit and will of our German people. Even before marriage was Christian, our people regarded it as something sacred; and the purity and solidarity of German family life was traceable to their high regard for marriage. Christianity served to sanctify and bolster that conception of marriage all the more. That is how matters remained down through the centuries. Even the religious revolt did not change things. The Protestants stayed by the religious character of marriage. That is how matters

251

still are today. The people do not want civil marriage.
As opposed to the vast majority of the German people,
those who represent the real backbone of our nation,
it is an infinitesmal minority of our urban population
who concur with this adventitious movement for civil
marriage; and these do so more out of prejudice and
the urge to follow fads than out of clear insight and
deep conviction. Here we have another indication of
how out of touch false liberalism is with the real
German people, how little it knows of their real thinking, and how it ignores their convictions.

The movement for introducing civil marriage seems
to me, therefore, to be one of the most unhappy currents of our time, which is calculated to wreak havoc
on society. I consider it the obligation of all
Catholics to rise up unanimously in the name of all
that is German and Christian to fight against it!

XXX Home - State - Church

1) The home, the state, and the Church are the three institutions in which a man begins life here on earth, lives all of his life, and finally dies. They are divine institutions which means, they are established by God. Of their essence they are independent of the human will in the sense that man cannot achieve his proper destiny outside of them.

2) Since the three institutions are from God, they cannot be in essential contradiction to each other.

3) The essence of these three institutions is determined by God, partly in the natural order of things as established by God, and partly in His supernatural revelation.

4) Their particular form and arrangement are partly left up to the will and determination of men who are endowed with reason and freedom for that purpose.

5) These human arrangements will vary according to time and place, and that is good and proper so long as they are essentially in order. This means that they must be in harmony with the Divine order in nature and with the express will of God.

6) So that they will not go beyond these bounds, we must never lose sight of the fact, in ordering each of these relationships, that it is not the only relationship among men, but that men are also involved in the other two sets of relationships.

7) Consequently, the particular arrangement of any of these societies must never be such as to interfere with the proper spheres of the other two; nor may there be any room for arbitrariness.

8) Instead, the three spheres must be clearly divided with definite agreement by means of laws and ordinances which show how far each extends in its rights and jurisdiction, and to what extent each

must recognize and respect the rights and competence of the others.

9) Nevertheless this demarcation ought to represent a free, respectful, trusting unity and not a nagging, reluctant affair fraught with anxiety and mistrust. It ought to involve a recognition of the indispensable role of each and of the common interest shared among them, and a readiness to assist each where necessary so that it can serve its proper purpose.

10) A total separation among them is simply inconceivable, as though the Church could fail to exert its influence on its members to get them to fulfill those obligations to the state and the family which God Himself has imposed; or as if the state could manage its affairs and pass laws which disregard the domestic interests or the religious perceptions and needs of its citizens; or as though the family could go on its way, oblivious to the laws of the state or the mandates of religion. I have taken these words from a valuable little book written by that blessed man Beckedorff in 1849. [39] I am pleased to be able to pay my respect here to this extraordinary man. There is no need to add anything, since he explained the relationship of these three Divine institutions on which the welfare of mankind depends in an inimitable and valid manner.

254

XXXI School, Freedom of Instruction, Its Scope and Conditions

No question is more important than the one dealing with the proper structuring of the schools, and none is less well understood by a large majority of our people. That is the unhappy consequence of centralization and dominance from the top which has deprived people of a proper insight and a clear understanding of their most important concerns. Our generation has grown accustomed to resigning itself to the requirements of school authorities in a sheeplike manner as though these represented the workings of some unescapable destiny. The more the best people and those with the most legitimate interest at stake, especially the parents, get out of the habit of exerting influence on the schools, the more the parties and factions and vested interests seize influence and try to make them serve their own interests. If we look closely at those who are currently taking public positions regarding the school problem and who are trying to bring about a new organization of the entire educational system by the state, we note that it is not the parents who are making the most noise about how children ought to be raised and trained. Rather it is the political parties, the exponents of abstract theories of education, and certain educators who are hostile to religion, who are making their voices heard and bringing their influence to bear. To the three institutions: the home, the state, the Church, they try to juxtapose respectively, the state, the Church, and the school. Schools, they tell us, have to be independent and exclusively state institutions; and the Church has to be separated from the state as well as from the schools.

In opposition to such a position, it is one of the most urgent needs of our time that Catholics, and above all the Catholic press should get a clear picture of what is at stake here regarding the school issue, and then they ought to work deliberately and in unison for a correct program. Above all, it is important to inform the parents of what their rights

255

and obligations are regarding the schools and to rally them against the intentions to which we have referred. They must be made to realize once again that there are no more sacred rights and obligations on this earth than those which they themselves have in the matter of schools for their children. It must be brought home to them how they jeopardize the welfare of their children in the worst way possible if they do not insist upon their rights in the way the school system is set up and operates.

We shall dwell first on the great danger that is involved when things move in the direction in which they are now moving. Then we shall indicate what the proper principles are relating to the organization of our schools.

The ancient pagans did not have elementary or public schools as we have them now. They had the most unconditional freedom to teach and to learn. Anyone who wanted to learn or to have members of his family taught was free to seek out any teacher he pleased. Beyond that there were also a few public institutions of higher learning which were more or less state-controlled.

Among the German peoples, the Church became the mother and foundress of schools. Wherever the Church established herself, she founded schools of all kinds and attracted children from all classes of people to herself to cultivate them and give them a better education. Compulsory schooling and taxation to support the schools were unknown in the Christo-Germanic age. Educational facilities were developed voluntarily, and parents were invited to send their children if they so wished and, one might add that the results were spectacular. In particular, excellent schools blossomed wherever there were monasteries. No sooner had the monks set foot in the most God-forsaken outposts and set up their huts, but that large groups of selected youngsters from among the German tribes flocked around them to learn what wisdom and knowledge they had to offer. A hundred years after the monks reached Reichenau, where no man could live until then, they had a monastery where 500 youngsters from all of the various Allemanae tribes were committed to a 16 year period of study. [40] The same thing was occurring all over. The monks tilled the soil with one hand and cleared the forests and cultivated every possible art; and with the other hand they cultivated the souls of our ancestors by planting the heavenly seed of Christendom in this fertile soil! By the end of the Middle Ages countless schools of every kind were widespread in areas which Christianity had first found totally without any kind of culture. Thus, a vast riches of educational facilities had been built up. The universities too are originally daughters of the Church; and the Church had nurtured such a cultural interest in that era that, for example, at the University of Bologna there were 10,000 students. At the same time during the time of Henry III, 30,000 students were enrolled at Oxford. [41]

Even after the Reformation, the same situation prevailed. Schools were regarded in the Peace of Westphalia as <u>annexum exercitu religionis</u>, i.e., as a necessary adjunct to the free exercise of religion. Even though the Church did, in fact, establish most of the schools, that did not really mean that only the Church had the right to found schools. The civil authorities also cooperated as, for example, by chartering universities; and basically, there was far more freedom to learn and teach. Yet, one did not have to resort to state authority to any large degree because of the presence of so many Church schools. On the other hand, no one would have considered the possibility of a legitimate Church that did not have the right to operate schools. That was true of Protestants as well as Catholics.

Once state absolutism reared its head, in particular since the 18th century, the viewpoint came to prevail more and more that the state ought to guide and regulate the entire educational process. Eventually when the old German Reich collapsed and the idea of an all-powerful state reached its crest, it was simply taken for granted that state authority was to arrogate to itself the exclusive right to determine educational policy and to establish schools. That principle could not be brought to bear completely in the area of elementary schools to which parents still had a very close relationship, and where church schools were most prevalent. The maxims of the modern state still stood in open and apparent conflict with the force of reality and the facts of life, try as one may to conceal that reality and the facts of life in every way possible. On the other hand, in the middle and higher schools the state has assumed complete authority, and the educational ministry in each state now dominated the entire educational program of the land, even though, in theory, the home and the Church were still to be taken into account.

Today even that consideration is to be swept aside, and the school is to become purely a state institution without any regard to home and Church. Liberal absolutism wants to purify and complete the work which the absolute monarchies began. Only the state may teach, or, since the state is only a concept, the person who represents it - the minister of education - who must always be an educationist. Educationists have to exercise a monopoly over instruction, training, and all of education. Thus, it is no longer up to the parents to determine how their children will be trained and educated. The teachers alone have this responsibility, and they no longer need to worry about the wishes of parents. The latter have only the responsibility to support their children and to pay the salaries of the teachers. The rest is left to the highly organized teacher caste which will then decide how children are to be brought up.

Such a system - now on the verge of realization - may well become a fact in the years just ahead, when at a given signal in the state assemblies it will be decreed to be an absolute requirement for culture and enlightenment in any truly modern state. It represents absolutism of the ghastliest and most damaging sort.

Even the present situation is far more harmful and unbearable than is widely recognized, and it

constitutes a severe infringement of parental rights
and also of the rights of the Church. It is already
discernible how the two camps are being formed into
which men are to be divided. There are those who are
under the influence of the family and who are still
predominantly Christian. Then there are those who
have been subject to the influence of the middle and
upper schools and who have already largely fallen prey
to modern unbelief. The family is still basically
Christian, and the home is still largely operating
on Christian principles. So long as the children are
at home, they are still influenced by ennobling Christian thoughts, sentiments, and practices. Even the
man who goes along with unChristian tendencies while
he is out in everyday life, when he returns home subjects himself for the most part, to Christian principles, and he demands of his family that they live
up to them. This is an undercurrent that still holds
society together, even though it is now in serious
trouble. Public life is already predominantly un-
Christian, and unbelieving, something for which our
school system is to blame. We may state it as a
principle that the more people receive their formative influence in the home, the more Christian they
are; and the more years they spend in the school
system, the more unChristian they become. Public
life today is dominated by the press, and the press
is the product of the modern school system. Even
in the year 1848 it was noted that a great percentage
of the young people who were later hunted down with
swords and torches were only doing the things which
their teachers, supported by the state and paid for
by their poor parents, had taught them. The only
difference between them and their teachers was that
they were more forthright and courageous. They
carried their false convictions not merely in their
notebooks, but in their hearts. Many parents are
now in the position where they may be certain that
after their children leave home and attend the upper schools, they will inevitably lose their Faith.
Even now the schools are so contrary to the home
and to the Church that one can find whole regions
where scarcely any teachers in the middle and upper
schools still believe in the divinity of Christ.
It seems that it would have been the first

responsibility of the public authorities, who control education, to fashion the schools not according to their own philosophy, but in line with the consciences of the parents for whose children the schools are, after all set up. But that is not what happened as a rule, and therein we have a grievous violation of parental rights.

Now, however, we find this program being brought to its full realization. The school is to be divorced in principle from the home and from the consciences of parents, and also from the Church. From now on the shifting opinions that happen to prevail at any given time among school officials will be decisive in the training and education of our children. If there has ever been a cause for common concern, it is this new educational policy with which we now stand face to face. Every Catholic home ought to receive a Catholic paper each day, which thoroughly explains this issue, so that our parents who love their children dearly will be alerted to what is going on and kept aware of their parental obligations. Then they will assert, in the name of parental rights, their authority to have the final word in the education of their children. If wild animals defend their young against hostile attacks, how much more ought our Christian parents watch over the souls of their children which God has entrusted to their care first and foremost, and protect them against the organized forces of unbelief which are running riot with our school system.

We have thus far described the condition of our schools and the dangers that they pose for us at the present time. Let us turn now to the principles of education that we believe correspond to right reason and to what our Church teaches.

1) The three great institutions, the home, the state, and the Church are at one and the same time formative factors for all men. Each contributes in its own way to man's character formation. The state has a great influence not merely insofar as it conditions a man for his civil and political life, but

because in a far more general way it is of the essence of the state's responsibilities to promote a peaceful setting and to assure justice, both of which have an unmeasurable influence on people.

2) The school, however, is an indispensable means to fulfill the cultural function not only for the sake of the home, but also for the state and for the Church. He who tries to exclude one or the other of these three institutions from the school prevents any of them from fulfilling its divinely appointed role. The school is not an institution that operates independently of the home, the state, or the Church. Rather it is a dependent helpmate for each of these. That, essentially, is the position of the school assigned to it by nature and by religion; and that gives the lie to contemporary currents which are bent on depicting the school as independent of the home and of the Church. The home, the state, and the Church all require schools which correspond to their own needs. They may not, without gross injustice, be denied the cooperation of the school.

3) F. J. Stahl lists the following as the special rights of state authority: [42]

"a) The right to demand a certain level of education for all of its citizens, notably, elementary schooling, and the right to prescribe accordingly that all children must either attend a public elementary school or receive equivalent training elsewhere.

"b) For all who wish to enter teaching as an occupation - not merely to supplement what a father is doing, as a private tutor - the state may require certain, definite moral qualities and also certain public tests and proofs of ability to determine whether they are generally qualified to serve as school teachers.

"c) The right to require of those who wish to serve as state officials, practice medicine, law, etc., that they attend public institutions (secondary schools and universities)"

261

The last mentioned right of the state exists
without a doubt but it does not flow from principles
which the authorities develop, not always too clearly.
Dr. Stahl, in the course of his discussions, adds
the restriction that public institutions ought not
to cause a conflict with the consciences of the
parents, since it is an inviolable paternal right not
to have to entrust the son to a school which goes
against the religious convictions of the father. We
concur fully with this view, but we believe that the
principle only makes sense if the father, in the
event of a conflict in conscience with the public institutions, is in a position to secure the required
education for his child in some other manner. If
that is not the case, then he is not in a position
to exercise legitimate paternal authority. Only on
those conditions can we recognize the right of the
civil authorities to require a certain program of
education for the various professions and to determine by examinations whether the candidates have fulfilled the requirements. Any use of compulsion regarding the manner of achieving the required level of
competence would be totally unjustified.

So far as the other two rights of the state outlined by Dr. Stahl are concerned, we agree fully with
what he says.

The first has to do with the state's authority
to mandate a certain level of schooling. It is true
that the Church has always sought to bring about compulsory education through an appeal to the consciences
of parents, in a manner which is in keeping with true
liberty - in this case - the freedom of the home.
The Church never introduced compulsory education by
the use of exterior force, although she never stated
in so many words that one may not operate in this
manner. The introduction of compulsory schooling
backed by exterior force has therefore always encountered considerable opposition among Catholics
where the notion of personal liberty was well entrenched. Nor would our Germanic ancestors have
taken kindly to compulsion in this matter. Though
there are many, therefore, who do not accept the
right of the state to forcefully compel schooling,

we cannot share their view. We feel, rather that the state has an inherent right to mandate a certain minimum level of elementary education for all of its citizens. We hold also that the state is entitled to require that parents, who cannot have recourse to an alternative means of securing this education for their children, must use the public schools. That is of course, provided that such schools do not conflict with the religious convictions and consciences of the father of the family.

The second right too, properly belongs to the state authority in a nation where there are several religious creeds. Where there is a state-established Church, the state must have the assurance that nothing will be taught in schools operated by the Church which will in any way endanger the state. Where a state recognizes various religious creeds, the state must have the right of overall jurisdiction. The limits of such jurisdiction, however, stem from the nature of state authority itself. The state must have the right, in such cases, to assure itself that nothing is taught in the schools which goes counter to natural morality or homage to the one true God. It may also see to it that the teachers are capable of providing the generally mandated level of schooling.

4) Even though we cannot subscribe to unconditional academic freedom in states where all creeds are treated on an equal basis, and though we cheerfully and totally accept the state's right to supervise education, we have to defend staunchly conditional academic freedom as something which goes along with freedom of conscience, the rights of parental authority, and true scientific inquiry. Whoever will guarantee to the state that they will not disregard morality and fear of the Lord in the schools, and that the teachers who are employed in providing the minimum mandated education will have respect for the demands of morality and religion, such a person has a full, unconditional right to establish a school for his own children or for the children of parents who want to entrust their youngsters to him for their education. Only then can there be talk of real academic freedom. State monopolized learning, as

despotic liberalism tries to introduce it, is no academic freedom but the education of caste and class, according to the rule and measure of those who sit perched atop the educational bureaucracy established by the state. The most urgent need of the times is an ordered freedom of inquiry whereby Christian truth too will once again be placed in a position where it can develop its excellent body of knowledge and oppose it to the irreligion of the state-monopolized school system. Academic freedom, therefore, so long as it remains within the limits that we have discussed, is a sacred, unalienable right of man, of the home, of the Church, and of science, which the Catholic press ought to campaign for tirelessly.

5) Beyond that, the state is obliged to structure the public schools, which it establishes, not according to subjective whim, but with due regard for the religion of parents, so that attendance at state schools will not infringe on the consciences of parents.

The justice of this demand flows naturally from the right of parental authority which has the prior responsibility for the kind of formation that children will receive. The obligation of the state becomes all the more urgent when it introduces some measure of compulsory education. Stahl says about this: "Once the state school is deChristianized or simply in open conflict with the leading accepted confessions, then its monopoly or dominance is no longer legitimate, either directly in the common elementary schools, or indirectly in the institutions for training public servants. Then the right of conscience prevails. One cannot force a father to entrust his children to an influence that is hostile to his religion. Then the Church has just as much right to undertake the task of education separated from the state."

There is no need to point out here how massively the exercise of state authority in this area of public schools comes into conflict with the religion of parents, and to how great a degree the consciences of the parents have been simply disregarded. It is vitally necessary that the parents be made aware of what is going on.

264

The demand for conditional academic freedom does not imply an urge to set up separate institutions alongside the state's public schools. Though we regard it as in the interests of freedom of conscience for the Church to operate certain institutions of its own, we would have to consider it as very unwise to develop a completely separate system of Church schools alongside the state's schools. That would be a definite sign of a kind of opposition of interests between Church and state which is contrary to God's will and therefore can lead to no good end. I feel, rather, that most of the schools, especially elementary schools, ought to serve the common purposes of home, state, and Church; and with a minimum of good intention, the three institutions could easily unite their interests in these schools. The more that is the case, the more beneficial the efforts of such schools will be.

7) On the other hand, a school system as envisioned by modern liberals, one that is independent and separated from home and church and where compulsory schooling is required, directly for the lower schools and indirectly for the higher levels- because attendance would be mandatory as a matter of fact to gain entry into public service and the professions - such a system represents the worst and most tasteless manifestation of the absolutist spirit, and the most flagrant violation of conscience. The majority of our people are in no position to avail themselves of private schooling for their children at the lower levels where compulsory schooling is mandated. And in the upper classes, countless parents find themselves in the position where they have to prepare their youngsters for public service. They all end up, therefore, being forced by indirect or direct compulsion to deliver their children up to schools which go against their consciences and do not enjoy their confidence. The apostate Emperor Julian deprived Christians of their right to establish Christian schools for their general education, and this gesture has come to be regarded down through history as one of the most reprehensible, repressive measures by which Christians have ever been confronted. The conduct of that emperor, however, represents a mild kind of repression compared to what false

265

liberalism has in mind for Christians, since compulsory schooling was not yet required in those times. Julian only wanted to deprive Christians of access to higher education. The state school, as the liberals intend it, is a kind of educational prison into which the children of Christian parents are to be herded so that they can be effectively robbed of their Christian Faith.

The educational issues, therefore, are of the utmost importance, and the Catholic press must be alerted to what is going on. It must combat the false principles of absolutist liberalism and stress true principles with reference to the rights of home and Church. It must arouse the consciences of Catholic parents and make them aware of the rights which they have to insist on from school authorities, unless they wish to be delinquent in their most sacred responsibilities to their children.

Thus far, we have avoided the matter of private rights in the area of schooling. We have to point out, in conclusion however, that where educational endowments are deeded over to the Church, the Church has a very special strict right to administer schools which are thus endowed. To in any way infringe upon such a right and to divert Church funds from the purpose for which they were endowed represents a violation of justice that cries to heaven.

XXXII <u>Freemasonry</u>

It is not our purpose here to enter into a long
discourse on the origins, the development, and the
overall scope of Freemasonry. We can only discuss
it insofar as we think the Catholic press ought to
consider what Freemasonry is up to.

If we draw attention to this delicate matter
here, it ought to be made clear that what we say
about Freemasonry is not to be imputed to every
single Freemason. We are speaking only about Freemasonry as such, not of the conception of it by individual members. We also feel certain that the
complaints that we have to make about Freemasonry
do not at all apply to many individual Masons.

Freemasonry is unique in the whole world in
that it lays claim to significant privilege. It
alone, with few exceptions, is not discussed in
the press, and it does not wish to be in the lime-
light. We note how the press discusses everything
else and passes judgement, and that ranges from
Christianity with all of its teachings and institutions, to the state with all of its laws and
constitutions. And whereas the press delves into
the most intimate personal affairs of people, Freemasons alone seem to enjoy a "do-not-touch-me" aura
that is universally conceded in all of Europe. Everyone avoids speaking about Freemasonry as though it
were some kind of ghost.

This phenomenon is proof positive of the enormous power which Freemasonry exercises throughout
the world. It still has a certain dominant influence
in the press, otherwise one could not explain such a
state of affairs. At the same time, it is clear that
such a condition is unreasonable and intolerable.
Whatever one may think of Freemasonry, there is no
denying that it is of uncommon concern and needs to
be studied and known so that its moral and cultural
worth can be brought to the light of day. It would
seem that such a climate, where every kind of monopoly and privilege is dragged into the open and

267

judged in the forum of public opinion, whereas Free-masonry alone goes on enjoying the privilege of immunity from public scrutiny, cannot continue. If the opponents of Freemasonry are wrong, it can only be in the interests of the latter if its history and workings are brought out of the shadows and exposed to the light of day. However, if the opponents are right, it is in the interests of all of humanity that its harmful influence is once and for all exposed. If Freemasonry can bear the light of day, then let us finally put an end to keeping it and its members in the dark. We think, therefore, that this condition has to be changed and that the Catholic press must play the leading role in forcing Freemasonry into the open. For the present, I consider it the most urgent responsibility of the Catholic press with reference to Freemasonry. Only after its history and present status is discussed over a period of time with the same candor as all other human institutions, will anyone be able to pass clear and definite judgement on its worth and on its faults. Until such a time, Masonry has itself to blame if its opponents are unreasonable in their condemnation of it.

Aside from all of that, we have another reason for wishing to see the whole matter discussed and analyzed in the press. One of them is the position which Freemasonry takes as opposed to Christianity and in particular to the Catholic Church.

It has been established as the chosen task of Masonry to nurture and extol the purely human, that genuine, true and abiding good that is humanity; and for that reason it establishes a bond among men. To this point, there is no conflict with positive Christianity, which has precisely the same objective. It too wants to fathom man in his innermost nature and essence and to develop what is genuinely and honestly human in man. It wishes, as St. Paul says, to develop the whole man. Therefore, we would have no real difference between Christianity and Masonry, on this point. Such a difference could only arise over the interpretations of what is purely human and over the means to realize and further this humanity.

Masonry also proposes to recognize the purely
human, the morality, and the goodness in all religions,
and it wants to present an image of brotherhood as the
rallying point for members of all religions. Even in
this aspiration there is no real clash with Christianity. On the contrary, it is Christianity which
has really and truly held and propagated the teaching
to the whole world that we all have a common Father
and are brothers therefore, and that God wants to be
the Father of all men. It was the Catholic Church
which opposed original Protestantism's teaching that
man was totally corrupt because of original sin. The
Church taught instead that all religions, even some
of the pagan philosophical systems, contain something
that is good and true, and much that is genuinely
human. Catholic learning has probed deeply and lov-
ingly for real traces of humanity wherever these could
be found, no matter how obscured they may have become
by the effects of sin and evil in the world.

The essence of Masonry, on the other hand, is
that deism which arose in England toward the end of
the 16th century and spread from there throughout the
world. It is in this era that Freemasonry also appears
to have arisen; any earlier roots would be traceable
only to the kinds of secret organization that have
been found in various times and places throughout
world history.

Deism consists mainly in a denial of any supernatural Divine revelation in history, and it tolerates
no knowledge of God except from what is discernible
in nature and attainable by unaided human reason.
Deism had a certain merit, since it originated as a
protest against the suppression of reason as promoted
by the Anglican Church. The teaching that human nature
was totally corrupted, so that the human race was merely
an unreasoning and condemned mass of mankind, had to
lead to such reactions. However, that battle for the
rights of human reason, though justified in itself,
led to a no less grave injustice in that one now disregarded the rights of God and His loving providential
plan; and by the denial of any but natural revelation,
all of the continuing, living, relationship between
God and His creatures was disrupted. From such deism

there later evolved rationalism, naturalism, pantheism, and materialism. Yet we must not confuse deism with these systems of thought, because deism continued to insist on the existence of a personal God.

In these principles of deism we see set forth the essence of Freemasonry, both insofar as it contains valid elements, and insofar as it is in error. Masonry is correct in opposing the view of orthodox Protestantism by maintaining that, wherever men are to be found, true, genuine traces of humanity are discernible; but it is wrong when it denies all supernatural revelation. We are now able to see clearly the position of Masonry as related to Christianity. It has a close inner tie with all of the rationalistic Christian sects. So long as Christianity poses merely as a natural phenomenon in the course of history, Freemasonry is perfectly willing to praise it and Christ, and to hold the Bible in high regard. Freemasonry can without any reservation at all place Christianity at the peak of all purely natural manifestations of the human spirit, and to declare the Bible to be the first book of the Lodge as even containing the word of God in a certain sense. That is why the Bible is used in some lodges when an oath is administered.

On the other hand, Freemasonry comes into open conflict with that Christianity which has taught for 1800 years, that has been announced to the world as representing the supernatural revelation of God, and which implies the blessings of supernatural grace. We refer especially to the Catholic Church which stands foursquare opposed to what Masonry proposes. Masonry totally rejects the Divinity of Christ in the Christian sense, as a supernatural descent of God among men instead of some merely natural revelation of what is divine in the human soul. Thereby it rejects all Christian teachings, institutions and sacraments having a supernatural, divine character. There can be no redemption by a supernatural act of God; no Christian concept of Christ as a mediator between God and man so far as Freemasonry is concerned. The words of Christ, "No one can come to the Father except through me," has no relevance to the Mason.

270

Freemasonry can only assign relative merit to all religions, and it has to regard as excessive the claim of any religion to be the one true spokesman for supernatural Divine revelation. [43]

Specifically it must delcare the entire Catholic Church, which lays claim to a supernatural mission, to supernatural teaching, to supernatural sacraments and to a supernatural authority, as a presumptuous human contrivance of priestly craft and cunning. However, just as deism evoked other errors, which it did not sympathize with, Freemasonry is subject to the same pitfall; and though the latter manages to coexist with all sorts of movements that come along, even the most godless, it would be wrong to denounce Freemasonry itself as godless. On the contrary, it regards genuine honor to God as a part of its task, and it speaks often and fervently of it.

If we are at all accurate in describing the essence of Freemasonry as we have, it is clear that the Church has good cause to forbid membership to her own people and to regard anyone who joins the Masons as having fallen away from the Catholic Faith. St. John wrote in his first Epistle: "Not all prophetic spirits, Brethren, deserve your credence; you must put them to the test, to see whether they come from God. Many false prophets have made their appearance in the world. This is the test by which God's spirit is to be recognized; every spirit which acknowledges Jesus Christ as having come to us in human flesh has God for its author; and no spirit which would disunite Jesus comes from God. This is the power of Antichrist, whose coming you have been told to expect; now you must know that he is here in the world already." (I John 4:1-4). That is the Church's point of departure. The divinity of Christ is the central point, the heart and soul of her teaching. It lies at her core as the sun is the center of the solar system. Freemasonry can only be regarded by the Church as a teaching which, in St. John's words, "disunites" Christ and is therefore not of God but of the Antichrist. The impossibility of being a member in good conscience of both the Catholic Church and of the Freemasons is quite obvious to the extent that our enemies have recognized it quite forthrightly. Undoubtedly many Catholics have joined the Masons without being remotely aware of the inner contradiction. However, if Freemasonry is really serious about pursuing truth as it proclaims publicly, we deem it unworthy for it to engage in a pretense that contradicts its own nature. It ought to avert any increase in membership which is achieved by duplicity.

The second objection against Freemasonry arises from its caste-like structure that is combined with its influence upon civil society. We refer in particular to the "ancient obligation" of a Freemason which we often hear about, namely: "You are to appoint a Brother whenever you are in a position to do so, or recommend him so that he will be appointed." And even if such a rule did not exist in the formal sense, it is generally known that Freemasons will give preferential treatment to their Brother Masons when it comes to supporting and advancing them, with the result that young persons join the lodges to assure their own futures.

It is obvious how such a process endangers the rights and interests of those citizens who do not happen to be Masons. In all seriousness we are entitled to question whether prudence would not require that no judge ought to be allowed to join any secret organization because this could give rise to the suspicion that membership in such a brotherhood might prevent his passing impartial judgements.

It is even more suspect for Freemasons to hold important government positions. Or would a non-Mason not feel pretty awkward if he found himself competing with a Mason for a position, when those who were testing him and passing judgement on him were also Masons who were bound by an oath of brotherhood to help his competitor?

Yet another suspicion arises when influential public offices are held by Freemasons: whether state authority might not be misused for Masonic ends and purposes. The Freemasons cannot lay claim to absolute infallibility and perfection. They have to

272

recognize the fact that they too are human beings with human weaknesses. How easy it would be, therefore, if a substantial part of public authority rested in their hands, for them to use such power to achieve the aims of the Brotherhood! What position would that leave the entire Christian population in, if state authority that commands their obedience to the laws has become the tool of a secret society which can then wage war against the Faith of Christians which it regards as madness and superstition and serve ulterior purposes under the pretext of fostering the general welfare and public spiritedness!

The whole picture comes into still clearer focus if we consider this matter with reference to teaching positions. What happens if public officials are Freemasons and if teaching positions throughout the land are occupied by Masons, and if the teachers are bound by the same secret oath? Then every semblance of equality and of justice has to be drawn into question. What is inevitable is a secret internal warfare against the entire population which believes in a supernatural revelation. Such warfare, incidentally, goes counter to that freedom of religion which is so loudly proclaimed in laws and constitutions. We must then reach a point where, despite all solemnly safeguarded claims to equal opportunity for state positions, actually only Freemasons can aspire to such positions; and while there is talk of freedom of religion and free inquiry, actually, in the schools only the religion and philosophical viewpoints of Freemasons finds expression.

We could air our complaints against the caste-like posture of Freemasonry toward all other sectors of the population, the manner in which it promotes a society of the elite who are set apart from the common folk, even though the action of that elite determines the everyday lives of the commoners. We could explore in accordance with what was said earlier, how the whole constitutional structure of the state begins to operate, what with its pretensions to wide representation of all classes of the populace, once an all-powerful state authority that is in league with Freemasonry, and parliamentary majorities that are shaped by it gain unchallengeable dominance in it. We shall abstain from such considerations, however, so that we may take the opportunity to air one more complaint against Freemasonry.

It seems to us that Freemasonry, even if it is capable of avoiding certain extremes in its own lodges, offers a great pretext and training school for all manner of secret organizations; and it thereby poses a threat to the sound civil order of all of Europe. It may well be that the lodges are to a certain extent under the supervision of public authorities. Such supervision is of little merit, however, if the supervisory authorities are themselves Freemasons. Aside from that, the lodges themselves, even if they were of a mind to, could not prevent the appearance of other secret offshoots which could be even more powerful and energetic than they themselves are, and which could exempt themselves totally from the supervisory control of state authorities. In fact, it would appear to us that secret societies are in any case repugnant to well-ordered civil society, and that there is something unethical in their very nature. So long as Freemasonry constitutes a highly privileged secret society, the door is wide open to this repulsive anomoly of secret organizations - as we now experience it - slithering about in the subterranean recesses of our society. Also, it makes impossible any feeling of security in the transactions of everyday life, since one never knows whether he might be up against a lodge brother who is bound by oath to take care of his own. Freemasonry, along with its fellow secret organizations, proposes to be in full harmony with the spirit of the times; but actually such societies are in open contradiction to it because the times call for a great openness! I believe, therefore, that we would be fully justified in the name of this openness, to ask for an end to all of the secret activity.

Finally, we cannot refrain from suggesting that a careful scientific treatise on Freemasonry seems to be among the highest priorities of the present time. A strictly objective and critical presentation of the

origins, the history, the nature, and the practices
and symbols of Freemasonry, along with an examination
of its position and its influence in modern civil
society, would be a most valuable contribution.
Such a work would put an end, once and for all, to
all of the secrecy surrounding this organization and
make a sound judgement of it possible. Would that
some capable young scholar may undertake this important task.

XXXIII   The Unity of Germany

Inasmuch as the German question has become part
of the order of the day which is of concern to all
Germans, we cannot pass over it in silence; even
though, it is true, that we have discussed it in
some detail in other contexts. We regard a more and
more generalized exertion toward greater unity of the
German nation, not according to the French mode of
centralization, but with Germanic autonomy of the
various states, as legitimate. It represents the well-
founded aspiration of each and every German and of the
German nation as a whole, and it is as legitimate as
any political ambition can be.

The dissolution of the German nation and of the
bond which unified the commonwealth cannot justly be
attributed to one or the other rule, or to some single
state. A plethora of factors has been at work over
the centuries to bring about the present disunity,
and these factors were not the products of the noblest
human instincts; nor were they in the best interests
of the German people. Instead, they stemmed predominantly from egotistical interests and self-aggrandize-
ment as well as from unwholesome historical currents
that were aided and abetted, of course, by the equally
egotistical and nefarious policies of foreign powers.
It was no genuine, higher, universal need of the
German fatherland which brought about that dissolution.
Nor could the renunciation of the German imperial
crown by Emperor Francis have anything to do with
the right to German unity, since this was not the
private domain of the German Emperor, but the common
inheritance of all Germans. No matter how complicated the solution to the problem may be, and no
matter how objectionable some of the revolutionary
efforts and activities which fly in the face of
history and of actual reality may be - parading as
they do under the banner of unity and German solidarity while actually presenting the greatest possible
threat to such unity - nevertheless, German unity
remains an altogether sacred and justifiable ambition.

It has been proposed in some quarters that
German unity is an impossibility because there is
religious division; and that is supposed to present
an insurmountable obstacle. There is some truth in
the assertion, since the highest ideal of national
unity could only be achieved where there is unity of
religious belief. It is a fact that the religious
division, and the particularism and absolutism which
were the real eventual consequences of it, created
the most deep-seated kind of rift in German unity.
However, on this earth we are often in a position
where we cannot immediately attain the highest ideals,
and that does not justify our not trying to achieve
some less total perfection. As a matter of fact,
there is scarcely any example of national unity left
in this world that is based on this ultimate and best
foundation for unity. On the other hand, we believe
it is of the greatest importance for achieving unity
among the German states - and we wish to emphasize
this especially - that politicians will stop using
religion as a tool for achieving their purposes. It
isn't so much the religious division in itself which
is such a threat to German unity as the efforts of
certain parties to dominate religious groups by legislation and then to use them as means to achieve their
ambitions. Nothing would provide a greater assist
for achieving German unity than the honorable recognition of the principle of autonomy for the church.
There is no end of talk about how ecclesiastics have
gotten themselves entangled in temporal affairs. At
the same time little attention is paid to how the
temporal authorities have interfered for centuries
in the spiritual domain and used the Church to further
their own egotistical and selfish ambitions. What is
more, modern absolutist liberalism is following the
identical destructive course. On the one hand it upholds German unity, and on the other it brings with
it the threat of the worst and deepest kind of religious division. That is why all who are really interested in striving for German unity and in living
at peace with their fellow Germans in a spirit of true
tolerance, ought to work together to see to it that
the autonomy of the Christian confessions will receive
recognition. Let them see to it that the terrorism
by which the Catholic Church is threatened in the

278

press and in certain governmental chambers will not become the order of the day.

Finally, we can only regret the fact that some Catholics have become hostile or indifferent to the movement for German unity simply because there are those involved in the movement who are there less because they want unity than because they hate the Catholic Church. We believe, rather, that Catholics ought to be careful lest we appear to be strangers to what are German issues, despite the animosity which the Catholic Church encounters at present. Instead, we ought to make every effort to separate what is true from what is false also in this issue; and we ought to make it clear that we are not to be outdone in our love of the German fatherland and its greatness and unity.

XXXIV Conclusion

I

If we regard humanity and the history of mankind,
we are convinced beyond the shadow of a doubt that the
condition in which we find these throughout the course
of world history cannot represent their ultimate goal
and their highest destiny. How else would one explain
the restlessness, the striving, the pushing, the widespread and patent dissatisfaction that is to be found
in all nations and among all people? How would one
reconcile the surging and swelling that occurs through
all of history like the rolling of ocean waves? How
else could one explain the clamor for progress, blind
and unreasonable as it is, often enough. As gravity
is to the body, so the persistent yearning for another,
better, happier life, which is an inseparable part of
man's essential makeup, is to the soul.

II

The mysterious spiritual compulsion in humanity
is explained and clarified fully by Christ. He has
established himself as the teacher of the wisdom which
reveals all things to us in their true substance. In
his desperate yearning for that wisdom, Solomon once
prayed: "God of our fathers, Lord of all mercy, thou
by thy word hast made all things, and thou in thy wisdom hast contrived man to rule thy creation, to order
the world by a law of right living and of just dealing....wisdom I ask of thee, the same wisdom that
dwells so near thy throne; do not grudge me a place
among thy retinue. Am I not thy servant, and to thy
service born? Moral man thou seest me, the puny
creature of an hour, a mind unapt for judgement and
the making of laws. Grow man to what perfection he
will, if he lacks the wisdom that comes from thee,
he is nothing....wisdom was with thee then, privy to
all thy designs, she who stood by thee at the world's
creation, and know thy whole will, the whole tenour
of thy commandments. Let her be thy envoy still out

of thy heavenly sanctuary; send her out still upon thy errand, to be at my side too, and share my labours! How else should thy will be made clear to me? For her, no secret, no riddle is too dark; her prudent counsel will be my guide...Thy purposes none may know, unless thou dost grant thy gift of wisdom, sending out from high heaven thy own holy spirit. Thus ever were men guided by the right way, here on earth, and learned to know thy will....." (Wisdom 9).

That was really a prayer to God in the name of the whole human race, and God has answered that prayer in overflowing generosity. That wisdom which exists at the throne of God, which dwells in Heaven at the very Godhead, that Holy Spirit from on high personally came down to man in the person of Christ our Lord. He Himself became the teacher of those who dwell here on earth so that they could mend their ways, and He sent the Holy Spirit so that man would continue to learn what is pleasing to God. Along with true wisdom, He also bestowed upon mankind the greatest benefits which could affect its sanctification, Divine Love and the highest possible unity. His entire exalted task is summed up in the words which he spoke to His Father on the night before He died: "It is not for them that I pray; I pray for those who are to find faith in me through their word; that they may all be one; that they too may be one in us, as thou, Father, art in me, and I in Thee.....(John 17: 20-21). God in His mercy could confer no higher benefit on mankind. Therein is contained everything. God is the source of all truth, all love, and all happiness. However, mankind is enabled to share in these great benefits to the fullest extent only because Christ united man with God Himself.

III

This descent of Divine Wisdom and Love from Heaven has not enjoyed the triumphant success which it should have on earth among the human beings which they were to liberate and make happy. All too often men have rejected them; they loved darkness more than they loved the Light (John 3:19). They nailed Christ to the Cross, and the same spirit which inspired that foul deed has

worked unceasingly ever since to attack and damage
Christ's Church. It prevented the Church from sharing her boundless treasures of God's love and wisdom
with mankind. It has sundered Christianity itself
and severed members from the Body of Christ.

Hence, we see the tragic division of the Christian churches in the East and in the West, which has
so enormously impeded the Church in her appointed
task down through the centuries. Hence we have the
unfortunate split of the Church in the West, which
has for 300 years likewise eaten away at our own in-
nards and wrought great havoc. Hence there are the
countless divisions in Protestantism itself that were
prevented from proliferating even further only when
temporal authorities erected some kind of external
obstructions. Hence, there is, finally, the newest
enemy which has come into the world with deism and
which has infiltrated Christendom and destroyed it
from within. It began by rejecting supernatural revelation, i.e., by denying a relationship between
God and man that goes beyond nature and unaided
reason. Thereby Christ with His divine mission here
on earth was stripped of its meaning. He was no
longer the wisdom which dwells at the very throne of
God and condescended to reach down to mankind. From
that denial of supernatural revelation, the same
spirit of the times proceeded to the denial of any
supernatural order and finally to a denial of the
very notion of a supernatural God. That is the
spirit with which we now stand face to face. Serious
souls like the Protestant Guizot have gone so far as
to divide mankind into two camps. In the one are
those who believe in a personal God, and in the other
are those who deny God's very existence.

IV

This unhappy situation causes all the more concern to Christians over the division within Christendom. They are coming to recognize that the name-
less horror whereby, 1800 years after Christ lived
on this earth, fools are able to proclaim in the
very midst of Christian society that there is no God,
not only in their hearts but from the very roof tops

283

and from academic chairs, was made possible only by
the division within Christendom itself. Even Catholics ought to share in this deep suffering with all
of their hearts and souls. What a pathetic contrast
between what Christ wished when he prayed, "That they
may all be one; that they too may be one in us, as
thou, Father art in me, and I in Thee....," and the
condition in which Christianity now finds itself.

It is our obligation, so far as any of us is
able, to do everything in our power to bring about
the reunion of Christians. A structure, no matter
how great, is made of small stones, and no Catholic
should shirk from his obligation to work for this
reunion, no matter how little he feels he may be
able to contribute.

The first duty is to pray for the reunion of
the Christian confessions. May God show us ways and
means to spread this unanimous petition among all
Christian souls who yearn for Christian reunion, according to some universally acceptable plan. It is
a petition which carries with it the great promise
of Christ who Himself guaranteed: "Believe me, you
have only to make any request of the Father in my
name, and he will grant it to you." (John 16:23).
What great potency that prayer will have, therefore,
if all of us unite with Christ as our High Priest,
and join Him in that prayer which was his final and
ultimate petition here on earth, "Ut omnes unum sint -
that they may all be one; that they too may be one in
us, as thou, Father, art in me, and I in Thee......"
The whole idea has created much excitement in recent
years. Pray that it will receive an ever warmer, more
universal, more heartfelt acceptance. We appeal to
all true Christian hearts who read these lines to
become apostles and spread this word about the circles
in which they move. An attempt has been made recently
by certain leading individuals toward the reunion of
the separated brethren by personal meeting and dialogue.
As happy as we are about such efforts, we have to express misgivings as to whether it is in God's plan
to bless them with success. What would please us most
of all would be if men of all Christian confessions
could address themselves to the problem of establishing

284

a society for common prayer among all of those who still believe that Christ was the incarnate Son of God. We believe that God could not refuse to hear the common prayer, "Ut omnes unum sint - That all may be one."

The second method of working for Christian re-union consists in our avoiding all controversies among ourselves and in trying to depict the great super-natural truths of Christianity by the way we live our lives. Nothing so hinders the world - to the extent that good will is present - from recognizing the Divine truth in the Catholic Church as when the sins of her children prevent this truth from becoming a living presence in the world. Practically all of the accusations that are made against the Church are based on misunderstanding; and the sources of such misunderstanding are, by and large, the imperfections and sins of the Church's members.

It is not yet enough for us in our time to oppose the controversies and irregularities with untiring zeal. We have to strive to lead lives that reflect the highest Christian virtue and to present an example of the supernatural life that has been at all times the full blossoming of Christianity, to a world which has gone so far as to deny the existence of the super-natural. This has always been the great strength of Christianity, and therein lies its power to conquer the world. It is a rejection of the whole wonderful history of the Church to suppose that it is enough to just promote a condition of natural justice and to lead commonplace lives, avoiding the worst excesses, and that by such behavior we can overcome the spirit that is now dominant in the world. In every century, beginning with the age of bloody martyrdom and of the anchorites in the wildnerness - whenever Christendom achieved notable triumphs - the performance of its saints was the deciding factor. Holy bishops and priests, monks and lay people overcame the world, and they were the ones who spread Christ's kingdom. That is how it will always be. We have to break away from the comfortable pattern of routine living and abandon ourselves to the ennobling grace of truly holy living if we really hope to achieve what our hearts crave for, the spread of Christ's kingdom and the reunion of the Christian churches. The cultivation of such a holy life is, first of all, the responsibility of the religious orders, and that is the reason why we insist on the freedom to establish religious orders, because they ought to be seedbeds of sanctity. After the religious orders, the priesthood must be an instrument whereby the supernatural light must shine forth so that it may achieve the mission which Christ gave it. What a challenge faces us! Would that we might measure up to it. That will be accomplished best, it is my deep-seated conviction, if priests are again united in heart and mind.[44] That has always been the life-style prompted by the Holy Spirit in the Church for fostering the more perfect, supernatural, priestly life.

V

Whatever great zeal we may have for effecting a reunion of all Christian churches, we Catholics may never conceal the truth that such reunion can mean nothing else but a return to the Catholic Church.

The Catholic Church rests essentially on two principles which set her apart from every other Christian church, and their worth is reinforced by all manner of developments in our own time.

The first principle arises from the teaching that the Church is linked to Christ in this world by an unbroken apostolic succession. Christianity is essentially the continuing real participation in Christ, in His teaching, and in His grace. Overall, it is the continuing communion with Christ. However, Christ shares Himself with mankind by the instrumentality of the apostolate. It is totally incorrect to depict the priesthood as a barrier between Christ and the individual Christian, which makes direct contact between Christ and the individual Catholic impossible. That is an erroneous Protestant position, and it is not a valid conception of how Catholics regard the priesthood. The priest who distributes Holy Communion and brings Christ to the souls of the faithful is not a mediator between Christ and the soul. He is rather a dispenser of Christ's graces to the soul. The continuing visible apostolate in the Church of Christ

286

through all ages is like the channel by which the
teachings and graces of Christ flow, so that they
can reach all souls everywhere. We find reflection
of this concept of the Church in all of God's works.
The tree spreads life through all of its limbs on the
condition that they remain attached to it. That visible attachment is not the life of the tree itself,
because even after life has gone from the tree, its
trunk, its branches and its twigs still remain connected. The visible connection, however, represents
the channel whereby the inner life is transmitted;
and the twig which is separated can no longer share
in the inner life of the tree. The same is true of
the human body. Participation in the inner life is
conditioned by the external connection of the members,
even though that external linkage does not constitute the inner life-giving principle. It is only
the channel for such vitality; however when external
separation of the members from the body occurs, the
member is cut off from sharing in the inner vitality
that courses through the body. In saying this, we
do not deny the possibility of an extraordinary action of Divine grace and Providence upon the separated
member.

We could draw similar analogies from all social
and political relationships that men establish. That
is how it is with the Church which the Apostle Paul
refers to both as the body of Christ and as a community, and Christ is the Head of this Body and of this
community. (1 Cor. 12:27 and Eph. 1:22). The Church
possesses in the apostolic succession, which was established by Christ and continues to exercise the
same power He bestowed upon it until the present time
without interruption, an external link with the
Incarnate Christ. That link is the essential condition for maintaining our connection to Him who represents its inner life. The essence of episcopal consecration in the Church lies in what Christ told His
apostles: "As the Father has sent me, I also send
you." (John 20:21). That is why one bishop says to
another: "The mission which Christ has given me, in
the name of Christ and by His power, I now confer
upon you." It is therefore through the apostolic
succession that all of the Divine power which Christ

287

assigned to His apostles has continued in unbroken succession throughout the Church as long as it has existed. The inner vitality which she transmits by this external human instrumentality to all of her members who remain in proper union with her is the Divine life of Christ Himself.

These two sides of the Church are also expressed in her teaching about the sacraments. The Church herself is the great sacrament from which the seven sacraments radiate. As Christ appeared in human form, so Christianity now continues to appear in the form of an external human constitution which is directly joined to the person of Christ and has its origin in Christ. Just as the fullness of the Godhead was concealed in the human appearance of Jesus Christ, so all of the Divine treasures of Christianity are concealed in this external institution of the Apostolic succession. That is the reason why we place such great importance on the uninterrupted succession of our bishops back to the time of Christ. It is the same idea which Tertullian once expressed back in the second century when he called out to the false teachers of his time, the Gnostics: "Let the heretics step forward and lay bare the beginnings of their churches. Let them make clear the succession of their bishops, how one followed the others until they arrive at a bishop at their head whose predecessor was one of the Apostles or one of the disciples of the Apostles who travelled in the company of the Apostles. That is the proper way in which the Apostolic Churches prove their origins. As the Church of Smyrna traces the apointment of Polycarp to John, and as the Roman Church traces the ordination of Clement to Peter, that is how all of the rest of the churches trace their episcopal appointments back to the Apostolic origins." [45] At another point Tertullian demands of the heretics: "Visit the apostolic churches where the Apostles themselves had their Sees, where their own original writings were read echoing their very own voices, and reflecting their own images with complete authenticity. Are you close to Achaia, then go to Corinth; if you are not far from Macedonia, then you have Phillipi. Do you live in Italy, then you have Rome where we Africans too have our validation! How fortunate these churches are, where the Apostles themselves gave the universal teachings and

288

sealed them with their blood. Let us see what they
learned and what they passed on to us." [46] Again we
find Tertullian questioning the Gnostics because they
claim to be basing their false teachings on Scripture
which is the property of the Church and which only
the Church is the correct interpreter of. "Who are
you, and where did you come from? What are you up to,
inasmuch as you are not mine and do not belong among
my flock? By what right, Marcian, do you devastate
my forest? By what authority, Valentine, do you divert my springs? Who authorized you, Apelles, to remove my boundary markers? The territory is mine, so
why do you sow and graze therein at your pleasure?
The territory is mine. I have the original claim to
it. I was here before you, and I have written testimony to prove rightful possession. I am the successor of the Apostles as they ordered it in their last
will and testament, which they officially handed over
by their solemn testimony; I am the rightful owner." [47]

     In the same period, the great bishop and martyr
Irenaeus, who may be regarded as the common spokesman
for both the East and the West, expressed the same
truth when he said, among other things: "In determining who are the bishops of the Church, it is necessary
to find out whether their succession can be traced
back to the Apostles, as we have shown, and whether
they have received their episcopal authority in good
faith and with the approval of the Father." [48]

     The Catholic Church, therefore, cannot surrender
this exalted privilege. Just as the narrow strand of
wire is, in itself, insignificant even while it serves
as the instrument by which a human thought can spark
from one end of the world to another in an instant,
that is how it is with apostolic succession. Even
though the bishops, by themselves, may be mere pathetic human beings, they are nevertheless ordained, by
God's will, to be the bearers of heavenly graces.
They conduct the life that is in Christ - as conduits
and instruments - down through the centuries to every
soul that is destined to receive life.

     The second essential principle of the Church con-
sists in the assertion of a teaching authority which,
by virtue of a higher supernatural assistance, cannot

289

err in transmitting Christ's teaching. Protestants assert that we have our access to the world of God only through Holy Scripture. Catholicism, on the other hand, affirms that we hear God's word mainly and first of all through the Church's teaching. We only have to reflect on what has been said thus far to appreciate the deep and decisive difference between these two viewpoints. Therein lies, without a doubt, the whole essence and final cause of the religious rift. This difference is so great that it makes any blending of the two principles impossible, and therefore, reunion can only be possible if one or the other party surrenders its principle.

In the foregoing discussion we have determined that the concept of moral freedom - as Catholic moral doctrine affirms - is decisive for any kind of freedom in any area whatsoever; and therefore only such action can be termed free which is the result of full inner autonomy. Autonomy is the determining factor for liberty. It is freedom as understood in this sense which is the basis for true human dignity, and without it there can be no human action or activity in the real sense of the word, human. On the other hand however, as we have demonstrated, a proper use of freedom hinges on the recognition of some authority. Authority without freedom destroys human dignity in that it obliterates individuality. And freedom without authority destroys human dignity in that it disrupts the relationship of man to God and to his fellow man - which relationships are the sole sources of its full flowering and development. The ultimate problem for mankind, therefore, is finding a true and genuine authority which will not blot out individuality but nurture it and bring it to its fullest possible development. World history is replete with authorities which trample underfoot the fine budding of human individuality and thus debase human nature itself. On the other hand, there have been recurrent instances of the abuses of the rights which individuals have only because of the freedom which God gave them. Nothing is of more critical importance, therefore, than the need to determine whether God did in fact bequeath to mankind an authority which men can accept, so that they can work out a proper balance between authority and freedom and thereby reach their highest development. If there is no such authority, then mankind is indeed doomed to be buffeted between the abuses of authority and of individual freedom until the end of time!

Protestants believe that they have such an authority in the written word of God. Now it is a fact that in the whole New Testament, it is nowhere written that Christ had the intention of spreading His word only through the Bible. Instead He referred always to a teaching authority by which His gospel would be spread through the whole world. It is therefore a fact that the basic premise on which all of Protestantism rests is nowhere to be found in the Bible so that it must be regarded as great self-delusion for Protestants to believe that their entire religious conviction rests upon the word of God and is somehow traceable to some God-given legacy. In fact, what we have to do is to make a distinction between the letter and external form of the Bible and the Divine wisdom which it contains. The Bible is, in the final analysis, only the exterior array in which those who were sent by God along with the Son of God Himself clothed their thoughts. It remains for us to determine the truths which are contained in the external expressions which the Bible offers to us. Man can only base his religious convictions on the inner sense that these words contain. If we had in fact, as Protestantism maintains, nothing but the Bible, then the inevitable result would have to be that, though we have the external expressions containing inner wisdom that could be authoritative, we would once again find ourselves in a position of uncertainty. That is because these external forms of expression often allow a manifold interpretation and are capable of subjectivized meanings. Therefore we have no way of knowing whether the meaning we are getting reflects some particular human interpretation or whether it really reflects the higher Divine meaning. In a word, the Protestant bases his religion on a form which comes from God, truly enough. To this external form, which cannot directly make contact with his spirit and which cannot directly shape his convictions, he attributes a meaning which he himself constructed without the aid of any higher authority. Therefore, he cannot really be certain whether his whole system of religious thought rests on the sandy foundation of human opinions or whether it rests on the external rock of Divine revelation. Only Christ's contemporaries would have been so fortunate as to build their faith on the Divine foundation of His living gospel, whereas we who live after Christ possess only the dead letter of Christ's teaching and would have to give a purely subjective human interpretation to its content. Where such a viewpoint regarding the word of God can lead, experience has shown us. It is horrifying to see how in our own time the biblical expression which comes from God is used by God's enemies and by the enemies of His annointed, Jesus Christ, to deny God and Christ. Could that possibly be a part of the Divine plan of God who came down from Heaven to earth in order to bring us not the dead letter of wisdom but its living content? The Bible is, in the final analysis, only a Divine container. If Christ had left it to us humans to fill this container with spiritual content, it would have been inevitable that the Father of Lies would also have injected his poison so that he could have spread death instead of the life that was intended, under the mantle of this exalted word of God.

The Catholic Church believes instead, that it possesses a higher authority regarding the living word of God in the teaching authority that was established by Christ. This viewpoint is supported on all sides by Holy Scripture. Does not the New Testament mention repeatedly an oral transmission of the word of God? Does it not therefore establish a firm extended foundation for a higher conviction that is based, in the true sense, on the word of God? The teaching authority of the Church is, first of all, spiritually alive. Secondly, it is not a mere human construct, but it has a supernatural character because Christ and the Holy Spirit abide with it. When Christ sent the Apostles into the world to teach all nations, not to write books, he promised them, "And behold I am with you all through the days that are coming, until the consummation of the world." (Matt. 28:20). In the same context, He told them: "....and I will ask the Father, and he will give you another to befriend you, one who

is to dwell continually with you forever. It is the
truth-giving Spirit.....He who is to befriend you,
the Holy Spirit, whom the Father will send on my
account, will in His turn make everything plain, and
recall to your minds everything I have said to you."
(John 14:16, and 14:26). Only on the assumption of
such supernatural Divine protection could Christ have
spoken of the obligation to listen to the Apostles:
"He who listens to you, listens to me; he who despises
you, despises me..."(Luke, 10:16). On the same matter,
St. Paul said: "Everyone who calls upon the name of
the Lord will be saved. Only, how are they to call
upon Him until they have learned to believe in Him?
And how can they listen without a preacher to listen
to? And how can there be preachers, unless preachers
are sent on their errand?" (Romans 10:14-16) . St.
Paul concluded from this: "See how the faith comes
from hearing; and hearing through Christ's word."
(Romans, 10:17).

The entire doctrine of the Church's teaching
authority rests on these two thoughts, that the word
of God would continue to be a living presence in its
content and in its spirit, and that there would be
an abiding supernatural Divine protection so that its
content would be preserved in its full purity. Only
on the basis of these two prerequisites can there be
any talk of conviction based on anything but purely
human and subjective foundations. If anything which
is of a higher nature and which presents itself as
being authoritative and able to lend conviction ex-
ceeding man's own inner strength, wishes to gain entry
to the innermost sanctuary of a man's soul, it has
to be something that is first of all, spiritual.
It has to be a thought, because only a thought can
break through to the inner recesses of the soul, whereas the form remains standing at the door. Secondly,
it has to be a thought that carries with it the Divine
imprint, since only a thought that comes from God possesses authority over merely human thought. For that
purpose, we have the teaching authority of the Catholic
Church which, therefore, corresponds to the deepest
cravings of the human spirit. Only a Faith that is
built upon it constitutes a Divine action that places
the soul upon a Divine foundation. Authority and

293

freedom thereby find themselves united in total
harmony so that by the Catholic's Act of Faith,
what David sang about, becomes a reality: "See
where mercy and faithfulness meet in one; how justice and peace are united in one embrace! Faithfulness grows up out of the earth, and from heaven,
justice looks down. The Lord, now, will grant us
his blessing, to make our land yield its harvest."
(Psalm 84:11-14). Men either have no higher authority to guide their liberty, or else they have it in
the Catholic Church.

So that misconceptions may be avoided, it remains but for me to stress once again that the infallible teaching authority of the Church extends only,
as we said earlier to truths which Christ Himself
taught. Furthermore that infallible authority does
not reside directly with each individual bishop, but
in the bishops together and in union with the successor of St. Peter. As soon as an individual bishop
parts company with this collegial group, he cuts himself off from that mainstream of living truth which,
in Christ, flows through the entire body of the Church.

VI

The spirit of the world now wishes to replace this authority, so full of grace, with another. It deceives mankind about what genuine freedom is and wants to subject all men to the reign of its all-powerful law. It deceives men about the sweet yoke of Christ and about the Divine authority that was established by Him. It seeks to impose upon our necks a new human yoke that is constructed by parliamentary majorities with the solemn cooperation of the press. This represents a trend that has gained unprecedented momentum, and we can already see how the net is being hauled in so that any free movement by Christians will be virtually impossible in the future. Pray God that this little book will help to clarify what is happening and to alert all true Christians who happen to read it for combat! The most urgent and greatest need for the development of Christian thought and Christian living in our time is the independence of the Church under the kinds of general legislation that we discussed earlier, and also the proper relationship between the schools, the home, the state and the Church. The leading antagonist who opposes these just demands is absolutism in its old traditional form, and especially absolutism in its newest form - modern secular liberalism![49] Pray that God will raise up better and stronger voices to summon all who still have a German and a Christian heart in our nation to rise up and do battle for these great blessings and against these enemies. Let the clergy understand the currents of our time and not be satisfied to plod along in the accustomed manner, using the old shopworn methods; but let them defend the things that are of God with any and all means that are good and legitimate. The Christian people of our nation must be educated to an awareness of what the great issues of our time are. They have to be made to realize how hypocritical modern liberalism is. They must know their rights so far as the schools are concerned; they must recognize the infernal plan to place the schools at the service of the Anti-Christ. The matter must be announced from every pulpit. These thoughts have to find expression in countless publications. What great blows we could strike for the things of God if we had a little of the zeal that God's enemies display, and by which they rush breathlessly about the world to spread their poison into every last homestead.

But it is not only a task for the clergy! All men who love Christianity ought to work with the same spirit, in the press, in political gatherings, in all walks of life where God has stationed them. They ought to do battle for this great cause of mankind by any means that are at their disposal. If we are prepared to take action the moment a thief breaks into our house, if it is regarded as a disgrace to stand and do nothing when an enemy invades our borders, how much more disgraceful it is for so many to stand by idly while the greatest treasures of the human race are placed in jeopardy. Revolutionary absolutism is determined to seize power and then to plunge our dear, good German nation into the abyss of unbelief and barbarism. It is far more noble and worthwhile in the eyes of God to defend Christendom against these forces than to sit idly and praise the deeds of our ancestors who marched to Jerusalem to rescue the holy places, where Christ's blood was shed, from the hands of the infidels. He who sits on his hands while the battle is raging will one day have to hear the words at the judgement seat of God, which that master spoke to the idle workingmen: "How is it, he said to them, that you are standing here, and have done nothing all the day?" (Matt. 20:6). May these words, by God's grace, serve to shed some light on the issues and help to incite others to join in this battle!

NOTES

1
Translator's Note: This was Pius IX who reigned
as pope from 1846 to 1878.

2
"What you perceive to be true, attribute to the
Catholic Church and hold fast to it. What seems
to you to be false, consider it as coming from me,
a mere man, and ignore it."

3
Translator's Note: All English translations of
St. Thomas Aquinas' Summa Theologica here and
throughout the text are from the three volume
English edition of the Summa published by
Benzinger Brothers: New York, 1947.

4
We recommend to all who are serious about getting
at the real truth in these matters, Möhlers
Symbolik. In this immortal work its author succeeded so admirably in combining the earnest pursuit of truth with loving moderation.
Translator's Note: The author was referring to
Johann Adam Möhler, a Catholic German theologian
who lived from 1796 to 1838.

5
See: Geschichte der Universität Erfurt, by
Dr. Kampfschulte. See also: Die Reformation,
ihre innere Entwickelung und ihre Wirkungen im
Umfange des Lutherischen Bekenntnisses, by J.
Döllinger: Vol I, esp. p. 410 ff.

6
The man who was responsible for the original split
among the Christian churches made it clear time
and again that during the period of the Reformation
this was the cardinal issue between the reformers
and the Church. That was nowhere expressed more
clearly than in his book about the lack of free
will (De Servo Arbitrio) where he took issue with
the polemical work which was directed against him
by Erasmus of Rotterdam who was defending free will.
In his introduction he praised Erasmus, because
the latter had acknowledged that in his campaign
against the Catholic Church Luther was not primarily
concerned with such issues as indulgences, purgatory,

and the veneration of Saints, but above all with
the question of free will and free cooperation
with grace. Having done that, he proceeded to
establish as the very basis of his whole teaching
the absolute absence of human free will; and he
did so with recklessness and a hostility that
was without equal.

7
See: Chapter·XXVI

8
Translator's Note: The Sachsen Spiegel referred
to here was the leading law book of the Middle
Ages. It was the work of a Saxon Knight Eike von
Repgau who, between 1220 and 1235 A.D. assembled
the entire body of law that was then contained
in the customs and traditions of the Saxons. His
work became the basis for much subsequent Germanic
law.

9
Dig. de Constitut. L. I. tit. IV. See Ozanam: La
Civilisation au cinquieme siecle. Tom. I. pag. 192.

10
Wolfgang von Gemmingen at the Westphalian Peace
Congress. Cf. Döllinger's Kirche und Kirchen,
p. 55.

11
Dollinger: Ibid. pp. 93-155.

12
Alexis de Tocqueville: L'Ancien Regime et la
Revolution: Paris, 1857.

13
Oevres de Fénelon: Paris, 1851. Tome I, pag. 155.

14
"In servilem degenerant anumum et pussilanimes fiunt
ad omne virile opus et strenuum." De regimine
princip. Lib. I, cap. 3.

15
De la Centralisation et de ses effets: Paris, 1861.

16
Barrot lost sight of the main reason - the growing
lact of religious sense, which is also an unmistak-
able by-product of state absolutism.

17
Geschichte von Mainz während der ersten franzosischen
occupation 1792-1793, by Karl Klein, published by
Verlag bon B. v. Zabern in Mainz, 1861.

18
   Tocqueville: op. cit. Chap. II.
19
   Translator's Note: The original text includes
   several footnotes which simply present the original Latin of Tacitus' Germania. These are
   omitted here, since the textual paragraphs to
   which they refer are themselves literal translations from the Latin.
20
   L'Eglise et la Société Chrétienne en 1861: Chap. 7.
21
   Suarez: Tract. de Fide Disp. 18 Sect. III, n. 4.
22
   Ibid. n. 5.
23
   Ibid. n. 7.
24
   Ibid. sect. IV, n. 9.
25
   Ibid. n. 10.
26
   Fénelon once said to the pretender to the British
   throne: "Sur toutes choses ne forcez jamais vos
   sjets à changer leur religion. Nulle puissance
   humaine ne peut forcer le retranchement impenetrable
   de la liberté du coeur. La force ne peut jamais
   persuader les hommes: elle ne fait que des hypocrites. Quand les rois se mêlent de religion, au
   lieu de la protéger, ils la mettent en servitude.
   Accordez à tous la tolérance civile, non en ap-
   prouvant tout comme indifférent,mais en souffrant
   avec patience tout ce que Dieu souffre, et en
   tachant de ramener les hommes par une douce
   persuasion. Oeuvrès de Fénelon: Paris 1787,
   Tomme III, pag. 530.
27
   Ecclesia in neminem judicium exercet, qui prius
   per baptismum non fuerit ingressus. Conc. Trid.
   Sess. IV. c. 2.
28
   Suarez: op. cit. 18 s. IV. n. 7.
29
   Ibid. n. 3.
30
   Suarez: Tract. de fide quo. 19. sect. III. et V.

31

   That, in fact, is how the Church has always
   dealt with schismatic Greeks and Protestants
   ever since they became historic realities;
   and it is completely untrue and scurrilous to
   propose to Protestants that they should be prepared for forcible conversion to the Church.
   Yet, surprisingly, that is the ludicrous case
   that is being made even now by those who agitate
   against the Concordats.

32

   See the pertinent historical work by Cardinal
   Xinenes von Hefele.

33

   Cf. Becanus: De Fide Tenenda Haereticis.

34

   "Hypocritical protests about freedom by people
   who never really understood what freedom is all
   about, while at the same time they punish the
   noblest expressions of freedom by exile! What
   madness and what an abomination," That is what
   St. Peter Damien already said some 800 years ago.
   "A man has a right to dispose of his property,
   but he does not have the right to bequeth it to
   God! He can give all of his possessions to other
   people, but one denies him the freedom to offer
   his soul to God, who gave it to him!"
   Montalambert: The Monks of the West, Vol. I,p.215.

35

   Dico, Papam non posse dispensare in impedimentis
   de jure naturae (matrimonium dirimentibus). S.
   Alphons. de Ligor. Theol. Mor. lib. VI, n. 1120.
   Translator's Note: Earlier editions of this work
   have the following as a footnote while later editions include it in the text: The Church always
   operates on the premise that there can be no contradiction between what the Church teaches and all of
   the laws governing the natural order, since both
   are the work of God and of the same Divine intelligence. Therefore these can only be in total
   harmony.

36

   There is nothing that the Catholic Church demands
   less than blind faith. She teaches instead that
   the true religion and the Church are equipped with
   such evident proofs of her Divine origin and truth

300

that anyone who makes use of unbiased reason
will be convinced that She is the one true
Church. To the extent that non-believers are
responsible for their unbelief, therefore, it
is not because they have put the Church to
the test, but because they have employed dishonorable and invalid criteria to Divine revelation and have therefore lost the Faith.

37
"Me of Athens, wherever I look I find you
scrupulously religious. Why, in examining
your monuments as I passed by them, I found
among others an altar which bore the inscrip-
tion, 'To the unknown God.' And it is this
unknown object of your devotion that I am
revealing to you." (Acts 17:23).

38
There is no doubt but that unbelievers too
can count among their numbers outstanding
intellects. Nevertheless, they cannot measure up, either in sheer numbers or in true
greatness, to the wise men of Christendom.
Above all, it is necessary to point out that
the prevalent conditions among unbelievers
is one of division and doubt. Christians,
on the other hand, have used their freedom
and come up with remarkable unity in all
essentials - something that can only be explained in terms of possession of the Truth!

39
Das Verhältniss von Haus, Staat und Kirche zu
einander und zur Schule: Berlin, 1849.

40
Leben und Wirken des heiligen Meinrad. This was
a commemorative publication marking the millenial
jubilee of the Benedictine Monastery at Maria
Einsedeln, published in 1861.

41
See: Hurter: Innocenz III, Vol. IV, p. 596.

42
F. J. Stahl: Recht und Staatslehre, p. 498.

43
One proof is sufficient to verify what we are
saying. In the most recent second edition of
Katechismusreden by Herman Fries, published as

a <u>Manual for Freemasons</u>, we find J. von Br. Oswald Marbach (Grandmaster of the Hair in the St. John Lodge, Baldwin of Linde in Leipzig) accused of resorting to biblical quotations far too often. Such use of the Bible conflicts with the principles of Masonry because: "The Bible is not a book of religion as it is for the Church, but a symbol of belief and of religious conviction." Marbach concedes this point, but he feels that the profusion of biblical quotations does not conflict with the principle. He continues: "But, my Brothers, I hear echoing in the hearts of one or the other brother the doubt: 'What happens to the reputation of Freemasonry which does not recognize any difference between creeds and embraces as brothers, Christians, Jews, Pagans, and Muslims, anyone who is a human being - now that we are dependent on the Bible to order and direct our faith.' O, my Brothers, would you let yourselves be put to shame by your Muslim brothers who do not have the Koran lying on their altars, but the Bible? I tell you, any pagan or Muslim who would be affronted by the biblical quotations that are heard here in praise of God and of truth is no real Mason, no matter what symbols, passwords, and handshakes he knows and uses. And I tell you further, if any Christian comes to these halls and denounces you for some word you use from the Koran or from Sophacles, or from Goethe, to praise God in spirit and in truth, he is no Freemason. That is because all writing that contains God's word is useful for teaching, for correcting, for improving, and for chastising in justice. The Bible is where God is. But where is He and who is to judge....? etc."

44
See: Lettre de Monseigneur l'Eveque d'Orleans au sujet de la vie et des opuscules d'Holzhauser par l'Abbé Gaduel. Orleans, 1861 Pp. I-XXII.
45
Tertullian: De Praescript. c. 31.
46
Ibid. c. 35.

[47] Ibid. c. 36.

[48] St. Irenaeus: <u>Adv. Haeres</u>. IV. c.26, n.2.

[49] Translator's Note: The German words, "dem ungläubigen, modernen Liberalismus..." are expressed here as, "...modern secular liberalism."

The Labor Problem and Christianity

by

Wilhelm Emmanuel von Ketteler

Bishop of Mainz

1864

Translator's Note

The work, <u>The Labor Problem and Christianity</u>
(<u>Die Arbeiterfrage und das Christenthum</u>), was,
like the previous one, written originally as a
book. It was first published in 1864 by the
<u>Franz Kirchheim Verlag</u> in Mainz; and it went
through three editions in short order. A fourth
edition appeared in 1890. Unlike <u>Freedom, Authority and the Church</u> which dealt with problems of
the political social order, this one dealt specifically with the economic order. Like the previous
work, however, this too found an echo in the teaching of a Roman Catholic pope - now in the person
of the great Pope Leo XIII.

The problems of the working class addressed
by Bishop von Ketteler remained unsolved; in fact,
they were more widespread by 1891 when Leo XIII
issued his famous encyclical <u>On the Condition of
Labor</u> (<u>Rerum Novarum</u>). Once again, according to
the biographer, Ludwig Lenhart, we have a public
acknowledgement by this influential Pontiff, who
once referred to Bishop von Ketteler as "<u>Son grand
predecesseur</u>," that, "It is from him that I have
learned." Anyone who has studied the many social
encyclicals of Leo XIII along with the better
publicized <u>Rerum Novarum</u>, will recognize the significant concordance in the teacings of the two men.
While Pius IX may be seen has having fired the
opening defensive salvo against the emerging post-
Christian world of the 19th century, Leo XIII already moved to the offensive by his many positive
directions on how society could be reconstructed
along lines which correspond with Christian teachings. It is clear that these teachings were first
applied to problems facing the modern world by
Bishop Wilhelm Emmanuel von Ketteler in <u>The Labor
Problem and Christianity</u> and in the shorter works
which came after it.

The original work included a statistical appendix in three parts. It is quite lengthy and
ranges over forty-seven pages in the original text.

The material, while impressive in its extent and in the manner in which it was presented, is not included here because of its dated historical nature. The three parts of the appendix were:

I. The Numerical Ratio of the Working Classes to the Total Population.

II. The Income and Expenditures of the Working Classes.

III.Regarding the Life Expectancy of Workers.

308

Foreword

On all sides voices are raised expressing concern over the plight of the workingman and offering suggestions for improving his lot. There are even widespread organizations which have as their purpose to work for the betterment of moral and economic conditions of the working classes. Meetings are held and periodicals appear bearing the designation, "Friends of the Worker," "Catechism for Workers," "Workers' Journal," etc. Speaking as a Catholic bishop, I now undertake to add also my views on this subject to those of all of the other spokesmen with their various proposals. If I too assume the title, "Friend of the Worker," and beg all Christian men who have the interests of the working class at heart to listen to and weigh my words on the subject, it is proper that I preface my remarks with a few words justifying my intrusion into this area, and explaining why I am entering the discussion. Many are probably of the opinion that as a bishop I have no business getting involved in such matters. Others may feel that as a Catholic bishop I merit the attention of Catholics only. I think otherwise.

I believe I have a right to express my opinions on the condition of the working classes, if for no other reason but that we are dealing here with the material needs of the Christian people. That places the whole matter in the category of Christian charity. Our Divine Savior established a permanent bond between the Christian religion and everything which has to do with alleviating the spiritual and corporal distress that people suffer. The Church at all times and everywhere has remained true to this assignment. The practice of Christian charity in various Christian works of mercy has always played a large role in the activities of the Christian Church. It is in the Church that we find the origin of such splendid concern for men in need. Every question that concerns itself with providing relief for people in distress is therefore essentially a Christian and a religious one in which the Church and all of her living members ought to become intensely involved.

I am further justified in getting involved in this matter because I must make clear what the position of the Church is, and what her teachings as well as her own particular remedies for this important problem are. Every Christian who is not content to live in total oblivion of the vital currents of our time ought to be sure that he is well-informed on this matter. The objective is to elevate the cultural and economic condition of the working class, and certain proposals are offered to achieve this objective. What could be more important for us than to know whether such proposals are in harmony with Christian principles, whether we are in sympathy with them, whether we may support them or not, and what special remedies Christianity has to offer for the cultural and economic betterment of the worker's condition. These are all questions which stand in an important relationship to our Christian religion, and on which I therefore, as a bishop and as a Christian, I am obliged to pass judgement.

However, my involvement in this matter has even deeper roots. I feel that the remedies that have been offered until now, and which for the most part not only ignore the Christian message but also reveal a misunderstanding and even a disdain for it, can only be truly helpful for the working class to the extent that they are brought into harmony with Christianity. Christ is the Savior of the world not only because he purchased the redemption of our souls. He also brought the answers for all other human problems, be they civil, political, or social. In a special way, He is also the Savior of the working class. The fate of the working class is ultimately in the hands of Jesus Christ. It was Christ who lifted the worker up from his former status as a slave. Without Him, all the efforts of the so-called friends of the workers cannot prevent their status from once again sinking to the condition that prevailed in pagan times. In what Christianity has done for labor, you have one of the clearest manifestations of Christ's Divine power and origin! A look back at the condition of the worker in the pagan era makes it clear that whatever progress labor has enjoyed, it owes to Jesus Christ. And so, as the architect is entitled to a voice in matters relating to the structure of

310

the cathedral that he has built, so Christianity
is entitled to a voice when there is discussion of
the condition of the working class. That is why a
servant of the Church has a perfect right to express
himself in the matter.

I have not only a right but an obligation to keep
a watchful eye on the concerns of the working class,
to make proper judgements about them, and to express
myself publicly when the occasion demands it. My episcopal status not only does not bar me from doing this,
rather it brings with it a special obligation to get
involved in the matter. When I was consecrated a bishop,
the Church put certain questions to me before She conferred on me the fullness of the priesthood. "Will
you show love and mercy to the poor, the homeless,
the thirsty, in the name of Our Lord?" I answered,
"I will." By the words of Our Blessed Savior, "As the
Father has sent me, I also send you..."the bishop becomes a representative of Christ. Therefore the Church
asks of a priest before She confers this office on
him, whether he has the intention of acting as Christ's
representative in bringing the love of Christ to all
classes of men who are in need of help. How could I,
therefore, after making this solemn promise, remain
detached from a question which has to do with the essential needs of such a large class of mankind? The
worker problem is of great urgency for me since it
touches the well-being of the many members of my
diocese who belong to the working class; and far beyond
this limited jurisdiction, it involves the welfare of
all workers with whom I am bound by Christ's love.

I feel justified, therefore in addressing my
words to all those in Germany who have dedicated themselves to this important question in a truly Christian
spirit. Even though the religious division has regretably erected a wall between us which still stands
fast, Christian charity knows no boundaries. We share
a common belief in the Son of God, which still binds
us together in an important sense; and this common
belief provides us with the opportunity to join hands
in a common effort to help alleviate the plight of the
working class.

When I undertake to discuss the condition of labor and the means to improve this condition from a Christian viewpoint, that is still a far cry from any suggestion that what I am saying is the final word on the matter. The surface has barely been scratched. I only wish to make one small contribution to the discussion. I would like to give proper emphasis to the Christian dimension in this discussion, which until now has received altogether too little attention. All in all, the condition of labor represents one aspect of that great social problem which is an inevitable consequence of the false religious, political, and economic principles stemming from the anti-Christian liberalism at large in our time. The problem is now only in its infancy. It will go on developing. Its grave consequences and its sad implications will become ever more obvious, until it will become painfully clear to all what has happened. Then others will treat the subject exhaustively and, by benefit of hindsight, substantiate the truth of what I am saying here. I refer to the truth for which all of human history provides the evidence, that only Christ and Christianity offer the remedy which the world and, especially now, the working class are looking for.

312

I   The Importance and Dimensions
    of the Labor Question

The so-called labor problem is essentially 'a
question of the worker's livelihood. Therefore it
is first of all a question of providing for the
basic needs: food, clothing, and shelter. Secondly,
it is of critical importance because it pertains to
the largest percentage of mankind. [1]

Therefore, the problem of labor has a far
broader significance than all of the so-called
political problems. He who reads the daily press
and observes the goings-on in parliament easily
gets the impression that the political questions
of the day are the really vital questions that confront mankind in our time. That is a big mistake.
The actual political issues concern only a small
portion of the nation, namely those who labor with
the pen, those who write and talk the most and who
control the press and dominate the speaker's rostrum;
and even in this group we are talking only about a
particular party which is in a position to exploit
the issue as an exclusively partisan concern for its
own benefit. This party controls both media: the
speakers platform and the press; and it uses them
to the utmost for propagating the notion that only
its own formula for healing the ills of mankind has
any merit whatsoever and that all else is scarcely
worthy of mention. It is constantly promoting the
same old message through both media. Our papers
faithfully reproduce all that takes place in parliament, and parliament faithfully echoes what is written in the papers. All of these long-winded and
monotonous discussions scarcely have any bearing on
the life of the working class which goes about earning its bread by the sweat of its brow. All that
these masses of the people, the workers and their
families, say and think and do, all that is of importance in their lives, all that has any influence
in improving or worsening their essential living
conditions, all of this scarcely comes up for discussion in the self-important political forum. The
only exception occurs when the political parties

313

find it in their immediate interest to exploit the
worker for partisan political purposes. But then the
workers are merely being used to serve the alien interests of those who falsely pretend to be the champions of the working class. The worker becomes a
pawn of partisan politics, and when the partisan goal
is achieved he is left to go on his merry way and once
again fend for himself, while his own condition is no
better than before. That has gone on now for over a
century.

Political parties have always pretended to make
the interests of the people their own. Time and again
politicians have summoned the people to the ramparts
at the critical moment. There the hapless masses have
had to do battle, up to and including shedding their
blood for the partisan cause. Invariably when the
victory was won, the condition of the people themselves
remained as desperate as it was before. All of the
so-called great achievements offered clear proof that
there was only a scant connection between what the
parties considered important and the well-being of
the masses. The people have been deceived by the
political parties, specifically by the dominant liberal party. The word was that all of this political
squabbling was in the best interests of the people.
Instead, the people's interests were in fact suffering setback after setback. In this sense, it is easy
to pose as a "friend of the people." All one needs
is the gift of gab in parliament and a certain willingness to publish long opinionated columns in the
papers; then the counterfeit title can be won. The
real friend of the people once said, "By their deeds
you shall know them." All that has changed. Now you
will know the friend of the people by his words and
by his slogans. By exploiting the dominance that
they enjoy in parliament and in the press, such persons try to persuade the people that their true interests are the political questions of the moment;
and in this manner people are shamelessly persuaded
to believe that their interests are best defended
by such endless speech-making and by long-winded,
tiresome publications. Many hallowed names in the
liberal party owe their widespread reputation in
Germany entirely to such false posturing, when in

314

truth they have accomplished nothing of merit for
the people.

The problem of the working class is something
else again. It is truly,and with no exaggeration,
of the greatest and most widespread importance. It
involves the most urgent needs of the people, matters
which concern the worker daily and constantly. They
occupy his attention totally and at all times. The
care of himself and his family, i.e., providing food,
clothing and shelter for himself, wife and children,
those are matters which concern him above all else,
from morning until night. They are the real source
of his joys and sufferings. The problem of the working classes is, to repeat once again, a question of
sustenance. It is a question of nourishing by far
the greatest part of mankind. Any person who has
anything worthwhile to contribute toward solving that
problem, we welcome with open arms as a benefactor
of the working class.

II The Unemployable Person

Among workers there are always many who are not
able to work. Since the worker is totally dependent
upon the wage from his daily labor, unless he has been
able to set aside savings, he will immediately find
himself lacking even the bare necessities for himself
and for those who depend upon him. Such unfortunate
persons are simply no longer able to help themselves
and must now depend upon support from their fellow
human beings. We must point this out so as to make
clear the connection between the poverty of many
workers, and Christianity and Christian charity.
It is true that some owners of enterprises and also
certain societies have made it their business to
look out for unemployable workers on purely humanitarian grounds, and without any specific Christian
motivation. It is proper that we recognize such
efforts, but in terms of the total needs of such
people this is a drop in the bucket. Practically
all of the poor of the world belong to this category
of unemployable workers; and it is a fact that virtually all of the immeasurable resources that come
into being all over the world for helping the poor,
including the countless hospitals, poor houses, institutions for the aged and infirm, have been inspired and founded because of the influence of the
Christian spirit. The present century is still the
beneficiary of such Christian capital and Christian
institutions, even though we tend to be forgetful of
these Christian origins, and sometimes even take them
out of the hands of the Church and entrust their administration to forces that are anti-Christian and
hostile to the Church. The ruling liberal party is
especially fond of expropriating the huge sums of
money that were accumulated by the Church in Europe
through the ages for helping the poor, and of blot-
ting out any memory of their origins. Only one bond
between them and the Church and Christendom remains
indissoluble, namely the force which first brought
them to life! Pre-Christian, pagan society had no
institution to provide for destitute workers. Such
wretched souls were left to their own resources, often
to perish in their misery. Where modern paganism provided such institutions, it received the impetus to do

317

so from Christianity. The pagan spirit itself is not capable of such action, except under extraordinary conditions or in individual circumstances when it is desirous of competing with Christianity. And that is how things will undoubtedly remain. True concern for the unemployable workers will always originate in the Church and with such persons who within the Church have captured the true love of Christ for their fellow man. Woe to the unemployable workers if it ever becomes possible to wipe out entirely the influence of the Church and Christendom! In such an event he will promptly find himself in the pathetic circumstances that prevailed generally in the pagan world before Christ's time.

Christendom provides for unemployable workers, however, not merely through the accumulation of charitable funds and the establishment of institutions for the poor. Far more important is the power of that supernatural love which motivates certain people to dedicate their lives and their talents to serving the poor in such institutions. Far more important than the gathering up of the helpless poor into such places is the loving care and attention which they receive there. Now there are just two possible motivations which would lead anyone to want to work in the institutions for the poor, the sick, and the infirm. Some regard such work as a means of livelihood, in other words, a paycheck. The meanest tasks are consigned to the most humble type of worker who, in other circumstances, would be employed as a domestic servant. Such workers perform in accordance with how they are paid. Since the work in such institutions is obviously the most unpleasant and difficult kind imaginable, work which human nature tends to rebel against, it follows that the most competent and capable workers would far rather work as servants in the homes of the well-to-do for higher pay and in far pleasanter conditions. That, all too often, leaves only the worst and least motivated workers to work in the institutions where the poor are taken care of. The poor hapless inmates must bear the consequences.

The other kind of workers who would serve in such circumstances are those who are less motivated by the

318

wage than by Christian charity. They often belong to that class which would not have to find employment in such lowly, difficult types of service. Yet they dedicate themselves to the unpleasant task due to the highest motivation which it is possible to have, that selfless Christian charity which sees in the poorest, neediest worker a brother in Christ and loves him as such! The difference between the way a person with such a disposition will care for the helpless poor, and how one who is working simply for a paycheck would perform is obvious and scarcely needs any further elaboration. But only Christianity is capable of providing such superior service to the poor, that true Christianity which draws its inner strangth from a living faith in the Son of God. Humanism is capable of a certain superficial imitation in raising funds and establishing institutions; but that genuine love of neighbor by virtue of which a man dedicates his very life to the service of the poorest of the poor is well beyond humanism's grasp. The Church has always had in all parts of the world and still has men and women who, though they often come from upper class families, have voluntarily dedicated their lives to working as the servants of the poor, needy working class, and ministering to their needs day and night. She can boast of thousands here and now who have served and who are still now serving the poor, whereas all of the secularist-humanist efforts together cannot instill such high motivation, cannot produce one Brother of Mercy, one Sister of Charity. They can only come up with a man or a woman who works for a paycheck. I will return to this theme later when I discuss the specific means which Christendom has to draw upon.

At this point, I cannot refrain from commenting on yet another matter. The Church properties which were confiscated during the secularization have enormous value. They have been incorporated into the state budgetary apparatus for the most part and generate income for the state which substantially alleviates the tax burden on the general public. The secularization was robbery, plain and simple; and it could only have done what it did by denying all of those principles on which the right to private property rests. The Church has relinquished her title to these properties permanently. By the same token, however, the poor have a right to the benefits that flow from such former Church property, since it is, both by virtue of Canon law and by the will of those who first provided it, the property of the poor. To some extent the state could make amends for this robbery if it were to use the former Church property as a kind of trust fund for helping the poor. Thereby we would simultaneously have the benefit of great institutions for accomplishing important tasks and we would also alleviate great need. Even if this thought seems inappropriate to some, let it nevertheless be expressed since, whatever else one may think of it, it is true. Let us turn now from the unemployable worker who is entirely dependent on Christian charity, to the problem that faces labor in general.

III   The Condition of Labor

In order to pass judgement on all of the remedies
that have been proposed for solving the problem of
labor, we must first have a clear insight into the
position which labor finds itself in with reference
to its wages and living standard, and to the reasons
underlying that position. We will concern ourselves
with the matter in this and in the following section.
The better the grasp that we have of these conditions
and of the reasons for them, the better position we
will be in to pass judgement on the value of the pro-
ferred remedies. It is because clear insight is all
too often lacking, that there is so much uncertainty
and confusion about the matter.

We will consider, in this section, the conditions
of the working class. Though we do our best to present
this picture here, we are not maintaining that what we
have to say has equal validity for all workers everywhere. Modern economic principles have not yet had
their full impact in all countries, nor have they fully
influenced all of the circumstances affecting the working class, so as to bear their ultimate fruit. Unfortunately however, what we have to say about the living
conditions of workers has already become reality for
far too many workers in far too many places. It is
the common ground upon which all labor finds itself
and will therefore lead to the same consequences
everywhere.

The satisfaction of the material needs of the
working class, the provision of all of the necessities of life for the worker and his family rests,
with so few exceptions that it only proves the rule,
on the worker's wage. And the wage rate in our time
is determined by subsistence in the strictest sense
of that word, i.e., the minimum food, clothing, and
shelter that a person needs to sustain a bare physical
existence. The truth of this proposition has been so
well established as a consequence of the well-known
controversies between Lassalle and his opponents that
only an overt intention to deceive would lead one to
deny it. [2] In it is contained the kernel of the

entire labor problem, as has been correctly maintained. On the one hand, it reflects the plight of the worker; and on the other, it provides the keystone for evaluating all of the proposals for improving the condition of labor.

This sad state of affairs becomes glaringly evident if we are aware of how human labor has been relegated to the status of a commodity which is subject, therefore, to all of the laws governing commodities. Just as the price of a commodity depends solely on the demand for it and the supply of it, so the wage for labor is to be determined by demand and supply. The law governing the price of a good is derived ultimately from the necessary costs of producing the good. Competition however promotes a state of affairs wherein everyone who produces a good tries to produce it more cheaply, then he can dominate the market and vanquish those producers who are able to produce the same good only at higher cost. Occasionally goods are even sold at below what it costs to produce them, and certain firms that are losing out in the competitve struggle manage to hang on in this fashion for a time. Ultimately they are headed for ruin, however.

All of this is regarded as applicable to labor and wage rates also. As the price of goods is based on their cost of production, likewise, the price of labor is based on the cost of the barest necessities in food, clothing, and shelter that are required to keep the worker alive. Just as the competing firm will do all in its power to reduce the cost of production in order to win over the competition, so, when there is an oversupply of labor, there is the tendency among workers to underbid their fellow workers and bring the minimum level of what they need to live down to a still lower level. The employers stand in the world's market place and ask, "Who will work for the lowest wage?" The workers underbid one another, depending on how desperate each is for work. That is how it happens that from time to time - as with merchandise - we find those terrible situations where this human commodity is offered for sale at a price which is below the cost of producing it. Translated into human terms, we find

322

a poor worker, desperate for work, accepting a wage
that is not enough to provide even the bare necessities for himself and his family. Eventually this
means that the man and his wife and children are
doing without that which is absolutely necessary
for living like human beings in matters of food,
clothing, and shelter. To do without these essentials - even if only for a few days - spells misery
and suffering! That is the condition of the working
class. Workers are dependent on the wage paid for
their labor, and this wage is considered just like
the price of any commodity. Its price is determined
daily by demand and supply conditions. The level
around which it fluctuates is subsistence. If
supply exceeds demand, then the wage falls below
subsistence. The general tendency, however, as with
all commodities, is toward ever cheaper production.
Here the cheapening of production means reducing the
necessities of life. Thus, in terms of this totally
mechanical, mathematical process it becomes inevitable that at times the price of labor does not even
cover the barest minimum needed for subsistence; and
large segments of the working class and their families
are destined for eventual starvation.

What a condition! Even if the full consequences
of these false theories have not become apparent everywhere, they will be. They will provide the proof of
how false the love of those friends of the people are
who reduced the working class to such a plight by such
false theories. We can no longer deceive ourselves
about this matter. The very subsistence of almost
the entire working class which makes up by far the
greater part of the human race in modern states, the
very question of daily bread necessary to sustain
the worker and his family is now at the complete
mercy of the caprice of the market placelike the
price of any other commodity.

I can think of nothing more reprehensible than
such a state of affairs. What a revelation it must
be for those poor people who are at the mercy of the
whims of the market place each day for all that they
need and all that is dear to them. That is the slave
market of our liberal Europe fashioned according to
the blueprint of our humanist, enlightened, anti-
Christian liberalism and Freemasonry!

IV Two Reasons for These Conditions

It was not always so. These conditions which
the working class finds itself in first arrived with
the advent of modern society. We are not yet passing
judgement. We are simply stating a fact. The fact
is that these fluctuations in the living standards
of the working class were unknown in past eras. They
put in their appearance when modern states were re-
structured after the French Revolution. Since that
time the worker's very survival depends upon the
daily wage for his labor which has become a commodity
whose price adjusts daily on the basis of demand and
supply; and it nearly always takes on a value that
sinks to the level of subsistence and sometimes below.

It is of overriding importance, therefore, that
we familiarize ourselves with the modern economic
principles from which these problems stem. We are
able to point them out with complete certainty and
accuracy. We need only to keep in mind what we have
already said and to ask the question how the labor
of a human being came to be regarded as a commodity,
and how the value of this labor came to be depressed
to the level of dire necessity. The price of a commodity is determined by demand and supply. Demand
and supply adjust acccording to competition in the
market place. Competition is at its best, however,
if all natural and artificial restraints are removed,
and this refers especially to such restraint as would
interfere with free trade in the market. Universal
free trade, therefore, implies unrestrained competition, and unrestrained competition reduces prices
to their lowest limit - the limit set by the costs
of production. If commodities can flow from all
parts of the world, the producer selling at the
lowest price will eventually dominate the market.
He will either drive all of his competitors from the
market, or else they will have to adopt the same low
price. The more widespread free trade becomes, the
more valid this principle becomes on an ever-widening
scale; and with the means of communication constantly
improving so that information about prices moves
rapidly from one part of the world to another, its

universal validity is more and more assured. Only the costs of transportation must be taken into account for they provide one last natural buffer against the law of free trade; and here the enormous progress in the means of transporting goods promises to remove even this last barrier.

Now if we apply all of that to the labor of human beings, which has come to be regarded as just another commodity, we have before us the real reason for the plight of the working classes. The wage for labor is determined by demand and supply. Demand and supply operate in the context of free competition, whether we are speaking of a commodity or of the labor of human beings. The most intense level of competition among suppliers of labor must inevitably push wages to the lowest possible level - a level which presupposes that labor is deprived of all safeguards. The abolition of all barriers to competition among businessmen is looked upon as no different than the removal of all limits on competition among workers. Unconditional and universal free competition must bring about a situation where workers compete wherever they are with no holds barred, with the same precise certainty that two times two equals four. This highest possible degree of competition must lead inevitably to a condition where the workingman's wage is reduced to the lowest possible level of subsistence.

We have now laid bare one of the reasons for the sorry condition of labor in modern states: unrestrained free competition. It is impossible to deny this as a fact. Labor is regarded as a commodity and in a condition of intense competition one buys a commodity at the lowest price from him who is willing to sell at the lowest price. Can anyone deny that this is the normal behavior on the market place? It is necessary that we emphasize this point time and again, since the political parties that curry public favor like to deny that this is the case. On the one hand, we have the great liberal party which for the most part draws its support from Freemasonry, from wealthy capitalists, and from among those rationalist professors and rank and file intelligentsia who dine at the tables of such

326

wealthy patrons, and who are beholden to speak and write each day in a manner which will please their masters. To keep up appearances and to deceive the ordinary people, this party takes on such catchy names as "The National League" or the "Progressive Party," at least until a still catchier name comes into vogue. On the other hand, there is the true radical party, which still tries to retain a modicum of independence from the great liberal party. Both however, are as one in proclaiming unrestrained free competition a postulate which is no longer open to question. Before we pass judgement on this postulate, we propose that even if free competition is the supreme law that liberals say that it is, then they ought to be consistent and not try to hide from people the fact that such competition inevitably and logically leads to the dreadful condition in which the working class now finds itself. Those parties are like the supposed friend who has pushed his comrade into the water and now stands on the river bank concocting various theories as to how the drowning man might be saved. For the benevolent effort expended in formulating fine theories, he deems himself a great humanitarian and a friend of the drowning man, without stopping to recall that it was he who placed him in his predicament in the first place.

I wish to make it clear that I do not propose to resurrect indiscriminately the restrictions imposed by guilds, especially as these eventually developed in their period of decline. Nor am I opposed to all efforts on behalf of greater freedom in enterprise. To make certain that there is no misunderstanding about this, we must examine the matter more closely.

Authority and freedom have this in common. They both originate in and have a definite place in the plan of the Creator. Both have a definite role to play in promoting the welfare of mankind. The problem is that, since they fall prey to man's fallible management, they never quite operate the way they were intended. [3] Instead, they are subject to abuse and exaggeration because of human weakness, and in some cases,

human greed. Authority comes from God, and wherever
and by whatever person it is exercised, it ought to be
in harmony with Divine authority. It is preposterous
to try to substitute some kind of popular will for
this authority. Yet, authority which comes from God
must be exercised by human beings, and regretably they
do not always exercise it in a manner which conforms
with what God intended. It sometimes becomes subservient to crass egotism and can lead to disastrous
consequences for those who are subject to it. That
inevitably leads to an extreme kind of reaction where
exaggerated freedom replaces it and is celebrated as
a kind of inherent necessity in the conduct of human
affairs. But freedom too has a necessary role in the
Divine scheme of things which cannot be denied. Again,
since it is subject to human manipulation, it falls
prey to the most unspeakable abuses. These abuses
appear in the form of insubordination and rebellion
against even the most fundamental laws and necessary
authority. The Christian recognizes a sinful condition in all of this rebellion. Abuse of freedom can
eventually lead to a general collapse which, as by a
kind of natural necessity, triggers the reaction
toward an opposite extreme. Thus, these two great
opposites keep clashing with each other here on earth
like the ebb and flow of the sea. It is a process
that continues throughout human history. Under the
circumstances, authority and freedom will fulfill
their God-given roles only when enough people harmo-
nize them and reconcile them in their own lives in
the way that God intended, and then, by extension,
in the various responsibilities which they are called
to fulfill toward their fellow man.

These basic considerations are applicable to all
human affairs and, therefore throw their light and
cast their shadows on the problems that we are dealing
with here. Guild restrictions constitute a restriction
of freedom, the freedom of enterprise in this case.
At the same time, however, they are a reflection of
that authority which has as its function to prevent
the abuse of freedom. Guild rules were designed to
offer protection to the workers - as a kind of contract
between the working classes and the rest of society. [4]
According to this pact, the working class performed

328

certain necessary services, and society, by placing
a restriction on competition, assured the workers a
higher wage than would otherwise have been possible -
so as to provide them with a decent standard of living and to protect them from day to day uncertainty
and insecurity. Whoever must earn his daily bread by
rendering necessary services to others has a moral
right to expect that his subsistence is not placed in
jeopardy from one day to the next by competition.
In other words, he has a right to a secure existence.
All other classes have such protection whether by
natural or artificial measures. Why should the working class be the exception? Why should the worker
alone be haunted from one day to the next by the fear
whether he will earn enough tomorrow to provide for
his family? Perhaps tomorrow an even more desperate
crew of workers will show up from some other area and
undercut me so that I am without work, and my wife
and children must go hungry! The wealthy capitalist
has protection a thousandfold for his business in his
very capital; and to an increasing extent, free competition at the level where he operates is a mere
sham. But the worker for some reason ought to be left
without protection; and to that end one castigates and
condemns guild restrictions.

We are not saying that the latter, as they came
to develop were faultless. Authority was abused -
which is no reason to overthrow authority. Guilds
were guilty of not keeping up with changing circumstances, thus they became quite abusive. They all too
often came to support inertia and selfish interests.
Prices became unconscionably high and quality often
suffered so that the consumer's rights were lost sight
of. Guilds needed to be updated and reformed. The
principle behind guild regulation, however, remained
sound, and it should have been preserved. In a certain
sense guild restrictions are to free enterprise as
authority is to freedom. Each is legitimate up to
a point, and then each is subject to certain restraints.
Guild restrictions became abusive and archaic to the
point where they represented mere class egotism; and
that is what triggered the cry for free interprise.
Free enterprise served to increase immeasurably the
output of goods, to bring down excessive prices, and

329

to improve the quality of goods. Thus it became possible for the poorer classes to enjoy certain goods and services that were formerly beyond their reach. But free enterprise too has its limits, its golden mean; and when these are transgressed, unwholesome consequences result just as they did when guild restrictions became irresponsible.

Thus far we have dealt with just one of the factors which has brought on the present condition of the working classes where labor is a mere commodity whose price is reduced to the level of bare subsistence. We must now turn to the second factor which has had a decisive impact in depressing the price of this "commodity," namely, the dominance of capital.

The supremacy of capital has - so far as the condition of labor is concerned - a doubly deleterious effect. <u>First, it reduces the number of independent workers and increases the number of mere day-laborers and workers who are entirely dependent on wages</u>. That is evident; and, given the prevailing economic principles, it is a condition that must follow with mathematical certainty. Thus, for example, the majority of coachmen in Paris lost their livelihood and had to take whatever work they could find. That occurred because a group of capitalists has taken over practically the entire transportation system of Paris. The same thing happens whenever a powerful building contractor or company, which has access to immense amounts of capital, moves in and takes over the building industry. Such people buy land, furnish building materials, provide the means to transport the materials, put up buildings and furnish them. Formerly, these various tasks were performed separately by various masters and craftsmen who are now reduced to the status of day-laborers. The same kind of thing happens in other industries. The greater the supply of capital, the more things move in this direction. If we stop to think what enormous amounts of capital have already been amassed in the hands of certain individuals and organizations, we can scarcely imagine the enormous power which capital will exercise as this trend continues. The number of mere

330

day-laborers and wage-earners must yet increase immeasurably since business will become more and more concentrated.

The second effect which capital has is to be found in the fact that as it is invested in machinery it will depress the price of merchandise even further.[5] The price of merchandise which capital produces, using machines, is no longer determined by the cost of supporting the worker, but rather by the original cost of the machine and the cost of its use. The worker must now compete with goods produced by machinery. He is confronted not only by competing fellow workers who must still eat, drink, and sleep as he must. Now he finds himself competing with machines which experience neither hunger, nor the need for sleep, but which work relentlessly day and night with energy that is measured no longer in human terms but in horsepower! The poor seamstress will sooner or later tire and have to stop working, but the sewing machine works with a speed that is beyond what countless human hands can achieve. Yet, the seamstress must settle for a wage which reflects what the machine rather than human hands can accomplish. That is the condition in all branches of industry, and we are only at the beginnings of what modern technology can accomplish. What do we have to look forward to when the implications of machine production for modern economies and human welfare, along with their merciless and relentless qualities, will have spread and taken their effect on all sections of the working class?

That is the condition of labor that has begun to unfold before our eyes, and those are the two economic principles of which this sorry condition is the result. It was the proper duty of governments to recognize the difference between what was abusive in guild restrictions and what was worthwhile. They should have worked out policies which incorporated the better features of guild restriction with legitimate freedom in enterprise. Alas, true political prudence seems to have become all too rare on this earth. Political leaders are leaders, typically, in the sense that skids lead a wagon that has begun to slide downhill. They are themselves led on and

331

captured by the spirit of the times and by party
loyalty, as these forces lead men toward decline.
They are effective, if at all, only in reducing
somewhat the rate of speed with which the decline
occurs. They failed to grasp the need to harness
these two forces - authority and freedom - for the
benefit of the working class, and we are therefore
headed irretrievably toward uninhibited freedom of
enterprise with all of its dire consequences. The
evil brought about by the excesses of free enterprise
will prove to be far worse than those brought on by
abusive guild restrictions.

One can scarcely imagine a more sorry situation
than the plight of countless workers standing in the
world market each day, offered for sale like any other
commodity for the price of the wage which must provide
their bread. They are plagued constantly by the uncertainty whether they, along with their wives and
poor children, will be without food, clothing, and
shelter, come tomorrow. Such a state of affairs
must eventually make mankind into a raging sea which,
lashed by savage winds, will one day burst out of its
boundaries and destroy everything in its path.

Having discussed the condition of labor with
reference to its means of livelihood along with the
reason for the problems that confront the working
class, let us now turn to the remedies that various
parties have proposed as a solution to the problems
and our evaluation of these remedies.

V <u>Proposals of the Liberal Party</u>

We can sum up the liberal party's proposals in
three categories, the first of which prepares the
ground for the next.

The first category embraces the following
proposals which are regarded as cures for what ails
society: 1) unconditional freedom of enterprise;
2) unconditional freedom of trade; 3) unconditional
freedom of entry, i.e., the right of anyone, regardless of what community, district or nation he hails
from, to settle in any area and to make his livelihood in whatever manner he chooses. This freedom
of entry extends, therefore, not only to all citizens, but even to all foreigners. It means also
the right of anyone to establish residence anywhere
so long as he has lived there continuously for a
certain period of years and has not had to depend
upon public welfare for his livelihood. It also
includes the freedom to marry as one wishes subject
only to the general civil requirements and without
regard to other customary restrictions on this
right, such as the prior approval of either the
community where the person came from or the one in
which he has now settled, or the investigation by
public authorities into his ability to support a
family in the occupation of his choice. 7

Such general rules prepare the way for a
second group of proposals, namely, the worker's
right to individual self-help, and the cultural
formation of the working class.

All of these propositions have their final
culmination in a third group of proposals which embrace the kind of workingmen's organizations that
are peculiar to this concept and which would be
called for in the interests of mutual social assistance.

Those are the proposals of the liberal party.
There is no denying that they involve a certain
amount of good intention to help the working class;

333

and they contain a certain amount of valid insight
into the workers' present plight. It is also true
that they contain a good deal of truth and justification. Their weakness, so it seems to me, lies in exaggeration, in inherent contradictions, and in a certain amount of muddled thinking. Underlying them are
false principles. What is true about them is not new,
and what is new is not true! In the final analysis,
these solutions are not at all capable of coming to
grips with the real problems which confront the working class. Permit me to substantiate my position in
specific terms.

    The first category of liberal proposals would
lead to a real atomization of the human society. It
rests on rationalistic-mechanistic premises which are
the stock-in-trade of the liberal party, and it is
simply an application of the materialistic principle
to problems besetting poor mankind. The materialist
regards all being, no matter how complex, as composed
of basic atomic particles. It is made up of them and
it eventually breaks down into them again. That is
the basic underlying principle that informs all of
modern economics. It would be a valid principle if
men singly and in their relationship to other men were
merely so many numbers. The whole is equal to the sum
of its parts and each part is equal to every other part.
One can rearrange these equal parts as one may wish,
and it makes no difference. If this were indeed a
valid concept of human society, then it would in fact
be true that one could disregard all distinctions among
men in the four corners of the earth and allow them to
mingle indiscriminately; unrestrained and unconditional
freedom would lack only the inevitable consequence.
For, if marriage were no longer subject to any condition at all, then divorce must also be allowed. This
means that the Christian teaching about the indissolubility of marriage would have to be viewed as justifiable, and it would have to be rejected by the majority
of some duly elected assembly. Such atomization however, such a reduction of human society to the status
of identical, individual, nuclear particles - an approach that is in perfect harmony with our materialistic outlook - would warrant the winds of chance
scattering these particles in haphazard fashion any-

where on earth.

The whole idea is totally false, however, as its
underlying principles are totally false. People are
not mere numbers, nor are they all of identical value.
Mr. Schulze-Delitzsch has himself maintained that absolute social equality is errant nonsense which contradicts nature. The manifold physical and intellectual
capacities of men are of infinite variety, and they are
immeasurably increased by the different cultural influences which operate in a vast variety of environ-
mental circumstances. It is true that man must support himself inasmuch as he is able, and that God has
given him the capacity to accomplish this end. But
it is not true that each and every individual is actually in a position where he can provide for himself.
It is even less true that each man is just as capable
as every other man to take care of his needs. Given
the immeasurable range of bodily and mental capabili-
ties of different people, as well as differences in
their cultural formation, all of which also change
with age in the same person, Providence itself has
given rise to the development of a wide variety of
organic structures in which man finds help and protection. Therefore, even though it may not be done
deliberately, it is a crime against humanity to do
away with all of these aids and to abandon man in his
individual differences and varying external circumstances to some naked, daily competition with the
rest of humanity. If the entire human race is to be
organized along the lines of such principles of unrestricted free enterprise, unlimited free entry and
freedom of movement, as well as complete freedom to
form and dissolve the family structure as one wishes, [8]
and if this liberal-rationalistic computerized society
is then allowed to run its inevitable course according
to uneluctable mathematical laws, the absolutely inevitable outcome would be that each day those digits
which do not perform up to a certain uniform level of
efficiency would have to be sorted out and eliminated
in the general free-for-all competition. Such a first
principle of society can scarcely offer a cure for
the problems which beset the working class. It will
rather aggravate an already intolerable situation by
calling into play the cruelest kind of competitive

335

struggle. Without fail, the worker's wage will be driven to the lowest level possible - the level of sheer subsistence; and indeed, even this wage will be paid only to those workers who are at the peak of their physical and mental powers. That would be the mathematical consequence of such a purely mechanical-mathematical process!

Yet, this group of remedies is only supposed to provide the underlying structure for social order. A second batch of proposals is appended, namely, the much vaunted self-help and the prospect of more training for the working class. I fear that these means of multiplying the loaves and fishes which the liberals have in mind are also doomed to fall short of the proposed mark.

The liberal party never fails to look askance at the charitable institutions run by the Church and by religious. Yet, it cannot deny that on occasion workers are rendered unable to work and require charitable assistance. The party also speaks of hospitals and homes for the incapacitated, but at the same time it always comes back to the deprecation of charitable actions and tries to persuade the workers that to avail oneself of the services of charitable institutions, as hitherto provided by the churches, is somehow degrading to human dignity. For example, the party views the great charitable organizations that operate in Belgium, and it shamelessly proclaims how much better these sums of money could have been put to use. It takes pains to propagate the opinion that while the accustomed Christian approach to helping those in need may have been well-intentioned, it was in fact misdirected and only served to encourage sloth. The approach proposed by liberal humanism, on the other hand, would eliminate such temptations to sloth and restore the dignity of honest labor. Hence comes all of the talk about self-help, which is repeated ad nauseam, and the supposed great beneficial effect which it would have for the worker. Hence we hear talk. also of how the cultural formation of the workers, under the watchful eye of the fathers of the liberal party, would boost their capacity for self-help in a manner that is both unprecedented and marvelous.

336

All of this is one-sided and in many ways untrue. The continued propagation of such unbalanced and false notions can only succeed in causing unspeakable harm to the working class. The great liberal party appears to be lacking in a sound conception of human nature and of its capacities. Superficial rationalism is responsible for this misconception. It understands the actions of machines far better than it perceives the actions and needs of human beings. In particular, it lacks completely any deeper insight into the workings of Christianity and of the Church, both of which it approaches full of prejudice. Specifically, the rationalist has no grasp of the supernatural element in Christianity, of its teachings, and of its helps. He cannot understand that whatever good he seeks to accomplish can ultimately be accomplished only by Christianity. Whatever, the Party's good intentions are, it will eventually succeed only in doing untold harm to the working class. Let us examine the basis for this assertion and then go into specifics.

First of all, it is not true that Christian charitable activity has promoted sloth. In concept and in execution, such activity is geared to helping those who are unable to help themselves. Abuses occur, but they are not ingrained in the Christian institutions. He who would eliminate all abuse would have to adopt a position which would inevitably result in extreme harshness toward those who are in genuine need of charity. The depreciation of charitable works is all too often a concealed envy, and such talk is meant to disguise one's own lack of concern for the neighbor in need. It is not Christian charity and the Church's concern for the poor which deserves the accusation that it encourages sloth and indolence. Such results are more peculiar to publicly sponsored charities that have been divorced from the Church, and where the poor are handed a pre-determined dole by some public administrator.

In any case, it is presumptuous and arrogant for the liberal party to posture as though it alone had discovered the meaning of self-help as well as the dignity which she proposes for the worker and now offers to the world as its own new-found truth. Such

337

pretense borders on the contemptible. The need for
self-help has always been obvious so long as there
have been people. God has imprinted the recognition
of this need indelibly in human reason; and so that
no one could forget it for a moment, He equipped man
with a natural law according to which he must eat and
drink in order to stay alive. Translated into plain
language, the need for self-help is nothing more or
less than the duty to work. Beyond that, God expressed the whole idea explicitly more than 6000 years
ago when he told man, "By the sweat of your brow you
shall eat your bread." Yet, it was reserved for
Christianity to bestow a full and proper dignity
upon this law of work which was engraved in man's
nature and decreed from the very beginning in God's
revelation. The true meaning and noble status of
work is the exclusive province of Christianity, not
of humanistic liberalism. Whoever wishes to understand work and through work to elevate the status
of the workingman must go through Christ to gain a
proper insight into the meaning of labor. The labor
of which we speak here has three peculiar properties.
It is a necessary means of earning one's bread; it
is a burdensome obligation against which human nature
tends to rebel; and it bestows a basic moral strength
which transforms and ennobles man. When the liberal
party speaks of the manner in which self-help, i.e.,
honest labor, and even more so of how diligence and
ambition dignify a man, it is still unable to reconcile these apparently contradictory properties of
labor. Only the deepest mysteries of religious faith
are capable of reconciling the often oppressive burden of labor with its finer ennobling qualities.
Liberals are scarcely dedicated to this dignity of
physical labor out of genuine charity; and virtually
all workers look forward to the day when they will no
longer be subject to the tedium of such work. From
a purely rationalistic point of view nice words about
the dignity of labor scarcely make any sense at all.
Among the pagans, labor was left to the slaves, and
without a doubt, if the world is refashioned according
to the principles of liberalism, the working class
will revert to this condition of slavery. Eloquent
speeches will not suffice to convince workers, on the
basis of purely naturalistic principles, that the lot

338

of those who must carry the burden of heavy labor on
their shoulders is an enviable one. If we are destined for nothing more than life on this earth, and if
the inner yearning for happiness has no other fulfillment than worldly pleasures, then the fate of those
who must go through life deprived of such worldly pleasures, eking out the barest subsistence by hard labor -
and by far the greatest part of mankind finds itself
in this position - is a cruel and contradictory absurdity in nature itself. This contradiction between
what the inner drives of human nature send a man seeking after, and the realities of what the mass of mankind is able to attain can in no way be explained away
by liberal prattle about self-help, the dignity of
labor, or even by various kinds of entertainment proposed for the working classes. Godless liberalism
cannot, by its teachings, prevent the eventual realization by the working class that its own position,
as contrasted with that of the more fortunate classes
of mankind, represents a monstrous injustice which can
only be explained in terms of improper political and
social structure that has its origin in the malice of
the upper classes. Such realization will inevitably
bring about a state of mind which affords a ready
audience for those "friends of the people" who promise
a satiety of earthly goods by simply making certain
changes in the political and social order. Right
now there is an as yet dimly perceived groundswell
of opinion that is so disposed; and that explains the
willingness of so many to follow demagogues blindly.
Given the premises of secularist unbelief, the lot of
the working class is and must remain a desperate and
unhappy one, where the workers are barred from precisely those pleasures which are extolled as the only
worthwhile ones, and which it observes its liberal
"friends" enjoying daily. A person has to be purblind
to not see the inevitable consequences of this philosophy. In pagan times, the outcome was one where the
slaves ended up murdering their masters, or else the
masters drove their slaves under the lash. That is
the practical and inevitable consequence of all concern for the working class which stems from purely
materialistic principles - principles which are the
liberal party's sole reliance.

339

Labor has, as we have seen, two seemingly
contradictory aspects. It has a burdensome, exhausting quality which man tends to rid himself
of whenever he is able. Every worker is conscious of this burdensome aspect; but labor also
has an ennobling, rewarding quality. The explanation of this paradox can be found only in Revelation and in our religious Faith. Our Faith teaches
us that the labor to which we are subject is the
consequence of sin and has to do with the relationship between God and man. Thus, work is in part a
punishment; but it is at the same time a means of
reconciliation with God. Furthermore our Faith
tells us that the Son of God, in order to expiate
for the sins of man, became the son of a worker
and became Himself a worker. Christianity, therefore, explains for us the reason why we must labor.
It also explains the paradox in work and the redemptive qualities and true dignity of labor.

Christianity also teaches us that there is
something beyond earthly pleasures, something
whose enjoyment is not limited to our finite
existence here below. The honest worker will
partake of that enjoyment to the extent that he
performed his duties worthily in this life and
to the extent that he suffered deprivation of
earthly goods patiently for the love of God.
There can be only two kinds of workers, Christian and non-Christian ones. Only the Christian worker has a sense of purpose which can
reconcile him with his lot in life. Only the
Christian worker has motivation in his work
which can ennoble him. Only he has access to
ideas which can satisfy him with an inner
peace and a kind of joy of the spirit that
make it possible to bear up under deprivation
of all kinds. All of these consolations are
lacking to the non-Christian worker. He has
to curse the blind fate which has made him subject to the cravings of earthly pleasures at the
same time that it has placed him in a position
in society where he cannot have access to the
means to satisfy them. His entire life is an
unsatisfied craving. He can have no other motive

340

for work but the attainment of the dire necessities and the remote chance that by a fluke of
fortune he may be able to enjoy a few years without hard work. There is absolutely nothing which
will make his work fulfilling or joyful. His
"friends" have already robbed him of the inspiration he could have derived from reflecting on Christ,
the Worker. It is sheer madness for the liberals
to imagine that they can lighten the great burden of
daily tiresome work in the sweat of one's brow -
the lot of most of mankind - by speeches about
self-help and human dignity!

Finally, the proposal whereby the liberal
party offers to improve the lot of the workers by
means of the cultural advancement of the working
class is also spurious. Societies for the cultural betterment of the working class are prominent these days. One tries to expand their activities wherever possible. A questionnaire designed to secure statistical evidence regarding
these activities put out by the liberal party
and circulated at the Fifth Session of the International Statistical Congress in Berlin gives
us an indication of the impressive organization
and extent of what such activities are designed
to accomplish for the working class. The societies were represented there under the modest
title: Association for the Development and En-
hancement of the Spiritual Capital of Their
Members. There followed a series of headings
under which information was solicited. Under
"Purpose of the Association, " the question
asked was whether that was fulfilled by:
a) courses of instruction; b) regular meetings
and lectures; c) through establishment and support of a library; d) through presentation of
exhibits in the natural sciences; e) through
sponsorship of scientific and technological
excursions; f) by providing stipends for trips;
g) through distribution of periodicals. Then
came the following list of questions: a) Are
family type meetings held? How often? Do
children participate? b) Are concerts held?
How often? Does the Society's choir participate? How often during the year? c) Does

the Gymnastic Society of the Association sponsor
tournaments? Competition? How often? d) Does
the Society have a theatre? What are its activities? e) Does the Society sponsor Christmas parties for its members? Etc....

We have presented these examples only to indicate the breath of activities envisioned by such
worker cultural-formation groups. They are designed
to embrace every part of the worker's life, both
its material and its intellectual side. They
extend even to his leisure and recreation and
to his family live. All are under the benevolent,
watchful eye of the proposed associations.

If we ask ourselves how such organizations,
oriented toward the cultural uplifting of the
working class, can achieve the aim with which
we are concerned here, to place the worker in a
better position amid the general competition
that prevails, to command a wage that is above the
bare minimum subsistence, we are no better off
than with the "newly discovered" formula of self-
help. These means cannot help in the slightest.
Proper trade schools where workers can learn the
technical skills of their craft and also round
out and complete their elementary schooling are
absolutely essential. To whatever extent such
worker organizations may fulfill that need, they
offer a worthwhile service. In this regard, however they are not especially helpful. The whole
range of their activities that we have indicated
above will, on the other hand, not significantly
improve the material welfare of the workers.

. We have to say, therefore, that the workers
are the victims of a cruel hoax. The great mass
of workers are daily subject to oppressive working
conditions. Even their children must all too often
seek gainful employment at an age when they ought
to be completing their elementary schooling. The
majority of the working class is physically exhausted by the daily toil to which it is subject.
Only the rare exception would be in a position to
take even minimum advantage of the dazzling array

342

of cultural-uplift activities, and only a minority of those present at lectures and assemblies would be capable of fully understanding what the gentlemen are trying to put across to them. As always, there is a select handful of uniquely endowed individuals who can derive some useful knowledge from these programs which would be of actual benefit in the conduct of their businesses. They represent a dwindling minority. However, at the same time that these activities are of only minimum utility in helping the working classes meet their real needs, those aspects of the programs which offer superficial entertainment and titillate the pleasure-seeking instincts find the widest participation and acceptance. The spiritual capital which is supposed to develop out of the activity of such organizations is most likely to accumulate and develop in such gatherings as serve the quest for pleasure. That is a definite outcome of these organizations, as is already apparent. It is not the proper means to secure a higher wage for the workers, and that is the announced objective of all, in particular of those who call themselves the friends of the working class. If one invites workers who barely earn enough to subsist on, to all of these family gatherings, amusements, concerts, theaters, dances, and gymnastic tournaments, he must, above all, if he wishes to deal with them honorably, provide new sources of livelihood for them. Otherwise one would contribute to the ruination of the workers and their families instead of helping them. In the last analysis, then, the worker-uplift organizations would not only not increase the workers' spiritual capital, but they would even destroy what is left of their material capital!

These dangers are enhanced even more by one other consideration. In the cultural uplifting process, which the great liberal party promises the workers, religion and Christianity are totally disregarded. They are ignored, but not to the extent that a certain bias against and contempt for Christian beliefs are prevented from coming to the surface at times. The great mass of workers is still bound to Christendom and the Church, for

343

for the most part. The leaders of worker-uplift
societies, however, stem for the most part from
those segments of our urban society which have
long since abandoned any adherence to Christianity
and belief in supernatural revelation. In these
circles there exists confusion and a bewildering
chaos of contradictory views regarding the basic
realities. They range from the crassest materialism to a kind of sentimental deism. Persons with
such philosophies are the ones who propose to act
as patrons of the working class, and they promise
to satisfy the workers' hunger. They will certainly succeed only in worsening the plight of
the workingman. But the temptation is great.
We have noted the impressive arsenal of means for
achieving the cultural advancement of the workers.
Problems of securing a daily sustenance and bread
for one's family are left to the working class;
and everything else is provided for by the leaders
of the worker-uplift organizations. Their lectures, their schools, their libraries and, in
particular, their scientific discourses and excursions, their theatres, their songfests, their
family and folk entertainment will all serve to
make propaganda for a culture which is itself
hopelessly sick and which is now to be foisted
on the workers. Even Sunday, when the Church alone
would be in a position to bring Christ into the
hearts of the working class, is now taken over
for the purposes of the worker-uplift societies.
As evidence, we offer the particular interest
which one party is already taking in the violation of the Sabbath. Thus we see these archi-
tects busily erecting a church of materialism
to elbow aside Christ's Church. The societies
which have as their ostensible purpose to improve the lot of the working man show another
and sinister, disturbing side. Their real purpose serves less to bring about an improvement
in the material welfare of the workers than to
exploit these workers for partisan political
purposes and to spread their anti-Christian
virus.

Let us sum up briefly what we have said thus far about the cultural uplift societies for workers. There is genuine benefit for the working class in such trade schools as might be established. It is also possible that a certain few, especially endowed workers, might derive some inspiration to seek further training in their craft or occupation. For the vast majority of the workers there would be no benefit, only damage. The quest for idle entertainment and conceit will be enhanced at the same time that Christian principles will be eradicated from their hearts. In their place will be implanted a desolate unbelief. Godlessness and immorality will thereby be spread, and those passions will be awakened which make poverty unbearable and rob the worker of all consolation and whatever satisfaction he may still derive from his labors and exertions. Most men already find tiring the struggle to wrestle with the ever present problem of providing food, clothing and shelter to satisfy basic needs. The liberal party now takes it upon itself to train the worker in such a way that this struggle will become unbearable for him. The rich have, along with their godlessness, at least the minimal consolation that can be derived from their superficial satiety of worldly things, and they can try to fill the emptiness of their hearts with these baubles. To deprive the workers, with his empty hands and exhausting day's work, of his God and of Christ, is to subject him to despair or abject brutalization. That is the inevitable consequence of worker cultural-uplift societies.

We turn now to a third group of remedies by which this party proposes to improve the lot of the working class. These are meant to be the crowning achievement of the whole liberal system, and they are intended to demonstrate its humanitarianism and effectiveness. The first group depicts for us the long list of freedoms whereby the human race is to be relieved of all limitations in its everyday activities so that its energies may be directed into more constructive channels. The second group shows us the great forces whereby man, thus freed, is to be brought to his ultimate fulfillment; namely,

345

by self-help and a new cultural formation. The third group, which is designed to crown the whole program, offers the concept of <u>social self-help</u> and <u>cooperatives</u>, which are its natural outgrowth. Schulze-Delitzsch, who is the leading spokesman for these associations, has outlined for us the scope of their activity.

In addressing myself to a criticism of these proposals and their usefulness for improving the condition of the working class, I shall express my thoughts in the following propositions. First, what is valid in these ideas is not new; second, they present what is true in the worst possible way; third, they do not remotely come to grips with the problem which they promise to solve, namely, a thorough-going, genuine improvement in the material welfare of the working class. Closer examination will bear out my claims.

First, what these ideas contain that is true, is not new. It is true that when people band together for achieving an objective their individual strengths are enhanced and complementary. It is true that this principle is also valid as applied to workers. When they band together into an organization or a cooperative, they fortify themselves with one of the most effective means to combat and alleviate material needs. But here we are faced with the same problem as with the notion, self-help. As no one has ever doubted the need to work, so no one has ever really questioned the effectiveness of organizations and cooperatives for boosting the power of the individual. Organization is as old as mankind, and that is precisely why one has to invent new names for it, like "social self-help," in order to sell these ancient ideas to the poor as the brand new creation of some great new-found humanitarianism. Such ideas date back to the time when the first herdsman banded together into tribes to achieve common aims by joint efforts. They date back to when the first agricultural communities were organized and laid the foundations for community enterprises. Even more basically, the first family was already a cooperative organization for social self-help. One ought to be especially

346

careful not to try to persuade us Germans that the principle of social organization is a brainchild of the modern humanitarianism. Whatever the German spirit has given rise to over the widest possible range of human endeavors has taken on a cooperative form. One expression of this communal effort in which the Germanic way found expression was to be found in the guilds. Guilds represented the form in which social self-help, to use the contemporary term, developed in accord with the German national spirit in that area, where the working class found itself engaged in specific industries. The family, political communities, the state, Christian communities, guilds and corporations, and countless other social organs all stem from one simple idea. According to a law of man's nature, men must band together if they wish to achieve their various purposes and satisfy their pressing wants.

We have to point out, however, that the liberals are in a certain sense contradicting their own philosophy when they advocate the cooperative idea. Self-help, as understood by the liberals, is opposed to cooperation. Social self-help is no longer merely an aid for the proud, self-sufficient individual. It is rather a humble acknowledgement that the individual alone is not sufficient unto himself. The term, social self-help, has a good ring to it inasmuch as it signifies the help of one's colleagues; but this notion, properly speaking, is ruled out by the principles of liberalism. Let us consider for the moment only the first group of its proposals, according to which a man is supposed to be left entirely on his own and dependent on his own abilities. No one should aid him. That would constitute an offense against his dignity. His pride, which measures his true worth as a man, rests on his ability to take care of himself. That is how the concept of competition is supposed to reach its full development. Each man is on his own; and it is every-man-for-himself as he competes on a world-wide basis with every other individual to the fullest extent of his physical and mental capacities. That is self-

347

help in the strict sense of the word as understood in the liberal system of thought. It represents the real measure of human worth. Now if the individual man turns to others for help, that is an open admission that he is not self-sufficient and that he requires the support of others for his fulfillment. Social self-help is help with and through one's comrades. It stands opposed, therefore, to the notion of self and individual for whom all the vaunted freedoms of liberalism are invoked.

Just as the cooperative idea stands opposed to the entire system of liberal thought and stems from a social philosophy that one is sworn to overthrow, nature and the natural law forces that system of thought into other non sequiturs. Limits are once again established for free trade and free enterprise. That is precisely what such organizations for social self-help imply, namely that they must afford some kind of protection against conditions that emanate from the situation where everyone is helping himself. Thus, free competition is once again restricted. A cooperative that procures raw materials for its members, for example, has as its purpose to preserve them from a free-for-all competition as well as from oppression by capitalists. It is designed to gain an advantage for its members over other workers who are dependent solely on their individual abilities. All of these associations represent, therefore, a reincarnation of tariff restrictions and limits on free enterprise by which one hopes to head off the consequences of unrestrained free competition. Liberals, if they wish to be fully consistent, ought to outlaw cooperatives rather than foster them. They stand in open defiance of the purity of modern economics and have a definite, darkly medieval, even ultra-montane flavor; which only proves that nature is more powerful than theoretical nonsense!

The simple truth is that the entire human race is basically a giant cooperative where all are forced to help each other and to acknowledge

348

each day that mere self-help is inadequate from
the moment of birth to the hour of death. Even
a charitable handout which a rich man offers to
a poor man is an expression of social self-help
in the proper sense of the word, just as is any
other act of mutual help and love that flows from
the complementarity implicit in human differences.

What is true in this liberal system of thought,
the idea of cooperation, is therefore not new.
What is more, it is directly contradictory to all
that liberalism stands for. I have asserted further
that the liberals offer us a truth in its worst
possible form. The principle of organization which
brings people as well as raw materials together into
powerful unity is a principle that is operative in
the plant and animal world, as well as for man and
for the human race, and, for that matter for the
entire universe. It originates, of course, in the
eternal intelligence and power and love of God,
and it shows up on earth in two forms. There is
a mere mechanical, external type of organization
bringing things together in a superficial, accidental manner; and there is the organic unification
which brings things together in a lasting substantial way. The modern cooperative principle would
fasten men together in mechanical fashion, whereas
God unites men organically as cooperatives formed
by men in ages past were united organically.

The family is such an organically united cooperative. It is destined to be destroyed by the
unconditional and unrestricted right to marry and
to divorce. The community is such an organic cooperative in which a variety of morally and spiritually binding powers are at work. It is destined
to be dissolved by the unconditional right to move
into and out of an area. Nations and states are
also such moral organisms in which countless moral
forces, like the idea of home and fatherland as
well as history itself with its mixture of good
and bad fortune, bind men together organically.
Obviously, national demarcations have to be transitory. They do not fit into the eventual scheme
of things. The first set of rules which liberalism

349

proposes makes it clear that their proponents
wish eventually to abolish all national boundaries. They are striving toward a kind of cosmopolitan world citizenry where every stranger
would have as much right in any German community
as the native inhabitants. The merchant guilds
and craft guilds were organic unities in the best
sense of the term. They bound together the common material interests, which the latter day so-
called self-help is supposed to foster, with
countless moral and spiritual forces into a
genuine living organism. These guilds have been
all but universally abolished. The obsesssion
of the liberals would seem to be to destroy anything that unites people organically, in living
and spiritual and moral and, therefore, truly
human fashion. Then these redeemers of the human
race would bind men together again by the superficial mechanical structures which they themselves
contrive. What they propose would be like reducing by some chemical process all plants and trees
and animals - all living organisms found in nature -
to atomic particles, and then to put them all together again mechanically. That, in truth, is the
kind of experimentation that the liberals would engage in with the human race. They propose this mad-
cap project to us as the non plus ultra of wisdom
and good fortune, for our admiration and gratitude.

Thirdly, the cooperatives which the liberal
party has given birth to are not in a position to
accomplish what they are supposed to accomplish.

The objective is to help the oppressed worker,
who has been reduced by the experiments of the liberals to a condition where he is dependent for his
very survival on a daily wage. That wage offers
him a bare subsistence, and he has to struggle for
it like a beggar each day in a market where labor
is treated like any other commodity, as subject
to the caprices of demand and supply. It has become painfully clear in our time that the cooperatives proposed by the liberals as remedies are not
up to the task. In this respect the charges of
Lassalle stand unrefuted and are, in fact, ir-

350

refutable. The loan associations [9] can only help
those few workers who operate their own businesses.
They are useless for the great masses of workers
in the strict sense of the word, i.e., those who
work for daily wages. For the small businessman
they offer certain advantages, but they can never
hope to restore this class of people to a higher
level of well-being and enable them to engage in
competition with capitalists and large scale enterprises. The same holds true for raw material pro-
curement associations. [10] They have little value
for the worker who works on materials that do not
belong to him. Even the small independent operators
will derive minimum benefit. The more such associations proliferate, the more they will affect the
general market price of raw materials, and the less
benefit anyone can derive from them. Only the consumer will then still gain something in the process,
and the worker will gain only inasmuch as he is a
consumer. Furthermore these organizations, given
the cumbersome nature of the leadership of associations, could scarcely compete with capital which
stands ready, cash-in-hand, when it comes to the
purchase of raw materials. And even if they could,
the small manufacturer, having paid the same price
for his materials, would still have to compete with
manual labor against the machine production of the
large-scale enterprise. To go on speaking about
the ability to compete under such conditions is an
exercise in delusion.

The consumer cooperatives render a certain
general service to the extent that the day-laborer,
wage earner, the factory worker, can be a member of
such an association. They buy in greater quantities,
avoid certain middleman profits, and secure better
merchandise than the individual might be able to
purchase in haphazard fashion in the general stores.
Therefore they provide for their members better
goods at lower prices - an undeniable benefit.
Quite aside from the fact that such cooperatives
help in some way to alleviate the plight of the
worker, though they are a far cry from resolving
it, it is also a fact that the advantages of consumer cooperatives are not likely to be lasting ones.

351

Just as with the producer cooperatives which pro-
cure materials for small producers, when these
associations multiply, the workers will still have
to sell their services for less in times when the
supply of labor exceeds the demand for it. Thus,
although they buy their necessities at lower prices,
the condition of the working class will be no better
and no worse than it was before. That is because
as small businesses go under, there will be more
people on the labor market.

We have now pretty well considered all of the
kinds of associations which the liberals propose as
the salvation of the working class. Beyond that,
they advocate certain measures which already represent a retrogression to those means regarded by them
with such contempt, i.e., those which smack of charitable activity to help workers who are unemployable.

After due consideration, I do not believe that
I am being unfair if I apply to all of these brain-
children of the liberals in their championing of the
working class the words of the Roman poet, "Parturient
montes et nascetur ridiculus mus." 11 I do not wish
to question the good will of these men. I do not wish
to deny that, as things stand and after having placed
the working class in its present lamentable condition,
even these cooperatives can accomplish some good.
What I do maintain is that the principles from which
all of these activities derive do infinitely more harm
than good to the true interests of the workers. Such
attempts to deal with the human race according to
the trite rationalistic scheme of things - whereby
all religion, all politics, all wisdom, and all
humanity and humanitarianism are reduced to a matter of addition, subtraction, multiplication and
division of the atomized humanity - are a crime
against human nature and against the Divine order.
They can only bring destruction and wreckage. I
maintain therefore that all of these proposals of
the liberals, instead of elevating the status of
the working class and improving its well-being,
threaten it with the greatest calamity.

In conclusion, to further fortify my position, I would like to present some of Schulze-Delitzsch's own criticism of the true worth of his proposals, as contained in his Deutscher Arbeiterkatechismus. [12] On page 74 he presents the complaints of the major part of the working class. First, there is the insufficiency of the worker's earnings; and second, there is the insecurity of earnings which put even the better paid worker in a position where he cannot look forward with a sense of security to his immediate future. On page 75 he cites as examples the business recessions and credit restrictions which followed the wars between England and the United States, and the great consequent hardship which the textile industries experienced there. Large numbers of workers were left without sustenance. That situation is well known; and we can only look forward with trepidation to what would happen to workers not only in England, but everywhere, if we were to find ourselves in a more generalized war sometime in the future! After these remarks, the author turns, on page 76, to those means whereby such evils can be avoided. As the best practical means for elevating the working classes from their misery and uncertainty, he proposes, workingmens' associations. At the end of the treatise, on page 166, he refers again to England and assures us that in England such workingmens' associations and cooperatives have reached a high stage of development. That, it seems to me, is the most devastating criticism of the author's whole scheme. If the workers' associations, as Schulze-Delitzsch proposes, are the best and only method for helping the working class, and if this method has reached such a high stage of development in England, and if a remote war far across the ocean was enough to leave great masses of workers hungry, then the fate awaiting our workers is indeed a sorry one. Therefore, let those weep who love the working class, and let those liberal sloganeers who present themselves as the saviours of the working class be silent and ashamed. They have reason to be very humble and modest about the worth of their efforts on behalf of the working

353

class; and they ought to abstain from any further
great speech-making which only serves to deceive
and do more harm to the workers.

354

VI Proposals of the Radicals [13]

In a general way we can express our opinion
in this way: Lassalle is right against Schulze-
Delitzsch, and Schulze-Delitzsch is right against
Lassalle. Each is right in his criticism of the
other, but both are wrong in the proposals they
offer for improving the lot of the workingman.
Both are right when they negate; both are wrong
when they affirm. That is, after all, the character of the worldly spirit. It can criticize, find
fault, tear down; but it can offer little that is
constructive, for the simple reason that it is out
of contact with the Truth and the Life. It is not
difficult to expose the error and insufficiency of
proposals that the radicals offer.

The faction which has as its chief spokesman
Lassalle himself, has rendered the undeniable service of laying bare with keen insight and discern-
ment the miserable condition of the working class,
reduced, as it is, to a lifelong struggle for bare
subsistence - a situation that we have described
earlier. The radicals also deserve credit for the
axiom that whoever wishes to sincerely and effectively help the worker must find ways whereby the
working class will have access to new and better
sources of income beyond the rock-bottom recompense
for its labor. The solution of this problem provides the very keystone for judging and testing
the validity of that party's proposals. It does
not deny that the measures proposed by the liberals
can have a certain palliative effect for improving
the workingman's lot; but it asserts that those
measures cannot really protect the workers from
the devastating effects of their competitive encounter with capital. In other words, the liberal
proposals cannot bring significant and lasting improvement for the working class. The radical faction therefore offers more potent and effective
remedies for this condition. Its proposed system
is starkly simple. We wish to present it in all
of its simplicity and then to examine whether it
is acceptable and capable of delivering what it

promises. Here is what it comes down to.

In every business, the total revenue is divisible into three parts. First, there is the daily wage of the worker which equals subsistence. Then there is the interest on capital which is used up in the productive process. Finally, there is profit in the strict sense of the word, which is left over from the sale of the product after the wages, interest on capital, and whatever other costs of doing business have been deducted. This profit goes to capital without the worker getting even the slightest share of it.

Such a distribution of profit does not seem to conform to natural justice or to any other reasonable criterion. The worker contributes his flesh and blood and uses up the most valuable of the earthly endowments he possesses - his health. Each day he uses up a part of his remaining lifetime. The capitalist, on the other hand, is contributing only a dead sum of money. It seems unfair, therefore, that surplus revenue should accrue entirely to dead capital and not to those who expend their flesh and blood in the productive process. It is true, there are other factors which enter into the ultimate determination of the exchange value of the product aside from mere labor and capital. They include the intelligence and greater diligence of management, as well as the energy entailed in selling a product. These must enter into the calculation and play their part in determining the eventual price of the product. A distribution according to abstract natural justice is therefore impossible, since the precise contributions of all participating factors defy normal cost accounting practice. They cannot be broken down into anything like their exact shares. Still, the accustomed manner of distribution contradicts a fair man's instinct for justice. Therefore, if one could discover a more equitable kind of distribution whereby the worker might get a decent share of business profits, so that his material means would include the wage sufficient to assure him subsistence and, in addition, a share of the profits so that he could live at a decent human level beyond mere subsistence, such a division of profit would be far more fair, and it would appreciably improve the workers's condition.

How are we to achieve this goal? Until now, the worker has always just been a day-laborer. Even the small businessman and craftsman are reduced to a similar level, where they find themselves having to compete with giant enterprises with their huge aggregations of capital. It would seem to be necessary, therefore, that the worker would become a co-owner of the enterprise in which he works. He would then get not only his daily wage, but eventually his share in the profits of the entire enterprise. Now since only capitalists can afford to buy shares of the enterprise, the problem lies in placing the poor worker in a position where he too can acquire capital and thereby assume the status of co-owner of the enterprise. The kind of competition which is supposed to obtain among all men through freedom of enterprise, free trade, free entry, etc., whereby they can develop their talents according to their fullest capacity according to sweet reason and natural laws, and thereby acquire their rightful share of what they produce, is, as we have demonstrated, pure fantasy. Competition is not among abstract persons of equal abilities, but among real people with the widest imaginable range of abilities. The people who compete do not enjoy equal status. Some of them are equipped only with their natural endowment, whereas others have command over capital and machines. Under such conditions how shall workers gain access to the necessary capital which would ensure them a share in the owner- ship and in the profits of the enterprise?

As a matter of fact, some few workers in France and England have succeeded in solving this problem. They are simultaneously workers and owners. The right set of circumstances, to- gether with exceptionally well-disposed entrepre- neurs, has produced some notable results. The success of such organizations has been considerable. They are known as Productive Associations, and they are unique in that workers are at the same time whole-or part-owners of the enterprises, so that they share in the profits. Intriguing as these Productive Associations are, however, it is a fact that instances where such a state of affairs can be brought about through the efforts of the workers themselves has been likened in its rarity to the good fortune of the occasional rare businessman, who rises from the status of second-hand clothes dealer to that of millionaire. Even in England such Productive Associations are a rarity when one considers the total working population; and even there voices are heard which declare their general applicability an impossibility. Spontaneous associations of this type will not, therefore, be up to the task of improving the general condition of the working class.

At this point the radical party, which is well aware of the state of affairs, steps forward and offers its remedies. To enable the working classes to acquire the necessary capital that would make it possible for them to become not only workers, but also owners of enterprises, the state ought to hasten to their assistance. It ought to either lend or give them the required capital. Parliaments, as they are now constituted, are not about to authorize such state assistance, inasmuch as only the propertied classes are represented in them. Those classes can scarcely be expected to assume this burden which will come out of their own hides, so to speak. Therefore, the working classes must work to introduce the system of direct representation. The nation would then directly elect men of their own kind and class; and it would be a simple matter to bring it about by majority vote that sufficient capital is made available to the working classes so that they may become owners of the enterprises in which they work. In this way the worker will finally get some genuine relief. With the help of capital made available to him by the state, he will be a simultaneously a worker and an owner. The enormous profits which now accrue to wealthy capitalists and merchants, enabling them to enjoy all manner of comfort and the

358

finer things of life, will then flow to the workers.
Thus it appears that we have discovered a way to
gain access for the working classes to all the
good things of this earth, and to abolish the
penalty of having to earn bread by the sweat of
one's brow!

What can we say about such proposals? Are they
legitimate? Are they practical and feasible? Are
they partly true? Let us consider these questions
one by one.

Let us examine first whether they are legitimate. Does the state have the right to use its
power in this manner? Is a parliament, in particular one composed for the most part of the propertyless majority, entitled to use majority vote
to tax private property in the manner that is proposed by the radicals? Doesn't such a procedure
represent an incursion into the private property
right?

Before we can resolve these most important
questions in a definite manner, we have to inter-
pose an examination of the nature of private property. We know that there are many who take the
property right for granted to the extent that they
are discomforted by any kind of discussion of the
right; and they try to avoid it. That is a fatal
mistake. In earlier times, there were many who
took authority for granted so that they never
bothered their heads about the foundations of
authority; and while they were themselves in possession of it they wielded it as incontestable
and self-evident and with reckless abandon.
They thus did more unintentionally by their
abominable abuse of authority, to undermine the
true principles of authority than their worst
enemies did. <u>Nothing is of and by itself indes-
tructible except God alone and His holy will.
Everything else has only a conditional existence
and justification. It is thus with authority,
and it is thus with private property</u>. Property
too has its conditional justification only in
God and in religion. Property, like authority,
has its deep and abiding roots in religion, in
the living God, and in Christianity which teaches

359

us about the true and eternal God. If these roots
are once cut off, then they are vulnerable as any
tree is whose roots have been severed. The tree
looks, at first, as though nothing has happened;
but it has lost its stability, and the first strong
wind will bring it down. The inner weakness of
authority has now become painfully evident. That
is due to the fact that its basic rootedness in
God has already deteriorated. Probably private
property will suffer the same fate. If the principles on which modern states are founded are correct, which make them neutral as regards religion
so that only the right to deny God is regarded as
basic to human formation, then what a majority in
parliament decrees has to be accepted as right.
And no one may argue that an attack on the property
right by the popular will is improper. Let us
have a clear understanding on this point.

Private property has its foundation in the
natural order of things with its eternal, unchangeable principles. Man needs nature for the satisfaction of his wants, and he can make use of
nature, its powers and its resources to satisfy
his essential needs only by recognizing the fact
of private property. If there is to be peace and
order among men regarding the use and exploitation
of the goods of the earth - and peace and order
are the first principles of civilized living among
the nations - then private property has to be accepted as a natural right in the same sense as the
right to breathe. To deny it would lead to a war
of all against all, and make an end to prosperity
in all of the activities of men and of nations.
The slogan: "All property is theft...." is therefore, contrary to one of the first and most basic
laws of nature.

As vital as that point is, it is not yet
adequate to put property rights on a sufficiently
firm foundation. For even if ownership, in itself,
that is to say, the distribution of the valuable
things of this earth to particular persons who then
have a right to use and dispose of such things to
the exclusion of others, is a right that is rooted

360

in natural law, still the right to own, in the narrower sense, as it comes to be applied in various particular circumstances in a particular nation, is not directly and immediately rooted in nature. It is the outcome of man's own activity. Our books on civil law, which are supposed to spell out in detail the natural law of private property, are not authored by nature but by men. They give expression to the law-making power of each nation. The particular form which the law-making power that effectuates and ordains the natural right of private property for each nation takes, possesses infinite diversity. In our state where the constitutional forms of government are in effect, the law-giving faculties are three-fold. The motives which were operative in giving expression to the property right in a particular nation during the course of history, as well as the sources from which these motives originated and which determine the particular legal form in which these norms are finally clothed, are equally various. History itself has taken a hand in this process with all of the numerous uncontrollable influences that it is capable of exerting on man's thought processes. Every race of men wishes to proceed on a reasonable basis. But in its concept of reasonableness each is already influenced by some general outlook by which it is unconsciously motivated and shaped, in the same way that one breathes without thinking about it. The particular national character of a people also influences and introduces particular peculiarities into the development of the private property right.

Finally, and above all, religion and the religious culture have a most decisive influence on both the grasp of natural law, on its foundation in general, and on the legal structure and firmness of the property right. Specifically, supernatural revelation as it comes down to us through Judaism as fulfilled in Christianity gave us the ultimate and finest clarification regarding the natural order of things. How desperately fallen human nature requires supernatural assistance to properly grasp these natural principles for human existence is readily apparent. Without

361

it the human spirit ultimately reaches a point where it has doubts about everything, even the clearest principles of the natural order of things. It even reaches a point where it is uncertain of its own existence and the existence of God, who is the Source of every thought of which a man is capable. If a man is once able to deny the very purpose and means of thinking, what certitude can remain for such a pathetic soul?

The command of God, "Thou shalt not steal," as handed down to us from Revelation, has given immeasurable support to the natural law of private property. In making this a matter of conscience it has offered greater support to the property right than all of the law courts on earth. Furthermore, supernatural revelation by its teaching on Divine Providence,has had a far-reaching influence on the full development of the right of private ownership as that right works itself out in practice. Men are capable of realizing that it is not mere chance but divine wisdom which determines that one man is born the child of a day-laborer, while another is born into a wealthy family. And by the teaching of Christian charity a measure of warmth is added to the otherwise austere, cold notion of property rights, inasmuch as the stingy property owner, in a certain sense, becomes the debtor of his poor neighbors.

Religion exercises yet another kind of great influence on the property right. As we saw, private property has its foundation in natural law which is essentially independent of man's caprice. Natural law merely allows a man the choice to accept it, or to reject it and thereby to work toward his own destruction. On the other hand, the positive law which embodies this natural law in each nation gets its expression and its explanation from the mouths of men - be they individual rulers, members of a ruling class, or the people gathered together in their parliaments. It is of critical importance, therefore, what grasp these men who are called to make laws have of their competence and authority to do so. But this grasp is dependent again upon their religious values. The slogans, "Law is the will of the king," "Law is the will of the king and of the nation," "Law is the popular will," all lack substance in that they do not get to the heart of the matter. There is a double meaning in them which is of the greatest significance. Some believe that when they utter the slogan, "Law is the will of the king," they have made the ultimate and decisive distinction between that and the statement, "Law is the popular will." That is a false assumption. Whether law represents the will of the king or of the people is, in the final analysis, unimportant. What counts is whether law represents the will of God or mere human whim. To restate that in more precise terms, the question is whether the men who operate as lawgivers and who give expression to the body of the law which is to bind a nation are acting only according to their own will and the will of those who appointed them, or whether they operate with full awareness that they are duty-bound to give expression to the Divine plan for order.

It is this conception which divides men into two groups in our time, and it must separate them according to their religious convictions. The one group, those who believe that there is a personal God and that He is the origin of all things, and who believe in Revelation and in Christ and the truth that through Him we will be able to gain understanding of even the natural order of things, such men will regard the will of God as the ultimate source of all law as well as its norm and its sanction. The others who deny a personal God as well as any connection between human law and the lex aeterna, the eternal law that resides in the eternal mind of God, and those who deny supernatural revelation and Christ can only resort to the fickle will of the people as the source, norm, and sanction of law. Since there is no such thing as the general popular will, and since one could not identify it in any case, one has to rely on a fiction and interpret either the will of the king as being the will of the people, or else the will of the parliament, or of a national assembly,

363

or all of these together as representing the popular will. It is necessary that I develop this theme so that I can apply a valid test to the remedies proposed by the radicals.

If there is no personal God, or if it is true that the question of God's existence poses a scientific problem, and if it is truly the viewpoint of all European governments who now allow professors in their universities to present this issue before our German youth as a dubious scientific postulate, if materialism and pantheism are valid notions, and if all of those who adopted the latitudinarian approach to religious beliefs are right, in other words, if the great liberal faction is right, then the private property right and all of the laws regulating it represent purely and simply the will of men and nothing more. I can see no valid reason therefore why anyone could protest if the masses of the people who have no property should decide one day by majority vote that the owning classes should lend them some of their wealth. In fact, it would seem inevitable that they would presently go a step further and decide to expropriate part of the property of the wealthy. That can even occur without drawing the validity of the natural right to property into question as a consequence of a certain tendentious interpretation of that right. Everything will then depend upon the will of the majority which will now also have the final say regarding the inheritance right. It would be up to the majority to decide whether and to what extent there is a natural right to inherit property.

The so-called modern state rests entirely on this principle. Then how can one expect to forestall the eventual consequences of the principle as applied to the modification of the property right? The party which is now in control of the press - and all law-making bodies never tire of announcing to us the good tidings of this new kind of state which, with total disregard of all tradition or all earlier agreements, and in particular without any respect for what is owed the Christian Church - upholds as right only what

364

the constitutent assembly decides by majority vote.
It views even the continued existence of the king
and his council of ministers along with the parliament as an antiquated anachronism which ought to
be eliminated as promptly as possible. They are
right, of course, if those professors are right
whom princes and kings have provided for the German
people as their teachers. The absolutely inevitable outcome of this whole system is a parliament.
What this parliament decrees is law, and whoever
invokes his conscience, his religious beliefs, his
traditional rights, or Christ and God in opposition
to parliament is guilty of high treason. He has of-
fended against the majesty of the popular will. Why
in heaven's name would one expect this majesty to
remain subservient to the money bags of the wealthy
liberals? If it has the power to run roughshod over
our consciences, mock our religion, and deny God
and Christ, it is preposterous to expect that this
new world order will hold still all of a sudden
when confronted by the wealth of millionaires, as
though entranced by it. No, never. God will see
to that! It will not happen that way. We must
drain to the dregs the consequences of what we have
brewed for ourselves, no matter how bitter the
taste. If these liberal majorities are able, by
their sovereign will, to decree out of existence
the millenial status of the Church and to heap
scorn upon it and at the same time quash the Christian conscience with all of its fine ramifications,
then before long other majorities will follow who,
on the same grounds and with the same kind of majority action, will demand not only millions in
subsidies for the workers' organizations but even
more radical measures. Based on the philosophy
of the liberals and that kind of wisdom which is
dispensed in the name of political science from
so many lecture halls, one does not have to waste
time debating about the validity of Lassalle's
proposals. They represent simply the most humble
beginnings of far more significant things to come.

Those who believe in God and follow Christ
have an altogether different approach to the matter. They hold that men should not make laws

arbitrarily but rather that laws must be based on and reflect the divinely established order. They hold that laws derive their power to bind not from the will of man but from the eternal will of God. They ask not simply what the majority has decided, but whether the majority had the right to decide so. In other words, we believe that the determination to help the working classes by such a device transgresses the legitimate God-ordained limits of what state law-making powers are entitled to do. It invades territory in which the state has no business.

In support of our misgivings, we shall prefix certain notions about the natural limitations on the right of private property as these have been developed in Christian learning. According to the unanimous opinion of Catholic theologians, the property right never goes so far as to allow flagrant disregard for the extreme need of one's neighbor. Here the impact of religion and theology is brought to bear on the right of private property in a spectacular manner. That right is in no case and for no person an absolute one! It comes from God in whom are to be found the source and measure of all things. According to this yardstick all things are measured, and the role of all things is determined. Religion proceeds from the source of all light and it pursues the rays of that light wherever they may lead to determine what the correct rule and measure is. In the Christian view, God alone is the absolute owner while man owns things only conditionally according to the measure that God has decreed. God made all mankind depend upon the resources of nature for satisfying its earthly wants; but he also established the natural law according to which private ownership is the only way in which man's dominion over nature can achieve the goal of the really dignified development of human culture. As firmly as theology insists upon the right of private property, so it also insists that this right cannot obstruct the higher right according to which all men are dependent upon the goods of nature. It holds therefore that any man who finds himself in extreme need may, after all other means are exhausted, satisfy his extreme need wherever and however he can. It is on that basis that the state enjoys the power, as it is everywhere exercised, to require that communities, i.e., property owners in a community, make provision for their poor. That is simply another way of saying that men must surrender enough of what they own to provide for the poor who are in extreme need.

Beyond this the theologians do not speak of compulsion to take care of one's fellow man in need. There is only the moral obligation to do so, the obligation in Christian charity. The property owner can be forced by a court of law to fulfill all of his legal obligations. By the levy of taxes he can be required to provide for the general revenue and pay for public functions. Beyond this I don't believe that he can be forced to give of his own goods to improve the lot of his fellow man. It is here that the distinction between obligations in justice and in Christian charity becomes apparent. The obligations in charity are just as binding as the obligations in legal justice. The owner who does not give alms in situations where he clearly ought to do so is likened in Christian teaching to a thief. On the day of general judgement when everything will be taken into account and when eternal justice will have its day, eternal reward and punishment will be meted out as Our Lord has promised, according to how the obligations in Christian charity were fulfilled. Here on earth, however, He did not assign the full scope of justice to the state, to be made effective by the power of the state exercising external force, but only that minimum amount of justice which was necessary to preserve order and peace on earth among men. Man is thereby given the degree of autonomy that is necessary to exercise his freedom for weal or for woe; but at the same time limits are established without which the abuse of freedom would generate widespread chaos and strife. That is the wonderful divine economy established for man here on earth. Compulsion by the state goes only so far as is required for the protection of all and to guaran-

tee order. At that point the zone of freedom
begins, including the freedom to own property.
But this area of freedom to own is again bounded
by an area of obligation, obligation in its highest and noblest form, whereby a man, recognizing
his duty and his relationship to his God and to
his fellow man and to his worldly possessions,
gives of his possessions in the exercise of charity toward his fellow man. Man's actions in the
sphere of strict legal justice, to the extent that
these are elicited by courts of law and tax collectors, are still but scarcely human activities.
Free self-determination is barely in the picture
where pure and simple compulsion is operative.
This is still a primitive condition, and the simple
observance of legal justice is on the lowest level
of moral activity. Whoever is content with the
fulfillment of strict legal obligations still
operates at the lowest level of human existence.

Beyond this area of compulsory human justice
is that higher justice which will one day be the
object of general judgement but which is nevertheless entrusted to our own exercise of freedom and
self-determination here on earth. Where this
higher justice is concerned, man does not have
his eye on parliamentary majorities, legislation,
and tax collectors, but simply on the will of God
whom he recognizes as the highest and ultimate
good, and as the Lord of all things. Here he will
not be dragged before a court of law where sentence
is passed on him by some strange judge. He sits
in the court of his own conscience and sentences
himself, according to the laws of God and of Jesus
Christ, to render the Christian corporal works of
mercy and to hand over a share of his property to
his fellow man as a holy burden. This kind of
action, which is so essential to freedom and to
free human activity and I would even say, to the
dignity of the human person, would be abolished
by the projected state assistance that will come
by majority rule. It is worth recalling here how
the state in the Middle Ages when it was still
basically Christian, contrasted with the modern
state in this area of individual freedom. In that

368

age immense contributions were forthcoming for social purposes, for science and religion and for furthering the esteem and dignity of the civil community, on a completely voluntary basis out of a sense of personal obligation. [14] Today, all of these functions can only be financed by an ever-expanding system of taxes and compulsion, under the burden of which various states are in danger of collapsing, and where free self-determination and discretion have been virtually eliminated. We are witness to the fact that such an idea of taxation and compulsion is an ever-growing phenomenon and that the modern trend is bankrupt of any notion of true human freedom. Christianity brings the individual to full freedom, while the modern spirit destroys individuality even in its relation to private property.

No matter how benevolent the proposal of the radicals may appear, namely to help the working classes by majority decisions that would pass laws and impose taxes, we believe that the proposal is not justified and therefore not genuinely benevolent. We believe further that it does not lie within the competence of the state authority to invade the right of private property in this manner and for such a purpose. We believe that by such action the state will be moving in a hazardous and destructive direction, and that if one congress has once voted to help the working classes by modest subsidies, other congresses are bound to follow which will make still greater incursions, by majority rule, into the basic right to own property. We do not fail to appreciate the consequences that derive from the principles of the modern state. But we hold that these principles themselves are deleterious, and we believe that they contradict the order which God has established and made known to us in the principles of Christianity.

Aside from the propriety of radical proposals, it is well to examine also their effectiveness. Is it really possible to help workers by and large, by such state intervention, that is, by making them entrepreneurs and thereby materially improving their status?

369

The misgivings which the liberals have, fearful as they are that state intervention violates the principle of self-help and is therefore to be avoided, has been rejected by their opponents as invalid. It has been correctly pointed out that wealthy companies and great industrial enterprises have succeeded in getting state assistance for themselves time and again, sometimes in the form of guarantees of their bond issues, e.g. the railroads, and sometimes through direct subsidies, without any qualms of conscience. To regard state intervention on behalf of the working class as improper while tolerating it for the wealthy owners of the wealthy capitalist class must therefore be regarded as a crass inconsistency. The objection that such support is only justifiable and acceptable when the general welfare of the whole state is involved is also a bit lame. It is difficult to argue that the public interest is more deeply involved in, for example, the construction of some railroad than in some undertaking where the welfare of a large sector of the working class is appreciably enhanced. This whole approach suffers from a further great inherent inconsistency inasmuch as the liberals regard it as damaging to the workers' capacity for social self-help to offer them any material assistance, while at the same time they feel themselves called to offer the workers the benefit of their great economic wisdom. Nay more, they force it on them. Yet, they do not regard such assistance as damaging to the working class's capacity for self-help. For example, at the Sixth Congress of German Economists (September 14-16, 1863) which concerned itself with the interests of the working class, there were among the 137 participants 25 state officials, 11 professors, 16 lawyers, 8 bankers, 14 editors, 30 who had doctor's degrees, 16 merchants, etc. The entire working class was represented by two craftsmen. It is interesting that these gentlemen do not regard it as an interference with the principle of self-help so far as increasing the intellectual capital of the workers is at issue, while they express alarm when someone proposes to help them increase their material capital.

370

Nevertheless, we are convinced, for other reasons, that the proposals by the radicals are not suited to bringing about the desired improvement in the workingmen's welfare. What the proponents offer in defense of their feasibility is, in our opinion, as weak and wide of the mark as are the arguments which liberals offer in opposition. The idea that all workers, including workers in the strict sense, as well as those who as tradesmen and small businessmen find themselves in similar circumstances, can by self-help all gain access to the means for becoming partners in enterprise and can thus simultaneously become workers and owners is simply not realistic. Even if we accept the eventual possibility of this process, it would take many years in any event, and it would require a smooth and uninterrupted evolution that presupposes, among other things, a harmonious political state of affairs. That, in itself, would be asking too much, and we could therefore pass over the other objections in silence. Let us suppose for the moment that the plan of the radicals is to be put into operation. The mass of workers, who comprise the majority of our total population and who are to be rescued from their plight, depend for survival entirely upon a fluctuating wage. They are to become partners in the great enterprises where they are employed and thus get a share of the profits. For this purpose producers' cooperatives are to be formed, and the state is to furnish the capital for the undertakings. Let us suppose further that spokesmen for the working class are to be elected nationwide in direct elections, and that their task will be to discuss and decide on measures whereby the project is to be carried out. They will have to consider first of all how much state aid is to be forthcoming in the first year and which branches of industry, which producers' cooperatives, will be first in line to have access to it. The worker representatives will have to mingle with the workers in various sections of the country, listen to the wishes of their voters, and make promises and commitments. At the same time the majority of our citizens will have to be convinced of and ready to accept the consequences of the idea that there is no objective right or wrong, but that whatever the majority of the law-making body rules, even about wealth and property, is right.

Enough said. It is clear that the entire plan is impracticable inasmuch as we cannot expect an orderly, calm, harmonious political development to result which would redound to the benefit of the working class. Rather one would have to be prepared for general class struggle and frightful revolution which would lead to everything but the desired outcome. All of the passions of which the human heart is capable would be incited to the flash point, and the workers themselves would be tempted to unbridled greed. Each individual worker as well as each branch of industry and each worker's association would consider itself as entitled to prior consideration for the greatest share of what is to be meted out. Each popular representation would present the demand of his own constituency as of primary importance; and, given the cowardice that is already apparent among so many of our elected representatives in the face of aroused public opinion, no one would dare speak up in the parliament for some sensible, objective norm for action. Anyone who can observe disinterestedly how far the various interest groups are from any kind of equitable harmony of interests, which incidentally would be in their own best interests, could draw his own conclusions as to how far such a process would be removed from anything like an ideal solution. It would instead set the stage for virtual warfare where the unvarnished greed and the basest passions would manifest themselves. Whoever is of the naive opinion that this program would proceed in peace and tranquility, that those workers who would be required to wait for their subsidies until some time in the future would wait with saintly patience until their turn came, such a person does not understand the human condition, nor human passions. He is even in danger of falling prey to the plans of these dreamers who desire to help mankind according to their short-sighted rationalistic grasp of things as inspired by their vague humanitarian impulses, while they are actually doing untold harm and bringing about great misfortune.

372

We can therefore entertain nothing but the gravest misgivings regarding the propriety of the radical party's proposal to help the working class by massive state subsidization. So far as its practicality is concerned, we regard it as hopelessly unrealistic.

It remains for us to examine the proposed method for extending state aid to the working class, namely, direct election. Even though this matter is not directly related to the problem that we are discussing, it is nevertheless associated with the working class problem and of great intrinsic importance. Actually, the working class has virtually no say in politics and in the affairs of state except via the electoral process; and that is another good reason for our analyzing matters pertaining to the electoral process.

The constituent assemblies are supposed to provide a true representation for the nation at large and for those interests which are to be protected and fostered by the power of the state.

The idea that such a representative body having certain rights along with the proper organs of state authority is desirable for the development of organized political society is so universally recognized, that it has surfaced in almost all nations and in all ages, more or less, even though sometimes in a most tenuous form. It belongs to those arrangements whose inherent justification is a matter of agreement among all peoples, who at the same time have provided the last proving ground for its justification. In a special way popular representation has been a part and parcel of life among the Germanic peoples. Their free German ancestors did not know the meaning of absolute state authority!

However, the particular forms in which the idea of representation for the entire nation or for those who enjoy full freedom and political competence according to the measure of their actual position in the life of the nation is

realized, is more effective the more it reflects
the given condition and the prevailing general
culture. It is less effective and less adequate,
the more detached it is from these realities. The
most satisfactory form of representation, therefore,
at least so far as its basis and principles were
concerned, was the old Germanic organization according to functions. It is true that these reflected the ancient functional structure and were
not so accurate a reflection of actual evolving
conditions. They fell out of step with the general
development of the nation and therefore required
some significant modification, like the suit of
clothes which was tailored to a body which gradually
outgrew it. We should have tailored a new garment
according to the same principles, but suited to
present-day conditions. That, we did not do.
In fact we abandoned the ancient Germanic traditions in favor of new French fashions, not only
in apparel, but in the design of our new political constitution. The form and the evolution
which it has experienced has departed so far from
the norm of truly representing our particular
national realities, that it scarcely reflects
these at all anymore. Let us examine this development more carefully.

The legitimacy of a constituent assembly
rests, as we have stated, on the prerequisite
that it represents the true interests of the
entire nation according to its own indigenous
mode of operation in the political sphere.
That prerequisite is recognized even legally
and constitutionally. It is incorporated into
the basic law of the state by the legal fiction
that the deliberations of these bodies are to
be regarded as reflecting the intention of all
citizens together. It is most noteworthy that
human society could not exist without certain
universally accepted fictions, i.e., notions
which one accepts as ideal truths even when it
is not at all certain that these truths will be
realized in every-day life. One such legal
fiction is associated with legally binding court
decisions. This one is so essential that any

374

kind of juridical order would be virtually impossible without it. In this case, the fiction lies in our acceptance of legally binding decisions as absolute law. On the basis of such law we then conduct our subsequent actions even though everyone knows that it is possible and that there are occasions when such decisions do not conform to what is objectively right. We tend to erect law itself into such a legal fiction. We regard existing civil law - in fact, we have to regard it - as an expression of absolute law even though anyone who has taken the time to observe changes in civil law must acknowledge that this assumption is unwarranted. Our whole being is totally dependent on the Absolute, on the Infallible, on what is Right and True in itself, i.e., on God - who alone is the eternal subsisting Truth and Right. As a consequence of this dependence, we transpose the absolute and infallible God into our midst in all of the affairs which God has placed under our jurisdiction, because without Him we cannot subsist, and with Him we begin to compensate for our own inadequacies. There is only one area in which God has spared us from this uncertainty, in the area having to do with our most essential aspirations and relationships. There we deal with eternal, fundamental truths which are the mainstay of all other truths; and there God has given us a tribunal whose decrees do not bring us the true and the absolute in the form of fictions that are subject to error. We are speaking of the infallible teaching authority of the Church whenever it interprets the truths which the Son of God Himself revealed to man.

The notion that an expression of the popular will by representative bodies actually reflects the will and the thinking of the people belongs in that area of necessary fictions which we need in order to carry on the affairs of men in the here and now. It is precisely because all of these fictions are legitimate that we flirt with catastrophe when they are perverted by lying and deception. Woe to the nation where the presumption that what the courts decree

375

corresponds to objective right provides the go-
ahead for deliberate injustice! Woe to the nation
where the tacit presumption that positive law gives
expression to eternal justice becomes a sham whereby injustice is camouflaged! But woe also to that
nation where the presumption that the parliamentary
assemblies represent the nation as it truly is in
its various classes and interests, and at its best
in all of its thoughts and aspirations, has become
a lie, whereby some secretly sworn party tries to
push through its plans, its interests, its philosophy and its wishes under the pretense of representing the popular will.

Unfortunately these conditions are no longer
some mere horror story. They are more or less a
reality ever since the evolution of the modern
state in French raiment. One can scarcely imagine a legitimate idea so out of step with the
given realities, as the proposal to represent
the people in their every day affairs by a constituent assembly is out of step with the actual form
which constitutions have assumed in some nations.
Let us consider a country where there are two
governments. One is an open one which is dominated by the landowning nobility. The other re-
volves around certain professors who are in league
with secret societies. Both governments operate
throughout the nation. The secret one has adapted
itself to the established jurisdictional pattern
and spread its influence throughout all of the
communities. Down to the lowest level wherever a
town council operates, this secret government has
circumspectly drawn confidential agents into its
net in each and every community, and these have
become the blind instruments of the hidden government. They may operate in close harmony with the
established government, but only so long as it
happens to be the willing tool of the hidden
government. The latter has also penetrated and
assumed control of the entire electoral system,
and it can therefore lay great emphasis on the
electoral process since the organs of the established government are subject to its manipulation, assuming that this kind of collusion exists.

Finally, by its influence and money, it is in control of the press, with insignificant exceptions. The subservient press must constantly echo the refrain that the existing parliament is the true and faithful representative of the people.

Such speculations are no longer mere insane fantasies. What a sham, what a cruel betrayal of an entire nation, what a havoc such a state of affairs would wreak on the entire social fabric! Let us recapitulate the whole plot with special reference now to Christendom and the religious convictions of a Christian people. Popular representation rests on the principle that the nation, as it actually exists and operates, is represented. It therefore enjoys a general confidence that its majority decisions are, in fact, the true expression of the popular mood. Now suppose a state of affairs has developed in the constitutional makeup of a nation like the one we have just described. A party appears which stands fanatically opposed to the whole body of Christian belief which prevails in the nation. This party proceeds instead from premises that are cosmopolitan, rationalistic, and materialistic. It hates and rejects the Christianity which the Church teaches and to which the nation is committed. By its pervasive influence it organizes an assembly of secret party faithful and exploits to the full the constitutional fiction that the Assembly speaks for the popular will. It does all of this in such a manner as to spread its hatred of Christianity and the Christian beliefs of the people to all sectors of society, into the legal structure of the nation, the school system, etc. We repeat, what a lie, what a cruel betrayal this would be. What a crime against society and the true welfare of the nation!

We do not hesitate to repeat that a state of affairs that is in many ways similar has already developed in many German states. A far-flung party is already hard at work corrupting popular representation in the manner that I suggested and twisting the very idea of popular representation to its evil partisan purposes whose realization would spell the very destruction of our German nation. The constituent assemblies even now often fall far short of being the valid expression of what they are constitutionally supposed to be representing. They often represent not the nation, but a party which is a stranger to the true interests of the nation at large. In particular, it is noteworthy that the Christian nation with its aspirations, its rights, and its particular philosophy has already been effectively excluded from the chambers of government in certain states, whereas party members have gained the exclusive say and dominance. In this ever-growing adulteration of the whole constitutional process we perceive what has to be reckoned as the greatest, most far-reaching peril that has perhaps ever confronted the Christian, German nation. It is a peril that is magnified the moreso by the intrinsic truth of the representative principle.

The great moral corruption which now threatens the constitutional processes of the modern state has its point of origin in the electoral system. It is not our task to give an exhaustive analysis of this complex problem. But we are convinced that the electoral system which we now have, together with the electoral college serves ever more to deliver the constituent assembly into the hands of that party which surpasses all others in danger and in energy. Although we confess to certain reservations about the method of direct election as proposed by the democratic party, we do not hesitate to express a preference for such direct election over the present corrupt system. Direct elections have certain weaknesses. Demagogues can take advantage of them to mislead the people. Also, since the liberal party has already prepared the ground by its falsehoods, so that stirred up passions rather than conscientious deliberations have become the moving force in the public life of our nation, direct elections can bring about great misfortune. Yet, the majority of our people still believe in God and in Christ.

Most people still recognize the Ten Commandments
and the voices of their consciences. We hold
fast to the conviction, therefore, that our
German people, having experienced such misfortune
would soon come to realize what was going on;
and when that realization dawned, following a
struggle in conscience, we would again be saved.
It is true that our Christian people can be deceived by the electoral process. But when I
discount that segment of our population in some
cities, which has already sunk to unbelievable
levels, the nation, by and large, still has in
its Christian faith a healing power which the
rank and file of the liberal party with its
crass materialism no longer has. Though we are
not prepared to embrace whole-heartedly the principle of direct democratic elections as a stirring ideal, still we would not hesitate to en-
dorse it as preferable to the present electoral
system which leads us to an ever greater corruption of the whole national fabric and threatens
to deliver us to government by a hidden and in-
accessable power.

VII   The Valid and Practical Means for
Helping the Working Class

The proposed remedies of the liberal party,
and likewise those of the radicals, are obviously
not suited to solving the great problem of our
time and to improve the lot of the working class.
In fact, it was the principles of these parties,
for the most part, which reduced the worker to
the circumstances in which he now finds himself.
These remedies will not protect him from the consequences of the free-for-all competition which
has made him dependent upon a bare subsistence
wage, and even that is only assured for one day
at a time.

Even though the intentions of many members
of these parties are, each taken by itself, benevolent enough, and even though their activity may
occasionally bring about some monetary and limited
improvement in the workers' situation, none of
their proposals are remotely capable of averting
disaster for the working class, let alone of providing a real remedy for their problem.

Is there no real means of helping the workers?
Must we accept the conditions of the working class
as we have described them here, passively, help-
lessly, as though they were prescribed by an inevitable fate?

England is held out to us as a model that we
ought to imitate because of its political freedom
and also for its development of workers' cooperatives. Yet in England we witness the most frightful deterioration of the conditions of the working
class and therefore of the majority of the population. The ultimate in political freedom and the
fullest development of the cooperative movement
among the workers cannot avert the deterioration
of social conditions. The mortality rate of the
working class gives a valid insight into these
conditions. The higher the mortality rate of a
particular class, the more its physical well-being,

its nourishment, and its health have diminished.
In some English cities, the population is divided
into three classes: the wealthy, the middle, and
the poorer class. In the wealthy upper class, the
average life span ranges from 35 to 44 years;while
in the lowest class it is between 15 and 19 years.
It is significant that when Lassalle cited these
hair-raising statistics in Frankfurt, there were
cries of, "Enough." That indicates how accustomed
a portion of our populace has grown to hearing
flattering oratory, and how smug and immune it has
become to the truth, no matter how important it is
that they hear it. Such figures appear to me to
be far more valid than an endless effusion of
euphemisms, for presenting a picture of the real
situation and of the capacity of all atempts that
have been made thus far to help the working class
out of the miserable condition in which modern
economic principles have placed it.

In the Alsatian city of Muehlhausen, the
mortality rate among the children up to one year
old, of weavers and spinners, was just double that
of the children of merchants and mill owners. Half
the children of these workers died before they
reached the age of one. In a sampling of one hundred factory owners and merchants, thirty-two lived
beyond the age of 50. Out of 100 weavers, only
eight, and out of 100 spinners, only three passed
their 50th birthday. In an English factory town,
the average lifespan before the factories appeared
was 31 years and eight months; and afterwards it
sank to 19 years! There can be no denying that the
general health and vitality of the working class
have progressively deteriorated under present conditions. In Germnay, matters are not yet so bad
as in England. Cigarmakers in Berlin still have an
average life span of 30, whereas in England, in
some cities, they have an average span of 15 years.
But we are moving in the same direction. The
workers of our time are still the children of our
German peasantry, and they are, therefore, endowed
with health and vitality. How long will this last?
How long before we find regions of Germany, until
now inhabited by a healthy, strong race of men,
where there will soon be nothing but a degenerate

weak, race of cripples leading a neurotic existence?
A French writer has broken down the inhabitants
of North America into three classes: the black
workers, i.e., the slaves; white workers - the pro-
letariat; and finally, the rich aristocracy, or
big money-men. All of the proposals of the liberal and radical parties will not preserve us
from these consequences of modern economic theory.
If there are no other remedies available beside
those which the great liberal and radical parties
propose to us, Germany will eventually find itself
in a condition where there are just two classes of
men; the rich stock-market men and speculators
with all of their parasitical activities on the
one hand; and on the other, the masses of workers
who are totally dependent on them and reduced to
proletarian status.

Is there no way out? Must we let our German
nation drift into this new slavery and look on
while at the same time our nation is persuaded
that such madness represents progress, freedom,
enlightenment, and bliss?

Certainly not. Christianity, with its healing
powers, has provided the solution to all problems
ever since it came to earth in the person of the
Son of God. That includes problems which have to
do with providing for the temporal wants of men,
inasmuch as that is possible on this earth. God
has ordained that Christendom will always and
again encounter great tasks; and by solving them
it manifests its origins and its Divine power.
It was Christianity that broke the spirit of the
old slavery, a task that seemed virtually impossible. Before Christianity, any notion of a
common origin of all men, of a common high destiny and a unique value of every human person had
all but vanished from the earth. The Greek acknowledged only the free Greek; the Roman, only
the Roman citizen, the Civis Romanus, as possessing full human dignity. The idea that a slave
too had an immortal soul equal in its origin and
in its destiny to their own, never entered their
minds. The slave was regarded as an animal and

treated accordingly. Christendom restored to this vast segment of mankind its human dignity. The Christian spirit transformed a large part of the rural slave population into our German peasant class, and the urban slaves became our German free burghers. The Christian spirit was responsible for accumulating vast resources with which to support countless institutions of all kinds to provide for the needs of the poor. The anti-Christian spirit of our times is well on the way to restoring the old slavery in new form. It has a formidable helpmate in the godless, materialistic, contemporary science. To proceed as though man were mere matter is bound to bring about nothing but a cold, hard relationship between man and his fellow man.

Do we not tread matter under foot and use it as it suits our needs? Do we not slaughter and butcher animals when our needs require this? Now if man is nothing but a higher form of matter, a further evolution from the plant and the animal, what is to say that we are not to treat him as anything more than a plant or as an animal which we tread underfoot or slaughter, but rather that we have to respect him as a human being and to love him? Greed will soon break down the defense which a sentimental humanism tries to erect. The new slavery reinforced by such crass materialism threatens to be vastly more gruesome and cruel than the old. When the great Christian thinkers of old opposed the ancient slavery, they spoke thus to the pagan masters: "God gave man dominion over nature, over animals. He did not give him a similar dominion over his fellow man. You stand before God as the equal of your fellow man." When peace was concluded between the German orders and the recently converted Prussians, the papal delegate spoke the following sublime words: "The new converts have been taught that all men are equal so long as they do not sin, that sin alone makes a man miserable and enslaves him." The new materialistic philosophy now strives to uproot these great principles from the heart of man by putting man on a par with the animal. In so

384

doing, it claims for itself the ultimate in enlightenment, and it will inevitably restore a
condition where man may be treated as an animal!

The entire burden of this development has come
to bear on the working class. Therefore it is once
again the task of Christianity to liberate the
world from the new form of slavery and thereby to
actuate its own God-given power and give testimony
of its always renewed vitality. I have no doubt
that the awareness of this great task will become
ever more widespread. The spirit of Christ from
which Christian charity transmits itself into the
hearts of all Christians will make them more and
more aware of the plight of the workingman. We
cannot say for certain whether the current precipi-
tous decline of the working class into proletarian
status must continue to its ultimate consummation
before we recognize the full consequences of secularism and blind humanism. It is also impossible
to recognize at this time what new means Christian
charity and the Christian spirit will come up
with to bring another great triumph for Christendom
out of the contemporary social distress. Far be
it from me to attempt to outline here and now all
of the ways and means which Christianity will bring
to bear on the task, or to try to present some kind
of completed system. I am satisfied to be able
to contribute to awakening Christian hearts and
inciting Christian charity toward a solution of
the great area which God has entrusted to them
for a Christian solution. If I now presume to
point out certain means whereby the Christian
philosophy can be of assistance to the working
class, those would only be modest proposals. It
is my earnest hope that men, more capable than I
am of coming to grips with this critical question,
will soon undertake to come up with a solution.

Above all, I would like to emphasize and reiterate what has to be the underlying principle
of the whole approach of Christianity and the
Church to this problem which besets the social
order. They cannot offer direct and superficial,
more or less mechanical devices and arrangements,
but they must work principally and preferably

through the spirit which they infuse in mankind. That is how Christianity overcame the old slavery by simply inspiring mankind with its Divine idea and by the spirit of charity. Masters were thereby moved to free their slaves voluntarily, and by the same token the spirit of entire nations and of legal structures was transformed.

That is how it must be when we begin to solve the social problem of our time. The causes of the workingmen's plight as we have discussed them to this point, and the evil consequences which flow from them are rooted in a departure from the Christian spirit that has marked recent centuries. The human spirit is no longer enlightened by the highest and eternal truths. Therefore it has fallen prey also on the more pedestrian level of political and social principles to false ideas, sterile abstractions, and that liberal fanaticism which is unaware that society is a living organism and which has a great capacity to abolish and destroy, but which can construct nothing.

What is more, since the spirit and strength of Christendom no longer holds egotism with its accompanying passions in check, we now have to experience the development of such ominous conditions in the social order. The cure for this can and will come only from within. To the degree that eternal truths once again enlighten men's spirits, we will once more discover the correct principles and their proper application in the economic scheme of things as well as in the political sphere that is so closely related to it. In other words, having searched for and found Divine wisdom, we will also be blessed with true social and political wisdom. Then governments and legal systems, instead of fostering destruction along with doubt and confusion, will make possible and foster a healthy new order in social and economic affairs, through a reorganization of industries and communities and of all other vital organs that is based on their true nature and purpose. In this connection, I would like to refer to the point of view expressed so well

386

by the outstanding Professor of Economics at Lyons,
Perin, in his research on wealth and poverty. He
states that just as the Christian spirit is a spirit
of love, it is also a spirit of self-denial, and
that the general well-being of society is therefore dependent on and conditioned by this spirit,
which makes possible self-control and limitation of
the ego, stemming from higher religious motivation.
In order that the power of the wealthy will not
oppress the poor, it is necessary that the rich
exercise self-restraint. They must not indulge
themselves in everything that a purely egotistical
exploitation of all the means normally available
to the wealthy makes possible. By the same token,
it is the spirit of self-denial and humility which
Christianity alone engenders in men which can
bring about in the working class the diligence,
thrift, and contentment that are necessary for
the genuine well-being of both workers and their
employers; and modern secularism perverts that
into something diametrically opposite - a spirit
of greed and discontent. Make no mistake about
it, truly successful associations, such as the
producers cooperatives that were discussed earlier,
will only be possible among workers who are motivated by a living Chrisitianity. Likewise only
genuinely Christian capitalists and captains of
industry will be inclined to enter into any kind
of profit-sharing arrangement with their workers.
I would turn now to a consideration of certain
factors which I regard as especially essential.

The first kind of assistance which the Church
is in a position to offer the working class is
the establishment and administration of institutions to take care of unemployable workers. We
have already noted how shabbily the great liberal
party, treated Christian charitable institutions,
so as to further its own preferred solution to
problems, the much vaunted self-help. Yet that
same faction has now begun to include the found-
ing of institutions for unemployable workers within the scope of its activities. This kind of
activity will nevertheless remain, in the future
as it has been in the past, the proper sphere for

Christendom, the Church, and Christian charity. Practically all endowments, houses, and institutions which render such services at the moment in Christian Europe owe their origins to Christianity and the Christian spirit. What humanism has done in this area is, by contrast, insignificant. Even today, any worker who has become unemployable and dependent upon others for assistance, owes to Christendom a debt of gratitude. Though he may no longer be aware of its largesse, Christendom is responsible for what help he may get in any of the numerous refuges of the poor, such as hospitals, poor houses, or invalid asylums. Christendom was not only responsible for raising the necessary money for these institutions, but also for providing the kind of care which is offered the unemployable worker there - a loving care of which only Christianity is capable for consoling the afflicted in the best way possible. The poor worker has not yet found real help just by the mere fact of having been accepted in an institution. It is the kind of loving, tender care he receives there that matters.

I do not deny that humanism may succeed in establishing adequate and decent institutions. These depend, however, upon outstanding, unique personalities who set the tone for such institutions; but that tone will typically survive only during the lifetime of these persons. In fact, the mere fact of having to compete with Christian institutions forces the humanists to exert themselves to the utmost to provide individual exemplary institutions. These may be furnished especially well and therefore give the appearance of being on a par with Christian institutions. By and large, however, all of such parties, which now pose as wishing to help humanity without benefit of those supernatural graces and gifts which God provides through the Christian religion, will never succeed in doing more than merely take in workers who are in distress. They will not be able to offer them the kind of loving care that only Christianity can offer.

The deeper aspects of caring for the sick and disabled are infinitely complicated. As he grows older, the unemployable worker requires ever greater care and vigilance. His body weakens, as do his mental faculties. His faults and failings, the bad habits acquired during his lifetime, become ever more apparent. He has a tendency to uncleanness, sometimes to a frightful extent. He tends toward indolence, dipsomania, and he becomes petulant. There is probably no place where the whole sorry condition of human nature so comes to the fore as in that type of institution. He who expects to survive in an atmosphere that is charged with all manner of moral and physical human weaknesses, and to offer loving, tender care to the inmates, must come with a heart fortified by something beside mere human concern and love. Where this is not the case, even the most benevolent attendants, not to mention the worst among them, will eventually fall by the wayside. They will gradually grow accustomed to human suffering and they will eventually even fall prey to the danger of treating the inmates in a coarse manner which no longer in the least reflects real charity.

From all of the years that I have been able to observe institutions of this nature, I have become convinced that despite all of the humanitarian principles so loudly proclaimed by their sponsors and officials, most institutions that operate under purely secular sponsorship suffer from severe inherent defects. Many of them are in a neglected condition where one finds, on the one hand, filth, indolence, and slovenliness, and on the other hand, a calloused indifference toward all of this misery. Constant operation in the environment where there is continuing and daily care for the poor, the sick and the invalids is a taxing enterprise which is simply too much for mere unaided human nature. Even parental love and devotion to parents often break down under the strain of continuing care for the sick and aged. How often does one find an aged father unable to get loving care from his own children whose care for him has grown more or less calloused by years of living with the pathetic condition? How would anyone expect decent care by people who are working merely for the paycheck in cases where even the love of children toward parents falls short? Only the supernatural love which Christ pours forth into human hearts can provide the necessary strength for extending the kind of continous care that is required for the poor in institutions designed to be refuges for human misery.

I am aware that one liberal party has sworn enmity against the Christian charity practiced by Catholic sisters. We first experienced the non-plus-ultra of such animosity in Vienna, later in Augsburg, and again here in Mainz. I am also aware, however, that this hostility is not the product of loving concern for the poor, the sick, and the needy workers. It flows from purely partisan, political considerations; and I am aware that there is nothing more vile, more inhumane, more unhumanitarian, than this animosity. I have experienced it first hand here in Mainz, and I can give an eyewitness account of the despicable tactics whereby, out of sheer hatred of religion, an attempt was made to deprive the poor workers in our hospitals and homes for the infirm of the most loving care that they could receive this side of Heaven. I shall yet take the opportunity to lay bare what I have experienced in this regard without pulling any punches and as a lasting lesson, for the sake of the poor and their welfare. Christianity and the Church will go on, despite all such hostility, in doing the loving work of the Good Samaritan toward all unemployable workers. They will thereby continue to do a part of the work of alleviating the sorry condition of the working class. Those in our Church who minister unto the sick and the poor are the true friends of the working class. They extend more love at the bedsides of the sick and the aged than all of the idle prattlers of the liberal parties put together, whose love finds expression only in speech-making and in spewing anti-Christian, partisan hatred.

The extent to which care for incapacitated work-ingmen is the exclusive province of Christendom becomes undeniably clear when one considers that the celebrated high cultures of ancient paganism, like those of the Greeks and of the Romans, did not know such care. Our new pagans are unable to come up with one example from antiquity of an institution providing care for the slaves. There is not a single passage in the works of any of the pagan authors which offers a shred of evidence suggesting an awareness of such activity in pagan times. That is most revealing and noteworthy. Care for those who cannot help themselves is the exclusive province of Christianity. It was so in the past, and it will be so in the future. Humanism can try to imitate, but it succeeds at best in offering a poor caricature of this specifically Christian activity. The conditions of our time offer an incitement to all Christian souls to resolve more than ever to provide institutions which will care for unemployable workers. They offer a special challenge to all Catholic religious orders to dedicate themselves to the administration of such institutions. They can thereby offer such a display of the power of Christ's love in their charity toward poor aged and sick workers as to put the Father of Lies to rout by the power of love.

The second means which the Church has to offer the working class, to help it out of misery, is the Christian family based on the solid foundation of Christian marriage. The Christian family provides the worker with three essential advantages which are also of important significance for his economic condition.

One great danger which confronts our working class is the dissolution of all social organisms that protect and preserve his individual life. As just one example, we cite the first group of remedies proposed by the liberal party. How far this dissolution process will go in the future, we cannot say for certain, but even the family is not safe from it. Among the liberal proposals there is even now to be found one which would free the right to marry from any kind of restrictions.

There is no denying that in some regions the process of concluding a marriage contract has been made unnecessarily difficult. Yet, a certain amount of restriction is called for not only in deference to Christian principles, but by human reason itself. Otherwise this state of life may be entered into without sufficient serious consideration, and the family structure will suffer damage. Contemporary agitation to make marriage a purely civil arrangement and to separate it entirely from the Church is, however, also a danger to the family. The stability of the family is rooted solidly in religion and in the Christian teaching about marriage. In particular, the concept of the Catholic Church which regards marriage as a sacrament and holds that it can only be dissolved by death furnishes the best possible foundation for its stability. Once you consider marriage simply as a civil affair - assuming this viewpoint can be put across to the masses of the people - then the Christian family and Christian marriage are finished. Marriage would then be like any other civil contract. It could be dissolved by mutual agreement, and the number of grounds for divorce would multiply indefinitely. This trend will be successfuly resisted by the Church and by Christianity working through the informed consciences of a Christian people. We will never reach the point, whether by the introduction of civil marriages or by facilitating easy marriages and easy divorces, where this divinely ordained organism which brings such immeasurable benefits for all members of the family will be destroyed.

Another danger facing the working class is to be found in the effect which a depressed living standard has on the health and life expectancy of the worker and his family. This is the inevitable consequence of poor nourishment, poor air, and a generally wretched existence. But it is not merely nourishment, air, and the kind of houses people live in which determine their physical well-being. Another factor plays a far more important part, namely a chaste moral standard. Chaste morals have a physical effect on even the most recent generations. When we encounter the bloom of good health among people who are lacking in adequate nourishment, the main reason for it is a chaste, pure set of morals. A nation where malnutrition and poor unsanitary living conditions are combined with wantonness and immorality is destined for collapse. Even the noblest nation cannot survive this combination for long. The degraded conditions of slaves in ancient pagan societies was chiefly due to such a state of affairs; and the despicable moral conditions of these poor wretches, in turn, occasioned their being treated like animals by their masters.

The claim that certain nations are safeguarded from such degradation by nature is totally unfounded. Such an idea is already based on the pagan conception that people are naturally divided into two groups: one is destined for a good life and for a higher level of culture, while the other is doomed to servitude and an animal-like existence. Poverty and wantonness together can cause any nation to revert to the basest level of paganism. Abundant proof is readily at hand in any of the large cities of Europe. The factors which promote such decay would wreak particular havoc among the entire working class if one succeeded in depriving the workers also of the institutions of the family and of marriage. All too many workers have already been reduced to the crudest level of existence by the prevailing economic principles. Destroy the family and you add the final poison of immorality with all of its deadly, devastating consequences.

It is painfully apparent that there is already an unclean spirit at large in the world around us. How many publications are already in its service, checked only by the fact that our nation is still basically Christian. Immoral amusements are offered daily, in fact, in the organs of the liberal party. These earn high praise as the true means to the full and good life. The liberals glorify immorality and all of the shenanigans that jeopardize Christian marriage and the family. The theater

393

in big cities, where culture is supposedly fostered, and the elegant novels that are written for these "cultured" classes, as well as the stuff that is disseminated and pawned off on people in papers even in the small towns, what is it all but shallow trash which abundantly portrays sensuality and even marital infidelity? In the face of all of this the Christian Church becomes an object of hate because it remains true to its Divine commission to battle against immorality.

Of course, whenever some religious person slips into a violation of the moral code, there is universal jubilance in the press which is quick to exploit such failings to the fullest extent as a weapon against religion. Every peccadillo is triumphantly reported so that the nation and the world is gradually robbed of its belief in a higher morality and in the possibility of chaste living. The advertisements in many papers offer a kind of catalog of depravity each day, and they present to people a detailed knowledge of all of the many secret ways in which vice manifests itself. In England, the trend has escalated to a point where there are papers dealing exclusively with filth, continuing revelations and fiction, as well as a kind of lonely hearts column for the people, for the working class, and for the servant and domestic classes. Hundreds of thousands of copies of this trash appear regularly. I have no doubt but that where such conditions exist among the working classes in England, they are partly responsible for having reduced the life span among certain classes to fifteen years.

What do we have to look forward to in such circumstances, where the unconditional freedom to enter into and dissolve marriage contracts were introduced, and where civil marriage in keeping with the spirit of the Enlightenment would become the prevailing mode? It is inevitable that workers are huddled together. They come to work together in great numbers, and they return home in the same way. They live together in great numbers in worker tenements. In the process the sexes are thrown together in close contact. What would happen to these workers if

Christianity no longer exercised an influence through its teachings on purity and chastity and sin, and if, instead, one counselled the working classes at every opportunity to marry and divorce as often as they please?

Impurity is a danger that puts in an appearance early in life. In youth it often exercises its most terrifying influences and is hardest to keep under control. Only a father and mother with truly Christian hearts, fortified with such refinement as Christianity makes possible, can with the aid of those means which religion offers preserve the youthful plant from this withering blight and nurture chaste offspring. Marriages that are contracted frivolously and dissolved just as frivolously are unable to provide the necessary protection for the poor children who stand helpless in their ignorance before this peril. What would become of all of the children of workers that would result from such lightly contracted, easily dissolved marriages and of children daily exposed to the dangers of temptation and bad example? Reduced physically to a bare subsistence level of living and lacking the care and supervision of loving parents, they would be the ready victims of lasting damage to their lives that results from immorality, and they would therefore hasten all the faster their own physical and spiritual destruction. This represents no mere figment of the imagination, but is already becoming a recognizable reality wherever modern principles have had their effect among the working classes and have begun to erode the solidity of marriage and family life. One cannot help but view with grave alarm the prospect that this trend will make further inroads among our German workers.

The force of Christianity and of God who stands by His church in all of His might will prevent that. Christian marriage with its high ideal of indissolubility and sanctity will provide the powerful antidote to this poison that threatens the human race. The Church will preserve marriage for the working class, and the

Christian family along with Christian motherhood
and fatherhood. That, make no mistake about it,
is the first and most necessary precondition for
the solution of the working class' problem. So
long as our workers still have the benefit of the
Christian family, so long as a man is blessed
with a Christian wife, the woman with a Christian
husband, the children with Christian parents,
and the parents with good Christian children who
still observe the fourth Commandment, just so
long will the working class have the benefit of
an insurmountable barrier against ultimate disorder.

Even the worker's meager wage is, in a certain sense, increased in a Christian family, and
that is the third advantage which Christianity
offers. We do not mean that the worker actually
earns a higher wage, of course, but that his wage
is made to go further. The money which the worker
turns over to a Christian wife takes on a higher
value, by virtue of her prudent management, than
in the hands of some frivolous female; and the
money which a good Christian man brings home goes
much further than the money of the irresponsible
fellow who squanders it in dissolute living at
the local pub. All of this is even more applicable
in hard times, as when there is unemployment or
illness. How valuable the Christian family is
for the worker and his children at such times,
what with its inner stability and its unlimited
capacity for sacrifice and love. Those are the
benefits of Christian marriage and the family for
the economic condition of the working class. The
Christian family provides for it the best and
most vital of all possible associations for the
preservation of his well-being. Without this
association, all others, call them what you may,
would be useless. The Christian family safeguards the working class from the consequences
of impurity even before birth, in the lives of
the parents. It does so later through the period
of youth and throughout life, placing the working
class under the protection of the heavenly Mother,
the Mother of all purity. It makes the working
man's meager wage reach much further through the

careful management of a good Christian wife.
In this respect, I do not hesitate to maintain
that Christian marriage and family, based as they
are upon the teachings and on the life-giving
grace that emanates from the Catholic Church,
are, taken by themselves, already of infinitely
more worth for solving the problem of the working
class than all of the proposals and exertions of
the liberals and the radicals.

The means whereby Christianity assists the
workers lie in the truths and teachings which offer
genuine culture to the working class. When the
liberal party promises a higher culture to the working class by its teaching about self-help and its
cultural organizations, to the extent that Christianity is left out of its approach to culture
the whole thing becomes a hollow and fraudulent
delusion. Only Christianity promotes genuine
culture. The contrast between the means to a
culture offered by a rationalistic scheme of things
and Christianity is like that between a crumb of
bread that has fallen from a table and the great
lavish bounty on the table itself. Christianity
with its immeasurable healing power is unknown to
the rationalistic schemers, and if they then lay
their hands on a few crumbs that have fallen from
the Christian festive table, they hold these up
for all to see as though they had suddenly discovered a new, unknown remedy. All the while,
what they present is just a miniscule particle of
what Christianity offers to humanity.

Christianity gives a man conscious possession
and the full use of all of his powers. It alone
has restored to man his full human potential.
Paganism did not understand the value of the individual human person. The Romans and the Greeks did
not recognize the worth of all the rest of the
human race. The Greeks did not even acknowledge
the equal status of half of their own people, since
women were regarded as a lower caste of human
beings. The value of the child was not appreciated
by them, and it could be sold or even killed for
any number of reasons. The full dignity of a
human being was accorded only to the citizen, and

his worth was measured by the contribution he could make to the community. As an individual the human being scarcely counted.

The pagans knew no working class having inherent, equal human rights. It was Christianity which first restored to mankind, by its teachings, true human dignity. The Apostle said, "Here is no more Gentile and Jew,; no more circumcised and uncircumcised; no one is barbarian or Scythian, no one is slave or free man; there is nothing but Christ in any of us." (Col. 3:11). St. Paul was speaking about the equal dignity which was the patrimony of all Christians. He could have said something similar about the dignity which all men have because their souls are created in the image of God. The former however, was a noble, wonderful, revolutionary teaching which stood in total opposition to what Jews and pagans, Greeks and barbarians, free men and slaves held regarding human dignity. Christianity spread this doctrine throughout the world. Thus a bright ray of light from above found its way into millions of the souls of the unfree and of the slaves. They had grown accustomed to the lowly state, in which they found themselves practically on a par with animals. They awoke, therefore, as from a deep sleep, and they once more became aware of the idea of a soul from which their human dignity and high destiny stemmed.

Christendom, however, was not content with spreading the doctrine of human dignity by hollow speech-making. It spread the whole truth in a manner which men would come to understand and accept. That is the big difference even today between Christianity and humanism. The latter also promotes the idea of human dignity, but without ideas, without truths which get to the bottom of the basis for this human dignity. Christianity, when it tells a person about his dignity, makes it clear to him that even if he stands at the bottom rung of the social ladder: "Deep inside of you, hidden by the wretched shell which covers you, there is a likeness in your soul of great beauty and eternal value; it is an image of the eternal, everlasting God, and a reflection of His eternal beauty and glory. This image in you is the cause of the deep yearning that you feel, which persists even in your worst miseries like some inexplicable homesickness. It bestows on your soul a mysterious, insatiable craving which drives you onward and which would allow you no rest even if you could take flight to the stars and claim the galaxies in your name. This, our human worth, resides in you like a jewel hidden away deep in some mountain, buried under immense layers of earth, as it were, beneath all manner of human misery, tribulation, and depravity. It is for this reason that the Son of God came down to earth, because he saw this precious jewel buried in the recesses of the earth. He came to rescue the image of God in you from the slavery of its earthly bonds and, by His teachings and graces, to elevate it once more to the dignity and glory of the sons of God.

That is how Christianity addresses itself to the question of human dignity, to the Jew as to the Gentile, to the Greek as to the barbarian; to the master as to the servant. And that is how it finally came to pass that the words of the Apostle were fulfilled: "There is no more Gentile and Jew...; there is nothing but Christ in any of us." Thus, when Christianity speaks to all mankind of its dignity, its teaching is consistent and complete. Humanism and the great liberal party, which has abandoned Christendom, also speak of human dignity. But when we inquire what the basis of human dignity is, they have no answer. Spoken by a materialist, a pantheist, an atheist, words about human dignity are hollow prattle. They can neither enable a man to lift himself up, nor motivate him to treat his fellow man in a manner that befits human dignity.

By its teaching about the dignity of the human person, Christianity has provided for every class, especially for the working class that languishes in slavery, above all an awareness of the obligation to develop one's capacities to the fullest. In the

doctrine about the immortality of the soul, and in particular by its deeply ingrained teaching about a conscience, which is so intimately connected with the doctrine of personal immortality, we have the deepest, most potent motivation for the fullest possible development of all of one's abilities and for the use of all of one's energies. The self-help of the liberal party is, once again, a crumb fallen from the table of Christendom. Certainly a man has an obligation to help himself. This is true not only because his material existence requires it, but also, and far more importantly, because his spiritual welfare calls for it. It is basic to his nature that he gains a share in all that is great and good only to the extent that he has exercised due diligence in developing and applying his own abilities. Sloth is, therefore, according to Christian teaching, one of the seven capital sins. As the old proverb says - "Idleness is the devil's workshop." [15] Man attains to true self-help - or to express this more adequately - to the full use of his strengths and abilities in body and in spirit - not by repeating _ad nauseam_ the term "self-help" in cultural uplift societies established for workers, but by vitalizing motives that are capable of inspiring him to action to overcome his sloth and to put all of his energies in harness. The liberal and radical parties can offer no better motivation than hunger, or, as the radicals propose, by arousing in the working class a thirst for all manner of the good things of this life. This unnatural craving is then supposed to goad the worker to greater exertion. How woefully low all of these men have sunk who abandoned Christianity and its eternal principles!

Christendom, however, not only bestows on the worker a deep insight into human dignity and the most effective conscientious motivation to develop one's abilities to the utmost, it also gives him what consolation he requires to carry on the struggle when he finds himself in reduced circumstances and subject to all manner of deprivation. Pascal said that the man who gives way on the principles

400

of Faith because he cannot fully grasp them, also
surrenders the true and clear understanding of
all other circumstances which he encounters in every
day life. He casts away the first link in the chain,
because this link is a mystery to him. But as he
surrenders the first link, he turns the world round-
about him into a chain of dark mysteries. The believer, on the other hand starts out with a mystery
which he accepts, because God Himself, who gave us
our being and our existence, is a mystery in His
being. Having humbly accepted that first mystery,
the whole world lies before him as an open book.
The unbeliever, in rejecting all mystery, rejects
the first Mystery of all. He consequently wanders
about during his whole life in an abject, mysterious darkness regarding his origins, his being,
and his destiny. The believer humbly accepts the
first mystery from God; then his origin, the nature
of his being, and his destiny all become trans-
parent and clear to him.

That is how things stand with the worker and
his destiny. If he has cast aside what is most important, namely - revelation or the world of God -
as a worker he will find himself ever more entangled
in a tortuous, irremediable mass of contradictions.
He is told of nature and nature's ways until he
gains the impression that whatever happens in human
life is inevitable as is the case with trees which
grow, thrive, and eventually perish. Yet, for all
of its alleged natural simplicity, he finds his
life laced with all manner of complexities. Christ
has said, "The poor you will always have with you."
And so it is. We shall always have poor, many poor
among us. In fact, the majority of mankind will
go on earning its bread by labor, and, with few
exceptions, men will be denied a surfeit of the
sensate pleasures of this world. All promises to
the contrary are nothing but sheer fantasy and
cruel deception. This marginal existence which
will always remain the lot of the working man,
this burdensome toil by the sweat of his brow
from early morning until late at night when he
retires exhausted, this daily struggle even under
favorable conditions for so much food, clothing,
and shelter as man is entitled to for a decent

living in the proper sense of the word, this mode of existence, which only rarely affords the worker a taste of the much advertised pleasures of the earth, represents a flagrant contradiction to the inherent yearning in man for happiness. <u>That is, if man's life is limited to his earthly existence and if worldly pleasures are the be-all and the end-all of what is to satisfy his inner craving.</u> Such is, of course, the philosophy which secularist liberalism embraces and by which it wishes to capture our working class. What good, then, are meetings for workers with fine speeches? Of what avail are such cultural offerings as libraries, concerts, theaters, folk festivals, etc.? The worker has the same built in yearning for happiness as the wealthy capitalists, the captains of industry, the money-men, who try each day to satisfy this yearning by all manner of worldly baubles. Concerts, folk festivals, and libraries will not quench that thirst, however. If there are no other pleasures but earthly ones and no existence but this fleeting mortal one, then the workers by and large - and they comprise the vast majority of mankind - will be miserable, unhappy, and pathetic people, <u>who lack even the foggiest notion of how to explain their own existence and this paradox in their lives.</u> They are human beings just as the wealthy are. They have the inherent need, just as the wealthy have it, to be happy. Yet they are excluded from all of the supposed satisfactions of their needs that are available to the rich. Instead, they are invited to a folk festival one evening of each week, or to a lecture. At the same time they are expected to labor by the sweat of their brows at exhausting labor - the exact opposite of sensate pleasure - in order to provide a surfeit of those earthly goods for a tiny handful of people, goods to which they themselves are denied access. For a worker in such circumstances life must be an abominable absurdity that defies any rational explanation. It must represent a monstrous injustice inflicted on him by his fellow-man, and it must choke him up with hatred toward those who have the things that he cannot have.

Here we see a hundred factory workers toiling to provide for some rich, liberal, captain of industry, who has perhaps robbed them of their Faith, with all of the earthly pleasures. He may get as much of these worldly goods for his enjoyment in one day as all of his workers together get in a year; and they have the same appetite for them as he has! Consider then what thoughts must run through such a worker's mind toward the end of his life. Consider how he weighs on one side of the scale all of his working days, his toil, his worries, his unfulfilled cravings. On the other side he weighs the paltry sum of the earthly pleasures which he might, in fact, have enjoyed in drunkenness, andnot without reproach. Now, he must say to himself, my life is over and all during my lifetime I had an irrepressible yearning for happiness and peace of soul which I must assume nature implanted in me. I have come to believe that there are no other means for satisfying this yearning than earthly goods. Yet I have been denied these goods, and they alone are goods. My innermost being has been frustrated, therefore, and my very existence remains an unfathomable enigma to me. That is the cultural formation which secularism holds out to the working class.

How different it all is for the worker who is blessed by the enlightenment of Christianity. Christianity is, in fact, for all classes; and God wishes that all men will be made whole and saved through Christ. By the fact, however, that the Son of God became a worker, He served notice that He had a very special kinship to that sector of mankind which is effectively excluded from a surfeit of worldly pleasures. The worker who has the Faith believes what Christ tells him, even if he cannot grasp God's mysterious plan, because he knows that his spirit is in harmony with God's Accordingly, in matters that really count, he has his bearings; and he knows what he has to know as he works, as he journeys through life, and at the hour of his death. He has clear concepts and principles to guide him, to clarify and mollify for him the yearning of his soul for happiness and peace,

403

as well as for his labors and deprivations. He has
a conception of life which he embraces as true and
which provides him with a consolation and peace of
soul in all of his tribulations. He accepts the
parable of Lazarus and the rich reveller; he believes
in a personal survival in the hereafter; he accepts
the intrinsic value of daily toil at his job at
something beside its mere mercenary value, and as
labor that will be rewarded by the God of justice
Himself. He learns from experience that there are
higher goods of the spirit that transcend food and
drink and the theaters and concerts or folk festivals proposed by the liberals for him - goods which
offer a preview of eternal bliss. He experiences
first hand the largesse of Divine Providence which,
time and again, comes to his rescue in periods of
privation. He finds in every word of the gospels
consolation, peace,and true joy. In the life-
giving sacraments and sacramentals of Christianity
he finds support and strength. As he sees the Son
of God at work, and poor, he gains an appreciation
of poverty and work, as having more merit than idleness and wealth. Ultimately he has the consolation
of his belief in an all-just God who will one day
weigh on the scales of Divine justice, the thoughts,
words, and the deeds of the entire human race, and
who will then, without respect to person, render
to each what he deserves for all eternity. That
is the banquet of eternal truths to which Christianity invites the working class. Standing opposed
to these are the partial truths of the liberals
and of the radicals, which are mere crumbs off
the table of this Christian feast.

Christendom, finally, nurtures those virtues
in the cultural formation of the working class which
are so necessary even for its material well-being.
They are virtues which serve to enhance his meager
wage and make it reach further. It provides the
worker with an inner joy, a peace of mind, which
lightens his burden, inspires moderation, thrift,
and discretion; and it thereby improves also his
material welfare. It offers him an appreciation
of family life which make hours and money wasted
at the corner tavern abhorrent to him. It preserves

404

him from the baleful influence of evil passions, and it thereby keeps him healthy and vigorous so that his work is that much less burdensome to him.

That is how Christianity provides for the workers the true means for self-help, in that it induces the full unfolding of all of his latent energies. It offers him genuine culture, in that it presents him with truths and virtues which alone can cultivate what is best in man.

The fourth aid which Christendom furnishes for the improvement of the material condition of the working class is to be found in the social forces of Christianity itself.

Consider first the workingman in his personality, in his individual capacities and talents. The Divine Teacher likens men to stewards who have been entrusted with certain talents, one with five, another with two, and still another with one. Each is obliged to make the most of his talents in his own given situation. The slothful servant who buried his talent, was finally called to account by his master. That is how Christianity has counselled and urged all men and all workers to use and exploit all of the capacities of body and soul with which God has favored them. The liberal party calls this self-help, and presents it to the world as its own new-found discovery - something that we have discussed earlier.

The worker is also considered with respect to his relation to his fellow man. His entire nature develops to its fullest in a twofold manner: On the one hand, in the development and unfolding of his own capacities, and, on the other hand, in the giving and taking of assistance in his relationships with his fellow man. That is the social, the cooperative side of his being; and it is just as vital a part of his nature as his individual personal side. It is only when both of these aspects of his nature are kept in harmony that man reaches his full development according to laws laid down for him by his Creator. The liberal party calls this social self-help, a hopelessly inadequate expression, as we have already demonstrated. If by this expression we mean that the worker, banded together in associations, should help himself without recourse to any outside assistance, that is to say that the association, as such, ought to reject all outside help, then we have here an arbitrary absurdity which is worthless. That interpretation would stand in open contradiction to the whole thrust of the liberal party which offers its unceasing moral and intellectual support to workers' associations. If workers help themselves, and if their association helps itself so much as possible, while avoiding resort to outside help simply as a compensation for their own lack of ambition, then they have a natural and reasonable right to accept help wherever and by whomever it is offered, so long as it serves their proper interests. The cooperative principle is, after all, basic to human nature; and Christianity can do nothing but offer its most enthusiastic support to all contemporary efforts to help the working class by this device. It would be colossal nonsense for us to pretend hostility to this principle simply because, for the moment, it is being pushed all too often by men who are strangers to Christianity. The air remains God's even when the atheist breathes it, and the bread we eat remains nourishment provided by God even when the baker who prepares it is godless. That is precisely how things stand with the principle of cooperation. It is rooted in the Divine plan and is basically Christian, even though the men who nurture the idea fail to recognize God's will in it and also abuse the principle in various ways.

The principle of association is not only justified, per se, and worthy of our support. As a matter of fact Christianity alone has the ennobling forces needed for it to reach its full potential and to make it capable of yielding genuine benefits for the working class. In this regard, it is as with liberalism's attempt to provide cultural uplift for the workingmen. What the liberal party proposes as its own are mere crumbs that have fallen from Christianity's bounteous table. Just as the

406

great truths which constitute the workers's personality and individuality are contained in Christianity, so Christian principles include the great
ideas and constructive forces which can erect cooperative associations into healthy and vigorous
corporate bodies. It is appropriate to refer to
certain associations as corporate bodies. The
body is the ultimate union of its members, which
are bound together by the highest life-giving
principle, the soul. We,therefore refer rightly
to certain associations as corporations, since
they, in a certain real sense, contain a soul
which truly unites the members of the organization. That is the specific peculiarity of the
Christian principle of association. Even though
the immediate purpose of an association is a completely mundane one, dedicated to the needs of
every-day living, it nevertheless is possessed
of a higher consistency and binding force when
it is based on Christian principles. In the
area of human social relations Christendom has
a special mission and importance. It has far
greater competence to accomplish what liberalism
proposes to do for healing our national ills by
modern principles of organization. Let us examine this problem more closely.

The Divine command: You shall love the Lord
your God above all else and your neighbor as yourself, contains, as St. Augustine said, three fundamental commandments: to love God, to love oneself,
and to love one's neighbor. He who loves God
above all else, said the Saint, needs never fear
lest his love of self will become inordinate.
That is because self-love which, when it is perverted becomes the source of all evil, will then
be regulated and ordered by the law of God so that
it will remain within the bounds which God's Divine
plan - the source of harmony in all human affairs -
has ordained for it. Love of self as kept in check
by the love of God will, in turn, provide the proper
measure for love of neighbor. The man who loves
the eternal and abiding God above all else will
have, by virtue of this love, the best of all possible rules for love of self; and he will reject
out of hand everything in his own self which does

not conform with the law of God. He will likewise possess in this love of self, which is cleansed, enlightened, and sublimated by the love of God, the best possible rule and measure for the love of his neighbor. Nothing more perfect or nobler is conceivable to the human spirit than the fulfillment of this command in the order that it is commanded - Thou shalt love thy neighbor as thyself - and as it was expressed in the words of the same Divine Master: "Do unto others as you would have them do unto you," and inasmuch as we are required to observe this command toward all persons without exception. All of Christendom with all of its teachings is merely an enlargment of this single commandment, and all of the graces provided by Christianity are simply aids that human nature - so damaged by inordinate self-love - requires, so that it may ascend once more to the heights of Divine love as expressed in it. That is the energizing force, the higher vital principle, which Christianity imparts to associations that are in conformity with its principles.

Whatever the various reasons which bring people together into associations - workers may band together to improve their material welfare, others may do so for social or for scholarly purposes - once they come together as Christians motivated by a Christian spirit, there is a higher purpose. A more spiritual, holier bond holds them together; and, even though unconsciously, it bestows a kind of spiritual energy upon the association that turns a mere organization into a living corporate body. That was the case with those associations which operated in an earlier era when the Christian spirit still prevailed. Even without their realizing it, the men who organized for a wide variety of purposes found themselves bound together by deep, inner, moral, spiritual ties which gave rise to a real corporate body. Therein lies the fundamental difference between the principle of organization that is operative among Christians, and that which is pervaded by the modern spirit. In the latter case, associations are simply groups which have no bond

408

other than the single, immediate purpose for which they were formed. A consumer cooperative furnishes cheaper bread for its members; a savings and loan association provides capital at lower interest rates; a producers' cooperative provides materials for production at lower cost to the members, etc. The specific purpose of the organization is its be-all and end-all, and there is no other bond which holds its members together. Self-seeking represents a constant threat to the rights of one's fellow man, and it represents an ever-present danger to the achievement of the end for which the organization was formed. On the other hand, where men gather together in a Christian spirit, there exists - whether they are aware of it or not - another higher bond which is independent of the specific purpose of the society and which offers a warmth and light to it that affects all of its members. The source of this light, and life, and vitality is contained in their common Faith and in the love that flows from it. They are branches of the tree of life which God planted on this earth, even before they are members of this more recent society. It is from the greatest, most durable of all bonds that the association, for whatever purpose it is formed, takes on an inner strength, an inner living principle. The associations that operate on Christian principles are, in a word, living organisms that are sustained by an inner life-giving principle. The associations that modern liberalism sponsors, on the other hand, are mechanical assemblages of people who are thrown together merely for some superficial, utilitarian end. Whatever future it may have, therefore, the cooperative idea belongs to Christendom. The ancient Christian associations have been destroyed, and we are hard at work obliterating the last remnants of these splendid organizations. We want to build something new, but this new structure is nothing but a miserable shanty, built on sand. It falls to Christianity to begin rebuilding anew. Only it can instill in workingmen's associations a proper meaning, a true sense of purpose and a true usefulness.

Thus far, among the attempts to help the working class by forming associations, we have spoken exclusively about the attempts made by the liberal party. These are almost entirely along lines proposed by Schulze-Delitzsch. We have yet to discuss two other kinds of organizations which were meant for the craftsmen. They too can take on real significance and therefore merit the full support of Christians.

We refer first of all to the organization of trade unions which has occurred in recent times and which has as its purpose to once again bring the craftsmen together into solid organizations. The idea behind this movement is completely meritorious and it requires serious attention. We extend to it our cordial support and would only wish that, as it is now constituted, it could bring about the desired results. If the governments, not under the auspices of the liberal party from which I expect nothing of value in any area, but independently and simply out of an awareness of what is good for the class of craftsmen, would provide a framework wherein the latter could once again attain to its necessary degree of independence and healthy organization, we would view that as one of the greatest and most beneficial measures imaginable. It appears, however, that we must resign ourselves once and for all to a total lack of any creative undertaking by present-day governments. It is therefore all the more important for all constructive and creative Christian forces to rally to the support of this effort to restore the class of craftsmen to a recognized status, in whatever way that we can.

The second undertaking which we have to draw attention to in this context is the Journeymen's Society (Gesellenverein). Since these arose principally under Catholic sponsorship, we are justified in numbering them among the Catholic contributions to solving the problem of the working classes. What these associations have accomplished to date already exceeds all expectations and gives us an indication of what they can accomplish if

they are allowed to develop to their full potential.
God has taken on a partner who would undertake this
task for Him; and after He had elevated him to the
priesthood, he made this Reverend Father Kolping,
a one time journeyman, the true father of the class
of journeymen-tradesmen. May God continue to work
through him and bring this worthwhile project to
fulfillment. That will happen as the organizational
principle implicit in the Christian spirit progressively unfolds itself within these associations
and makes all of their members living parts of the
same organism.

As to the fifth aid which Christendom has to
offer to the working class, we refer finally to the
advancement of the producers' cooperatives by special means which only Christianity has at its disposal.

We have perceived producers' cooperatives
as the sharing by workers in the management of
business enterprise. In them, the workingman is
simultaneously a worker and an owner. He therefore
has a double claim to the earnings of the enterprise:
his wage as a worker; and his share in the firm's
profits.

It is not necessary for us to go into greater
detail here regarding the great value which producers' cooperatives have for improving the condition of the workers. We cannot tell now whether
it will even be possible to make all workers or
even the majority of them part-owners of the enter-
prices in which they work. Such cooperatives represent an excellent idea, however, which deserves
our earnest support. It is an approach which, to
the extent that it can be applied, offers the most
direct and obvious solution to the given problem.
It would open up to the worker, who now depends
for his livelihood exclusively upon a wage that
is reduced to bare subsistence by competition on
the marketplace, an additional source of income.

Lassalle would like to actuate this plan
through capital subsidies provided by the state.
We have explained that we regard this notion, if

411

one is considering it for universal application
by means of a direct legal enactment that would
tax the wealthy to provide the necessary capital
for the working class, as an incursion on the
private property right and as a transgression of
the legitimate bounds of the state's right to tax.
We also indicated that we would have grave doubts
about the practical feasibility of the approach
in a manner that would permit peaceful and orderly
development of the body politic. The distinguished
Professor Huber has proposed, in view of these
difficulties, that the project be undertaken by
the efforts of the workers themselves with the
help of voluntary assistance, and that it ought
to be tried in the smallest enterprises first.
The difficulty in getting producers' cooperatives
underway lies in acquiring sufficient capital.
The big entrepreneurs are the rich capitalists
and corporations which assemble millions in capital.
The thriving large corporations and capitalists
will make it impossible for these small cooperative associations to compete with them unless the
latter too can lay their hands on enormous amounts
of capital. Thus, small scale worker-run enter-
prices with meager capital or none at all will
be crushed and obliterated by the giant firms which
thrive and operate everywhere. Where would one
expect the workers to get the necessary capital?

If Lassalle's plan is both unjust and impractical, as we have no doubt that it is, and if there
is no other way than the one Professor Huber proposes, we would be tempted to throw the whole noble
idea of producers' cooperatives out as a nice but
impractical fantasy. At the very best, we would
have to resign ourselves to applying the principle
on a limited scale so that at least an appreciable
number of workers would benefit by it. It is
always worthwhile to save even one person among
many who are drowning. Yet, to save one man among
thousands of others who are drowning is a weak, in-
effectual kind of remedy when it is considered in
terms of the plight of thousands who are going
under for the third time. From a purely natural
standpoint, I would like to make this metaphorical
comparison with the establishment of producers'

412

cooperatives. I am afraid that the means that
the world has at its disposal are simply not
adequate to make possible a broad enough application of the cooperative idea, so that it would
measure up to the gravity of the problem that
faces the masses of the workers. Of what use
will it be for the great masses of workers if,
occasionally, a handful of their class scores
a breakthrough and succeeds in gaining the status
of partner-in-enterprise so as to share in profits
and thus improve their lot somewhat, while their
fellow workers wallow in misery?

Whenever I have considered these problems
and obstacles, I have been bolstered by the confidence and joyful hope that the forces which
stir Christian hearts will also become operative
in this area to aid the working class by making
the idea of partnership in production a reality
on an ever-widening scale. Large amounts of
capital will be required, and I scarcely expect
that such help for the working class will be
forthcoming all at once and on a grand scale.
Looking at the problem in perspective, however,
I nurture the hope that first one and then another Christian soul will come to grips with
the matter. Christianity has always been a
kind of force which works slowly from within
men's hearts, but which eventually and inevitably yields the greatest and most unexpected
benefits for curing mankind's ills. There
will no doubt be many pitfalls along the way
before the Christian remedy finds widespread
application. The Christian spirit required
centuries before noble, ancient, Roman families
were finally moved to release their slaves by
the thousands and to grant them their freedom.
Perhaps many a Schulze-Delitzsch will yet appear
and promise salvation for the working class,
before the dream castle which the last of these
men erects comes crashing down and dashes the
workers' hopes, to awaken them to the reality
that all was in vain. Perhaps the world will
even have to try out Lassalle's remedy to discover
for itself, after all of the anguish which would

413

have to result from this dangerous experiment,
especially if it falls into the hands of unprin-
cipled demagogues, that the democrats cannot help
them either, so long as they erect their philan-
thropic proposals on sandy humanitarian foundations instead of on the rock of Christianity.

Precisely how and when Christianity will
come to the working class' rescue, we cannot say
for sure. On the other hand, we do know that
whatever is true and worthwhile and practical
in the idea of producers' cooperatives will be
brought to its full realization by Christianity.
Unfortunately, at the moment, the majority of
that class of men who are in a position to really
help the working class is pretty far removed from
Christianity. I refer to the wealthy businessmen,
industrialists, and capitalists who provide the
moving force as well as the financing for the
great liberal party. But even among these one
still finds the occasional true Christian, and
the others need not remain the way they are.
There was a time when the old Roman patrician
family, whose matron employed hundreds of slave
women simply to cleanse and adorn her body, stood
far removed from Christianity. Yet it came about
that the children of these families released the
slaves and covered all of Italy with benevolent
institutions for assisting the former slaves.
Many of them, out of love for Christ, even dedicated their lives to this service. Christianity
is that remarkable! He who is its enemy today
falls to his knees at the foot of the Cross tomorrow and pleads forgiveness; and the son of the
man who cursed Christ ends up shedding his blood
out of love for Christ. As it has always been,
so it will continue to be! Christianity is so
rich in its spiritual resources that, if it is
God's will to touch the hearts of men in this
area, it would no longer be difficult to provide
whatever enormous capital is necessary to bring
about partnership-in-enterprise on a grand scale.

There are two systems of taxation. One is
applied by the state, the other by Christianity.

414

The state taxes by exterior compulsion, by tax laws, tax levies, and tax collectors. Christianity taxes by the interior law of love; and the compulsion, the size of the levy and the tax collector are nothing else than a man's free will and his conscience. All of the great states of Europe are being progressively destroyed by their tax systems. It is out of the current fiscal mess, the present quagmire of iniquity and corruption, that a worldwide web of market speculation, with all of its attendant moral corruption, has developed. Christianity's tax system, on the other hand, has always been able to come up with a lavish abundance of whatever means were necessary for its undertakings. What immense capital Christendom has been able to accumulate by its voluntary tax levied on human consciences and on the hearts of good Christians! Consider all of the churches, all of the cloisters, all of the benevolent institutions for all manner of human infirmity and weakness, all of the parishes and dioceses established all over the world, all of the endowments set up to care for the poor of the world, all of the schools up through the university level that are supported by voluntary donations! Recall that almost all of such undertakings were established and supported by voluntary giving, and you begin to appreciate the tremendous vital force of Christianity. That is true not only of the Christianity of old, but it is still true today. Think of the benevolent institutions which have been established by voluntary contributions. What an enormous accomplishment! Such voluntary taxation, as motivated by the Christian spirit, has in just the last five years resulted in 23 million marks for the Holy Father. Whatever our enemies may think about the use that is made of those gifts, they have to at least admit that a church which can get such results has a significant power over the souls of its members, which they themselves do not possess. Is there any reason why Christianity should not also be able to come up with the necessary remedies for the plight of the working classes?

415

It was the supernatural fire which Jesus, the Son of God, brought into this world, which has enkindled in men's hearts the zeal for all of the works of charity that Christendom has produced. It is the fire of which Christ said, "I have brought a fire into this world, and I will nothing but that it continues to burn." That is the source of all Christian works. From this bonfire of Divine love sparks leap forth, first into one heart then into another Christian heart, to enkindle the flames which make possible the great self-sacrificing efforts that are needed to bring about great endeavors. Therein lies my hope, my trust for the future. The more the world fails in its vain attempts to help the working class, the more certainly the day will come when God will come to the workers' rescue through the saving grace of Christianity.

Please God, that men will soon arise who will seize upon the useful idea of partnership-in-enterprise in God's name, and put it on a firm Christian foundation so as to rescue the working class from its sorry plight. A large number of workers in very many factory areas are now employed by godless men and dependent on them for a wage. They are in double jeopardy. They depend on the daily wage he offers them for their subsistence - a wage which could be withheld at any time. They are also faced with the danger that their rich employers may deprive them of their Faith and of their clear consciences for this rotten wage. That is the most depressing spectacle that is associated with such latter-day slavery. How many captains of industry take advantage of their dominance to uproot the Christian Faith from the hearts of poor people who have to work for them? I say, "have to work for them," because it is preposterous to claim that their workers accept employment of their own free will. This is the kind of double-talk and hypocrisy that is rampant in the liberal economic system with its so-called free competition. The poor worker lives in his home town, near the factory. He is told that there is free entry and free exit, and that he is free to go elsewhere to earn his bread. How, pray tell, can this poor man with his wife and children take to the road to look for other employment? Even to go without wages for one day threatens him with starvation, never mind the prospect of his spending weeks on the road looking for more suitable employment, even if he could afford the cost of such a journey. He would be doomed to beg or to starve. There is no free entry or free exit for him since he cannot afford it. Rather he is bound by natural laws to stay close to his home town. The liberal party beguiles him further by telling him there is free enterprise. Pick an enterprise anywhere in the wide world and free yourself from your dependence on the daily wage paid to you by an employer. Another lie! The poor worker of whom we speak is the father of a family. He has worked the first ten and best years of his life in the factory where, given the intense division of labor, he became adept at some particular mechanical operation and none other. It is an operation that would be of no use to him anywhere else. His working life will be no longer than forty years at best, and he may already be showing symptoms of illness at a time when his family's needs are greatest. No matter how much the liberal party preaches to him about free enterprise and mobility of labor, for this man - and that is the condition of the vast majority of workers in the world after they reach a certain age - these do not exist. If he does not want to starve, he must remain with his family in this neighborhood and at that particular kind of work. He must go on working for this particular employer, and that "must" is as binding for him as it was for any slave who found it enforced by the lash and by the ball and chain. That is the plight of countless numbers of workers who are employed in factory districts.

The plight of these poor persons, dependent as they are upon the will of their employers and painfully aware as they are of this dependence, is often enough taken advantage of so as to contribute to their moral and religious ruination. All the while speeches are made about humanity and toleration. Who does not know of such employers whose great work houses are nothing more

than institutions where our poor Christian people,
in particular our Christian youth, learn to mock
religion and to adopt every possible bad habit
and succumb to immorality?

What a wholesome influence it would be if we
could begin to introduce a Christian-oriented
partnership-in-enterprise in these centers of
white slavery, where our poor Christian people are
victimized by unChristian captains of industry.
If only it were possible by the practice of Christian charity to scrape together the necessary means
for setting up an enterprise, and then to invite
workers to work in such an enterprise with the
understanding that whatever profits are not needed
for maintaining the enterprise, and whatever must
not be put into a reserve fund will flow to them
as an expression of Christian love. The effect
would be tremendous, and the accursed influence of a
godless industrial system on the working class
would perhaps be broken once and for all. May the
attention of all Christian thinkers - all men motivated by the Christian spirit to consider the plight
of the working class and the means to help them -
be turned to this grave problem. May God awaken
men who have the insight and the capacity, to work
toward this goal. If we were to make a beginning
in the kinds of industry which do not require huge
amounts of capital, and operate on a modest scale
at first, a start would be possible. There are
classes of people also in our time who have the
motivation to help their fellow man. Their nobility in former times was responsible for a large
share of the grants which supported the monasteries
of the Church as free-will offerings. I could
think of nothing more Christian or pleasing to God
than the formation of a corporation which could
move into an area where the plight of the workers
is especially desperate and establish a cooperative
enterprise on a Christian basis.

To further this cause, it is necessary, first
of all, that the idea of producers' cooperatives
should be aired thoroughly on all sides so as to
determine the best mode of establishing such associations

Only after the need for them becomes clear among
the workers themselves as well as to others outside working class circles, after large numbers
of persons become convinced of their enormous
usefulness, and after they gain an understanding
of the proper means and the proper methods for
establishing cooperative enterprises, can we expect that attempts to bring them to reality will
multiply.

419

VIII Concluding Remarks

The purpose of this work is to demonstrate to the workers as well as to all others who are concerned about the condition of the working class, that Christianity alone is able to provide a genuine solution to the problem. Without the help of Christianity, whatever other efforts there may be, the plight of the workers will grow progressively worse until it approaches again the sorrry condition that prevailed during the pagan era. History itself is the unassailable witness to the truth of this entire thesis. All that I have maintained is fully borne out by historical developments.

The cultured Greeks, whose civilization is still proposed to us as a model society, contemned manual labor. Industrial activity was viewed as degrading and beneath the dignity of free Greek citizens. The idea of self-help by labor along lines proposed by some today was unknown to them, and all manual work was reserved to the slaves. The gods of the Greeks, so much praised by the most beloved of all German poets, had no heart for slaves or, for that matter, for manual laborers. In Athens, according to the census of Demetrius Phalereus, there were 20,000 Greek citizens and 400,000 slaves - not counting female slaves. Sparta had 36,000 citizens, 244,000 helots, and 120,000 Perioici who were, for all practical purposes, slaves. Corinth had 460,000 slaves and Aegina had 470,000. The Greek philosophers taught that slavery was natural to mankind and that it was therefore not possible to ever abolish it. It would last for all times. It never occurred to them that the entire working class might one day reach the dignified level that it did by virtue of Christianity. The slave was chattel for them just as was any other material object that they possessed. He was an instrument serving the needs of his master. The greatest and noblest philosophers concurred in the opinion that the slave was basically degraded and ignoble, so that he had no other motivation beside fear and pain. Even the idealist Plato admonished the Greeks to be

421

strict with their slaves and to keep them in line
with harsh treatment. He viewed it as a sign of
good breeding to regard slaves with contempt.
That was the status of the working class when the
Greek gods reigned on Olympus!

In Rome, the situation was similar. Romans
regarded slavery and labor in the same way. Originally husbandry and certain skilled crafts were
still held in high regard; but before long any
kind of farm work, handicraft, or mercantile activity came to be slave labor. All of the activi-
aties which are carried on by the working class in
our Christian societies were consigned to slaves.
In Rome, as a matter of fact, the treatment of
slaves was much worse and more horrible than among
the Greeks. Atrocities were commonplace in all
parts of the world under the dominion of Rome where
paganism prevailed. And we are talking here of
atrocities which in our own time, given the dominion of the Christian ethic, would arouse world-
wide indignation. The slaves were purely and simply
means for satisfying all of the pleasures of their
Roman masters. That is how one explains the terrible spectacle of Romans enjoying themselves at
games where slaves were thrown in with hungry lions
and tigers to be torn to bits before their eyes.
And what of the gladiatorial combat for which slaves
were trained to battle by the thousands while the
Roman mob took pleasure in watching them open gap-
ing wounds in one another, in hearing their death
rattle, and in observing their mortal agony? That
was the fate of the working class under the Roman
gods.

The picture was pretty much the same so far
as the working class was concerned in any and all
pagan societies, and that includes our German ancestors. The Germanic tribes also regarded manual
labor as the work of slaves. They busied themselves with warfare and the hunt, or else they engaged in drinking bouts and dozed in drunken stupor.
It is noteworthy that even agricultural labor,which
was once held in high esteem by the early Romans
and which was later to be endowed with a certain
nobility in the German states, so that it gave rise

to the peasant class which became the pride of
the German nation - even that kind of work was
regarded with disdain by the ancient Germans.
Slaves and women had to tend to agriculture.
The German slaves who were used to working the
fields were already far better off than their
Roman counterparts.

The singular exception to such degradation
was to be found in the Jewish nation, and that
was already indicative of the Jews' Providential
mission. Even there, we find slavery in a certain
manner of speaking. However, just as Judaism
stood in the midst of the nations as a witness
and reminder of God's mercy, and just as it led
the way to the Redeemer of the world, so it was
the destiny of the nation which was to give birth
to the Messiah to also provide a kind of preview
of the abolition of slavery by relieving slavery
of some of its pagan degradation and horror.
Jewish slavery was unique in the ancient world,
just as was the Jewish regard for labor. The Jew
worked alongside his slaves. He accorded to the
slave the same right to rest on the Sabbath as
he himself enjoyed; and he was obliged to recognize certain basic human rights of slaves. [16]

Christ has freed the world from all of these
pathetic conditions. He has not only redeemed
men's souls from the bonds of sin and deception;
He has at the same time bequeathed to the working class a new, truly human mode of life here
on this earth. The eloquent wisdom of Holy Scripture:
God made man in His image: He created him in His
own image and likeness...," was practically lost
sight of in the pagan world, so steeped in the degradation, the pathos, and the misery of the masses
of the people. Christ once again spread the good
news to all men, including the poorest and the most
wretched. With Divine power, He burst the chains
that held the slaves, chains so firmly forged that
one and all regarded them as natural to mankind.
By His redemptive act, these formidable chains
began to drop from the ankles of their victims.
Note, however, that the manner in which the emancipation occurred was even more remarkable than the

act itself. The perceptive Möhler remarked so wisely that it may have been Christendom's most remarkable accomplishment <u>to have brought about the release of Christians from slavery without a single violent revolt</u>.17 Church history does not recount a single incident where slaves, acting according to the teachings of their Faith, tried to free themselves by violent overthrow of their masters or by even murdering them.

The Apostle Paul has shown us by example how Christendom was to solve this problem. The slave Onesimus had fled from his master and come to Rome to become a Christian. St. Paul sent him back to his master, but he sent him with a message to Philomen that was written in a manner that was to make it the emancipation proclamation for all slaves in the Christian world order. If the Christians would treat their slaves as the holy Apostle asked Philomen to treat his runaway slave, then slavery would have come to a rapid and peaceful end. "As thou dost value thy fellowship with me, make him welcome as thou wouldst myself: Do not think of him any longer as a slave; he is something more than a slave, a well beloved brother to me in a special way" (Philomen 17:16). Those were no mere words, for St. Paul added: "I write to thee counting on thy obedience, well assured that thou wilt do even more than I ask." (Philomen 21:22)

This "more," Christians have done, by and large. They not only treated their slaves as brothers in Christ, but eventually they extended to all of them their freedom. That is how Christ overcame slavery, by announcing the eternal truths. Just as the body that has been healed of its illness gradually sheds also the external symptoms of disease, the swelling and the skin eruptions, that is how it is with Christendom, as it begins to have its healing effect on the human race. It is a Divine leaven placed in the human race that eventually permeates the entire race of men with its redeeming qualities. Its healing power works from within until the effects reveal themselves also on the exterior. Exterior chaos has its roots in interior disorder. Christianity cures the soul first, because man's soul is the seat of all of the external woes that afflict him. That is how the bonds of slavery were gradually melted away over the course of centuries by a remarkable, inner, spiritual process. By the Middle Ages, slavery was all but eliminated in all Christian nations. From that time on, we witness the evolution of the Christian working class in place of the slavery of pagan times. We see cultivated a class of Christian craftsmen and a whole new appreciation for the dignity of labor. What had been a disgrace to the pagan was regarded by the Christian as a school of virtue and an honor.

History supports our claim that only Christ and Christendom have been genuinely helpful to the working class, and that only this same Divine force can sometime in the future resolve the problem that now besets the hapless worker. Yet, I must deal with an ambiguity that could be read into these words of mine. In Rome there was a great temple known as the Pantheon, i.e., the temple of all of the gods. In this temple altars were erected also to the gods of those nations which Rome conquered during its campaign for world domination. These deities attained the high honor of being admitted into the company of the Roman gods, and that is what finally bestowed upon them their full legitimacy as gods. The so-called Enlightenment is today erecting such a Pantheon once again, and <u>it expects Christ to take His place there among the gods of all of the nations</u>. One is willing to honor Him alongside the gods of Greece and Rome, alongside Zoraster, Confucius, Cakya-Muni, and Socrates, as well as the deities and false prophets of our own time. That is how we honor Christ and Christendom in our time. All of the wise men of the world are supposed to be accepted as His equals. If Christians are willing to be taken in by this ploy, then one is even willing to concede that Christ was the wisest of all of the wise men. That is the grand deception which is to be perpetrated against us Christians in our time. These are the sheeps' clothing under which the wolf is to gain access to our midst. Every lie is now

modified by the words, Christian and Christianity.
Men have found a way to use these holy words in
any context whatsoever. Since Christendom began,
it has encountered a plethora of enemies. It has
had to fight to the point of bloodshed for the
purity of its doctrine, for its institutions, for
its laws and for its sacraments. Given the present
hypocritical use of the word, <u>Christian</u>, there can
be no real enemy of Christianity. Every false prophet and every preacher of some new mad cult has
the privilege of declaring himself a true Christian.
Even those hangmen's assistants who hung Christ on
the cross are now able to regard themselves in this
exploited sense of the word, as Christians, friends
of Christians and admirers of Christianity. That
is the great fraud that is just now being perpetrated against the working class. The world is
full of people who in a figurative sense are again
nailing Christ to the Cross, and whenever the true
believers rise up to defend Christ against them,
those false humanists plead that they are the
true spokesmen for real and authentic Christianity.

That is the truly pathetic plight, the worst
kind of enmity that Christianity has ever had to
face. If the roll were called of all of those who
attack the Church of Christ in the name of Christ,
then we would be surprised to find the names of a
crowd of Jews as well as of a band of brazen atheists,
all of them masquerading daily before the gullible
folk as champions of Christianity. What I am saying is that, when I have spoken out on these pages
about the blessings which Christendom has to offer
the working class, I am speaking of that true Christianity which rests on a belief in the Divinity of
Christ, which draws its strength from His Divine
power and blessing, and which, by this power, has
changed the world. The other false something-for-
everyone-Christianity is a counterfeit which did
not conquer the old slavery and is likewise unable
to protect the workers of our time from the insensi-
tive force of greed. If the ancient Christians had
permitted their God to be placed alongside the false
ones in the Pantheon, they would not have suffered
bloody persecution. They would have been tolerated

426

in the Roman empire as were the servants of all of
the gods of other nations. But from the very beginning, Christianity insisted that it was the only true
religion, and it based this affirmation entirely and
exclusively on the belief in the Divinity of Jesus
Christ. For this truth Christ Himself died on the
Cross. For this belief Christians freely took the
opprobrium of the whole world on their shoulders.
All of the others who pretend to be Christians are
like those who hung Christ on the Cross,while at the
same time they masquerade as His followers.

Only Jesus Christ, Son of the Living God, can
help the working class now and in the future. If
belief in Him and in His message once again penetrates the world, then the working class problem
is solved. If, on the other hand, the belief in
Him and in His Divinity is obliterated and if the
ideas proposed by the liberal party become widespread, then all grandiose proposals for rescuing
the working class will come to naught, and the
workers will once again find themselves in that
pathetic condition in which they suffered during
the reign of the gods of the Pantheon. Pray God
that the working people will come to realize this,
and that they will part company with those "friends,"
who wish to rob them of their belief in the Divinity
of Jesus Christ. The latter are the workers'
greatest, most treacherous enemies. They are the
advance guard of the movement which will forge new
chains to put around their ankles.

The conviction that only that brand of Christianity can help the working class, which is rooted
in Jesus Christ - in whom alone, as the Apostle wrote,
is found the fullness of the Godhead and who alone
possesses the supernatural and Divine power - leads
me to my second conviction. It is this second conviction which brings us to our final conclusion. I
refer to the belief that only the Catholic Church,
which alone is founded by God, is able to contain
and sustain the full, true, heritage of the Christian
belief with its acceptance of the Divinity of Christ
and the boundless blessings which this belief brings
with it for all of mankind. Yet, all that I have

427

written until now is addressed not only to Catholic
Christians, but to all of those who share our belief
that Christ is the Son of God and who have a heart
for the working class. I had to risk narrowing the
circle of my readership by such a presentation as
this. I have to resign myself to this, as I am always painfully aware of the unwholesome consequences
of that division, just as I am convinced that so
many of the problems now facing the world are so
hard to come to grips with because of this sorry
division! The problem of the working class is one
of the great issues of our time, and on its resolution depends the future well-being of the human
race. I have no doubt at all that it would be easy
to solve, if we did not have to reckon with the
great division in Christianity. God grant us what
we may all affirm in the Apostles Creed, which we
still all pray, "I believe in one, holy, Catholic
Church."

        Finally, I could have fortified further the
theme that was referred to at various times in our
discussion of this problem. I refer to the remarkable similarity between the developing political
and social conditions in our time and political
conditions in pagan times, on the one hand, and
the link between these conditions and the doctrines
of modern materialism, on the other. How disastrous both systems can be for the working class if
all of these contradictory forces can develop themselves fully! I could have pointed out how neither
a vague and generalized humanism nor a vague and
generalized Christianity can erect a dam against
the full fury of this destructive flood of ideas.
Only the positive teachings and dogmas and the
genuine forces of Christendom, the supernatural,
clear truths of our Faith can do that. All of
the measures proposed by the modern liberal party
are formulated according to materialistic teachings about matter, about the modification of
matter and about the mechanical laws of matter
as being the foundation of all existence. At the
same time, all of the political ambitions of the
modern state are based precisely on the notion
of the ancient state which recognized neither

428

individual nor corporate freedom or independence.
It accepted neither personal conscience nor personal
individual worth. A man was judged according to
his political viewpoint and his position in the
decision-making process or power structure of the
state. In the light of these ideas one is able to
penetrate the secrets of modern economics and of
the modern progressive state; and one can thus again
appreciate what all of our false liberal attempts
to help the working class are bound to lead to. I
have to forego such analysis in the interests of
brevity. I have to be satisfied with just having
drawn attention to them.

NOTES

1
By "worker," we mean not only worker in the ordinary sense of the dependent day-laborer or wage-earner. We include also those who, although they own their small shop, are nevertheless working with such a small amount of capital that they find themselves in the same condition as the wage-earners. For example, there are many handicraftsmen, merchants, tradesmen, and small landlords and land-owners who must live mainly off their daily earnings.

2
Translator's Note: Bishop von Ketteler was referring here to Ferdinand Lassalle (1825-64), a German socialist who founded the General Association of German workers in 1863. Lassalle first coined the expression which came to be known in the English language as "the iron law of wages," which he used to describe the subsistence wage theory proposed by classical economists.

3
We rely here on the teaching of the Church as derived from Revelation, because this teaching, according to our Faith, is rendered infallible by special Divine indult.

4
The word contract is used here to mean a bilateral arrangement which is based on the nature of the situation as it was intended by God, rather than on some explicit act by two contracting parties.

5
I am not condemning the use of machines. The use of natural energies in the service of man represents a triumph of the mind over matter. Used properly, it can lead to an ever greater emancipation of man from need and from the druggery of physical labor.

6
Translator's Note: The author apparently is using the term party here to mean an ideological faction. The National Liberal Party was not founded until after the War of 1866, while this book was first published in 1864.

431

7
Resolution of the Sixth Congress of German Economists
held in Dresden, September 14-16, 1863.
See: <u>Arbeiterfreund</u>, Vol. 3, 1863, p. 353.

8
Translator's Note: The German word <u>Rechenmaschine</u>
used here would today be best expressed in terms
of the computer.

9
Translator's Note: The term used in the German
text is <u>Vorschussvereine</u>.

10
Translator's Note: The term used in the German
text is <u>Rohstoffvereine</u>.

11
Translator's Note: The words are Horace's and
they translate: <u>The mountains are in labor and
they give birth to a ridiculous mouse</u>.

12
Translator's Note: This would translate as: <u>The
German Worker's Catechism</u>.

13
Translator's Note: Here too the author used the
expression, Radical Party, and he may have been
referring specifically to the General Association
of German Workers founded by Ferdinand Lassalle in
1863. It is more likely that he was once again using
the word <u>Partei</u> to refer to an ideological faction,
as in the case of the liberals. The Social Democratic Workingman's Party was not formed until 1869
by Wilhelm Liebknecht and August Bebel.

14
There are a number of smaller cities in Germany
where funds were set up in those times for hospitals,
schools, churches - funds which are still in existence. Some of these funds were of considerable
magnitude when one considers the size of the communities, e.g., certain imperial cities in the south
of Germany.

15
Translator's Note: This translates the German
proverb which reads: <u>Müssigang ist aller Laster
Anfang</u>.

432

16
We cannot neglect to make the following observation with reference to this matter. In all of antiquity, only the Jewish slaves, by virtue of the force of supernatural revelation and the preparation for the coming of the Redeemer, were relieved of the obligation to perform heavy manual labor on one day of each week. Everywhere else slaves were required to bear the oppressive burden of their work, day in and day out, without a break throughout the year ahd throughout their entire lives. With the triumph of Christianity, Sunday rest as well as rest on the numerous holy-days came to be a prime means for alleviating the back-breaking burden of servile work. Various Church Councils issued decrees that obliged one and all to accord to the serfs the same right to rest on these days and on the vigils thereof, as was the right of every Christian. What is more, the decrees were sanctioned by heavy ecclesiastical penalties. With what joy these poor people, who had until then never known surcease from the hardest conceivable kind of labor, must have greeted the Church's decrees. In our day, regretably, we have to report that wherever Christianity is in decline, the salutary influence of such Christian benevolence is on the wane, and ancient pagan conditions, at least in their incipient stages, have begun to reappear. How many domestic servants, factory workers, journeymen, and railroad workers, already find themselves in a position where they enjoy no break in their work week! The cause and effect pattern is perfectly obvious here.
17
Translator's Note: The author is referring to the Catholic theologian, Johann Adam Möhler (1796-1838).

433

The Labor Movement and Its Goals in Terms
of Religion and Morality

by

Wilhelm Emmanuel von Ketteler

Bishop of Mainz

1869

Translator's Note

        This is the first of a series of shorter works
by Bishop von Ketteler. It was originally an address
to workers at the Liebfrauenheide near Offenbach on
July 25, 1869. The Franz Kirchheim firm published
it in the same year under the German title: <u>Die
Arbeiterbewegung und ihr Streben im Verhältniss zu
Religion und Sittlichkeit</u>. Here we find a catalog-
ing of specific workers' demands which the Bishop
found fully justified. However, he added certain
warnings lest their desperation lead the workers
to abandon Christian virtues, and also lest they
follow those who offer to solve their problems but
lead them instead to a worse state of affairs.
The address affirmed that whatever legitimate
demands the working class may wish to make find
full support on the basis of Christian principles
of justice and charity. Like <u>The Labor Problem
and Christianity</u>, this work too found an echo in
the Leo XIII encyclical <u>On the Condition of Labor</u>.

437

After spending some fourteen days among you, beloved inhabitants of this Main River region, I have invited you all to come together for one more great gathering at this place. I was especially eager that you workers would put in an appearance today. This is a wonderful and holy place, centrally located and afforded solitude by beautiful forests on all sides. Your ancestors used to come here seeking consolation, strength, and help in their times of need. The new altar with its miraculous image of the Sorrowful Mother, recently erected by you, proves that you are devoted to the pilgrimage place as your dear forebears. I am grateful that you have responded to my invitation in such great numbers. Before me, I see a great contingent of workers of this industrial area, together with their families. It is a great joy for me to see you all reunited here one more time before I must take leave of your company.

I had urgent reasons for extending an invitation in particular to you workingmen. You make up the greater proportion of the population in this region. Your villages have either been converted to factory neighborhoods, or else you have felt the need to migrate in great numbers into the industrial cities that surround the area. I have an abiding and deep concern for all that pertains to your well-being. The deep love that I have for you motivates my concern, and this love has been growing over the many years that I have been honored to serve you as your bishop and to visit and get to know you. My concern is motivated in particular, however, by my awareness that I represent Him who was Himself a workingman and who chose to be the son of a carpenter so that he could be close to the people and have compassion for them in their need. The mother of this Divine carpenter's Son, whose image we honor here, will certainly approve my addressing myself to what we call the problem of the working class in its relationship to religion. That is because she lavishes her maternal affection in a special way upon the men and women who make their living by

439

daily toil, and shares with them in their tribulations.

My viewpoint on what I wish to discuss with you is self-evident. The working class and, specifically, the factory workers are confronted in our time by a movement which gathers momentum daily. You yourselves are perplexed by this movement, being true children of the Catholic Church. Your deep faith became apparent to me whenever I spent some time among you in your communities, and it has been a source of deep consolation and great joy to me. Neither the pressures of the harvest time nor having to forego your daily wage at the factories have deterred you from taking part in all of the festivities. On the other hand, you are unable to remain indifferent to the currents that stir around you. Eventually, every Catholic worker has to ask himself, which of these forces which are making their presence felt throughout Europe and beyond are legitimate, which are not, and what danger is contained in them.

To what extent can I as a Christian and as a Catholic participate in such movements without damage to my religion and injury to my conscience. To what extent must I remain aloof? What dangers must I avoid? A conscientious worker must have a clear notion about where he stands in such a complex situation. I would like to answer these questions for you as briefly as possible, but with complete candor, in fact, with that total frankness which the truth demands and which alone is worthy of Him who is Truth itself and as whose representative I stand before you. In the course of my presentation, it will become clear to you that whatever is good and legitimate in the labor movement of our time can only be realized to the extent that it remains firmly tied to religion and morality. Without religion and without morality, all efforts to improve the lot of the working classes will be futile. It is of the utmost importance that we grasp this truth.

Let us turn to specific details. I shall
deal first with the principal objectives of the
worker and the demands which they are making, and
then I shall analyze their relationship with religion and morality and point out whatever dangers
there are.

The basic objective of the labor movement,
that which provides its motive force, in fact,
its very essence, is the effort to unite, to organize workers so that by solid united effort their
interests may be promoted.

This direction to which workers are now inclined is a direct consequence of the economic principles which have come to prominence since the time
of the French Revolution, and which, in fact have
acquired a kind of unchallenged dominance in our
part of the world. Given these principles, the need
for workers to organize has become an inevitable,
natural consequence. Religion can do no less than
bless the endeavor, hope that it will serve to solve
the workingman's problems, and offer support. The
unconditional freedom in all sectors of the economy -
no one can deny this, especially anyone who considers
such freedom as necessary and who nurtures the conviction that it will ultimately be productive of the
best possible results - that freedom has been directly responsible for plunging the working class into
its present desperate condition. All former bonds
were abolished, and as a result, the worker was isolated and dependent entirely upon himself. Each
worker stood unprotected, equipped only with his
capacity for work which was his sole means of support.
Confronting him stood the massive power of high
finance which became the more dangerous, the more
those who controlled it were without scruple, without
religious beliefs, and therefore bent only on pan-
dering to their own egotism. The principles of
modern economics produced opposite results so far
as the potency of human labor and the money power
of capital were concerned. As I mentioned, the
worker was isolated and left to his individual resources while the money power, on the other hand,
was centralized. The working class was atomized
into individual particles, so to speak, with each

441

individual powerless by himself. At the same time, the money power was not so fragmented into small modest accumulations of capital. Instead, it tended to centralize into greater and eventually massive fortunes. A Rothschild, who left 1,700,000,000 francs to his children, was the inevitable consequence of such an economic philosophy. A union of people was replaced by a union of money in frightful dimensions. It is in such soil, i.e., where the money power proceeded to spread unchecked, that the working class was plunged into unspeakable misery. For well nigh 40 years, therefore, the bulk of the working class of England has already been mired in the swamp-land of moral and physical decadence.

It is from the same England where the corruption began that the greatest pressure to organize labor originated. By such collective effort workers may protect their rights and interests and this is entirely legitimate and beneficial, if the working class is not to be completely vanquished by the power of centralized capital.

Yet it is already apparent there how attempts to unify the working class can yield no lasting benefits without reference to religion and morality. In attempting to organize, the workers need help. They cannot accomplish it all by themselves. They have need of leaders and people who will guide them. Who can guarantee that these leaders and representatives will not turn out to be their deceivers and betrayers if they are without religion? Such leaders speak incessantly of how great capitalists exploit workers mercilessly for their own egotistical purposes. But the leaders are themselves human beings possessing the same human nature as the capitalists. If a person who has the power of capital at his disposal ruthlessly exploits his workers for selfish purposes, being oblivious of God and religion, who is to say that one of these so-called friends of the working class and folk heroes will not turn around and use the workers simply to serve his own interests, if he is a man without a conscience, or without God or religion? Just as the monied classes exploited the workers, so demagogues who not only have no respect for Christianity, but who in fact despise it, will also turn on the workers and use them.

You see before your own eyes how often bitter hostilities break out among the very men who hold the leading positions in the labor movement - something that is occurring right at the present moment. Note how these men then become guilty of the same selfish tactics of which they accuse the capitalists. How could it be otherwise? Without religion, we all fall prey to egotism; it makes no difference whether we are rich or poor, capitalists or workers. We will take advantage of our fellow man as soon as we have the power to do so.

No matter how justified the aspirations of the German workers to organize may be, real benefits can only be expected if the leaders of the labor movement will cease their hatred of Christianity and adopt a position which is at least respectful and amicable toward religion and the Church. That ought already be clear to us when we observe the great difference in the results achieved by the labor movement in England and in Germany. Even though the English working class was in worse shape than the German, so far as the dire consequences of modern economic philosophy are concerned, the efforts to organize the working class in England are vastly superior to our own. That is due first and foremost to the great respect shown in England toward the significance of religion in solving social problems. In Germany, on the other hand, the spokesmen for labor make a public display of their hatred for religion.

Let us pass now to a consideration of the specific demands which the working class hopes to achieve by means of organization. We will note the relationship of each demand to religion as we analyze them one by one, and also how the whole labor question is basically a religious one, whereas godlessness is at the same time the working class' greatest enemy.

443

<u>The first demand of the working class is for</u>
<u>an increase in wages that reflects the true value</u>
<u>of a man's labor.</u>

The demand is fully justified. Religion too
requires that human labor is not to be treated as
a commodity which is valued simply according to
supply and demand. That is how labor is to be ap-
praised according to the economic principles of
which we spoke earlier, which abstract from all
moral and religious considerations. Labor is not
only regarded merely as merchandise, but, in addition, the man offering his labor for sale is considered merely as a machine. As one buys machines
as cheaply as possible and then uses them day and
night until they are completely depreciated, that
is how such a system proposes that a man ought to
be worked, until his strength is used up. It is
a state of affairs that has reached frightening
dimensions in England. It gave rise to the English
trade unions which spread rapidly. The principal
weapon of the trade unions against capital and
against powerful entrepreneurs was the strike.
Many have maintained that the strike, because of
the disruptions which it causes in the business
and the loss of wages which workers suffer during
the course of the strike, does more harm to the
workers' cause than it is worth. This is not true,
overall. Strikes have resulted in significant wage
gains, as the English writer Thornton proved deci-
sively. Since the trade unions began their activities, wages have risen by as much as 50% in certain
industries, in others by 25-30% and in all other
industries generally, by at least 15%. Thornton
also demonstrated that even as a result of strikes
which workers appeared to have lost, wage increases
were granted soon afterward; so the defeat was not
as decisive as it sometimes appeared. In Germany,
labor unions have been formed after the pattern
of these English trade unions, and not a few of
you are members. The struggle to get a decent increase in wages is legitimate, it goes without saying. It is a requirement of justice and of Christianity that the workingman is entitled to a just
wage.

444

It is absolutely proper to insist that human labor ought to be rewarded according to different principles than machine labor, or, to say the same thing in other words: human labor and the workingmen ought to be again accorded their rightful dignity of which the principles of liberal economics robbed them. Yet, here again, dear workers, we have to point out to you that this effort will only be truly worthwhile and yield durable benefits so long as it remains on secure religious and moral foundations. There are two ways in which moral and religious principles come into play in this area.

First of all, do not lose sight of the fact, dear workers, that increasing wages also has its limits; and even at its uppermost permissible limits we are talking only about a modest income. The natural limit of the workingman's wage is set by the profitability of the enterprise in which he is employed. The capital, both material and non-material that has been invested in the business, will quickly be withdrawn to more profitable directions when wage demands become excessive to the point where the return on capital is inadequate. At that point you are unemployed. The rate of wages, therefore, has its limits, regardless of how well you are organized; and it would be most damaging for you not to realize that, given the many irresponsible suggestions that "the sky is the limit."

Whenall is said and done, even the best wage possible will yield an adequate and satisfactory level of living only, provided that you live a life marked by temperance and thrift. These precious qualities, temperance and thrift, will only thrive among the working class where genuine religious values play a key roll in the lives of the workers. It is proven time and again that the welfare of the working class depends not merely on the level of wages. There are districts where industry generates high pay rates, but where workers are in desperate straits. At the same time we find other areas where workers have attained a better level of prosperity despite the fact that their wages are lower.

One of the greatest dangers facing workers in this regard is drunkenness and the pursuit of pleasures stimulated and nourished by the ever-present saloons and taverns which abound wherever large numbers of workers are concentrated. The proliferation of such haunts is condoned by governments to the extent that they themselves have lost a proper respect for religion and morality. In fact, I heard a politician say that the multiplication of such establishments is in the state's best interests since they generate tax revenue. Saloons represent parasitical growths in the sense that they bleed the workers of their money. They are a baleful venture calculated to deprive the workers of their hard-earned wages. A brief episode of intemperance is all that is necessary to nullify the most satisfactory level of earnings. What good is a high rate of pay to a man who has become a slave to intemperance? Yet, how great is the temptation facing the worker in the present day and age. There has probably never in world history been work which is so strenuous, so demanding, so monotonous as the factory labor of our time. You see a large number of workers engaging in prolonged labor of a kind where all of their tasks are so interrelated that if one lets up for a moment, all others are immediately affected in the performance of their tasks. It is not hard to understand how a man toiling for long hours in the same shop, at the same machine, at the same repetitive task, would finally seek relief from it all by plunging himself into intemperate drinking or debauchery. It takes a strong moral character to remain thrifty and temperate in such circumstances and to avoid seeking relief from monotonous labor in saloons with their low-life form of entertainment. Only religion is capable of instilling in workers the strength of character that he needs to remain thrifty and temperate. If wage increases are to be of real benefit to you, therefore, dear workers, it is necessary that you lead truly Christian lives.

You also need religion and an ethical sense for your efforts to raise wages, to keep your demands within proper bounds. We have pointed out

446

that wage increases have their limits. It is
extremely important in our time therefore, since
worker efforts to improve their material circumstances are becoming ever more widespread, that
they will not overstep their proper limits.
Workers have to be careful not to let themselves
be used for ulterior purposes. <u>The objective
here is not class conflict between employers and
workers, but appropriate harmony between the two
groups</u>.

The godlessness of capital which exploits
human labor to the breaking point must come to
an end. It is a crime perpetrated against the
working class and robs it of its proper self-
respect. Such a mode of conduct is apt only
for such people who seriously propose the theory
that man descended from the ape. But we must
also battle against godlessness creeping into
the ranks of workers. If the movement to raise
labor's wages transgresses its proper limits,
catastrophic conditions are sure to result which
will only boomerang with effects that will bear
down with special weight upon the workers. Capital,
in the final analysis, can always find new outlets,
even if the business in which it is presently invested collapses. If nothing else, the abominable
condition of indebtedness which modern states
find themselves in provides an outlet for any
speculator who has money to invest in the exchange
and in government securities. The worker, on the
other hand, does not have such an easy time finding other employment when the business which hires
him goes under. Beyond that we have to consider
the small businessman. He suffers far more than
the large capitalists when wage demands become inordinate. I am speaking of modest enterprises of
middle class shop-owners down to the level of
master craftsmen and their journeymen.

A working class which keeps its demands within proper bounds, which does not permit itself to
become merely the tool of men with evil ambitions,
and which avoids falling prey to the selfsame greed
which it detests and campaigns against when that is

447

practiced by capitalists, such a working class has
to be a decent, religious, Christian one. The
money power bereft of all religious values is
evil incarnate. But the same applies to workers
if they gain the upper hand at the expense of their
religious values. Both breed catastrophe.

The second demand of the working class is for a reduction of the hours of work.

I am not in a position to pass judgement on
the length of the working day in this area. What
I do know, though, is that both wages and the hours
of work are under the sorry influence of contemporary
economic principles. The economics of our time ab-
stracts from morality and religion. In other words,
it dehumanizes man's economic activity with the result that instead of capital being in the service
of mankind, it rather serves to depress wages to
the lowest possible level, at the same time that
it lengthens the hours of labor to the ultimate
limit which a man can endure. Although human labor
simply cannot bear twenty-four hours a day continuous operation like the actual machine, it is nevertheless treated, in the present system, as merely
human machinery and driven to the limits of its
capacity. Wherever and whenever the hours of labor
are driven beyond the limits of human endurance and
beyond what proper considerations of healty and
sanity would dictate, the workers have a perfect
right to fight the abuse to which the moneyed interests subject them, by collective action.

But here, too, my dear workers, the ultimate
merit of such efforts depends on morality and religion, if your actions are to produce lasting benefits.
If the worker uses the time which he gains to better
fulfill his duties as a father, to look after the
house, his property, and to keep them in good order,
then such time is used to good advantage. If, on
the other hand, he spends his spare time hanging
around the streets, all too often in bad company,
or lounging around in a tavern, then the extra
time is of no benefit either for his health or
for his economic well-being. It will only serve

448

to hasten his spiritual and bodily ruination and
make it all the more certain that he will squander
his pay.

The third demand of the working class is the provision of days of rest.

This demand too is fully justified. Religion
not only supports you in this, but it made precisely
the same demand long before you did. God ordained
it when he commanded men to keep holy the Sabbath.

In this area, too, the principles of modern
economics as well as the party which propagates
them have perpetrated a crime against humanity which
cries to heaven. And they continue to do so on a
wide scale to this very day. It is not only the
great captains of industry who are guilty here of
forcing their workers to work on Sundays. Even
craftsmen of all kinds, landowners, as well as
those who hire domestic servants deny their help
the right to Sunday rest. Guilty also are those
public officials who do not have the backbone to
stand up to the wealthy, to stand by the defense-
less workers and enforce the laws that are on the
books. The hypocrisy which results from so-called
liberal economic principles has more recently been
brought into the light of day by certain leaders
of the labor movement, and rightfully so. The
money powers have always paraded this kind of exploitation as the noblest benefaction to mankind.
They reproach the Church for its insistence on a
day of rest, calling this an inhuman intrusion on
the rights of the working class. How often these
hypocrites have talked of the Sundays and Holydays,
proclaiming with sanctimonious pretense how much
wage payment it would all add up to if men would
but work on these days! How benevolent, these
money men are for making such earnings available
to the working classes; and how hard-hearted the
Church, which wants to deprive them of it. To
this sham, the spokesmen of the working class
party have responded that there is yet another
way to make such earnings available to the workers
without requiring that they work themselves to
death in the process. Why not pay them as much

for six days labor as they were earning for seven?
Then the worker will earn just as much, at the
same time that he is better able to live like a
human being. Who can gainsay the wisdom of this
proposal, and who can fail to recognize the lying
and deception in the proposal of the money men,
which is still so often heard in Bavaria and Baden?
If the latter are right, wouldn't it be downright
inhuman to permit people to sleep? After all,
look how much money you could earn during the night
while you waste your time sleeping. Just as certainly as a man requires a certain period of rest
during the course of 24 hours, he also needs surcease from labor during a continuous seven-day
period. He needs this not only for his spiritual
well-being so that he can set aside a day to recall that he is a child of God, but also for his
bodily well-being so that he remains healthy and
strong. Just as a man who hires a worker for a
day at a time is obliged to give him the opportunity for a night's rest and to pay him accordingly,
so the factory owner who hires a man for an entire
week is obliged to give him the weekend off to rest,
and to pay him accordingly. Rest time is to be regarded as part of the work day, since the need for
rest resulted from labor, and inasmuch as rest is
a necessary prerequisite for whatever work a man
will yet be expected to perform.

It is not enough, dear workers, that days of
rest are championed by organized labor. You yourselves have to take care, so much as it is within
your power not to violate the Sabbath. Even while
organized labor is campaigning for Sunday rest,
there are always those workers, unfortunately, who
work on Sundays not because of dire necessity but
because of greed, simply to earn an extra dollar
whenever and wherever they can. Such workers sin
not only against God's law; they also sin in the
strict sense of that word against the working
class itself. By violating the Sabbath in their
greed, they give employers an easy excuse for depriving other workers of their Sunday rest. Would
that all workers may one day unanimously insist on
this as a basic human right, and that includes every

450

worker from the domestic servant who is exploited
mercilessly by hard-hearted heads of households,
down to the last railroad worker whom filthy rich
railroad companies begrudge the right to a single
day of rest. What good are the so-called human
rights contained in Constitutions - which are of
little relevance to the typical workingman - when
the moneyed interests are in a position to contemp-
tuously disregard these basic social human rights?

No matter how religion stands by you in demanding the day of rest, dear workers, and no matter what efforts the labor movement makes to secure
this right for you, all will be in vain if there is
not underlying the demand a basic religious motivation that stems from the Divine command, "Remember,
thou keep holy the Sabbath day." For it is a fact
that the Sunday as a day of rest will only be of
real benefit for you, whether we are speaking of
your health, of recovering your energy for further
labor, of the good of your souls, of a genuine contribution to your cultural aspirations, or finally
of your families from whom you must be absent most
of the week, and of the bolstering of a true family
solidarity, if you are upstanding, Christian workers.
The Sunday at rest will only be really meaningful
to you if you are living lives that are in harmony
with what your Church and your religion proposes.
Otherwise the day of rest may simply contribute to
the ruination of the health and well-being of the
worker and of family life. The expression, "blue
Monday" is suggestive of what Sunday without religion does to people. In some regions Sunday has
actually contributed to the delinquency of the
working class, and it has proven detrimental even
to its material well-being.

What a contrast one sees in the way a religious family spends its day of rest and what takes
place otherwise. I do not have to elaborate. All
of you are well enough aware of examples of what
I am talking about. A day of rest that is spent
in taverns, with bad companions, in drunkenness,
in debauchery, and in nocturnal revelry is ruinous
to the health, the economic welfare, the family

451

life of the workers. It will prove to be as much
a curse, as a Sunday spent in the way Christians
ought to spend it proves a blessing to him in all
of these respects.

A fourth demand of the labor movement is the
ban on child labor in factories, while children are
of mandatory school age.

I regret to have to report that not all working class people are equally insistent upon this
demand. There are those who, unfortunately, out
of their own greed, send their children into the
factories. I have to say, therefore, that this is
a demand by only certain spokesmen for the working
class. Specifically, the head of the Cigarmakers
Union in Germany, Fritsche, who is well known to
you, demanded in no uncertain terms before the
Parliament of the North German Federation that
the labor of school children ought to be forbidden
by law. He was able to support his testimony by
relating his own painful experiences, having worked
in factories from his tenderest years.

Fritsche pointed out that, among other things,
the morals of minors are placed in great jeopardy
by factory labor. Regretably, his pleas went un-
answered. Laws were passed to limit child labor,
but it was not prohibited outright. I protested
this development and saw in it a triumph of crass
material considerations at the expense of vital
moral principles. All of my own experiences support what the worker, Fritsche, maintains as regards
what becomes of school children employed in factories.
I am not unaware of the excuses that are offered
for child labor. Nor am I unaware that even certain persons who regard themselves as sympathetic
to the working class are willing to make exceptions
to the general rule against children working in
factories. Some would even propose that children
have an obligation to help their parents, as they
have always done so around the house and on the
farm. The enormous difference between such family
chores and factory labor has to be apparent to anyone. By factory labor the familial instincts are

already obliterated from childhood, an effect which is of the greatest danger to the working class in adulthood as we shall discuss presently. Aside from that, the child is deprived of any opportunity for wholesome play which is so important for a normal childhood. What is more, its health is impaired and its morality is placed in extreme danger. I regard child labor in factories as a contemptuous abomination of our age, a crime perpetrated against children by the spirit of our age and the greed of the older generation. I deem it a gradual death sentence for both the bodies and souls of our children. Children are being asked to sacrifice the joys of their youth as well as their morality for the sake of material gain. What is more, all too often they are required to earn bread for parents who, because of their own corrupt condition, are in no position to provide for their children. I rejoice, therefore, over every word that is uttered in defense of working children. Religion, by virtue of its great love for children, cannot condone child labor. I beseech you most earnestly, dear workers, to throw your whole-hearted support behind this demand of the labor movement, and to give force to your expressions of support by seeing to it that you do not permit your own school age children to work in factories.

The fifth demand of the working class is to prohibit female labor, especially the employment of mothers, in factories.

The Frenchman, Julius Simon, deeply devoted to the well-being of the working class, wrote in his book, The Female Worker: "Our whole system of economic organization suffers from a horrible atrocity which is mainly responsible for the downfall of the working class and which must be eliminated, whatever the cost, if we are not to destroy ourselves. I refer to the destruction of family life." He makes reference to what Michelet said: "Female worker, a horrible expression not found in any language before our time, inconceivable in any age prior to our iron age, can single-handedly obliterate whatever other progress we hope to achieve in our time." The man is telling us that we are on the road to ruin when the mother

453

is no longer a mother, but an employee!

"The woman who has become a worker is no longer
a woman. She no longer leads the hidden, protected
modest life in the bosom of the family which is so
vital for the well-being of the woman herself as it
is for the soundness of the entire family structure.
Such a woman lives no longer under the authority of
her husband, but under that of a boss, among other
female workers of dubious moral qualities, and in
constant contact with men, severed from her own
husband and her children. In such a working family,
husband and wife are absent for fourteen hours. One
cannot speak of a family any more. The mother cannot nurse her own children, and the mortality rate
among children rises alarmingly. Children three
or four years of age run around the streets, hungry
and cold. When mother and father finally return
from work at seven in the evening and find themselves all together in one room that they call home,
the parents are exhausted, and the children are
famished and apathetic. Nothing is ready. The
room was empty all day long, with no one at home
to do what had to be done and to keep things clean.
There is no fire in the stove, and the mother is
tired and lacks the energy to prepare a decent meal.
Her own clothing, like that of her husband and
children are in disrepair. That is the pathetic
picture of a family - a kind that is the product
of our factory culture. It is not surprising if a
man, faced with the prospect of returning to such
a dismal, dingy hovel, where he is greeted by half-
naked children and a woman whom he no longer really
knows because she is mostly absent from the home,
prefers to stop off at the tavern to squander his
earnings and dissipate his remaining energies. That
is the plight of all too many working class people.
It represents a colossal blight on our so-called
great industrial society."

So writes Simon, after many years of travel
about the factory regions of France where he was
able to observe women at work in factories and the
resultant destruction of the family. He arrives
at the conclusion that all attempts to raise wages

454

are futile unless morals are elevated, but that the uplifting of morals depends on the restoration of the family life which has been so disrupted and impaired by modern industry and factory production. "Terrible," he exclaims.

"Subsistence falls short in the household far more often because of the father's failure than because of industrial abuses. Blue Monday devours a quarter, sometimes half of a man's weekly wage. Then the best paid workers, who could provide a decent living for their families, are almost universally addicted to alcohol. Economic welfare depends more on morality than on the wage. The evil is basically a moral one, and the problems that need to be resolved require that the worker has to get himself back on the straight and narrow path. One can do the worker a far greater favor than to put more money in his pocket. Far better to cultivate in him a respect for thrift and morality. When the workshops are full and the taverns empty, the problem will be largely solved."

All of these abominable conditions, which Julius Simon describes as prevailing in French factory districts and which are even more widespread in England, have not yet come to prevail in our own industrial towns on such a scale. For example, women and mothers are not employed in factories hereabouts, by and large, at least so far as I am aware. The recognition, however, of how extremely important the welfare of the family is for the well-being of the working class shows us again how intimately religious values are tied to the many objectives of the labor movement. We realize that these objectives can only be realized in and through the context of religion. Religion also requires that a mother is to fulfill her obligation to her husband and children in the confines of her home. All that Julius Simon has to say, and anything that any friend of the working has ever had to say anywhere is merely an echo of what you yourselves have heard since earliest youth from your church extolling the sacredness of family life.

It is an unassailable truth that the problems of
the working class are first of all moral problems
that are inextricably related to sound family
structure. Accordingly it is beyond question
that they can only be solved by religion. The
closer you are to your Church, the better your
women will be, the better mothers there will be
for your children, the closer your family ties
will be, and the more these solid family ties
will serve to protect you from the temptations
that confront workers everywhere, in the form of
saloons and taverns and debauchery.

The sixth demand which is often pressed among
spokesman for the working class, one which is closely
related to the previous one, is that young ladies
are also to be excluded from work in factories.

Various reasons are put forth. One is that
young girls are, by and large, able to work for
less, since their needs are less. They are therefore used in great numbers by employers to lower
the wage rate below what a man with family responsibilities requires to live on. In England, as a
consequence of the dominance of purely materialistic economic principles, the situation became
so unnatural that men stayed home and took care
of the children, while women, instead of taking
care of their children worked in the factories.
The second and main reason put forth as to why
young women ought not to work in factories is the
bad effect on the morals of the workers' daughters
and therefore on the families of the future.
Workers and their leadership have often offered
testimony in recent years to indicate the gravit-
of this problem. In their assemblies they have
said something like: "We want good and wholesome
families among the working classes; to have such
families we need virtuous, decent women and mothers;
we are not about to get such women if we send our
girls into the factories and expose them to the
virus of immorality and brazenness." I cannot
tell you, dear workers, how impressed and overjoyed
I was to hear these sentiments voiced by the workers
themselves. Ten years ago before the labor movement had made much headway in Germany, one could

456

hear such thoughts expressed only from the pulpits of our churches. The liberals had no conception of any such moral dangers confronting a working girl. Even when girls became totally depraved by the working environment of the factories, the liberals posed with hypocritical righteousness as their benefactors, on the grounds that the girls were given the opportunity to earn money. The grave danger which factory work poses for the morals of working class girls and therefore of working class families is being more widely recognized even among factory owners. That is a happy turn of events. It shows that, with the problem of the working class as with so many other problems, we are dealing basically with religious and moral values. Concern for the integrity of young girls is, according to an official report about the actions of the panel of judges at the Universal Exposition in Paris (1867), a main criterion for deciding on a winner. Numbered among the methods to assure that integrity, were segregated workshops for young girls, strict supervision of such places, homes for girls who have no families, separate lunch rooms and female supervision of female labor.

My dear factory workers. God has thus far spared you from the worst consequences that factory work could cause among the daughters of the working class. The factory system is not so old and well-established here; and genuine Christian, family life is still prevalent enough among us to provide real resistance to these moral threats. I can vouch for it and do so with great joy, that very many of our young female workers are still exemplary young maidens. That is not to say that we can ignore for a minute the dangers that confront the morals of your daughters. These dangers are probably greater hereabouts, because virtually nothing is done to safeguard the moral standards. Most of the measures mentioned above, like segregated workshops and the supervision of women workers by responsible female supervisors are totally absent in most instances. I can only urge you, dear workers, to get behind and support whole-

457

heartedly these efforts to safeguard the morals of your daughters. Join in, one and all. This is a general working class problem. It is a sacred duty incumbent upon the working class. Finally, it is a religious duty.

The honor of your daughters is your honor, fathers, brothers! The disgrace of your daughters is your disgrace. The chaste morals of your daughters is the precondition of the chaste morals and blessing of your families, dear workers. Whoever attacks them attacks not only your own honor, but he also destroys the future of the family. You men, therefore, have an obligation to cooperate in fighting this evil, whether on the way to the factory, or in the factory itself. They are your daughters. Accursed be the father who stands by and tolerates the forces that corrupt his daughter. Join in the battle, you brothers. It is your sisters that we are talking about! Shame on any brother who can stand by and watch while his sister is dishonored. The same is true of the entire community. The misfortune that befalls these girls befalls the whole community, for they are your children. In a special way you older virtuous maidens ought to help along. Out of humane and Christian concern you ought to help to protect your younger sisters from these grave dangers which threaten to rob them of what is a young girl's greatest treasure, of her good reputation, her purity, her high calling. Accordingly you must not tolerate any shop foremen who use their position to accomplish the devil's mission, i.e., to corrupt the morals of female workers. Above all, do not permit yourselves to become accomplices of such supervisors out of selfish interests, such as the fear of losing your jobs. All too often we find workers who, though well aware of the nefarious activities of such immoral supervisors, cannot muster enough nerve to confront them about their misconduct. Consequently, these wretched, corrupt scoundrels continue to get away with seducing the innocent without anyone lifting a finger to stop them.

Thus, dear workers, you see the many faceted and close connection between religious values and the weal and woe of the working class and its demands.

Everything which religious teaching has inculcated
in your daughters, your children, from the earliest
childhood until now, serves at the same time to preserve their morals and to protect them from danger.
These teachings serve to raise them as is necessary
if we are to have a generation of truly virtuous
wives of workers, good mothers of workers' children,
in other words, if we are to have a solid basis for
a virtuous family structure among the working classes.

Dear workers, I have now discussed certain of
the principal demands of the working class, which
are of the highest urgency and with reference to
which the relationship to religion was most clear
cut and demonstrable. I am well aware that I have
not exhausted the subject. There are certain other
demands which are important to you. I could speak
about the various associations which have been established to protect workers savings, and others
which provide consumer goods at lower prices. They
too could be discussed in the same context. I could
make mention of these organizations which go beyond
the trade unions that have as their main objectives
simply to raise the wages of workers. There are,
for example, those which promote a sharing of the
firm's profits among the workers, whether by having them become part owners of the enterprises,
or merely by simple profit-sharing arrangements.
I would like nothing better than to be able to
discuss such partnerships-in-enterprise with you.
I am convinced that they could easily be introduced in the cigarmaking industry, since this industry does not require huge capital outlay. [1]

On every side one can point to examples of
where the justifiable demands of the workers have
a firm support in ethical and religious principles.
I have to warn you, however, against being taken in
by those demands which are not in your best interests
either because they are excessive, or because they
represent vague, fanciful, socialist pipe dreams.
Such demands serve rather to indulge the conceits
and vain ambitions of certain leaders. They serve
to make the workers the unwitting tools for dubious
political intrigues which will eventually lead to
their downfall. I cannot go into these problems in

459

detail now, but I do wish therefore to make you
aware of certain special dangers which this gives
rise to.

Beware, dear workers, of all those who mock
religion and who try to talk you out of your religious convictions and the fulfillment of your religious obligations. Such persons are your greatest
enemies because, as we saw, whatever is in the best
interests of the working class has its foundation
in morality and religion. Anyone who says he wants
to help you, at the same time that he lauches an
attack against your religion, is beyond any shadow
of a doubt either a liar, or else he doesn't have
the slightest idea as to what the workingman's
problems are all about. There are men among us
who act as though they had the magic power of
turning the mockery of religion into bread and
money with which to solve the nation's problems.
Preposterous! In the process, all of their
thoughts, words, and actions come to be directed
against us Catholics. Their quest for freedom
and for progress, their patriotism, their enlightenment, their devotion to the people and for their
welfare all become the occasions for blasphemous
attacks against religion and specifically against
Catholicism. Beware of such people. They are not
leaders of the working class; they are liars and
betrayers.

Secondly, beware of bad, immodest thoughts.
Never indulge in them voluntarily. To do so is to
take the first step toward total corruption. There
are many occasions for such thoughts, because nowadays you are thrown daily into the midst of society
in your youngest most impressionable years. You
children, even while you are in school and come
from families where you are perhaps never exposed
to a wrong word and where there is never offered
an occasion for immodest thoughts, suddenly find
yourselves thrust into the middle of all of these
temptations. If you once give into them, you are
on your way to losing the purity of your hearts.
The corruption in your society will ever increase,
and your passions will become stronger until you

460

become victims of secret and even not so secret
sins which are both harmful to your health and
destructive of your morals. These sins will toss
you from one abyss to the other until you stand
before the ultimate abyss of all! Mortality
rates are especially high among the working class,
and there are many reasons for that. One of the
principal ones is immorality!

Beware of immodest talk, bawdy songs, bad
books and pictures. What I said about impure
thoughts applies also to them.

Dear young workers, men and women, for the
same reason I urge you to avoid getting involved
prematurely with companions of the opposite sex.
You probably feel sometimes that your religion
is too demanding, and that too much is made of
these occasions of sin which you keep hearing
about from the pulpit. Is not immorality often
portrayed as simply a minor shortcoming that goes
along with being young, and are not the Church's
admonitions regarding impurity depicted as un-
duly stern and even sinister? If only you will
take to heart what I have told you, which is in
complete harmony with what the workers themselves
wish for their families, then you will come to
realize that what religion asks of you in the
matter of morality is the greatest boon to humankind. On the other hand, everything that is in-
jurious to purity is the bane of mankind at its
unspeakable worst! You demand pure brides, and
chaste wives because you want model mothers for
your children. Such women are the angels of their
families. Blessed be the man who has such a wife;
blessed be the workers' children who have such a
mother. How do we expect to have such women for
our families if we are careless about our early
acquaintanceships? They are a threat precisely
to that precious gift of virginity which would
prepare a young woman to be a dutiful wife later
on. Consider the girl who soon, upon finishing
school, begins to indulge in dirty conversation
and entertainment. She fills her heart with
filthy thoughts and images, as she becomes ever

461

more brazen. She becomes involved with bad companions, wanders about the streets from tavern to dance hall. By her conduct she has lost all claim to respect. Among other things, she doesn't know the meaning of the word thrift; and whatever she may have earned, she squandered. Finally the inevitable happens, and at the tender age of twenty or twenty-one she has to solve her problem by marrying the first thing that comes along. Such marriages are doomed from the start, and they are destined for misery and unhappiness of the kind that we described earlier.

Now consider another kind of girl who has kept herself chaste until her twenty-fourth year, and who has a reputation as being diligent, moral, and spotless. By her thrift she has put aside a little something; what a contrast! She has her pick of good men who will compete for her affection. She is everything that a virtuous working class expects of a worker's wife. If you want chaste brides and decent women, therefore, shun premature relationships which lead to nothing but spoiled worthless young ladies, who are poor prospects for working class families.

Finally, dear workers, be on guard against intemperance and drunkenness. Stay away from those establishments which thrive on separating the workers from his hard-earned pay. The frequenting of taverns, the habit of looking for pleasure, fun, and relief from the monotony of labor in such places is, according to all who have studied the way to improve the lot of the working class, in whatever country, one of the greatest threats to the worker's welfare. The panel of judges at the Exposition in Paris concluded, in their consideration of what is to be done to eliminate vice, that drunkenness is the principal problem. They proposed organizations that would abolish, or at least carefully supervise drinking establishments.

Those are the words which I wish to leave with you, dear workers, as I conclude my stay among you. They are intended to be an expression

of my heartfelt love for you and of my deep concern for your problems. You see now that, also
as Catholics, you are in a position to get involved in and support many of the objectives that
the labor movement is promoting without violating your religious principles. You also understand now, however, that all of these objectives
are futile if religion and morality do not remain
their foundation.

1
A capital investment of 20,000 dollars would be
sufficient to begin a cigar making enterprise
with worker participation here in central
Germany.

The Charitable Concern of the Church for
the Working Class

by

Wilhelm Emmanuel von Ketteler

Bishop of Mainz

1869

Translator's Note

This paper bore the German title:
<u>Sozialkaritative Für sorge der Kirche für die
Arbeiterschaft</u>. It was presented before the
Conference of Catholic Bishops at Fulda on
July 26, 1869, just one day after the previous
address was delivered at Liebfrauenheide. In
published form it first appeared in the
November 6, 1869 edition of <u>Christlich-Sociale
Blätter</u>. An Italian translation was printed
in Venice the following year. We have here a
serious and systematic inquiry into precisely
what the so-called social problem was - here
termed, the most complex and urgent problem of
the time - and an answer to the question whether
the Catholic Church could and ought to have become involved in its solution.

The topic deals with the so-called social problem, a most complicated and vital issue in our time. The questions we have to address ourselves to are these:

1. Is the problem also present in Germany?

2. Should the Church get involved? Can the Church do anything?

3. What are the remedies?

4. What practical measures can the Church take to apply the remedies?

I

Is the social problem also a reality here in Germany?

The nature of this social problem can be presented in the following propositions:

1. After the abolition of those regulations which formerly protected the craftsman in his trade, with the introduction of the free enterprise system, free competition, free entry, and with the abolition of usury laws, etc., capital, together with the advent of machine production and the application to it of the principle of division of labor, further aided by improved transportation and communications media, has secured enormous dominance. As a result, not only the craftsman but also the small businessman, merchant, and landowner, all of whom rely mainly on human labor input, are no longer in a position to hold out in competition with the power of capital which becomes more and more centralized.[1] Eventually these men must give up their independence and become piece workers or wage earners in some factory; or else they work as day laborers or sub-contractors who are also dependent on someone else. As a consequence of these deveopments, the middle class which is the mainstay of the state as well as of the Church, is on the way out.[2] It is being replaced by a

471

phenomenon that is peculiar to our time - a mass of propertyless and joyless proletarians who are disgruntled and frustrated.

2. The relationship between worker and employer is no longer based on moral principles that call for respect for human dignity; and there is no longer any evidence of the beneficent influence of Christian charity. It is now governed exclusively by mercantile considerations whereby one tries to reduce costs to the lowest possible level so as to compete as profitably as possible with other producers.

3. From this perverted situation, a whole range of material, physical, and moral abuses confront the workingman.

a) The worker's wage is governed not by his actual needs or by his contribution to production, but by an "iron economic law" which, under the influence of demand for and supply of labor, always pushes the wage down to the level of bare subsistence.

b) The worker does not even have the assurance of the continuance of this pathetic wage. Business fluctuations, sickness and old age, all threaten him with a loss of earnings, so that he is left helpless.

c) The worker - with rare exceptions - is barred from being able to lift himself from his depressed and hopeless condition, as the independent craftsman is still able to do.

d) There is nothing about the kind of labor performed by workers in our time which is uplifting for their mental or moral dispositions. A man works and exerts himself, but he does so not for himself but for some capitalist. Given the crass, materialistic spirit which prevails in our industrial society, the man is regarded as a commodity; and his worth is calculated on the same basis as machinery, i.e., he is a kind of living machine. As a result, he even comes to look upon himself in these debased terms as a piece of machinery. The

472

inhumane long hours along with the soul deadening
monotony of his work brutalize him. The hopeless-
ness of his condition, his insecure future, the
feeling of helplessness arising from his isolation
from his fellow man, all serve to ennervate his
manly spirit and rob him of his self-confidence.
It is hardly surprising, therefore, that his heart
is more and more choked by a level of dissatisfaction that borders on desperation, and that he
develops a bitterness and a hatred toward the
upper classes which enjoy to the point of satura-
tion, the goods of this world that he produces by
his toil.   .

e) Add to all of this the miserable living conditions, the worker's pathetic hovel that
he calls his home, the shabby clothing, the sub-
standard nourishment, and you begin to understand
the excessive use of alcohol, the erosion of family
life, the debasement of womankind, the neglect of
children.

f) If we are content with the accustomed
pastoral concern, the grace of Christendom is a
closed book for these poor workers, by and large.
They will remain beyond our reach, both unreceptive
and unapproachable. [3] It is necessary to first
make provision for humanizing these brutalized masses
before there can be any thought of christianizing
them. [4]

The more a country becomes industrialized in
the modern mode, the more generalized and deplorable these conditions become so that the workers
live without anyone caring or offering a helping
hand in circumstances which are a reproach to human
dignity and which are calculated to ruin him together with his wife and children in time and for
all eternity. What a lamentable state of affairs
it is when we see in that El Dorado of industrial
progress, England, at the same time as there are
enormous annual increases in national wealth, the
names of poor people who died of starvation in
the daily obituaries! Surely this is a state of
affairs unparalleled in the annals of Christian
civilization.

473

So far as Germany is concerned, it is true that social evils have not reached the intensity that we find elsewhere, as for example, in England. But the danger is present, and we have industrial areas where such problems show signs of beginning. What is alarming is the lack of any prospect that the modern industrial system is to be replaced in the foreseeable future by something better. It appears inevitable that this wretched system must run its course here in Germany too, with capital increasingly concentrated in the hands of a few, with large-scale factory production moving in on a massive scale to overwhelm small businessmen and independent craftsmen with the resultant increase in the numbers of dependent workers and propertyless masses. We have to be prepared for such a development since there is no power on earth that can stop its arrival. Given the same causes in Germany as elsewhere, we have to expect the same effects.

II

Should the Church get involved in this problem?

The answer has to dawn on us without a moment's hesitation. If the Church cannot help, then we have to despair of a peaceful solution to the social problem. "Where are we to go for a new force of loving concern - since that is what the problem is all about!" [5] As Huber relates, this was the agonized cry of one of the outstanding leaders of the Rochedale pioneers. [6] Moral devastation and the lack of moral remedies constitute the root causes of the social problem. That is why only Christianity is in a position to help. It alone can penetrate men's hearts with healing graces which are able to bring about an inner renewal among the masses of mankind. Even Huber, a Protestant, recognizes that the Catholic Church has a mission to fulfill in this area. He says the Catholic Church is in a better position than the Protestants in this regard because it is better equipped with the means that are necessary. It is better organized also for practical action, having more laborers in the vineyard, what with its many and widespread religious congregations, both

lay and clerical, and also since its religious
are, or at least could be, in closer relationship
with the ordinary people. [7]

The Church can and must help. Her vital interests are involved. It is true that the Church
is primarily concerned with the spiritual welfare
of men, with announcing the basic Christian truths
and with the nurturing Christian virtues and true
brotherly love, not with the problems of capital
and industry.

But it is precisely the Christian ministry
that is at stake here. The Church cannot exercise
its proper ministry toward millions of souls if it
ignores the social problem and is satisfied to confine itself to the traditional pastoral role. I
quote Huber again, as he writes: "By this persistent, and with few exceptions, purblind posture of
ignoring the conditions which affect the spiritual
and physical well-being of millions, by being content to deal with the problem in the same old way
with the accustomed routine rather than to confront
the social problem with vigorous pioneering efforts
and measures that bespeak real Christian charity
and formation, the Christian Church, in fact the
whole world, is placed in greater danger than from
so many issues over which the Churches engage in
interminable sectarian bickering. [8]

The Church must help in this problem. The
social problem cannot be separated from the teaching and pastoral office of the Church. First of
all, is it not true that the Magisterium of the
Church sitting in Councils repeatedly concerned
itself with the abuse of capital as that occurred
in the social context of the times, as when it condemned usury and unlawful interest taking on doc-
trinal grounds? Why should the Church not wish to
involve itself in a situation, in the modern context, that is comparable to that one?

Secondly, the social problem touches on the
deposit of faith. Even if it is not immediately
apparent, the leading principle of modern economics

475

which has been aptly characterized as, "The war of all against all," stands in direct opposition to our Faith; and it merits foursquare condemnation on dogmatic grounds. Why? Because it contradicts the basic natural law, not to mention the Christian teachings of love for one's fellowman. If this is not sufficient proof, witness the results in nations where the economic system based on that principle has reached a significant state of development, so that there has been bred a factory population of physical, spiritual, and moral cripples who are beyond the reach of Christianity's saving graces. It also stands in flagrant opposition to basic humanity, let alone Christian dignity, just as it stands opposed to the destiny of material goods, as intended by God, to serve the needs of all mankind. It plays havoc with family life which was intended by God for the propagation of the race of men, including their proper nourishment and upbringing. Above all, this abominable principle flys in the face of the mandates of Christian charity, which is intended to govern not only the dealings among individuals, but also to serve as the guideline for the organization of society and social relationships in general.[9]

Certain limits must be established if free competition is not to become a general "Sauve-qui-pent,"[10] a field of battle where the weak are devoured by the strong. Even economists of a liberal bias have come to admit this. For example, Roscher in Leipzig writes, "As with any freedom, it is also true of economic freedom that external force can only be dispensed with if stringent self-discipline takes its place.[11]

3. Furthermore, it is within the competence of the Magisterium to rise in opposition to the materialistic conception of things, according to which man is treated no longer as a person, but as representing a certain amount of labor - a machine - and whereby he is regarded as a commodity which one exploits for egotistical purposes. In this milieu, it is up to the Church to confront the employers with St. Paul's stern admonition: "The man who makes no provision for those nearest him, above all for his own family, has contradicted the teachings of the faith, and indeed

does worse than the unbelievers do." (I Tim. 5:8)

In this matter, Lassalle maintains that the master-slave relationship was even better than what prevails now, in that it was still basically a human relationship. The slave was regarded as a moral being and treated accordingly, i.e., not as a mere machine.

4. The Church must get involved in this social problem in an especially urgent manner if it expects to fulfill the mandate of Christ that it is to work for the salvation of mens' souls. At stake here are the souls of vast numbers of the working masses who find themselves placed in a proximate occasion of sin (Occasio Proxima Peccandi), or very close to falling into such an occasion. When the fulfillment of their Christian obligation becomes a moral impossibility, we have to do all in our power to extricate the working classes from such a moral wasteland.

5. Out of consideration for simple Christian charity (ex caritate), the Church is obliged to come to the workers' rescue, since these are in desperate need with which they themselves are no longer able to cope. Given such a situation, we have the strict obligation to help, an obligation that bears down with special weight upon the Church, because the Church professes her readiness to help any and all who are in need including those who are not numbered in her fold. She has to help out of the fulness of her charity and mercy. Otherwise the unbeliever-worker will taunt her with the accusation, "What good are all of your fine teachings and consolations about a better life hereafter if you are willing to stand by and let me and my wife and children succumb to starvation and neglect. You are not genuinely interested in my welfare. It is something else you are after." [12]

6. The Church, by coming to grips with this task which is beyond merely human capacity, a task which demands the greatest loving concern possible in the present century, must bear witness before the whole world that she is the institution established

by Christ to solve men's problems. She must prove again the words of the Son of God that his disciples will be known by their works of charity.

7. Finally, the Church must get involved in the workers' problems, because otherwise they will fall prey to other elements which either are indifferent to Christendom or are downright hostile to it (as Schulze-Delitzsch or the Social Democrats), or which, in any case, operate outside the Catholic Church.

III

What are the remedies?

One could offer the excuse at this point, that the problem facing the workers and the solution to it are still too intricate and not yet clearcut enough for the Church to come to grips with the matter with sufficient serenity and certitude, so that there would be some reasonable prospect of success. Not so. The issue is a ripe one. It is painfully obvious that no power on earth can hold back the forward motion of the modern economic system with its centralized mass production techniques that promise to spread to all sectors of the economy. It is equally obvious that the troubles afflicting the workers will go on spreading apace with this development inasmuch as there seems to be no help coming from any other quarter.

Whereas the entire system cannot be overthrown, one must do what one can to soften its ill effects and to come up with appropriate remedies and see to it that the workers also share in whatever benefits the system is capable of generating.

How that is to be accomplished is a question that cannot be answered, if one is willing to settle for the largely fruitless theoretical disputations that occur among certain political parties and workers' organizations. However, there are satisfactory answers to be found elsewhere. In fact, the problems have been resolved admirably

478

in certain individual cases on the practical level, where benevolent industrialists and Christian men have achieved excellent results by fostering or forming organizations and institutions for promoting the welfare of the workers.

France, for instance, offers us many proofs of how the disadvantages that come with factory production can be overcome without harming the legitimate interests of the industrialists. What has been accomplished in this regard in Alsace is absolutely remarkable. Les Institutions privees du Haut Rhin; notes remises au comite departmental pour L'Exposition Universelle de 1867 par A Pennot offer some very significant information. The official report by the award panel of the Paris Exposition of 1807 is of even greater interest. It was compiled by the then Minister of Trade and Agriculture, Alfred LeRoux, and has been translated by Dr. Steinbeis (Stuttgart 1868). The Report deals with "The Promotion of Concord in Factories and Factory Districts, and the safeguards of the welfare, morality and mental well-being of the working class."

We see from what has already been accomplished that right-thinking Christian men are able to alleviate the material plight of the working class, to come to grips with their physical suffering and the threat of moral collapse, and to generate an air of serenity along with the blessings that come with true Christian family living in working class circles. If similar approaches were made everywhere, the working class problem would be solved, by and large.

The magnitude of the problem and the intensity of sufferings among the working class call for a proportionately wide range of measures and structures for dealing with the problem. The panel of judges at Paris listed these as follows: [13]

I. Institutions to protect against need and improverishment.

1. Insurance programs to cover sickness and injuries which may be financed by a tax on workers

or on industry. In Aachen, six such funds were
established in 1854, and they have at their dis-   14
posal something like 100,000 dollars. In Wesserling,
there are also six similar funds which disbursed
1,570 francs in 1864 and had a total reserve of
106,187 francs. Four of these funds also distributed retirement benefits in the amount of 140 francs
a month to some 79 aged and invalids. The insurance
program of the Belgian Society <u>Vielle Montagne</u>
already has a reserve fund of 600,000 francs.

2. <u>Hospitals</u>. The Niederbronner Sisters of
Mülhausen, for example, have opened a hospital that
can take care of 60 to 70 female factory workers
for a nominal payment of from 12 to 20 francs a month.[15]

3. Maternity Assistance. [16]

4. Care for Infants.

5. Contribution to Life Insurance Programs.

6. Retirement Pay.

7. Widown and Orphan Benefits.

8. Burial societies.

9. Baths and Laundries.

10. Consumer Societies and Credit Unions.

11. Provision for health and safety in workshops.

II. <u>Institutions for the Elimination of Vices</u>.

1. <u>Suppression of Drunkenness</u>. The mining industry at Höganäs in Sweden got into such difficulty
because of widespread deterioration among the workers
that the company, to save the business, announced
that it was prepared to make whatever sacrifice was
necessary to elevate the moral conditions of its employees. Widespread alcoholism was just one problem
along with every manner of entrenched vice that usually

480

accompanies it. To come to grips with the problem, a chaplain was appointed, and the religious level of the workers was bolstered to the point where scarcely a case of drunkenness is to be found there now. It is said that the establishment of a Temperance Society in the area would now be superfluous![17]

2. Saloons should be kept distant from factory areas, and where they exist they ought to be carefully supervised.

3. Measures agains concubinage. In a 'few years time in the factory region along the upper Rhine, 2000 cases of concubinage were terminated, and 4000 children who were born out of wedlock were made legitimate largely by the efforts of the Society of St. Francis Regis.[18]

4. The elimination of Blue Monday.

5. Good example by employers.

6. Proper discipline in workshops. By proper discipline and cultivation of a decent religious atmosphere, a man named Mame, in Tours, found it possible to employ 530 female workers in his printing establishment with scarcely one or two situations arising in a year's time which called for any disciplinary measures.[19]

7. The reform of a certain few especially bad malefactors.[20]

III. Institutions for elevating the intellectual and moral level of the workers.

1. Taking pains to provide religious instruction and religious services. The erection of chapels. In Stein near Nüremberg, a separate parish was established for the personnel of a pencil factory. The Church cost in the neighborhood of 118,000 francs.[21]

2. Provision of schools, shop training, libraries, study halls, etc. Hundreds of thousands have been spent for these purposes in factory districts. These constitute the fundamental basis for reconstituting the working class, according to the panel of judges referred to earlier. The high expectations were not entirely disappointed. For example, a factory in Zornhoff (Lower Rhine) employs some 1000 workers representing a population of 4000. Thanks to the concern of the factory owner, Goldenberg, these workers have distinguished themselves for their high moral and religious standards. Despite the proximity of the big city and the constant contacts with it, there is hardly ever a child born out of wedlock.[22]

IV. A Restructuring of the Workers Organization, and of the Method of Wage Payment with a View to Improving the Conditions of the Workers.

1. Working in harmony.

2. Premium pay. Krupp in Essen has distributed some 200 payments in the amount of 512,000 francs to his workers for exceptional performance.[23]

3. A system of promotions whereby the worker can achieve something like the status of master workman.

4. Increasing pay according to length of service.

5. Profit-sharing.[24]

V. Measures to help the worker become more settled and permanent.

1. Advances for buying a home, a piece of land,[25] a few head of cattle. In Mühlhausen (Upper Rhine) the factory owners have actually built a small friendly worker city, Dollfus an der Spitze. There are 800 houses, each with a small garden; and by 1867 about 684 of these had been bought by workers. The government subsidized the undertaking by a grant of 300,000 francs, also in high hopes of beneficial results.[26]

482

2. Provision of groceries and other necessities of life at modest prices.

3. Sacrifices must be forthcoming when necessary to avoid periods of unemployment.

VI. Developing the Habit of Thrift.

1. Savings institutions.

2. Encouraging the habit of regular deposits, etc.

VII. Harmony between Workers and Employers.

1. Avoiding strikes and other interruptions of work. Such are not likely to occur in factories where the welfare of workers is properly cared for.

2. The perseverence of the enterprise in times of political unrest. During the uprisings of 1848, the employees of von Diergardt, whom we mentioned earlier, instead of joining in the unrest greeted their employer with expressions of gratitude and a vote of confidence. That was in the Viersen area. [27]

VIII. Continuing Good Relations.

1. Some sense of tradition and loyalty among workers toward their place of employment.

2. Personal contact between employers and their workers.

Some outstanding examples could be offered. Thanks to the concern of Count von Laderel, the working population of 1000 people in his Boric Acid plant at Larderello in Tuscany have been loyally devoted to their employer for nigh unto 50 years since the firm was established. There has been no sign of antagonism in that time. Le Roux confirms in his report[28] that the prosperous fortunate families who make up this highly moral and enlightened community feel themselves a part and parcel of the industrial enterprise where they work.

483

IX. A Link between Agricultural and Industrial Work.

1. Factory workers ought to have the opportunity to do some gardening whether they are living
in rent, or own their own homes or just a small piece
of land.

2. There is the possibility that a large industrial enterprise could own a large section of
agricultural land and either cultivate it or parcel
it out to its workers for cultivation.

This kind of link between agricultural and
factory work tends to solidify family ties. It
binds a wife and children to their own homestead,
aside from being good for their health; and it also
provides somewhat of a buffer against periods of
unemployment as when there are business recessions.
The Stumm Brothers at Neunkircken, among others,
have introduced such a system.[29]

X. Taking Care to Preserve the Innocence of Young
Girls.

1. A decision not to employ young girls in
factories, even if it may appear economically ad-
vantageous to do so. Several industries have adopted
this rule.

2. Segregation of the sexes in the shop.

3. Strict and continuous supervision.

4. Separate dining facilities.

5. Suppression of illegitimacy, etc.

XI. Concern for the Duties of Wife and Mother.

1. Acceptance of the role of housewife as the
legitimate role of a woman.

2. Provisions to be made by the shop owner and
others so that a woman can tend to her household duties.

484

Safeguarding the family as God intended it to be must always take first priority. Without the blessings of good family life, there can be no question of salvaging the working class. No one has expressed this more emphatically than Julius Simon of Zurich, in his book, <u>The Female Worker</u> (Translated by Dr. Fr. Nessler), especially in the fourth section entitled: <u>Salvation through the Family</u>.

We now add to these provisions, another one:

XII. <u>Measures that ought to be enacted by the proper legislative authorities</u>.

1. Abandon the practice of employing young children in factories.

2. Strict limitation on the hours that young people are allowed to work, in the interest of their proper physical and mental development.

3. Segregation of the sexes in workshops.

4. Closing shops which pose a health hazard.

5. Limitation of the hours of labor generally.

6. Sunday rest.

7. Compensation to be paid to workers who, through no fault of their own are disabled while on the job, whether temporarily or permanently.

8. Legislative encouragement and support of worker organizations that are in the common interest of workers such as the law of the North German League protecting the legal status of industrial and commercial associations, passed on July 4, 1868.

9. State enforcement of the labor regulations by the appointment of official factory inspectors. [30]

In outline form, these represent the means and the institutions whereby the drawbacks of industrial society may be eliminated or at least minimized and the welfare of the workers advanced. The sooner such measures are universally adopted, allowing of course for local differences, the sooner will the social problem be solved.

IV

What role can the Church play in propagating such worker associations and protective measures on a wide scale?

1. It is not the proper role of the Church to set up such associations and to enact such measures directly. That is beyond her official competence. Nevertheless, the Church can render great service in this direction by offering benevolent encouragement, support, and recognition, and by providing instruction and educational programs.

2. The Church must first of all arouse an interest and a concern for the working class among its clergy. To a large extent, the clergy remains indifferent, because it is unaware of the existence and magnitude of social evils and of how great a threat they represent. The clergy is also in the dark about the nature of the social problem and its implications, let alone the remedies.

The problem of the working class must therefore no longer be omitted from the philosophical and pastoral training of the clergy.[31] It would be advisable, in fact, to pick certain clergymen who show a disposition for such things and train them in economics. Provide them with the opportunity to travel to France, for example, where they may observe some of the measures and institutions designed to help the working class. It appears that in France the relevance of religious and moral factors for coming to grips with the problem has gained more recognition than elsewhere.

486

3. Special care must be taken in assigning priests in industrial sections, to see to it that they have a proper disposition and competence for pastoral activity among workers.

4. What would be most desirable would be the kind of man who would dedicate his entire life to an apostolate of the workers, as that blessed Father Kolping devoted himself to the welfare of the journeymen craftsmen.[32]

Such a man must be afforded the spare time to make a careful study of the worker problem, to look up the pertinent literature in France and England as well as in Germany. Then he would be in a position to see first hand the problem confronting the workers and to pass judgement on the proposed remedies. Thus fortified with a knowledge of the facts and the great charity for the working class, as well as with a persevering patience, he could undertake his apostolate. He could then play an active role in seeing to it that appropriate worker organizations are established in his own province. Eventually, he could visit the industrial sections of Germany, establish contact with clergymen in the area, as well as with sympathetic industrialists, offer public lectures where he would take the part of an apostle-of-peace between workers and employers to counteract the animosity between capital and labor. He would have to appraise the situation dispassionately but with complete candor, inform workers and industrialists of their rights and obligations in a spirit of charity without prejudice toward particular personages or systems, all the while avoiding purely controversial positions. He would confine himself to presenting and recommending measures that are clear beyond question, practical, and suited to the local circumstances. Finally, he must spread the knowledge of any and all worthwhile progrmas for solving the labor problem, both inside and outside Germany. By the spoken and written word he must make these known and contribute toward the institution of similar measures by his own experience and knowledge in whatever way

487

he is able. Yet, he ought not to saddle himself
with the immediate responsibility of heading up
such programs, since that would limit him too
much in his general mission. His proper sphere
of activity would be to provide the necessary information to the workers and to inspire in them
a firm, virile resolve and trust in God. He may
then win over many other kindred spirits to this
working class apostolate, men with a true Christian spirit whom he could unite and prepare for
action. Such an apostolate, in the hands of the
right man would certainly yield a rich harvest!

Should we sit and wait for someone to come
forward on his own initiative to undertake this
apostolate. Certainly not. We would probably
wait in vain. Such an effort cannot be undertaken
on a part-time basis. It cannot be left to
chance. It calls for full time devotion by a
competent man; and it is precisely the most competent who, busy as they normally are, would be
the last to propose themselves for yet another
activity.

There would be a better chance of succeeding
if the German bishops offered encouragement for
certain men to involve themselves in the solution
of this all-important worker problem. Chances are
that the one or the other person would step forward, who is inclined in this direction and who
could then receive the proper training.

It would not seem advisable to set up some
ecclesiastical structure covering the whole of
Germany all at once. Such an artificially contrived organism, I fear, would be lacking in real
inner vitality. Also, the solution of the worker
problem is generally of a more local nature. The
situation and the difficulties that call for solutions vary greatly from place to place, and the
appropriate remedies therefore must be suited to
each different situation. A vast centralized
organization like Father Kolping's Gesellenverein
is not called for in this case. It is well to
note that if Kolping, as closely as he wished his

488

organization to be bound to the Church, nevertheless
rejected any proposal to establish it as a canonical
confraternity, the same reservations are even more
valid in the matter of establishing workingmen's
organizations.

5. This does not mean that each and every
diocese should not undertake without further delay
the designation of one or the other man. For that
purpose he may be either of a religious order or
of the secular clergy. Such a man ought to be commissioned to inform himself thoroughly about the
worker problem, to gather precise information about
the factories and factory workers in his particular
diocese, to find out what their situation is with
respect to their physical, intellectual, moral
religious, well-being, and to ascertain what measures and institutions are available for dealing
with the workers' problems. Furthermore a conven-
tion of such men, as appointed by their dioceses
either at the state level, or one covering all of
Germany, ought to take place. Each can represent
and report for his own diocese so that they can
all share information regarding the measures and
programs that show promise toward solving the
worker problem.

6. The press should certainly also be used
to arouse widespread interest in the solution of
the problem facing the working class. Along lines
that are in harmony with Christian principles.
Christlich-Sozialen Blätter which appears in Aachen
could very well serve as the medium for such purposes.

7. The annual assembly of all Catholic associations in Germany, as, for example, the one to
be held next year in the industrial city of Düsseldorf,
can provide an occasion for promoting an interest
in the problem of the working class among ever-
widening circles of people.

NOTES

1
Cf. Schüren, Zur Lösung der sozialen Frage, Leipzig, 1860.

2
Cf. Moufang, Die Handwerkerfrage, Mainz, 1864.

3
In many Catholic regions, the conditions described here are not yet in evidence among the workers; or at worst, they are in their incipient stages. Elsewhere, especially in large cities, one finds them in their advanced stages, even here in Germany. We must first devote some attention to restoring a semblance of humanity to these dehumanized masses before we can begin to think about Christianizing them.

4
Huber: Die latente Assoziation. Cf. Marlo: Organization der Arbeit, I, p. 102 ff.

5
See: Die Genossenschaftliche Selbsthilfe, p. 36.

6
Translator's Note: The Rochedale Society of Equitable Pioneers, founded in Rochedale, England in 1844, was one of the earliest consumers' co-operatives which established the first principles of cooperatives.

7
See: Historische-politische Blatter, 1862: Vol. 49, p. 628.

8
See: Huber, The Rochedale Pioneers, Foreword

9
Keen and benevolent historians are coming to recognize this more and more. Cf. Geschichte der Volkswirtschaftlichen Literatur im Mittelalter by Dr. H.C.W. Contzen, p. 69 ff.

10
"Let him who can, save himself."

11
System der Volkswirtschaft: Stuttgart, 1871, I, p. 175.

12
Cf. Katholik, 1868, Vol. 20, p. 343. Also: G. Ratzinger, Geschichte der Kirchlichen Armenpflege, p. 413 ff.

491

13

See the above mentioned official report of
LeRoux, p. 205 ff.

14

Pennot, <u>Les Institut</u>., p. 59.

15

Cf. LeRoux, op. cit. where he discusses the institutions established by Karl Metz in Freiburg im
Breisgau.

16

Ibid. p. 86 ff.

17

Ibid. p. 74 ff.

18

Pennot, op. cit., p. 93.

19

LeRoux, op. cit., p. 66. The moral tone among the
young ladies employed in the factory of Baron von
Diergardt is also above reproach. See: LeRoux, p.24.

20

See: LeRoux, op. cit., p. 24.

21

Ibid. p. 93.

22

Ibid. p. 59.

23

Ibid. p. 83.

24

See: <u>The Industrial Partnership System</u>, Augsburg,
1868, which describes a system that W. Bochert,
owner of a large brass works in Berlin introduced
into Germany.

25

Cf. <u>Der Arbeiterfreund</u> by Brämer, Vol. 2, 1864:
"<u>Über Baugenossenschaften</u>, " pp. 182-228.

26

Pennot, <u>Les Cites ouvrieres du Haut-Rhin</u>, and <u>Instit.
privées</u>, pag. 39. seq.

27

LeRoux, op. cit., p. 23; cf. also p. 102.

28

Ibid. p. 95.

29

Ibid. p. 88.

30

The results achieved by the English Factory Laws of 1836-1866 demonstrate how effective state intervention can be in this matter. See: Ludlow and L. Jones, Die arbeitenden Klasse Englands, trans. by Holtzendorff, Berlin 1868.

31

Cf. Stöckls, Lehrbuch der Philosophie, 2nd ed., Part II, Section 197 ff.

32

Translator's Note: Father Adolf Kolping founded the Kolping Society (Gesellenverein) which, among other things, established "homes away from home" for journeymen craftsmen. Bishop von Ketteler made the acquaintance of Father Kolping while the two were students in Munich, and he encouraged him to carry out his idea to establish such homes.

Liberalism, Socialism, and Christianity

by

Wilhelm Emmanuel von Ketteler

Bishop of Mainz

1871

Translator's Note

This very important essay was originally
delivered as an address before the Twenty-First
Congress of Catholic German Societies held in
Mainz on September 11, 1871. It was first pub-
lished under the German title: Liberalismus,
Socialismus und Christenthum in the Christlich-
Sociale Blätter of October 1, 1871. The Franz
Kirchheim firm of Mainz also published it in the
same year. Due to stylistic changes in the
German language, the title is written in modern
references as: Liberalismus, Sozialismus und
Christentum.

We find in this work a particularly damning
indictment of liberal capitalism. Its author
made the straight-forward assertion that if
liberal capitalism was correct in its premises,
then the socialists were justified, because they
carried those premises to their consistent conclusions. Bishop von Ketteler undertook to demonstrate step-by-step why this was so, at the
same time that he explained how both the premises of liberal capitalism as well as the
socialists' pretensions for offering solutions
were false. Liberalism, Socialism, and Christianity, more than any other of his works, established the position of the Catholic Church
at the "center" between the liberal capitalists
on the "right" and the socialists on the "left."

497

At the very time that everyone craved peace and quiet following the recent glorious but bloody war from which our nation emerged victorious, a new, bitter struggle broke out for us Catholics. Although nothing is more urgent for the successful development of our new German Reich than religious peace -as our past history so clearly shows - virtually all political parties, without any provocation whatsoever by us Catholics, have pounced upon us so as to destroy religious peace in the worst way possible, by enkindling and fanning everywhere the flames of sectarian strife. As painful as the whole phenomenon is in terms of both our religious feeling and our love for the German fatherland, whose best interests we see so recklessly endangered by it all, we are nevertheless not taken by surprise. We are ever aware that struggle is the inevitable fate of man on this earth. Mankind's entire history provides the best proof. Truth and justice are preserved and spread only by struggle. The great men of history are the battlers for justice and truth. Nothing can be more unwarranted, therefore, than to complain about ceaseless struggle. Nothing could be more misleading than to view this battle as a peculiarity of our time and as a consequence of its particular wickedness.

Nothing is more crippling to our efforts than to take the position that there was a good time in ages past when truth, justice, and virtue prevailed among men without any need for a hard struggle. The exact opposite is true. Actually, the fact that the Catholic Church now, as always, stands at the center of the arena is the surest evidence that it is the true church of Christ, the Church founded by Him whom the spirit of the time lifted up on the cross.

It is all the more important, therefore, that we Catholics give a good account of ourselves in the battle. For that reason it is necessary, first of all, that we understand clearly what is going on and what the best means are for carrying on effectively the struggle for right and justice in our time. Every age has its own peculiarities, but the

great principles are ever the same. The man who
knows only the lofty principles, and does not come
to grips with the specific problems of his time
ends up beating on air, and his thrusts mostly
go over the heads of his contemporaries. All too
often that is our way of doing battle, and it represents our great weakness. There is a reason for
it. We belong to the Church whose very mission it
is to be the treasure house of all of the great
basic truths which are the mainstay of everything
that is worthwhile and necessary for the welfare
of mankind. That is why we are all too prone to
rest with those great principles which, while
excellent, are not sufficient for hitting the
nail squarely on the head. And that is what
must be done now in our time.

Your actions here, gentlemen, will certainly
help us to clarify the issues and to arrive at
practical conclusions for coming to grips with
the real problems that face us here and now. By
way of introduction, it may be useful to analyze
liberalism as it stands in relation to the Catholic Church.

Liberals are like those who bear noble titles
but who do little to bring honor to their great
names. Liberalism is an exalted term. Who does
not wish to be liberal in the proper sense of the
word? Liberalism implies generosity, fairness,
lack of prejudice, open-mindedness. It suggests
the pursuit of true freedom, etc. There is also
implicit in the term the notion of genuine humane-
ness, real Christianity - all of which finds its
true fulfillment in Christ's Church. Nothing is
more liberal than the Catholic Church, in the
true sense of the word liberal. But all of this
is a far cry from what the world means by liberalism. What the world takes to mean liberal is almost the exact opposite of what the word really means.

To fully understand contemporary liberalism
we have to examine the various phases that it has
gone through over the past half century. First there

500

was liberalism in its infancy. Then we find liberalism in its full adult maturity. Ultimately we find another kind of liberalism in the recalcitrant offspring of mature liberalism; and in this latter form it causes much grief to its parents to the extent that the latter would gladly disown it and blame the whole thing on us Catholics. Their efforts come to naught, however, because the offspring clings to its parents, demands its rightful inheritance, and can prove that it is its legitimate progeny. I refer, of course, to <u>socialism</u>. The first distinction between liberalism in its youth and in its maturity was made clear by national liberal spokesmen in the Reichstag. They highlighted the difference by contesting the freedom of the Church as upheld by the Center Party - a freedom that had been honorably acknowledged and defended by early liberalism. The distinction is becoming ever more painfully clear to us. The neo-liberals are overthrowing much that the earlier liberals upheld and insisted upon! Equally significant, however, is the relation of mature liberalism - one might better call it senile liberalism - to its unruly offspring, socialism. It is worth our while to probe into the legitimacy of this offspring.

Let us try to clarify the changes that have taken place by examining the earliest phase of liberalism.

Early liberalism, specifically, that of 1848, was less a closed, complete system than it was a weapon against the absolute state that had become more and more prevalent throughout Europe since the 16th century. Present-day liberalism, on the other hand - mature liberalism - is to a far greater extent a completed, closed system. It claims for itself the full and absolute truth, which is precisely why it feels impelled to spread its gospel everywhere to all of mankind. Its political philosophy is to its disciples, as revealed truth is to us Christians who regard revelation as coming directly from God, the eternal Truth. Whoever gainsays them is exiled. Their system represents truth and certitude because they say that it does. Whoever

501

dares to contradict it is immediately denounced
as an enemy of all modern culture, of humanity,
of reason. That is because humanity, culture,
and reason are what the liberals say that they
are; nothing more, nothing less. Whoever does
not accept their interpretation of culture and
reason is a child of darkness, an ultra-montane
on whom the truly cultured person looks down with
disdain and arrogant contempt. Absolutely no opposition is tolerated. They refuse to pay any
attention at all to the Church, to the feelings
of a Christian people, to millenial traditions,
to treaties among nations, to the most solemn
decrees of princes. The liberal system represents the absolute bearer of all culture, of
all right, of all reason, of all knowledge.
All else must be subject to it. Whatever contradicts it is unreasonable. No proof is required.
The liberals have spoken, and having spoken, anyone who insists on being "unreasonable" must be
brought into line by the police state. The infallibility of the Church is nonsense, because
the liberals have told us so repeatedly in all
of their newspapers. Therefore everyone must
believe it. The infallibility of liberalism is
another matter. That is self-evident and requires
no proof. It is the supreme act of reason to follow blindly this infallible coterie of liberals.

There is a second difference between earlier
and present-day liberalism. The early liberals
campaigned for the freedom of all men, whereas
the liberals of today impudently oppose the freedom of Christian men whenever these refuse to accept some article of faith proposed by the liberals
as infallible. It is true that the early liberals
did not fully understand what freedom means.
Liberty is to some extent a complex concept, and
it has to be understood in a variety of contexts.
Above all, it must be viewed also in its relationship to God, so that it can be understood in its
fullest dignity. In that sense it is something
that all men by their very nature, even if unconsciously, strive for as a great transcendant good.
The early liberals conceived of liberty in the one-

502

sided sense that had been proposed by the French liberals. In their struggle for liberty they also followed the pattern of the French, in that they were concerned with securing a few limited political rights. That was but a pathetic fragment of what true liberty is all about. The men who pursued this kind of liberty, however, were honorable men who recognized the same freedom for their opponents which they sought for themselves.

Unfortunately, the present-day liberals are still coasting on the honor of these early liberals. They have the undeserved sympathy of many who do not yet realize that the old liberalism has shed its skin and is now something altogether different. Instead of freedom for all, present-day liberalism defends only the rightness of its own system, anything that opposes it is absolutely anathema. What is more, liberalism learned in its youth that if it supports the legitimate freedom of every man it would suffer setbacks, in fact it would fail to achieve its ultimate objectives. To its chagrin it has noted that the Church too, as well as the Christian nation, also knows how to use freedom, and that Christian life has experienced a remarkable resurgence after some of the earlier restrictions were eased. Now, lo and behold, the liberals are once again hankering for police measures, not indeed against themselves, but against the Christian people. They also know how to reconcile this mass of contradictions and to make them all self-evident truths! _Idem non est idem_. For the old absolute monarchies to resort to repressive police measures was flagrant injustice. That is because in those times repression was exercised not only against Christianity but also against liberalism. In any case, the ancient regimes were unjustified in resorting to such methods. But what was not permissible for them is now the unquestioned prerogative of a system which presents itself as sweetness and light, which is the depository of all culture, all right, and all enlightenment. How else do you explain the peculiar turn of events to where it is once again right and proper for liberalism to employ the methods of the police

503

state, such as martial law, preventive security measures, placet's etc., etc., when the objects of such methods are the Church and the Christian people. What princes were not supposed to do, that is permissible for liberalism once it becomes dominant. Anyone who cannot accept this is beyond help. Such a person does not understand the new culture of our time; he is a rebel who must be rendered harmless as soon as possible in the name of freedom.

This demeanor of modern liberalism was made clear beyond a doubt by one of its main spokesmen, Professor Bluntschli of Heidelberg. Speaking of a bill proposed by the electorate of Hessen for regulating affairs of the Church, he said: "To abolish the sovereign body which supervises the Church's actions would be a political impossibility. From it all reforms emanated, as Church history reveals. Once upon a time the Archduke of Baden rendered great service in the matter of church reform. The consistories were a kind of general staff which needed a good chief of staff. They required a prince like Bismarck and a Count like Moltke." In other words, one used to say that the Protestant Church as contrasted with the Catholic Church was the church of the people, and everything in it happened as the people willed it. However, now that we liberals are at the helm, this can no longer be so. Now we have to introduce a military-style regimentation into the church. We need consistories that are patterned after a general staff with military posture and discipline. In that way we will soon get the people to the point where we are now, i.e., where they will lose their faith because we have lost our faith. That alone will be reasonable since we alone are the spokesmen of reason.

One has only to apply this doctrine to the general approach of liberalism in order to gain a real insight into its noble aspirations. The ideal of liberalism is a general staff with a Moltke and a Bismarck; and this general staff is to oversee not only the activities of the Church

504

but of the whole state. All of which presupposes that there will always be a Moltke and a Bismarck, who will be the willing tools of liberalism. But the liberals would go further. They would go to Russia and bring back the police truncheon so that one can impose the use of reason on the ignoramuses who do not yet appreciate the absolute reasonableness of liberalism, and who will not render homage to it.

A third difference between the old and the new liberalism is in the relationship of the two to the money power. The latter is in a position to loan millions to the state in a manner that will earn still more millions for itself at the expense of the taxpayers. The old liberalism was, for the most part, innocent of such an alliance. The new liberalism of our time, on the other hand, is in league with the big moneyed interests. Its absolute culture, humanity, and reason are really bought and paid for in cash and at a profit. True, there are sterling exceptions, and it is equally true that money-making and venality have always been major factors in the corruption of men of whatever class and in widely varying circumstances. There has never been a money power, however, equal to that of our time; and the close alliance between it and liberalism with its absolute system is painfully obvious. That is why liberalism must include an absolute freedom for profit-making. The absolute dominion of money along with the absolute servitude of the Christian Church are inevitable consequences of the liberal scheme.

If we wish to summarize our anlaysis of the present-day system of liberalism, we may represent it as passing through three stages: 1) the state without God, 2) the state itself as God, 3) the battle against the true God by the state.

The most appropriate formula for this monstrous development is that offered by Hegel. "The state is the true, immanent God. It represents the divine will as a kind of contemporary unfolding, as taking on actual configuration and organization. The state is the genuine god here on earth; as the prime mover contains its own end, the state has supreme power over individuals. The people as represented in the state are the absolute power on earth." [1]

In such a scheme of things, the Church and Christianity naturally have no place. If the state is the immanent God, the only church conceivable would be one which is a creature and servant of the state. In order to fully appreciate the application of Hegel's thought to modern liberalism, we have to bear in mind that present-day liberals, with their military style general staff, have appointed themselves as the spokesmen for the people, even though they are actually light years away from the real pulse of the nation. That is our present plight. The actual immanent God on earth is the state under the dominion of liberalism. All mankind, Christians included, are to be forced into line by the state for its purposes, so that in the name of culture, enlightenment and humanity they will pay homage to the false earthen god.

The dear Lord always sees to it, however, that the trees which men plant and the towers that they erect will not grow into Heaven. Accordingly, He has permitted this false liberalism to give birth to a legitimate son. That son has already declared his father senile while proposing himself ever more boldly and persistently as the legitimate heir of liberalism. I refer, of course, to socialism. God has built a certain ineluctable logic into world history, which provides a guarantee that the great mistakes of mankind generate consequences that serve as an appropriate rod of correction and court of justice.

There is one painful truth that we have to come to grips with. If the principles of liberalism are valid, then socialism, which is in fact one of the most perverse aberrations of the human spirit, is fully justified. It is only because liberalism is false that socialism is unacceptable. If liberalism were correct in its premises, then socialism's conclusions would be valid. We had better reflect on this. If I am serious about liberalism's principles, then I will eventually fall prey to socialism. True, I would have misgivings about socialism's

506

ability to relieve the misery of mankind. Nevertheless I would, in order to be consistent, have to let
this dire experiment run its course as a consequence
of the principles to which I dedicated myself. It
remains one of the great privileges of us Christians
that we alone are privy to the means and know the
way, not, it is true, to abolish all earthly woes,
but rather to show the way to a measure of good fortune here on earth that no one else can bring about.
Without Christendom, we have only experiments; and
if I am a devotee of liberal principles, I had better
pay some serious attention to the principles of socialism. I propose to demonstrate how socialism follows
liberalism as its inevitable consequence.

Liberalism elevates the state to the dignity of
the immanent God. At the same time liberals go on
talking about the Christian religion and the Church.
This is patent nonsense. If the state is the immanent God, then the whole development of the Christian religions is simply a great mistake. That is
why socialists wish to have done with religion,
church and homage to God.

Liberalism wants to strip marriage of its religious, sacramental character. In its place it offers
a civil marriage ceremony. Socialism comes along and
says, if God has prescribed no conditions for marriage,
then we will certainly not permit any man to do so.
In that case, our own will is law, and our own change-
able inclinations represent natural law with which no
man may tamper.

Liberalism proclaims that there is no eternal
law that is higher than the state. The state's
decrees are absolute. The Church, the family, the
parent has no authority beyond what the state delegates to them. The property right, on the other hand,
is inviolate subject to certain exceptions. The
Church may be stripped of its property since its
right to property rests solely on state sufferance.
All Catholic institutions may likewise be deprived
of their property for the same reasons. Only one's
own property is immune from seizure. Socialism
replies: that is nonsense. If the state is the

507

source of all laws and rights, then it is also the
source of the private property right. Whatever
the state decrees about property, goes. Therefore
we demand a revision of property laws and inheritance
rights. The present condition, wherein all wealth
has been concentrated in the hands of the few at
the same time that the great mass of humanity must
live in poverty, is horrible and inhumane. Only a
man's own labor provides a title to ownership.
The present-day unconditional right to inherit must
be abolished. All land and natural resources belong
to all of mankind, etc.

If the premise, that the state is the immanent
God whose law is absolute, is valid, how can anyone
deny the state the right to revise the right of
private property? If the state does it, God has
done it - the immanent God - to use Hegel's words.
Then what the state does today is just as right as
what the state did yesterday, even though what it
did yesterday was just exactly the opposite of what
it does today.

Liberalism mocks the idea of eternity and the
consolation of religion. Material satisfaction is,
for it, the only goal of mankind. That is why it
urges the amassing of the riches of this earth so
that man can enjoy as much sensual pleasure as it
is humanly possible to enjoy. It sees no inconsistency in the fact that ninety percent of humanity
is denied even the basic necessities while the other
elite ten percent wallow in material comfort to the
point of glut.

The socialist comes along and responds: We
too laugh at the idea of eternity and a just reward hereafter for man's suffering on earth. We
too mock this fraud which is perpetrated by priests,
as you have so diligently taught us by your press
and in your schools. But if it is true that there
is no eternity, no life hereafter, and that our
destiny is confined to our lifespan here on earth
and whatever sense pleasures we are able to enjoy
in this life, it is massive injustice to exclude
ninety percent of humanity from such enjoyment for

508

the benefit of the other ten percent. All people
must be afforded equal access to the goods of this
world. All must labor equally for their share,
and all must share equally in the fruit of their
labor. The condition we have now where idle coupon
clippers bask, without any scruple at all, in wealth
which is almost totally denied to the working class-
especially when such wealth is the only ultimate
destiny of man on earth - such a condition is preposterous. That kind of pronouncement is false only
because what liberalism proposes is false, and because what Christianity proposes is right. There
is a life after death, and an eternity; earthly
pleasures are not the true and final destiny of man;
in fact, they will not suffice to make him happy.
The possession of God alone will satisfy man's inherent yearning. If the premises were correct,
however, the socialists would be right and liberalism
would be an inhumane egotism.

Liberalism wants to make all men equal. That
is its message to the world, and it promises to
abolish the inequalities that survive from earlier
more benighted eras. Accordingly, the liberals
have set out to destroy all class distinctions.
A strange thing happened. Instead of eliminating
inequality they have introduced a new kind of distinction among men that is more harsh than any other.
I refer to the crass distinction based simply on
riches and on how much money a man has. This is
crass because, unlike the class structure of earlier
times, it is not tempered by Christian teachings
and the old Germanic moral code. Each day the division becomes deeper and wider - a division based
solely upon money! Here too socialism stands behind
liberalism with clenched fist and goads it on its
well-worn path. Excellent, says the socialist!
All men are indeed equal, and we must see to it that
this equality is borne out in real life. The mere
abolition of classes will not help a bit if wealth
is so concentrated in the hands of a few that the
plea of equality becomes a hollow mockery in actual
every day life. You end up with a destruction of
social equality, with inequality in access to cultural advantages, inequality in the most fundamental

509

human right to the necessities of life. You destroy
equality in the whole political sphere because the
mere right to cast a ballot becomes a plaything
for those with enough money to buy and sell ballots.
You destroy equality by the enormous influence which
wealth confers on its owners in all circumstances,
public and private, at the expense of their fellow
citizens who have nothing. You even end up with inequality before the law about which you rave so, as
though this were the ultimate blessing of liberalism.
The rich man has the means to guarantee his rights in
a court of law, means which are undreamed of by the
poor man who can afford neither counsel nor appeal.
You destroy the equality of access to political office from which the poor man is effectively excluded.
You have even eliminated equality in the matter of
military service. How can you compare the one year
of voluntary service required of the wealthy, which
often as not is a pleasant diversion for him, with
the three years of mandated service by the poor day-
laborer or craftsman who must leave his normal means
of livelihood behind?

Finally, the socialist harps on the immeasurable difference in the share of material goods that
rich and poor get to enjoy - goods which, as we saw
earlier, are the only reason for man's existence.
Be still with your supposed freedom, you who have
by your economic principles nurtured an unconscion-
able concentration of wealth in the hands of the
few and at the same time reduced the masses of
mankind and their labor to the status of a commodity which must be offered for sale daily on
the market place. What the socialists have to
say to the liberals would be valid if what the
liberals have to say were valid. But it is not;
for both of them are a far cry removed from what
Christianity has to say, and that alone is valid.
Neither the liberals nor the socialists have any
idea of what true freedom is all about any more
than they understand the real meaning of equality.
Equality has to do mainly with something beyond
this world, and neither liberalism nor socialism
has any conception of such matters. St. Paul
was talking about real equality when he admonished

510

Philomen to receive his one time slave, Onesimus, into his household, not as a slave, but as his beloved brother, after the latter had been baptized and become a child of God. The more Christianity becomes prevalent, the more all men will become equals in the possession of spiritual goods. In the process, inequality in material things, insofar as earthly conditions permit, will also disappear. If liberalism were right in its assertion of the primacy of material goods, then the equality which it advertises would be a fraud and a deception. Its kind of equality would require as an absolute condition that all goods are to be held in common - an obviously unrealizable sham - because then social- ism, not liberalism would have triumphed.

Liberalism has proclaimed over the years, "Everything through the people." Hegel has said, "The people, organized in the form of the state, represent the absolute power on earth." With this watchword, the liberals have fought against the supremacy of God and made sport of our Christian motto, "By the grace of God." Now it is true that the expression, "By the grace of God," was at times horribly misused by absolute monarchies. Neverthe- less it contains that important ancient truth spoken by the apostles, that all authority comes from God. That is because every exercise of authority includ- ing human authority originates in and has its legi- timacy from God. It is God who has laid down a universal plan for order which includes all that is necessary for establishing that order here on earth, including authority and the force necessary to exercise authority. In this universal plan is contained the natural law for mankind's successful development.

With the slogan, "Everything through the people," liberalism has undermined and ultimately demolished the entire political order of old, along with its legal foundations. This magical incantation, however, led to cruel disappointment. The doctrine of liberal- ism, whether of the old or of the new variety, never did and does not now express the sentiments of the people. Liberals gained a degree of influence among

511

certain segments of the population through their predominance in the press and in the schools; but their doctrines did not originate with the people, rather they were forced on the people. There was never a party that was further removed in its ideology from the real people as they live and breathe at the grass roots level, in their homes, their towns, their villages and in the cities, than the liberal party. And the slogan, "Everything through the people," useful as it was for undermining the old order, had to remain nothing more than an empty phrase. Eventually, "Everything through the people" was perverted in practice to something like, "Nothing through the people and everything through the dominant liberalism!" It was all nothing more than a colossal lie, but the unwelcome offspring is already standing at the parental doorstep ready to compound the felony. "Certainly," it calls out, "Everything for the people." "You represent the ten percent who possess most of the wealth. We speak for the other ninety percent; the workers. We, not you, are the people, who, as Hegel said, possess, when organized into the state, absolute power. The state which Hegel erects into the immanent God whose will is the divine will - that is nothing more than we and our workers, not you and your capitalists and bankers."

Here again we have to repeat that if the principles of liberalism were valid, then socialism, not liberalism, would offer the right answers. That is especially true if we are talking about present-day liberalism as represented by Professor Bluntschli, who wants to govern the Church and the state by means of a general staff. On the one hand there is much talk of the people's state and the people's church along with endless repetition of Hegel's slogan, "The people as state are the absolute power on this earth." On the other hand, in actual practice, a small band of men arrogates and exercises, much like Bluntschli's general staff, supreme power over the people and pulls the wool over their eyes. This ambivalence cannot last for long. I say again, in the face of such monstrous falsehood, the socialists have a point. But they,

512

too, are on the wrong track because the whole
Hegelian scheme about the state being the immanent God and about the people as organized in
the state having absolute power is as nonsensical
as it is impractical. If the socialists were to
assume absolute power today and operate in the
name of the workers, by tomorrow they would be
guilty of the same hypocrisy, since they would
operate in the name of the people while exploiting them for their own purposes. That kind of
development emanates from the very nature of
things, which is more potent than any and every
false doctrine and eventually brings them full
circle to their absurd conclusions. Large
numbers of digits can be reduced to one because
there is a basic unity in every number. One
hundred can become one hundred times one, and
one thousand can become one thousand times one.
All is possible. But in order for the flowery
phrase, "All things through the people," to
become a reality, the people, the spirit of the
people, or more precisely, the will of the people
would require an underlying basic unity. That
is only possible if every man among the people
believes in God and subjects himself to the will
of God. I am saying it would only be possible in
a thoroughly Christian context. In a Christian
society it is possible to speak of the will of
the people in a fine and meaningful sense. A
nation without God, such as liberalism and socialism propose, a nation that has fallen prey to the
Hegelian madness and believes itself to be the
immanent God, such a nation has no unifying principle whereby it can be reconciled into a basic
unity. Instead, it is bedeviled by that sinister
force which all too easily comes to dominate the
human spirit, egotism. Egotism is divisive. A
nation of egotists cannot establish an authority
that will represent it in a truly communitarian
manner. That is precisely why all of the deified
states that are erected on this lie, of necessity
fall prey to some dominant party which exploits
the state for its narrow partisan purpose. All
talk of the popular will is fraudulent since only
the unity of varying party interests is possible

under such conditions.

That is our condition at the present time, and such are our opponents. Their great strength is in their solid organization and in the influence which they exert in the press and in elections. We have to fight them with similar weapons. A single good organization, operating in any of the specialized areas in this great battle with coherent thrust and persistence, is worth more than a thousand speeches. Let us also do battle and do it well! Christians are themselves old battle-hardened campaigners. At present, however, we are still like young eagles who try their wings for a time before they are able to take off on their long flight. The future belongs to Christianity - that is a foregone conclusion - not to liberalism or socialism. We may yet have to undergo some hard schooling before we fully understand what the stakes are for which we fight. Our weakness at present is in our campaign strategy. We have to select the proper weaponry before we can come to grips with our enemies. Our task is a staggering one, as difficult as the one which confronted the ancient Christians who had to do battle with the old paganism and who succeeded in converting the world to Christ. We are fighting against a neo-paganism. What else can one call the liberal Hegelian state, if not resurrected paganism, a triumph of paganism over Christianity? Just as the new paganism is trying to take over again the Capitoline Hill and take its revenge on Christian Rome which defeated the ancient paganism, so it expects to become dominant everywhere else. When we battle against liberalism, we are fighting for everything that Christianity means to us. We are trying to salvage not only the spiritual heritage of Christendom but even the temporal benefits that have stemmed from it, including even Christian motherhood itself, which nurtured us in our youth.

This battle is the noblest challenge that faces stout-hearted Christian youths today. There is nothing finer to which they could dedicate themselves as they prepare to undertake life's journey. God grant that many of them will receive

514

the great motivation that is required to undertake
this important mission. It is a campaign that ought
to appeal to every German man who loves his country.
What would become of our German fatherland if this
liberalism, that singlehandedly has laid waste a
great neighbor nation, succeeds in penetrating ever
more deeply the bosom of our Germany. Even the
German army will stop being what it is if the poison
of liberalism begins to infect it. Say what you
will, the successes of the Prussian and German armies
are attributable in large measure to the deep inroads that liberalism has made among our enemies.

This battle is the sacred duty of every Christian father, because it is being waged first and
foremost against the survival of the Christian
family, against Christian upbringing, and against
the authority that properly belongs to the father
in Christian families.

Finally, it is the bounden duty of all Christians to join in the battle. What is at stake
here is no less than Christianity itself, Christian
beliefs, Christian civilization, and Christian
culture. It is up to us now to prevent our fatherland from becoming a victim of that corruption
which has already undermined the nation from which
liberalism principally spread to the rest of the
world.

515

NOTES

[1]
Cf. Dr. Stöckl's article in the July 1871 issue
of <u>Katholiken</u>.

517

<u>Religion and the National Welfare</u>

by

Wilhelm Emmanuel von Ketteler

Bishop of Mainz

1876

Translator's Note

Here we have the first of Bishop Wilhelm von
Ketteler's last two lenten pastoral letters addressed to the Catholics of his Diocese of Mainz.
The original document was dated simply, "The Middle
of February, 1876," which we could assume was
February 15, because 1876 was a leap year. The
German title on the original manuscript was: Über
den Zusammenhang zwischen Religion, Sittlichkeit und
Volkswohlfahrt. That is how it is entitled in the
original publication of all of Bishop von Ketteler's
pastoral letters as edited by John M. Raich and published by Lehrlinghaus of Mainz in 1904. Later
publishers, like Mumbauer, designated the letter
simply as Religion und Volkswohlfahrt.

In this pastoral letter Bishop von Ketteler
offered an explanation of how virtuous Christian
living enhances the national economic welfare. He
pointed out that while other measures, like wise
legislation, are of themselves good and necessary,
they will not succeed in fostering the national
economic welfare unless virtuous living is also
operative. Specific virtues like thrift and temperance have an obvious reference to that economic
welfare. However the Bishop also explained quite
convincingly how other virtues like chastity also
contribute to it. The pastoral message is best
summed up by its assertion that the overall
welfare of a nation depends essentially on the
quality of its families.

521

During my episcopal visitation around the diocese last year I often spoke of the relationship that Christian virtues have to the economic welfare of the nation. When speaking of Christian virtues, one rightly regards them first and foremost as leading to eternal salvation. Unfortunately, not enough thought is given to their importance for our temporal welfare, and to the fact that they are for most men the necessary prerequisite for earthly well-being. The denial of this simple truth even goes so far as the proposal by the enemies of religion that Christian virtues hinder a man's pursuit of his temporal welfare. They suggest that religion makes men apathetic regarding their material needs as they center their attention on the hereafter. Even though the falsity of this position may be apparent to you, it will still be worthwhile to discuss with you the truth of what St. Paul wrote: ".....holiness is all availing since it promises well both for this life and for the next." (I Timothy 4:8). That is another way of saying that Christian virtues are the necessary prerequisites for man's temporal welfare. I determined to develop further for all of you in this pastoral letter what I had made mention of during the course of my visits to various communities during the past year.

At the moment nothing preoccupies our contemporaries more than the matter of enhancing the well-being of the working class. Praiseworthy as such efforts may be, it is too often forgotten that whatever means are employed for achieving these worthy objectives, they are inadequate without resort to what is most important, moral remedies. Nothing is less generally recognized than the fact that the problem of the working class is first and foremost a moral problem. I wish to demonstrate in this pastoral letter that it will be impossible to promote the general welfare of the vast majority of mankind, especially the rank and file, without promoting religion and morality. I will show how Christian virtues are especially suited to that purpose.

523

1. First, I must explain what welfare I am
speaking about. Holy Scripture teaches us that,
".....for my state of life, be neither poverty mine,
nor riches. Grant me only the livelihood I need."
(Proverbs 30:8).

It is clear that what the Holy Spirit Himself
teaches us to pray for can only be the best counsel
possible.

Riches, as such, are no blessing for us. They
can become one by the grace of God if, by that grace,
we use them wisely; that is, if we use them as a
means to spread the love of God to our neighbor and
do not allow them to lead us from God's loving ways.
In itself wealth is dangerous; it all too easily
leads us from the service of the true God to the
pagan worship of Mammon. What is more, it provides
us with the means to satisfy our inordinate desires.
That is why our Savior said: "Believe me, a rich man
will not enter God's kingdom easily." (Matt. 19:23).
But he immediately added: "Such a thing is impossible to man's powers, but to God all things are
possible." (Matt. 19:26). According to St. Paul,
even the inordinate craving for riches is replete
with danger: "Those who would be rich fall into
temptation, the devil's trap for them; all those
useless and dangerous appetites which sink men into
ruin here and perdition hereafter. The love of
money is the root of all evil. Some have been so
eager to get it that they have wandered away from
the Faith and have broken their hearts with many
sorrows." (I Timothy 6:9-10).

Holy Scripture also teaches us, however, that
dire poverty is dangerous. It brings with it many
pitfalls. It becomes difficult to raise children
properly, and it often leads to laziness, dishonesty,
lying, and malcontent. Many other dangers can arise
from extreme poverty. A household that is heavily
indebted is subject to many temptations.

Finally, the word of God tells us that a measure of well-being that falls between the two extremes, in other words, that provides a decent livelihood for our families without becoming excessive,

is best suited to the moral and religious life of man on this earth.

It is this kind of welfare, which I call the welfare of the people rather than the welfare of the rich, about which I shall now speak. It cannot be divorced from religion. Whatever other condition may be working in its favor, true national welfare will not be achieved on a wide scale without religion. A man can be rich without religion; in fact he can become rich by immoral means. A nation by and large, however, cannot live in a prosperous condition unless its morality rests on a solid religious base. Let us consider those particular virtues which are especially suited to promoting national prosperity.

2. Among them I list, first, the virtue of temperance. Temperance is one of the cardinal virtues. Brief reflection will make it clear that temperance is also an indispensible prerequisite for national welfare.

In its proper sense, virtue implies fitness, diligence in doing good, a persistent striving for what is good. Temperance, however, is the virtue which inclines a person to always seek moderation in all things. It becomes a Christian virtue when it arises by the grace of God and from our belief in Him, in other words, when it has God as its motivation and as its final end.

The Christian virtue of temperance, therefore, is the persistent striving for and, eventually, the constant inclination to seeking moderation in all things. The moderation we speak of here is that which is indicated both by reason and by faith. Through this virtue we are inclined to conducting our lives as guided by faith and reason, and to restricting, denying and governing our unruly passions and inclinations accordingly.

Thus considered, the importance of this virtue for decent moral living as well as for national welfare becomes obvious.

As regards the importance of temperance for decent moral living, it is necessary to bear in mind that a man, in the conduct of his human affairs, is capable of being governed by one of two masters. The one is reason, the other is comprised of his unruly inclinations and passions.

If he follows the one, he acts reasonably and morally; and that is why St. Thomas characterizes morality so beautifully as reasonableness in the daily transactions of men or, actualized human reason.

If a man follows his passions, on the other hand, he acts unreasonably as the animals do, since his actions are governed now not by reason but by blind instincts. Such a man is denounced also in Sacred Scripture as animalistic. True reasonableness, therefore, consists less in knowledge than in action. That man is truly reasonable, whose thinking and way of life are adjusted to reason and faith, not the man who thinks reasonably but who acts like an animal.

The indispensable means for applying this morality and this higher reasonableness to our every day actions is the virtue of temperance. Temperance gives a man the capacity to subject his unruly passions to the demands of faith and reason and to govern his actions accordingly. Intemperance, on the other hand, signifies moral weakness, even moral impotence, which makes of a man a wretched slave to his passions.

Now the virtue of temperance in the broader sense finds its application to the whole range of man's moral actions, since it provides the measure of moderation that is required in each human action. Yet, in the narrower sense, we usually restrict its application in every day life to moderation in matters pertaining to the senses, specifically in eating and drinking.

We scarcely need to demonstrate how very important temperance in eating and drinking is for the general welfare of a nation. Lack of moderation and gluttony are among the chief wellsprings of impoverishment. They not only spell the downfall of many working class families, but they may also bring to dire straits and misery those who enjoyed far greater material well-being. The intemperate fellow gradually loses all moral stamina which would enable him to regulate his needs and keep them in reasonable proportion to his economic means. Eventually he loses all control, and he sacrifices whatever he has to cater to his unruly passions. Who can adequately depict the untold misery that intemperance causes, the destruction of family harmony, the long-suffering of so many poor women who come face to face with poverty that becomes worse day-by-day, the pathetic plight of the poor children deprived of the necessities of life, the constant conflicts which arise from this wholesale destruction of family life! The great tribulations of mankind, pestilence, famine and war, do not cause such a vast amount of grief among men as does intemperance.

Indeed, how could intemperance exist side by side with national prosperity! Statistics show that the vast majority of mankind must be satisfied with a very modest income. It is that way now, and it will always be so, more or less, despite all of the best efforts of men. That is precisely why temperance is indispensible to national prosperity. That virtue alone provides man with the moral courage he needs to keep his appetites in reasonable harmony with his income and his means.

If temperance is lacking and insatiable cravings determine his expenditures, a man of modest income will be swallowed up in a bottomless pit. It is a matter of painful experience that the level of income alone does not determine the level of national welfare. There are places where, despite the prevalence of generally higher wages, one finds more poverty than in other places where wages are lower. Temperance makes the difference.

If we contemplate how poor and limited the share
of the world's goods is which the vast majority of
mankind gets to enjoy, as contrasted with the abundance which a few rich take for granted daily, it
is impossible to rid oneself of the conviction that
a deep-rooted moral disposition is necessary for
staying contendly within the limits of what these
modest means make possible. That is why temperance
in a nation, wherever it is found is so great a
virtue and is so pleasing to God. Parents ought
to take great pains to implant the seeds of this
virtue in the hearts of the children from their
tenderest years. To raise temperate children is
to raise virtuous children. Children that are
brought up to give in to their sensual impulses
and appetites are likely candidates for a life of
intemperance and debauchery. If sensuality rather
than reason and religion prevail in the child,
they will also run riot in the adult.

If we once appreciate the importance of
temperance for moral living and national well-
being, how can we but be disturbed by the wholesale
denial of this simple truth in our time? How many
there are who are no longer capable of understanding
the base animalistic implications of intemperance or
the great worth of temperance. How many of our young
are being swept along by the pestilence of intemperance, by the many forces that are at work in our
society!

3. I include among the Christian virtues
which are critical for national welfare, secondly,
the virtue of frugality.

Frugality is a direct descendant of temperance.
Without temperance, there can be no talk of frugality.

Not all frugality represents Christian virtue,
however. There are times when frugality is an abominable vice. That is the case when it stems from
inordinate self-love or greed, and when it entails
calloused disregard for the dire need of one's
fellow man. Frugality becomes a vice when it inclines a man to seek after earthly treasures like

528

the rich man in the Gospels, while remaining indifferent to what really counts. St. Paul calls athe miser an idolator and his hard-heartedness, idolatry. (Eph. 5:5).

Virtuous frugality is something altogether different. It stems not from the inordinate attachment to earthly goods or the indifference toward spiritual treasures, but rather - as is the case with all virtues - from reverence for God and from the desire to do His will in all things. It is not dominated, therefore, by a blind quest for riches. Rather it is moderated and governed by an appreciation of the Divine order in all things. Frugality is not a one time performance, but it is an established way of life developed by persistent practice. The saying of Solomon provides us with an excellent model of the kind of frugality that is pleasing to God, in the story of the provident woman. It is she who cultivates wool and flax and processes it with her own hands. By her great industry she sees to it that the entire household is provided with whatever it requires. She rises early in the morning to prepare a meal. She is out in the fields early, planting her crops so that the harvest will be ready in due time. She sees to it that everyone has warm clothing when cold weather arrives. In her generosity toward the poor, she is always ready with an open heart to help those in need.(Proverbs 31:10). Such providence is not miserliness, but rather a balanced kind of frugality that is pleasing to God. Holy Scripture also tells us: "Let him toil as he will, the sot's purse is empty; little things despise, and little by little thou shalt come to ruin." (Eccl. 19:1) The essence of frugality is regard for the insignificant. Our Savior Himself gave us an example of such concern for what seems insignificant when, after he had fed the 5000, he commanded His disciples: "Gather up the broken pieces that are left over so that nothing will be wasted." (John 6:12).

Virtuous frugality also involves avoiding inordinate luxury as well as a certain foppery and passion for ornamentation in clothing and in household furnishings. The "vigorous wife" in Proverbs 31:10 saw to it that everyone had extra clothing when winter came. To make abundant provision for real needs is not luxurious indulgence; it is rather prudent and praiseworthy. Luxury implies foolish and corrosive vanity. It seeks rather to impress others, often enough at the expense of genuine needs in the household.

We scarcely need to point out how essential frugality is for genuine economic welfare. Without it the latter is beyond the reach of the vast majority of humankind. He who insists on living from hand to mouth, that is to say, he who is quick to spend each cent that he earns, always operates along with those who depend on him, at the borderline of poverty. The first misfortune that strikes reduces him to the status of a beggar who must rely on others for his livelihood. And that is true no matter how high his earnings may happen to be. A couple of years ago there was an account in the papers of the sad fate of a certain man. As a poor but ambitious youth he left his home in the Odenwald region and attended a school of drawing in Heidelberg. Through diligence and hard work he succeeded in establishing a flourishing business with twelve employees. Regretably he began to lead a life of intemperance and debauchery and he indulged in a life style that soon went beyond his means. Debts piled on debts until, in desperation, he murdered his wife so that he could marry a woman whose wealth would put him in a position to pay his debts and continue his riotous life style. Similar cases, albeit not so spectacular and not all leading to such dire consequences, are occurring all the time. They bear witness to the inescapable rule of life that without frugality, no matter what a man's income is, economic welfare is out of the reach of most ordinary humans. At the same time, one could cite other examples of how men with modest incomes, by dint of the virtue of frugality, achieved a level of stable well-being. Virtually every community can provide object lessons to illustrate both such cases. Everywhere one can find families which - hard times notwithstanding - have managed to scrape together a decent measure of material well-being by hard work and frugality. One has only to see the children that come from such fine families. They are well fed, properly clothed, and clean, and it is obvious that they are being well provided for and grow up healthy and happy. How do you explain it? Easily. They come from homes where there is temperance, frugality, and fear of the Lord! At the same time one finds families everywhere steeped in misery and wretchedness, where children suffer unspeakable privation so that their frail bodies bear the impress of malnutrition and sickness. And how do you explain that? All too often it is due to intemperance, a lack of frugality and of fear of the Lord.

So we have demonstrated that frugality is essential to economic well-being. What can be accomplished with a modest income where frugality is the rule was brought home to me two years ago in a community where most of the people were entirely dependent on their wages for a living. In the year gone by, the inhabitants of that village alone deposited a total of 23,000 gulden in the savings bank - a tribute to their temperance and frugality. Savings banks can be good and useful institutions for fostering these virtues, and if they are run properly, i.e., for the welfare of the depositors rather than for all kinds of other purposes, they are to be recommended. The child that is trained to be frugal from its earliest youth has a priceless inheritance to see it through its later years, one which will pay interest for a lifetime. Parents ought to encourage their children in the practice of temperance and frugality. One way to do this is to put aside a part of the youngsters earnings in a savings account in their own name. This will get them used to the idea of setting aside a part of what they earn for the future.

4. The Christian concept of the proper choice of a state of life also deserves a place along with those virtues that enhance economic welfare.

When I speak of commitment to a state of life as a virtue, I am not speaking of virtue in the strict sense of that word. The concept of vocation is not so much a specific single virtue as it is a decent mode of life based on a proper orientation and on various other virtues.

An appreciation of the deep significance which the sense of vocation has for the national welfare of the individual depends first of all on the family to which one belongs. Secondly, we must understand the extent to which the family rises or falls with a sound or frivolous judgement in the choice of a state of life.

The virtuous family is interrelated in so many ways with the national welfare that it is scarcely possible to do justice to the matter here. We shall have to confine ourselves to certain main aspects of the relationship.

Everything that a man derives from his family from the cradle to the grave has a bearing not only on his eternal salvation, but also on his welfare here in this world. Countless numbers of people struggle through a lifetime of poverty, because they have been deprived of what is an essential condition of well-being through the failings of their parents.

In a certain sense body and soul are the instruments by which a youngster is destined to accomplish both his eternal salvation and the fulfillment of his temporal needs. If one is to accomplish these purposes, the instruments must be adequate. Whether or not they are up to it, whether the child develops in a healthy fashion in body and soul so as to be able to work out its economic destiny and welfare, all of this depends in an essential way upon the family and on proper parental care.

The very body, by which we are able to see the light of life, and which is our constant companion on life's journey through time and, in a sense, our own personal day-laborer who works for us, illustrates this point. True, it is God who is the ultimate arbiter regarding sickness and health, life and death. But just as certainly as no sparrow falls to earth without His permitting it, and just as He has a count of every hair on our heads, it is also certain that God allows natural causes to contribute toward the shaping of our destiny. The state of our health is therefore often dependent on the kind of parental care that we receive. There are many who suffer physical handicaps because of the sins, excesses, and vices of their parents. One has only to visit the wards of any hospital in our large cities to be appalled by the plight of so many helpless children that are abandoned at their tenderest ages by their parents. How can youngsters, who are from the start innocent victims of physical handicaps because of the debauchery of their parents, going to be able to achieve a decent measure of temporal well-being? The more we are inundated by our immorality, which corrupts our youth, the greater will be the numbers of such poor children that are victims of the excesses of their parents.

When all is said and done, a basically healthy body is not all that is required for making one's way in life. Such a body requires years of diligent care. No creature is so dependent for so long as the human being. An animal requires a certain amount of care so that it may flourish, and it is often the beneficiary of painstaking efforts in this direction. Man too is subject to this natural requirement. Only if a child receives proper nourishment, clothing and shelter as befits the human species, can it be expected to grow up healthy. If, on the other hand, the youngster grows up in poverty and misery during the precious years of its youth, if its tender body is subjected to hunger, the ravages of the elements, if it wallows in filth and squalor, in damp and miserable quarters, if it is deprived of every semblance of

533

the normal amenities of life, then its poor body
is bound to be sickly. It will scarcely be able
to avoid being steeped in abject poverty later in
life. A large number of children find themselves
growing up in just such circumstances in our time.

Having reached their fourteenth birthday,
what with their poor stunted bodies, such youngsters
are all too often forced by their parents to go out
and support themselves. The tragedy does not end
here. Rather these pathetic children fall among
bad companions and propagate their plight from one
generation to the next.

Still more crucial for a man's well-being than
the body is the soul, patterned, as it is, according to the image of God, and destined, as it is,
for eternal life. The soul must inhabit this body,
lead and guide it and subject it to its service.
At labor, the spirit that guides a man's work is
more vital than the mere plow or hammer which serve
as instruments. That is precisely the relationship
of the soul to the body. A wholesome soul must
reside in a healthy body so that work will lead to
true well-being. To that end, the soul requires
knowledge; and what is vastly more important, it
requires virtues. Whether or not the soul is so
equipped depends once again upon the family. The
family is the seed-bed of those virtues which a
child needs to lead a life conducive to well-being.
It can also be the hotbed of those vices which lead
to misery and poverty.

Even the mature man, standing now at the head
of his own family, requires its help for his well-
being. The most sensible, sober, and diligent man
cannot do the job by himself. He needs the cooperation of a good woman. Given a poor housekeeper, an
indolent, chaotic, self-seeking wife, there is no
way that he can conduct a successful household.
Likewise the wife. Even if she possesses all of
the qualities of that vigorous woman in Holy Scripture, she cannot ward off poverty by herself if
she has to contend with a husband who is the slave
of intemperance, who is more at home in the local

pub than in the bosom of his family, and who squanders the means there that are meant to provide the family with its necessary means of support.

So it is that the welfare of the nation – from cradle to grave – depends essentially upon the quality of our families. Overall national welfare can only exist if genuine Christian family life prospers in a nation. Of all the methods proposed for solving the so-called social problems and to improve the material lot of our people, by far the most critical is the fostering of solid family structures. Whoever does not recognize this and proposes all sorts of other remedies is a fool; and be his intentions good or bad, such a person is building castles on sand.

It is for these reasons that we appreciate the value of a sense of Christian vocation for national well-being. Whether or not we have good Christian families depends in the final analysis upon a sensible commitment to a Christian way of life. That is a truth that ought to be self-evident, but it is widely ignored today, so that its denial has become a principal source of all social evils.

For a sensible Christian state of life, the first test is whether the two main components possess the necessary moral qualities required for solid family structure. The task of the Christian husband and father, and of the Christian wife and mother are so great and so noble! They are the representatives of God for their children – and there is no higher vocation than to be God's deputies! What lofty qualities one called to such a high purpose should possess! How reasonable and proper it would seem to be for persons about to undertake that awful responsibility to ask themselves whether they have the requisite disposition. For the choice of a Christian state of life, one ought to undergo yet a second test; are the necessary material means present that are required for the support of a family. We are not talking about riches, but simple reasonable prudence to make sure that one's family will not start out in misery and poverty. We are suggesting a proper reflection about whether one can lay claim to the means of support that are necessary for establishing an orderly household.

How many families are begun, these days, without proper consideration of these questions? Before one aspires to any other state of life, one gives due thought to the necessary prerequisites. It seems that only in this most vital of all vocations, the welfare of which often determines the rise and fall of entire generations, men do not exercise even minimum prudence. Many marry after having spent their youth in licentiousness, without having cultivated a single one of the virtues that are necessary for an ordinate family structure. Instead of virtues, they come equipped with those specific vices that are certain to devastate their families and corrupt their children. They approach the married state burdened down with bad habits that make it impossible to get by on their income, even while unmarried. Instead of savings, they start out in debt. Smothered is that voice of conscience which would prompt them that entering marriage in such a state is an offense against right reason and against God, as well as a criminal transgression against what their family and their children have a right to expect from them.

What could be more sinful than to inflict upon a family the manifold misery that is the inevitable consequence of such unscrupulous recklessness? What could be more appalling than to be the cause of a state of affairs where poor children pass through an entire joyless youth in anguish and misery handicapped in body and in soul?

That is how critical a good Christian sense of vocation is for the national welfare. Good families are the cornerstone of a sound society. Nothing could be more detrimental to the national economic welfare, therefore, than whatever militates against a sound family structure.

536

5. Finally, we number among the virtues which are conducive to the national welfare, purity, or chaste moral standards. Chastity has an immeasurable impact upon the well-being of a nation. In fact all of the virtues referred to previously cannot operate in the absence of this one. Temperance depends upon chastity since both of these virtues infer a subjugation of man's baser nature to his reason. Temperance, as we saw, is the virtue which inclines a man to subject his dealings to the promptings of reason as enlightened by faith. It enables him to overcome all of the base, animal passions and instincts that conflict with right reason, so that he may practice moderation in all things. Nothing, however, increases a person's moral stamina more than chastity. Nothing weakens a man's moral fibre more than impurity. Impurity ennervates the person's moral fibre and delivers a man up to his blind, immoderate passions. Impurity and intemperance are companion vices.

Thus, thrift, for example, also suffers when there is impurity. Wasteful habits go along with it. Countless examples in every day life bear witness to the fact. Even the savings that have been scraped together over the years through hard work and temperance begin to evaporate on the day when impurity begins to take over. In their place, one finds debts, discord, and recklessness.

A sensible commitment to the Christian state of life depends on chaste living. Chastity gives a man the spiritual independence that he needs to make proper decisions based on sensible Christian considerations in all of the important matters that he comes face to face with in life. It gives him the deliberate calm - free as he is from the influence of his base passions - that he needs to come to grips with the big issues which confront a man as he goes through life.

Impurity on the other hand, robs a man of the capacity to make sensible judgements about the important problems that beset him, including a choice of the proper state of life. Instead, blind unreasoning passions becloud his judgement and plunge him, as well as those who depend upon him, into dire material and spiritual misery.

The total well-being of the family structure depends upon the purity of morals. It brings good fortune and blessings to all who are part of the chaste family. Only the chaste family gets to enjoy all of the peace and good fortune that God intended for the members of a good family. The chaste family alone is the seedbed of all natural as well as supernatural virtues. It alone is productive of that solid well-being that one is lucky enough to encounter on occasion. Impurity destroys all of this. Whenever it rears its ugly head, peace, good fortune, and serenity are driven out. Its presence makes the family a school for vice. Wherever it takes over, intemperance, profligacy, disorder, and eventually poverty follow as inevitable consequences.

That is how welfare and chastity on the one hand, and the dissolution of wealth and impurity on the other are linked together. I have been able only to give you a certain few illustrations; many more would be possible. The terrible consequences of this vice even for temporal welfare are so many that we can only scratch the surface.

It will never be possible to generate widespread economic well-being in a nation in the absence of deep-rooted chaste morals. At the outset, I have stated that the problem of the working class is mainly a moral problem. I could go a step further and state that it is mainly a problem of pure morals. The rich are often in a position where they can indulge in intemperate and unchaste practices and still remain rich. That is not to be regarded as an advantage of riches, rather as its pitfall. People generally, however, cannot surrender to intemperance and impurity without impoverishing themselves. God has so ordained it as a general rule that a people cannot enjoy temporal prosperity unless it is also virtuous.

538

Nothing is more beneficial and conducive to
human welfare, nothing is more apt for safeguarding
a person from his own weaknesses, as well as from
external dangers all through his life from infancy
onward, than chaste morals. Nothing, on the other
hand, is more destructive of human welfare than impurity. Nothing is a greater threat to a person's
spiritual and corporal well-being, and against nothing does he find it so difficult to defend himself than the depredations of impurity. Nothing
causes so much poverty, sickness and misery.

Safeguard well this most valuable of family
treasures - chastity - which, thank God, is still
much in evidence in Catholic households. St. John
saw Babylon as a harlot, "drunk with the blood of
Saints, the blood of those who bore witness to
Jesus." (Apoc. 17:5-6). This characterization of
a harlot drunk with the blood of Christians drives
home to us the painful truth that impure morals
and hatred toward Christ's Church go hand in hand.
Those are always especially perilous times when
the two appear together in order to lead men to
their destruction. We live in such a time! It
is a time filled with hatred toward the Catholic
Church, the great witness of Jesus on earth; and
it is a time replete with temptation to licentiousness and immorality. To despoil the morals of a
nation, however, two things in particular are
needed. It is important that you recognize these
means so that you may be in a position to safeguard
yourselves and your children from the perils of
immorality.

The one instrument for propagating immorality
is the promulgation of those false principles which
have as their purpose gradually to tear down the
horror that people have of the vices of immorality.
Whereas Christianity has always taught us that impurity is one of the most abominable of all sins,
men are now busily engaged in making excuses for
it. Whereas no instinct is more deeply ingrained
in the innocent soul than shame and disgust toward
impurity, there is a campaign underway to depict
impurity as something natural and respectable.

539

While no vice generates more misfortune and tears, an immoral world pretends to make light of this vice. These are corrupt principles which are abhorrent in the eyes of God as they are to a pure soul. Nevertheless they have an appeal to what is base in man due to his fallen nature. That is why we are always subject to its peril. So it has come to pass that men are careless about their choice of companions and even in their commitment to a state of life. God forbid that you ever permit yourselves to be swept along by these destructive principles.

The second means for the propagation of immorality and intemperance are the manifold opportunities that are to be found all around and which pose a great temptation in particular for our youth. In our time, the sad fact of the matter is that most sensible barriers that would have hindered the proliferation and lessened the dangers and evil stemming from this vice have been lowered. Chaste and pure morals once so dear to the German nation, this rich wellspring of so many other virtues and of so much good fortune, are to be found nowadays in the privacy of many family circles and in certain select fortunate communities. They have, for all practical purposes, been banished from public life as a whole. Brazen immorality and shameless innuendo are allowed to run rampant to corrupt and poison the morals of our nation so long as they conform to certain feeble norms. Desperate efforts are made to halt venereal disease at the same time that not a finger is lifted to prevent the propagation of this pest of immorality. Every imaginable kind of impurity in pictures, books, peep shows, bawdy plays, etc., proliferate throughout our cities and spill over into the countryside with the result that our good German people are contaminated, and brazen immodesty permeates all levels of our society.

Protect yourselves and your children from these great dangers. Keep the children, insofar as this is possible, within the family circle where they will cultivate good morals and partake of pure and wholesome pleasures.

6. From all of this, it is clear how religion and the national welfare are intrinsically related.

The primary reason for the relationship is the fact that only Christ teaches us the great truths which alone can generate true Christian charity, which protect the weak from oppression by the powerful, and which enable us to overcome selfishness and to cultivate true morality and virtue.

Christ teaches us to love God above all else and to love our neighbor as ourselves. He teaches us that whatever we do to the least of His brethren, we do unto Him, and that we are not to cultivate love of self at the expense of our neighbor. We are taught that we must do unto others as we would wish them to do unto us, and that God is the Lord of all and we are only his stewards. We are to be merciful if we wish to obtain mercy from God.

Those are the great social principles of Christianity which because of human frailty are, it is true, never fully applied. Nevertheless the striving toward their realization is always in evidence in the conduct of Christian peoples; and it is clear that they have brought great influence to bear in the lives of individuals as well as in the relationships among men.

As Christ binds men together, unbelief drives men apart. Without Christ, self-seeking reigns supreme. It has always been thus, but our own time provides special proof. Men are now proposing to us as the ultimate product of enlightenment and science a state of affairs where raw egotism would reign supreme and whose logical consequences would be a justification of the exploitation of the weak by the strong and of the poor by the rich. Indeed, if the principles of modern secularism are valid, then Christian concern for one's fellow man is madness, and the prevalence of the stronger over the weaker members of society is the true rule that governs mankind. According to the anti-social teachings that are now being propounded for our

541

acceptance, men were not created by a wise and
holy God; rather they evolved from the same blind
unreasoning mass that gave rise to the entire in-
sentient universe and included eventually mankind
itself. The basic principle of evolution, however,
is what they call the survival of the fittest. As
the stronger tree in the forest suppresses the
development of the weaker, and as the death and
decay of the weaker makes the stronger flourish
all the more, so, they tell us, it is with all
life on earth. Christianity proposes that the
basic law of human development is the love of God
and the love of neighbor which stems from it.
Contemporary science substitutes the principle of
the survival of the fittest, according to which,
the strong assure their true fulfillment and development by suppressing the weak. Where this new
principle of evolution will take us, we are already beginning to see in what goes on around us.
The usurer, who multiplies his wealth at the expense of thousands of his fellow men whomhe destroys, is the finished product of this modern wisdom as applied to society.

The second reason why religion is implicitly
bound to the national welfare is this: Only through
Christ and His grace and assistance can men success-
fully cultivate those virtues; temperance, frugality,
chastity, and industry, on which the well-being of
a people depends, as we have seen. Religion is not
merely a teaching about God, but a source of God-
given strength. Only by the supernatural aids of
religion can we cultivate true virtue. God has engraved the moral law not merely in two stone tablets,
but he has written them indelibly in the hearts of
men. That is why we have only to reflect within
ourselves to recognize the value and beauty of virtue. As a consequence of original sin and of his
own personal sins, however, man has yet another law
in his being, which, without God's help, is even
stronger than the natural law. That is why the
Apostle Paul wrote: "Inwardly I applaud God's disposition of my conscience, and so I am handed over
as a captive to that disposition towards sin which
my lower self contains." To the cry, "Pitiable
creature that I am, who is to set me free from a

542

nature thus doomed to death?" Paul replies, "Nothing else than the grace of God, through Jesus Christ our Lord." (Romans 7: 22-25).

That is the story of mankind. We all feel in our innermost being the joy that comes with genuine goodness and virtue. Yet we all have to contend with the contradictions in our nature which inclines us toward evil and base passions. In the struggle, good will overcome evil, virtue will triumph over vice, the spirit will conquer the flesh, and the love of God will prevail over self-love only if our hearts are one with Christ, so that his grace will provide us with the necessary strength.

The third reason why national welfare and religion are inseparable is found in the inner bond between religion, the family, and national well-being. Religion and the Church are the firm supports of the family. When God constituted marriage as an indissoluble unity and elevated it to the dignity of a sacrament by bestowing supernatural grace on married partners so they could live up to their high calling, He accomplished more toward assuring national welfare than all human institutions combined, which are designed for that end. The married state will only serve as the firm foundation for the family where it retains its solid tie with the Church.

If I have discussed in this pastoral letter the relationship between certain virtues and the national welfare, it was not my intention to convey an impression that nothing else is needed. I have not even mentioned one of the most necessary virtues, Christian industry. That is because I would like to deal with this separately on another occasion. But aside from these virtues, there are still many other factors which are essential for national well-being. The state has to cooperate by wise legislation. Far be it from me to downgrade other means to promote national welfare. I only wanted to pronounce the important truth which is so disregarded in our time: all other means are by themselves insufficient and religion and morality are the first and most important prerequisites for the general welfare of a nation.

Beware of those who promise you well-being and temporal fortune while at the same time they minimize the importance of your religion or even express open contempt for it. Don't fall for their promises. One cannot be an enemy of Christ and of His Church and at the same time be a true friend of the nation. Those who are enemies of Jesus Christ are even moreso your deadly enemies.

If I have encouraged you to strive for Christian virtues, which I suggested are conducive to national well-being at the same time that vice breeds poverty and need, I certainly was not speaking about the kind of poverty over which its victims have no control. Christ said: "The poor you have always with you." There is a kind of poverty that is caused by carelessness, indolence, and debauchery. But there is yet another kind of innocent poverty which is a consequence of living according to the holy and wise counsels of Divine Providence. We are obliged to honor such poverty and to join with it in spirit. Christ Himself has sanctified it by His example and by the evangelical counsels. It has been canonized by the voluntary poverty practiced by a long succession of great Saints down through the course of Christian centuries. Therefore, even while we strive in Christian fashion to work out a decent measure of temporal well-being, let us always remain mindful of the poor among us and approach them with true Christian love so as to help them in their need to whatever extent we are able. In a Catholic community, no poor person should be left without help.

There is a kind of wealth which has its origin in injustice, usury, and exploitation, and such wealth is evil and contemptible. There is another kind of wealth that stems from adroitness and diligence, or sometimes from inheritance. Such wealth is legitimate, but it is dangerous. Finally, there is a kind of well-being that is based on the fear of the Lord, virtue, and work, and which can only be kept intact by more exercise of the same virtues. I wish this for all of you, with all of my heart.

With all my love, I extend to you and to your children, my apostolic blessing. In the name of the Father, and of the Son, and of the Holy Spirit. Amen.

The Christian Concept of Work

by

Wilhelm Emmanuel von Ketteler

Bishop of Mainz

1877

Translator's Note

    The Lenten Pastoral Letter of February 1,
1877 was Bishop von Ketteler's last such letter,
since he died on July 13th of the same year.
Fittingly, it was a social pastoral message by
the bishop who came to be known as the pioneer
of modern social teachings by the Roman Catholic
Church. The Letter was entitled, <u>Über die</u>
<u>christliche Arbeit</u>, in the original German of
<u>Raich</u>'s edition of <u>Hirtenbriefe</u> published in 1904.
Thus, the Letter addressed itself specifically to
what the man had devoted a lifetime trying to
dignify and ennoble - work, and the class of
people which earns its livelihood by work.

Last year we examined the relationship between national welfare on the one hand, and morality and virtue on the other - relationship which we regard as beyond question. However, morality and virtue are, in turn, dependent upon religion. Therefore religion and national welfare are implicitly connected.

Two errors, in particular, stand in opposition to this truth. There are those enemies of religion who maintain that religion preoccupies itself with the next life rather than with man's temporal welfare, so that it tends to make men apathetic as regards the latter. Others don't go quite so far, but they do minimize, more or less, the value of religious belief for furthering man's temporal welfare. Instead, they rely mainly, if not exclusively, on external measures whereby they hope to solve the manifold problems that confront the human race. That is why some persons, who find themselves in need and in misery through their own fault, fail to recognize the real reason for their plight. Instead, they blame their fellow man or find the cause in external circumstances; and rather than acknowledge their own guilt, they proceed to fill their hearts with hatred and bitterness toward others.

Both positions are equally false. All truths taught by religion foster the temporal as well as the spiritual welfare of a nation. It is certainly true that religion does not deceive people with visions and promises of an earthly bliss which is nowhere possible; nor does it propose that men should believe the fanciful nonsense that stands contradicted by everyday experience, that earthly pleasures can really satisfy man's deepest cravings. Yet religion makes it obligatory for man to make prudent provision for his temporal needs, and it offers potent means to that end, without which all other remedies are all but useless. A nation that is truly Christian will also, making due allowance for its particular circumstances, be a prosperous nation. A people, on the other hand, which turns its back on religion and Christianity

551

will always fall victim to the phenomena that were in evidence among the ancient pagans; impoverishment of the masses along-side riotous living off wealth beyond measure by a chosen few.

This connection between religion and the national welfare was the topic of a previous pastoral letter.[1] Specifically I pointed out the relationship between temperance, frugality, chastity, and the prudent choice of a state of life on the one hand, and prosperity on the other. I indicated that in the absence of these virtues, neither legislation, nor an appropriate institutional framework of society, and not even the state are able to forestall the impoverishment of the masses. In fact, even where the latter arrangements are less than adequate, but where those virtues flourish among the people, a decent level of prosperity is likely to prevail. Thus, the old proverb is born out: "Where God bestows His blessing, all else abounds."[2]

There is one virtue, however, which is especially relevant for temporal welfare and which I have not discussed at length, and that is the virtue of Christian industry. It is so essential that I chose to treat it separately so that I could do greater justice to it.

We tend to overlook the particular virtue of Christian industry because, as with other vital but ordinary everyday phenomena, we tend to take it for granted. What is more commonplace than daylight? Yet it is one of the most beneficial works of God in that it reveals to us not only all of the creatures of this earth, but it also elevates our thoughts to the Source of eternal light and truth. What is more ordinary than bread? Yet bread is indispensable for our mortal life, and at the same time it is the image of the Eucharistic nourishment which was offered for the world's eternal salvation. Thus industry has a vast significance, and at the same time it is inextricably bound up with man's most vital concerns.

552

The true and full significance of industry
becomes known to us only by Divine Revelation.
Therefore we shall first consider what the Word
of God Himself says regarding work. Then we shall
draw further conclusions from that.

I. The Divine Law of Work.

What we find in the first pages of Holy Scripture clarifies at once, as nothing else could, the
entire history of mankind. There we find at the
very outset the basic and true reason for all subsequent developments. We have the solution of all
that puzzles and perplexes man throughout his journey
through time. We find there the key to the entire
human paradox: the nobility and the baseness in
man's nature, the craving for immortality and happiness alongside the reality of death and misfortune,
the explanation of why there is so much good at large
at the same time that there is so much evil, so
much love and so much hatred, so much justice and
so much injustice, so much truth and so much deceit.
There, finally, one finds the fundamental principles
whose acceptance or rejection determines the well-
being or misfortune of individuals as well as of
entire nations. Among these fundamental truths,
which are the key for understanding the story of
mankind's journey through time, are numbered the
story of the creation, the creation of man in God's
image, the origin of marriage, the Fall and its
consequences - mortality, as well as the Redemption
and its ultimate purpose - eternal life and happiness. Also numbered among these truths, however, is the law of hard work.

The scriptural quotation is familiar to you,
my beloved. After our first parents had sinned,
God said to Adam, "Thou hast listened to thy wife's
counsel, and hast eaten the fruit I forbade thee to
eat; and now, through thy act, the ground is under
a curse. All the days of thy life thou shalt win
food from it with toil; thorns and thistles it
shall yield thee, this ground from which thou
dost win thy food." (Genesis 3:17-19).

This law of work is the first which God imposed on man after the Fall. From that, if for no other reason, one ought to recognize the great importance of labor. Its validity extends to all of mankind just as we all share in the guilt of original sin. It represents the basic Divine mandate for enjoying the fruits of this earth. The destiny of man is conditioned by how well we observe the law or how badly we violate it. Let us examine further the specific implication of this law of work.

1. First of all, it is a law that binds all men. Adam appears here as the father and representative of the entire human race. Work is therefore a duty for any man. No estate, no class is exempt. Whoever shuns work violates the Divine plan for order and the first law which God laid down for fallen human nature.

2. Secondly, the law was imposed upon man immediately and directly. So long as the earth which God created to sustain mankind contains thorns and thistles and provides nourishment only by hard labor, such labor represents one of the first duties incumbent upon man. Woman must also share in the toil. Is she not, according to God's word, a helpmate to man, and is it not commanded that "thou shalt be subject to thy husband?" (Gen. 3:16). Her first and principal obligation is the raising of children and what is necessarily tied with the care of the household. That is the norm which God himself laid down for the division of labor. Every violation of it, since it goes contrary to God's will, leads to disastrous consequences.

3. The Divine law of work also requires hard labor. Even if man had remained in the state of innocence, he was not destined for idleness. Scripture tells us that he was commanded to cultivate and tend the "garden of delight." (Gen. 2:15-16). But his labor was to be pleasant, not marked by tedium and punishing exertion. That work was only to become burdensome as a consequence of the Fall, was clearly and

554

emphatically expressed by God Himself when he said: "All the days of thy life thou shalt win food from it with toil." The importance of this is clear from the fact that God repeated: "Still thou shalt earn thy bread with the sweat of thy brow until thou goest back into the ground from which thou was taken." (Gen. 3: 17-19). The expression, "sweat" indicates a kind of work that is unpleasant and tedious for man. And such work is destined to be a man's lot all the days of his life until he returns to the ground from which he came.

4. This hard work was imposed upon us by God as a punishment for sin. That is clear from the context of scripture; and lest there be any doubt, God expressed the connection clearly when He said, "Thou hast listened to thy wife's counsel, and hast eaten of the fruit I forbade thee to eat; and now, through thy act, the ground is under curse. All the days of thy life thou shalt win food from it with toil." For the same reason, because she had sinned, woman was destined to bring forth children in pain, and be subject to her husband. We must never forget that hard work is a penalty for sin. He who tries to avoid the pangs of hard work is attempting to dodge God's punishment on this earth and is going against God's will. Consequently the more he tries to avoid the punishment, the more he will fall prey to it, not only on this earth but in eternity.

5. Finally such work, with its tedium, sweat, and pain as God ordained it, is the necessary prerequisite for extracting the fruits of the earth. That is clear from God's words: "Thou shalt eat food from it with toil." He who will not exert himself will not have the right to eat. "Still thou shalt earn this bread with the sweat of thy brow." He who shuns the sweat of honest labor has not earned the right to his daily bread. The Apostle Paul expresses the same thought when he writes, ".....the man who refuses to work must be left to starve." (2 Thess. 3:10-11). He continues: "And now we are told that there are those among

555

you who live in idleness, neglecting their own
business to mind other people's. We charge all
such, we appeal to them in the Lord Jesus Christ
to earn their bread by going on calmly with their
work." Elsewhere St. Paul says, "We would only
ask you, brethren....to keep calm and to go on
looking after your affairs, working with your
hands as we bade you." (1 Thess. 4:10-11). He
is telling us to avoid getting involved in matters that are none of our concern, but to tend
diligently to our own affairs and thus earn and
enjoy our bread.

II. Further Explanation of the Divine
Command to Work.

We have examined the five conditions which
God Himself has attached to the law of work.
Before we turn our attention to how the law is
violated and what the consequences of such transgressions are, we have yet to examine more closely
certain implications of the law itself.

1. God is speaking about physical labor in
the specific context. It is clear, however, that
mental toil is included in the labor under discussion. Actually, we cannot separate completely
mental from physical labor, for, among other things,
it is impossible to win fruits from the earth without considerable mental reflection on how it is
to be done. What is more, man, by virtue of his
likeness to God and his lofty calling, is destined
primarily for mental labor. That is why St. Paul
recommends "double consideration" for those ".....
who bestow their pain on preaching and instruction."
Every true exertion in any of the various legitimate occupations that God has assigned to men is
pleasing to God, necessary for mankind, and useful
labor, therefore.

2. The work for which God has destined us is,
furthermore, a kind of punishment, but that in no
way exhausts the full meaning of labor. At the
precise moment when God pronounced this curse upon
mankind after the Fall, he connected with it the

healing merit of the Redemption that was to come.
God does not wish the destruction of sinners, but
rather that they convert and enjoy eternal life.
Blessing is the reward for punishment endured,
and rebirth follows death. That is true also of
work. The burdensome nature of work has persisted,
it is true, but by the merits of our Redeemer,
that which was merely punishment has become the
means for our healing and a blessing for mankind.
That is the twofold nature of work according to our
Faith. Through our daily toil, concupiscence is
to be overcome and sinfulness is to be atoned for.
Peace, joy, and tranquillity are the proper compensation for the toil and exertion that go with honest
labor. We cannot extol adequately, therefore, the
blessings of honest toil for the individual person
as well as for the entire human race. Work is a
bounteous source of life. A Christian working
people is a happy people, and a Christian working
person is a happy person. Without work there is
neither happiness nor inner peace.

3. Since the labor which God has decreed for
us is a kind of labor that involves sweat, toil,
and pain, it is necessary that we understand that
there are different kinds of labor. Only such labor
is pleasing to God which serves a true purpose and
which involves a degree of tedium and exertion. It
is only by such work that the Divine mandate comes
to fulfillment; and it is through it that we receive
the bounteous blessing that God has bestowed on honest
labor. This truth is so often misunderstood. Not
every kind of activity qualifies as Christian industry, only such as involves self-denial and sacrifice and which therefore bears the imprint of the Cross.

4. Neither are we to take the notion of eating in the mere literal sense. God ordained hard
work to be the prerequisite for earning one's bread.
Food, in the sense that the term is used here, represents the enjoyment of all of the earth's fruits.
A man is not to share in the earth's bounty which
God has placed at our disposal unless he has performed honest labor.

557

Another thought comes to mind in this connection. He who does not work ought not eat; in other words, he does not earn the wherewithal to sustain life. This applies not only to our physical but also to our spiritual and moral subsistence. Personal toil is the indispensable condition for the spiritual and moral survival of each and every individual. This truth is basic to the proper development of human character. With bread we are able to assist the indolent, lazy person who is threatened by starvation because he refuses to work. We are not able by our own resources to rescue the souls of the spiritually indolent, who are unwilling to undertake the tiring moral exertions necessary for the salvation of one's soul. That is an unalterable Divine law. Without hard spiritual exertion, the good seeds which God has implanted in us are stifled and eventually rot and perish. It is for this reason that it is impossible to train children entirely without their cooperation, that is, without considerable work and exertion on their own part. Where parents fail to impart a sense of obligation in their children, where children from their earliest youth are permitted to shun any kind of physical and moral exertion, they are doomed to be spiritual, moral weaklings despite whatever other benefits are subsequently lavished on them.

III. The Violation of This Law and the Consequences.

Having examined the Divine mandate to work, we shall now consider what happens when the law is disregarded. In the process we shall come to recognize many of the problems which now confront us, as well as what the real remedies for them are, and also the close connection between human welfare, morality and religion.

There is no command of God that men have turned their faces against more than the law: "Thou shalt earn thy bread with the sweat of thy brow..." Hard labor is abhorrent to the pleasure cult which is so attractive to fallen human nature. The craving is

insatiable and men would like nothing better than
to enjoy the fruits of the earth without toil. Man
tries time and again to enjoy the reward without
the burden of labor, and he is tireless in his efforts to thus thwart the Divine plan. We see how
among all pagan peoples those who are in power
strive to possess and enjoy all the good things
which the world has to offer, all the while avoiding hard labor which they impose on the sweated
backs of their exploited fellow men. Therein lies
the essence of slavery: on the one hand lavish enjoyment of the goods of the earth without lifting
a finger to earn it; on the other hand labor without a chance to taste the fruits of one's labor.
Among the ancient Jews, it was different since they
already had the benefit of Divine revelation. It
is also different when Christianity takes hold,
where Christians may bask in the light of Christ's
revelation. There the obligation to perform honest
labor again received due recognition. Yet, even
where Christendom prevailed the Church had difficult times trying to inculcate respect for God's
laws, because it must always contend with fallen
human nature. So we find that in the Christian
era the Church had to battle against that slothful
thirst for pleasure, which always tried in one way
or another to shake off the burden of the Cross and
to enjoy the fruits of the earth while circumvent-
ing the obligation of hard work which God had decreed.
The temptation to thus avoid God's law is now at
large with new force, and even by means unknown to
the ancient pagans. That is because the influence
of the Church and Christianity is woefully reduced
in our time. Indeed, to bring into subjection and
to enjoy the fruits of the earth without hard work
is a foremost objective of our time. Therefore we
cannot fail to recognize that the spirit of our age
is in its deepest origins a revolt against the original law of labor.

In such circumstances, it is quite immaterial
whether a man is rich or poor. Both, having once
abandoned their Christian principles, have the same
desperate desire to get as rich as possible, as
quickly as possible, in a manner, of course, which

calls for as little exertion as possible. As soon as such persons are in a position to do so, they imitate the pagan slave owner of ancient times; they transfer the entire burden of work, which is our common heritage because of original sin, onto the shoulders of their weaker fellow men; and they themselves enjoy the good things of the world to the point of satiety. This craving is not a fault of the rich exclusively and one that is lacking in the poor, as though the poor were possessed of a different human nature than the rich. No, it is a flaw - a part of human nature - traceable to the Fall of man, which rebels against God's law. Therefore wherever religion and Christianity are in decline men will more and more divide themselves into two classes, one of which will possess and enjoy the good things of the earth without working hard to acquire them, while the other propertyless class must perform the hard work that is necessary for the others to enjoy the fruits. Like any violation of God's law, that situation will lead to bitter social struggles and upheaval. However, as soon as a measure of peace is restored, wherever shallow enlightenment is offered as a substitute for Christianity, the same deep-seated division between rich and poor reappears. A world which rejects Christ and His Redemption will never rise above a situation where one group of men enjoys without toil the fruits produced by the other group, which is exploited to perform the hard labor that is necessary. That is a fact, all fantasies about fine new social systems notwithstanding. The worker, if he once comes to power - lacking religion - will surrender to the same impulses. He will enjoy the fruits which others produce, passing the burden of hard labor on to those who were his comrades before his rise to power.

We must be ever mindful of these truths so that we are able to distinguish the various transgressions against God's command to work, which we are now to consider. It is also necessary that we are aware of how the law can be violated not only in a crude fashion, but also in a more subtle

fashion. The more it escapes our notice, the more
dangerous the transgression of the law becomes.

1. The first kind of violation of the law of
work is the simple refusal to work. Holy Scripture
tells the idler: "Up with thee, idleness, go to
school with the ant, and learn the lesson of her
ways! Chief or ruler she has none to give her commands; yet in the summer hours, when the harvest is
a-gathering, she ever lays up food for her own
nourishment. And thou, art still a-bed; wilt thou
never wake? What, thou wouldst sleep a little longer,
yawn a little longer; a little longer thou must pil-
low head on hand, Ay, but poverty will not wait,
the day of distress will not wait, like an armed
vagabond it will fall upon thee! (Wouldst thou see
the good grain flow like water, wouldst thou see
poverty take wing, thou must be up and doing)."
(Proverbs 6:6-11).

Idleness is the destruction of economic well-
being, just as industriousness is its foundation.
No proof is needed for this assertion since everyday experience makes it plain enough. The source
of idleness is sloth which the Church numbers among
the seven capital sins. These are sources from which
all other sins stem. We have also the proverb which
says: "Idleness is the devil's workshop." Sloth
and idleness never operate in a vacuum. They bring
with them the neglect of our duties, specifically,
providing for the future, for posterity, for the
upkeep of the household, for the children. They
lead to recklessness, pleasure-seeking, intemperance,
impurity, dishonesty, lying, deceptiveness, and
theft. Sloth and idleness are like a stagnant pool
which serves as a breeding place for all manner of
vermin. Just as worms and rottenness fester in a
corpse, so all manner of temptations and sins fester
in a slothful person.

The crudest kind of transgresssion of the law
of work is, however, not the most perilous. That is
because overt idleness is such a contemptible thing
that only the totally depraved person can surrender
himself to it without a deep sense of shame. The

561

more subtle infringements on the law are more dangerous, and these have a certain element of progression in them where each step is worse than the previous one. Let us consider these next.

2. In the second instance we sin against the law of work when we do, in fact, work; however we do so not as God wills it but in a manner that avoids all tedium, i.e., without the sweat of one's brow.

We are guilty of this violation when we busy ourselves about many things, all the while dodging our proper responsibilities which we find unpleasant because they involve mental or physical exertion. There are yet other occasions when, even though we tend to our proper duties, we are very selective in devoting our energies to those among them which we find to our liking, and at the same time we shun others which we find burdensome even though they may be the most urgent.

Simply being busy does not, therefore, add up to Christian industry. One can be occupied with all manner of activities without being industrious in the Christian sense. Those persons whom St. Paul described as living in restless fashion and busy about the unnecessary no doubt regard themselves as industrious. Yet, the Apostle said of them that they are idlers, meaning that they do not wish to work as God wants them to. There were also those women about whom St. Paul said: "Meanwhile, they learn habits of idleness as they go from house to house; nor are they merely idle, they gossip and interfere, and say what they have no right to say." (Timothy 5:13). They, too, were busy, but the Apostle called their activity, "idleness."

Such activity does not represent true Christian industry and is all too often a disguise, whereby one seeks to conceal his basic laziness both from himself and from others. Some are ashamed to admit even to themselves that they are idlers. They may even be stern judges of idleness

562

in others, all the while oblivious that their own misdirected activity falls short of being Christian industry. They fail to recognize that they are neglecting their own proper duties whenever these involve tedium and penitential effort, and that, in fact, their activity is a kind of disguised pleasure-seeking.

That is why mere activity that is not honest labor does not earn the compensation that comes with the latter. The honest work of a God-fearing man performed in the sweat of his brow brings an immediate reward in the inner satisfaction that is topped off by an abiding sense of joy. Frenetic activity that is not true Christian industry does not generate such a reward. It is often mere boondoggling, an expressive term to describe how those people waste time, the most precious gift of God, which becomes burdensome to them simply because they cannot bring themselves to undertake the tedium of honest labor. The boondoggle occupies time only so long as it lasts, and as soon as it ends, instead of the sense of peace and satisfaction that true labor leaves in the soul, there is a sense of dissatisfaction and revulsion. Thus, mere activity distinguishes itself from Christian industry also in its consequences.

3. We also sin against the law of work when, even though we do not actually sidestep the tedium of labor, we resort to dishonest effort to gain access to those goods of the world which we could not lay our hands on honestly or without great difficulty and patience.

Dishonesty in pursuit of profit is closely linked to contempt for the Divine law of work. About this, St. Paul makes a penetrating and timely observation:

"And indeed, religion is ample provision for life, though no more than a bare sufficiency goes with it. Empty-handed we came into the world, and empty handed, beyond question, we must leave it; why then, if we have food and clothing to last us

563

out, let us be content with that. Those who would
be rich fall into temptation, the devil's trap for
them; all those useless and dangerous appetites
which sink men into ruin here and perdition hereafter. The love of money is the root of all evil
things, and there are those who have wandered
away from the faith by making it their ambition,
involving themselves in a world of sorrows.
It is for thee, servant of God to shun all this;
to aim at right living, holiness, and faith, and
love, and endurance, and kind forbearance. Fight
the good fight of faith, lay thy grasp on eternal
life, that life thou wert called to, when thou
didst assert the great claim before so many
witnesses." (I Timothy 6:6-12).

Thus, in a few words the course of world
history is summed up. Fear of God generates contentment. He who fears God works and is satisfied
with the return that honest toil yields for him,
while he who strives for riches, subjects himself
to all manner of temptation and finally loses his
Faith. Covetousness, because of its implicit connection with godlessness, is truly a "source of
all evil." We see the fruit of these evils in
all of their dire consequences before our eyes.
It is precisely among those persons, who with
hypocritical pretense combine greed and irreligion while trying to pass themselves off as cultured, that dishonesty in business has reached a
level that was hitherto unknown in the Christian
era. Nothing, not even the most essential means
of subsistence, is safe from the greedy depredations of these men who are impelled by such a
fraudulent spirit.

I would like to illustrate, by presenting
two specific cases, how sternly the Catholic
Church in times past reproached dishonest business practices as outrageous attempts to circum-
vent the law of honest labor. There was a time
when all interest-taking was forbidden. The reason for that ban was rooted partly in a specific
historical economic context which no longer prevails, but partly also in unsavory, usurious

564

undertakings that arose in connection with interest-taking. The latter were held in contempt and regarded as immoral, among other things, because they were recognized as attempts to dodge honest labor and to gain access to the fruits of the earth, while shunning the labor which God ordained as the proper means to that end.

A renowned Hessian writer on economic matters, Heinrich of Langenstein, who was a professor at the University of Paris as well as Vienna (d. 1397), dealt with this matter. At the very core of his economic treatise On Contracts he inserted the passage from scripture about "earning one's bread by the sweat of one's brow." He stressed repeatedly how wrong it is for men to seek to enjoy the earth's fruits without honest labor. "Among the progeny of Adam," he wrote, "there are always many who strive by all kinds of ruses to shun this burden of work, and who seek to enjoy a surfeit of useful and necessary things in idleness, while avoiding work. Some do it by theft, others by robbery, others by plunder, some by usury and usurious contacts. Still others resort to deceptions and an infinite variety of crafts for accumulating dishonest profits. That is how great numbers of Adam's children have tried and continue to try to acquire riches in idleness. But since such persons try to shun the burden of work which God in His justice imposed upon mankind, they thereby bring upon themselves the grave guilt of sin whereby they will one day burn in Hell after enjoying an apparent prosperity here on this earth. The prudent children of Adam do not operate that way. Rather, acknowledging with a sigh that the burden of work was justly imposed upon them by God as a result of their Father's sin and as the means to earn their livelihood, they meekly undertake the burden in the hope that this will gain them pardon for their sins, at the same time that honest work will earn for them both the goods of this world and of the next."3

The famous rector of the University of Paris, Johannes Gerson (d. 1429), said it concisely and simply in his tract On Contracts: "Man is born to labor and the birds to fly." (Job 5:7). It is therefore contrary to man's nature to attempt to live without labor, as is the case with usury and interest-taking; it is a fact that Adam was commanded even in the state of innocence to cultivate and look after the Garden of Eden, and after the Fall he was told to earn his bread by the sweat of his brow. [4]

All of this applies with equal force to the countless dishonest enterprises in our time, which, taken together, pose an ever-growing threat to the economic well-being of our society. We can only appreciate their full impact if we recognize that they signify a revolt against the law of work, as a manifold attempt to get rich without hard work, while passing the burden of labor on to the shoulders of the working people. The root of the development that we are now witnessing is in a rebellion against God. I refer to the gulf between rich and poor that was a hallmark of ancient pagan times and which is the inevitable outcome of the anti-Christian principles, of the counterfeit liberalism, and the false enlightenment of our times. Having denied original sin, it is inevitable that man wishes also to unload the burden of its guilt. A small clique of men wants to dominate the world and enjoy its fruits. In the process such men mock and deride Christ and His Church.

4. We have to keep in mind still another violation of God's law of work. We violate the law if we disregard the division of labor that God Himself has ordained.

In describing the Divine law of work, we have already seen that God did not leave the division of labor entirely to chance or to man's discretion. Rather God laid down certain principles which we are to follow. They are to be found in the very difference between man and woman. But there is a further development by virtue of the command which

566

God expressed to our first parents after the Fall. The man was ordered to cultivate the earth by the sweat of his brow and to make its produce serve mankind's needs; but womankind too shared in a special way in the penalty for original sin.

As man was to earn bread by his toil, woman was to take over the care and bringing up of children. And just as the man must do his work in toil and sweat, so the woman too shall experience sorrows and pain in begetting and bringing up children. (Genesis 3:16). These sorrows and pains are the means by which she will gain salvation, as the Apostle Paul said, "...if she will but remain true to faith and love and holy living." (I Tim. 2:15) That is womankind's role in the division of labor that was ordained by God from the beginning, and that is how she shares in the tribulations of life on earth. Whether or not man will enjoy good fortune and prosperity in this world depends on how well he complies with the Divine plan for order. The preferred roles for woman are being a devoted mother to her children and a good wife to her husband, thereby extending all of those blessings through the household which come with fulfilling the proper role of woman. Only to the extent that her primary role permits it, she ought to be a helpmate to her husband in all of his other undertakings.

How woefully men violate this division of labor decreed by God, and on which the well-being of the human race is so dependent in our time! How men flaunt the natural order of things before our eyes in this all important matter!

Among the offenders are those who lure the young maiden away from a domestic way of life, and encumber her with occupations that do virtually nothing to prepare her for her proper vocation in later life.

Also among the offenders are those who deprive the children and the home of proper maternal care which God intended, and who instead exploit these womanly energies for their own self-seeking

567

purposes. Modern industrial conditions, wherein
the natural order and the utterly indispensable
and vital vocation of wife and mother are perverted to a money-making role, are an abomination
before God and will produce untold harm for humanity. Women, therefore, who forsake the work which
God intended for them in order to earn money are
guilty of great injustice.

Those women who pursue worldly pleasures also
sin against the law of work when they reject the
true calling of womankind and fill their lives
with selfish activities that serve their own conceits and comfort.

Finally, we find among the offenders those
women who do everything possible to avoid the
pains and sorrows of motherhood, and in doing so
they themselves go astray, and they lead their
husbands far from God's ways.

IV. The False Conclusions That Are Drawn
     from God's Law of Work in Our Time.

We have yet to consider an error regarding the
Divine mandate to work, which is widespread in our
time and which is fraught with peril.

All goods which nature places at our disposal
directly, as well as those which we must earn by the
sweat of our brows, come from God; and they are designed to satisfy our ;needs. As we have seen, however, God intended for all of us to work by the
sweat of our brows and thereby to acquire a rightful share of these goods for satisfying our temporal wants. This truth, that was so clearly expressed by God's own word, is being misinterpreted
in our time so that unintended and downright
ruinous consequences result.

To stir up your awareness of these errors, let
me refer to developments that are close at hand.
In a few years we will commemorate the centenary of
the French Revolution. At the outset of that Revo-

lution, men were excited by the motto: "Liberty, Equality, and Fraternity." - words that strike a responsive chord deep in human hearts. They have also found their expression throughout Christendom in the proper sense; and wherever the teachings of Christ were propagated one spoke of these three qualities. But the word of Christ falls partly on good ground where it yields its fruit a hundredfold; partly it falls on rocky ground or among weeds where it is strangled. So it was with these fine principles. In the Christian era, they bore wonderful fruit. All too often, however, men turned a deaf ear. Regretably, that was the situation during the years preceding the French Revolution, so that there was little evidence at large of liberty, equality, and fraternity. The men of the Revolution did not fail in their esteem of these three qualities which had always been extolled in pulpits of the Christian churches. They erred rather in that they tried to introduce them by improper means, namely, by external force. Now external compulsion exercised by legitimate authorities has its place when held within proper limits. The nobler tasks of mankind cannot, however, be accomplished by the application of force. God intends that they be fulfilled by the exercise of human freedom. Resort to compulsion here, and you go astray so that eventually you accomplish just the opposite of what is intended. That is what happened to liberty, equality, and fraternity. These lofty human ideals were never trodden under foot more than during the time of the French Revolution. The Christian religion, on the other hand, is the divinely commissioned protector of genuine liberty, equality, and fraternity. It is through Christianity, not by state authority and force, and not by fire and iron, that they are to come to realization on earth.

The same thing is true of the Divine law of work. Man must work. He must work in pain and sorrow; he who will not work, neither let him eat. He who finds himself in possession of the goods of the earth should regard himself as God's steward and see to it that he distributes the goods of the earth bounteously among his fellow men according

569

to the law of love. The workingman is worthy of
his hire; those are all truths which the Church
has always taught.

The errors of the present have less to do
with the fact that men wish to make the law of
work and the value of labor operative principles.
That is a valid enterprise in perfect harmony with
the word of God from the first to the last page
of Holy Scripture.

The error is in the methods that are proposed
for bringing about a just distribution of the goods
of this world. Just as the French Revolution sought
to impose Christian ideals on the world by state
authority and bloodshed, so the present day inno-
vators are trying to realize the fruits of Christian charity, i.e., the proper distribution of the
goods of this world as intended by God, by altering
the political system, by state edict, by blood and
iron once again. That is the danger in such well-
intentioned movements. That is what is wrong with
them. They would end up as the French Revolution
ended up, completely frustrating the purpose for
which it was intended. Now as then, the consequence
would be untold conflict and immeasurable social
turmoil among men. And when the time of deep
troubles had run its course after frightful upheaval, as long as unbelief would prevail, the
powerful would, after as before, enjoy the pleasures of this world while saddling the working
masses with the required toil. All great ideals
can only find realization on this earth through
religion and through Christ and Christianity,
that is, to the precise extent that men bow before
Christ and become true Christians. They flourish
not in a climate of compulsion, but only where
freedom, nurtured and fostered by the Divine
teachings and graces of Christendom, prevails.

On the other hand, such departures from God's
ways can serve as terrible scourges. That is what
happened often; all too often. That is what happened at the time of the French Revolution, and
that is what is likely to happen once more in

570

our times. Ever since the all out campaign against Christendom and in particular against the Catholic Church was begun, our conditions in the matter of distribution of temporal goods and the manner in which they are made use of became completely contrary to what nature intended and to what was specifically ordained by God in the law of work. Whatever barriers remained against insatiable greed and boundless pleasure-seeking are relentlessly torn down. At the same time those Christian principles which make us aware of our obligations, which foster a spirit of charity, self-denial, and benevolence are suppressed more and more. In their perverted enlightenment, men ridicule the great Christian truth that man is merely the steward of God's goods which are therefore not here to satisfy man's passions, inflate his ego, and pander to his sense pleasures, but to serve God's holy purpose. Under the sway of this unChristian spirit, we are reverting to the kind of terrible division of mankind into rich and poor as it prevailed throughout the pagan era. It may well happen, therefore,that God will permit us to lapse into that abominable state of affairs, where rebellion against Divine order prevails and men are left to their own erroneous ways, so as to teach us a bitter lesson. But such punishment may turn out to be far more terrible than that which came with the French Revolution.

V. Christian Labor.

Now that we have considered the significance of the Divine law of work in the light of revelation and have seen how important it is in the destiny of mankind on this earth, we will investigate the concept of Christian labor.

To live a Christian life means to live as Christ lived. Therefore Christian labor means to work as Christ worked.

It is a significant stroke of Divine Providence that the Son of God, when He became man, chose to be the foster-son of a poor carpenter;

571

and He himself chose to work with him at the craft
until his thirtieth year. We are in a better position to comprehend that mystery if we keep in mind
what we have discussed thus far regarding the meaning of work.

As Christ Himself lived up to the law of work
and labored in the sweat of His brow, we too ought
to work. Hence, we can establish the following
Christian principles of labor.

1. We ought to work with a proper intention.

Two intentions are possible. One can work
with a view to temporal gain, to earn one's bread;
or else, one can work to do God's will. The first
intention is fine, but insufficient by itself. He
who works only for temporal gain has his reward in
this world, as Christ Himself said so often in appropriate circumstances, namely, in the form of the
temporal gain itself. (Matt. 6:2-6) It is important
that we combine both intentions when we work. We
ought to work to earn bread, but we should also work
to serve God and to do His will. That is how Christ
worked. "It is the will of Him who sent me," He
said, "not my own will that I have come down from
heaven to do." (John 6:38) Christ made this intention, to do His Father's will, the rule of His every
action. It ought to be the norm of all of our actions and labors. Therefore it ought also to be
the substance of our morning prayer with which we
begin our day. If we live in this manner, our labor
will earn for us both a temporal and an eternal reward.

2. We ought to combine our work with prayer.

Our Savior counseled us, "Pray continually."
(Luke 18:1). We cannot accomplish this in the
sense that we think constantly of God. It is possible, however, if we combine work and prayer by
turning our thoughts to God often during the course
of our toil, in other words, if we frequently renew
our good intentions throughout the day. That is how
Christ worked. While He worked, he lifted His mind
to His heavenly Father time and again.

By working in this manner, the most commonplace labors which we perform take on a value
beyond what they are worth in themselves. When
the Jews offered their sacrifices - their animals
and crops - to God, it was not the externals that
counted, nor the market value of their offerings.
Rather it was the deeper meaning, the intention
whereby they recognized and appealed to the
Sovereign God as the Lord of all things. The
external form of worship was only symbolic of
the inner intention to worship God - the highest
act of which man is capable. When the Blessed
Mother of God brought to the temple the customary
offering of the poor, a pair of turtle doves, the
externals of her action were not impressive. Yet
the sacrifice had a value in God's eyes that is
beyond human measure.

That is how it ought to be when Christians
work. Your crafts and occupations may be unim-
pressive in the eyes of the world; in fact, their
external worth corresponds in no way to the dignity of one who is a child of God. They take on
an entirely different significance when they are
performed in a truly Christian spirit. The purer
the disposition with which our labors are performed, the nobler is the task itself. Men judge
by externals. God judges our intentions. It is
possible for a man to do exalted work in base
fashion, for example, if he is motivated by pride,
vanity, self-seeking. Such work is contemptible
in the eyes of God. On the other hand, a man
can perform humble tasks, as for example day-
labor or the chores of a domestic servant, with
great dignity. God will recognize such work as
elevated and dignified. The noblest disposition
is to want to please, to honor, to serve, and to
love God by the daily performance of our assigned
tasks. We please God most when we unite our own
labors with Christ's sacrifices and lay them
before God as a continuous offering from morning
to night. That is how we ought to work; that is
how we ought to combine work with prayer. If we
perform our labors in this fashion, we will not be
disturbed if God has destined us for work which is

573

not exalted in men's eyes, nor will we be puffed
up if our occupations are held in high esteem by
men. Many of the labors of God's poorest servants
have infinitely greater worth by virtue of their
consecration to God than the great deeds of others
that are recorded in the history books. On the
day of general judgement our efforts in this life
will be accorded a different valuation than men
assigned to them. It is that judgement which
counts for all eternity!

3. **We ought to work well, with a joyous
heart, and with dignity and honesty.**

This goes without saying, if we work with a
proper intention, i.e., to serve and honor God.
Work often becomes burdensome for us because we
lose our perspective and see only the lowly external value of what we do, losing sight of its
deeper significance.

If we work for God, we work well, and we perform even the most menial tasks with great diligence. The story is told about St. Ignatius, that
he once encountered a Brother who was going about
his duties in a careless manner. Ignatius asked
him, "Brother, for whom are you working?" The
brother answered, " I work for God, for the honor
of God." St. Ignatius responded, "If you were
merely working for some human being, your work
would be unacceptable and slipshod. How much
worse it is if you are working for God." This
thought, that even when we carry out the most
menial chore we are doing it for God, can serve
as the most powerful incentive for us to do even
such humble tasks with great care.

Also, if we are working for God, we will
perform all of our labors honorably, taking great
pains to avoid even the slightest dishonesty which
is apparent only to God's discerning eye.

4. **We ought not to complain about the burdensome nature of our work.**

As we have seen, the burden of our labor is a
penalty, a penance, a thought we ought to bear always

574

in mind. When we confess our sins, the priest imposes a penance upon us. The burden of our work, on the other hand, is a penance that God Himself has imposed on all of mankind. He who suffers gladly the toil of his daily labors, ever mindful of the fact that they are an expiation for sin, such a person leads a penitential life. And even if he does not perform other dramatic acts of penance, he can fully expect that by his performance he has reduced whatever punishments he might have to suffer in the life to come.

We ought to remember too, that patient acceptance of the burden of work yields a harvest of blessings and graces even in this life, as we explained earlier. Inner peace and calm, inner satisfaction and joy are the rewards for the burdens of our labors which we can enjoy even in this life.

Finally, with regard to the discomfort of our daily tasks, we ought to call to mind often Christ Himself. If we meditate upon the life of Christ frequently during the course of our working day and dwell on the torments and agonies of our Savior, we will gladly bear our own burden without further complaint. We will recall that no one can number himself among the followers of Christ unless he sees in his own daily toils a sharing of the Cross of Christ.

5. Finally, we ought to perform our work in the state of grace.

All of our labors have merit only when they are done in union with Christ. This great truth is explained so vividly by our Savior in the parable of the vine and the branches. (John 15:1-ff). The branch lives only through the vine. Cut it off, and it wilts. By Christ's own word, that is the relationship between Him and man. He is the vine, we are the branches. Severed from Him all of our toil and labors have no value. Joined with Him we participate in the life and redemptive acts of Jesus Christ. Just as the life-giving juices flow from the vine to the branches, so, when we

are united with Christ, His infinite merits transmits themselves into our poor efforts and impart a
value that is related to the value which Christ's
own works have.

How is it possible to be joined together with
Christ in such a way that our poor works share with
Him in His redemptive task? You are all familiar
with the means: only by sanctifying grace. We can
now appreciate the immeasurable value of work performed in the state of sanctifying grace, and the
boundless misery of work performed where that grace
is lacking, in the state of sin. So long as we
have mortal sin on our souls, all of our works
and efforts are in vain and without merit before
God. They are made meritorious by the merits of
Jesus Christ, and we are cut off from participation in the merits of Christ by mortal sin. When
we are in the state of sanctifying grace, there
is a living relationship between Christ and ourselves as well as with all of our efforts, labors,
and sufferings. As the branch transmits life-giving
juices from the vine to even the tiniest twigs,
so grace and blessings flow from the infinite
merits earned by Jesus Christ to the last bead of
perspiration on the forehead of a Christian who
toils in union with Christ.

Those are the five rules of work that we must
observe in our daily tasks, if we wish to do our
work as true Christians and merit all of the blessings that flow from Christian work.

I have now concluded, with this and last year's
pastoral letters, my treatment of the virtues which
are essentially related to the national economic
welfare. We ought to recognize that a God-fearing
disposition and religion are beneficial not only for
our eternal salvation, but they are indispensible
prerequisites for our temporal welfare also.

The most wretched error of our time is the ongoing preposterious delusion that men can be made
happy without benefit of religion and Christendom.
There are certain truths which hang together like

links in a chain. They cannot be separated because
God has forged them together. These include the
following: there is no real morality without God;
there is no true knowledge of God without Christ;
there is no true Christ without His Church. Where
the Church is absent, the true knowledge of Christ
is lost. Where Christ is missing, the true understanding of God is lost. And where that understanding is lost, morality succumbs in the battle with
sinful self-seeking and sensuality, covetousness
and lust, and a proud life style. But where morality is absent, there is simply no way to promote
true human welfare. There is also no way to make
a nation truly prosperous. Men will be dominated
by their passions. Greed and sensuality will become tyrants that bring all to subjection; and in
the service of these tyrants, the strong will eventually exploit the weak, and the weak will eventually rise up against the strong. If the weak
succeed in overthrowing the strong, they themselves
will fall subject to the same tyranny and seek to
indulge their own passions. Thus the struggle
between rich and poor will continue without end,
and peace on earth becomes a mere chimera. That
is how inherently and inseparably religion and
morality are linked to the well-being of a nation.
It is true that a totally just distribution of the
goods of this earth will never occur. That is because God has committed the establishment of moral
order to free human beings, and in real life human
liberty is never totally subjected to the Divine
Will. Yet, in a truly Christian nation, the divisions between rich and poor have the best chance
of being minimized. The temporal well-being of
a nation depends ultimately on whether the little
people - the middle class and the working class -
enjoy a decent level of prosperity. Great poverty
and great riches, these are extremes that come to
the fore time and again where religion is relegated
to an inferior status. Welfare for the greater
part of a nation, that is a condition that is occasioned by the operation of morality and religion.

Above all, always hold work in high regard.
Do not judge labor by the standards of the world,

but according to the principles of your holy religion. Be sure to work always as a Christian ought to work, not merely for temporal gain, but in the spirit of your Faith. Engender in your children a respect for honest labor, and make every effort to do whatever you can to have them cultivate the virtue of industry in their young hearts. The spirit of our times works against us in this effort. The universal pleasure cult evokes a disdain for work. It stands opposed to the whole idea that God wishes us to work amid toil and unpleasantness. That is all the more reason why, dear parents, you must strive in every way possible to bring your children up with a respect for work and with a recognition that work is an obligation. Explain the matter to them so that they will recognize that God Himself gave us the command to work and not to shun honest toil. Be sure that they understand that burdensome Christian labor is the way to temporal well-being on this earth, as well as to true inner peace and eternal life. Amen.

NOTES

[1]
Translator's Note: Bishop von Ketteler was referring to his Lenten Pastoral Letter of the previous
year, 1876, entitled: Religion and the National
Welfare.

[2]
Translator's Note: The German proverb is: "An
Gottes Segen ist alles gelegen."

[3]
Henric. de Hassia Tractat. de Contractib. Inter
Opera Joann. Gerson. tom IV. Coloniae 1484. Fol.
185.

[4]
Joann Gerson de Contractib. Opp. tom. III.
Antverp. 1706, pag. 172.

<u>Christianity and Social Democracy</u>

by

Wilhelm Emmanuel von Ketteler

Bishop of Mainz

1877

Translator's Note

This work was found in unfinished form after
Bishop von Ketteler's death, which occurred on
July 13th of 1877. Parts of it were incomplete,
and there were, in fact, two slightly different
versions of it. The Bishop had also been considering two different titles until he decided on: Kann
ein katholischer Arbeiter Mitglied der socialistischen
Arbeiterpartei sein? - which translates - Can a
Catholic Worker Be a Member of the Socialist Workers'
Party? In a period not given to lengthy titles,
that came to be shortened, as in the Mumbauer text,
to: Christentum und Sozialdemokratie (Christianity
and Social Democracy). The incomplete manuscript
seems to have been published for the first time in
the third volume of biographer Otto Pfülf's three
volume work, Bischof von Ketteler in 1899. Pfülf
used the first of the two versions, for the most
part, while inserting brief portions of the second
when that seemed to him advisable for completing
certain thoughts.

Although incomplete, Christianity and Social
Democracy is a significant work. In it the Bishop
was lamenting the disappearance of those natural
intermediate associations which used to provide a
buffer between the state and the individual. He
thus provided a first glimpse at the principle of
vocational orders or organizations which even
Leo XIII did not yet directly propose, but which
Pius XI in 1931 included as an essential part of
his Encyclical Quadragesimo Anno (On Reconstruct-
ing the Social Order). Beyond that, Bishop von
Ketteler here anticipated that same Pontiff's
answer to the question whether a Catholic could
be a Socialist; and he was referring now to so-
called democratic socialism, or what Pius XI
termed less radical than the Communist variety of
socialism. Both men, of course, responded in
the negative. Such anticipation of what the
leading spokesman of his Church was to teach a

half century after the Bishop's death provides
another indication as to why Wilhelm Emmanuel
von Ketteler has come to be regarded as the
pioneer of the Roman Catholic Church's modern
social doctrine.

With the rapid spread of the Socialist Workers'
Party, the question whether one may become a member
of that Party becomes a relevant one for each and
every Catholic worker. Wherever he turns to find
work, he is urged to join the party. He has to be
able to answer this question for himself if he wishes
to appear as a reasonable and conscientious man.
This is a matter which concerns not only the worker,
however, it is of concern to any of our contemporaries
who is involved in the important happenings of our
time. It is the purpose of this writing to help
provide an answer to the question.

I feel all the more compelled to address myself to the topic because the labor movement has
undergone some significant shifts in direction
since I first wrote about this matter in my book
on Christianity and the Labor Problem (Mainz:
Kirchheim, 1863). What were then two distinct
German worker parties merged at Gotha on May 25,
1875 into the one party called the Socialist
Workers' Party. The combined forces have not only
gained considerable momentum because of the united
front they represent, but there has also been a
significant change in direction. The original
movement was predominantly a German movement concerned with the problems of our own nation, whereas
what we have now, proposes to embrace the workers
of the world; it is international in its orientation. The original movement was concerned mainly
with offering a set of practical proposals which
would serve to improve the lot of the working
class. The present-day party, on the other hand,
is preoccupied with a radical overthrow of the
present system with its particular organization
for the production and distribution of the goods
of the earth. In its place it offers the so-
called socialist society, at the same time that
more down-to-earth practical measures have been
pushed into the background. What I wrote earlier,
therefore, is no longer entirely applicable to
the changed situation, and it is necessary for
me to update that material.

585

To answer the question whether a Catholic
worker may become a member of the Socialist
Workers' Party, <u>we have to inquire first into the</u>
<u>ultimate objectives of that party</u>. Obviously
they are the determining factors as to whether
we may associate oursleves with the Party or not.
Every worker, in fact, any reasonable person ought
to know what the Socialist Workers' Party and the
masses of the people who adhere to it in our time
are after. It is the sole purpose of this article
to shed some light on the objectives of the movement, since nothing seems to me more pathetic
than the general confusion and ignorance that
prevails regarding this matter.

So that I may consider the Party's objectives with reference to our Catholic beliefs,
I propose to divide them into three categories:[1]
those which are fully justified; those which are
partly justified, but partly wrong; and those
which are totally unjustified, and downright
dangerous and evil.

I wish to emphasize, however, that I am
addressing these lines only to men of solid
Christian beliefs, not to nominal Catholics or
secularists. Anyone who does not stand firmly
on the rock of Christianity is unteachable.
Such a person will be tossed about hither and
yon from one erroneous fad to the next. There
is little hope for him, as he falls prey to
every temptation that comes his way.

I <u>The Justifiable Objectives of the German</u>
<u>Workers</u>.

The program of the Socialist Workers' Party
of Germany as announced on May 8, 1875, enumerates
the immediate practical demands for the German
workers in the last and shortest part of the whole
program under the heading: <u>The Socialist Workers'</u>
<u>Party of Germany demands within the context of the</u>
<u>present social system</u>. All of the demands are con-
tained in eight points.

586

The words, "within the context of the present social system," as well as the placing of these practical proposals at the tail end of the entire program, are highly significant. They indicate that the demands are not the main feature of the program, but some kind of an after-thought. They provide only a transitional program until such time as the real goal, the transformation of the system into a socialist state, is achieved. That is what the Socialist Workers' Party is all about, as is apparent from certain principles stated in the opening paragraphs of its program.

We had better pay close attention to the announced purpose of the socialist movement when we are arriving at our conclusions and making judgements about it.

An inevitable consequence of such a shift in emphasis is the fact that the realistic and attainable practical objectives of the workers have been allowed to recede into the background. They get only the most cursory and inadequate attention in the program itself.

＊ The problems facing the working class, which are the very real objects of valid concern, are in danger of being drawn into a web of nebulous revolutionary agitation. This eventually gives rise to the temptation to throw the baby out with the bath, so that the justifiable complaints of labor remain unheeded. Thus, the workers end up betrayed by their leaders. If one were to ask each worker individually for his honest opinion as to what ought to be done to improve his lot as a worker, you would get from him not some chimerical proposal for altering the social system, but rather the kind of specific practical proposals that we referred to earlier. That is the case, all the more so, because it is these proposals that provide the material that is exploited by agitators and which occupy the prominent place in all of the speechmaking before the people, even though it becomes a mere negligible appendix to the official Program. The people themselves are convinced that only these practical measures have any real meaning for solving the workers' problems. Still, the more the leaders become obsessed with entirely different objectives, the more the working class risks being exploited by them, and the more the achievement of their real, immediate practical measures becomes frustrated. * 2

The more importance we place on the latter, the less we can rely on the socialist program for their implementation. They deserve far greater extension and elaboration, so that the eight points referred to in that program will be included, but they will make up only a small part of what is necessary. The demands of the workers which are totally justified may be treated under three headings:

1) The achievement of an effective organization of the working class;

2) Reasonable support for worker alliances by the State;

3) Legislative protection of labor and the working class from all manner of exploitation.

I. The Organization of the Working Class.

In the dissolution of all natural associations among the great masses of the working population, we have a root cause of the difficult position the workers find themselves in virtually all civilized nations.

It is in the determination of the proper kind of organization to regulate the affairs of the working class that the root of the problem facing these people is to be found. That is true of all other natural classes of the population. One has to find the proper mode of organization to come to grips with all of the basic political problems of our time.

The dissolution of all of the ancient ties which held together the classes into which the population naturally gravitated began when the state insisted on being the one and only bond to unite all people, and viewed with a jealous eye all other lesser organizations as threats to its hegemony. That absolutist trends by states began with the absolute monarchies, and it has since spread with the French Revolution to all other forms of government. The forms varied, but the principles were always the same - the State is everything! Modern socialism is a genuine child springing from the same mother, as we shall see. The worker state that is envisioned by the socialists likewise lacks any kind of natural harmony among the various classes. It is a state comprised of an alliance of workers. In principle, such a state is therefore not social, but anti-social. It does not unite people in a manner which takes into account their great and varied differences, as would be the case in a natural kind of society. Instead, there is only the one bond holding them together, the State. That, however, is a kind of union which does not unify, any more than one could unify the different phenomena of nature by destroying their individual differences so as to force them all into the same mold. One would not be uniting them; rather one would destroy the harmony among them. It is the same with the human race. It too calls for the preservation of individual differences before we can speak about a healthy and normal society. It is no more possible to try to subject human nature to a drab uniformity imposed by the state than it is to eliminate the differences in purely natural phenomena. The individual differences in the human race give rise to class differences into which people gravitate naturally on the basis of their varied native endowments. Such different native endowments are obviously God-given, and they serve to separate things into different groups.

The absorption of all natural associations into the state structure has now reached its culmination in the liberalism of our time. The socialist worker state proposed by the socialists would carry this destructive trend even further. The liberalism we speak of has now come of age. It refers to itself as "national liberalism." We would call it "money liberalism," or, what comes to the same thing, "Jewish liberalism." Nothing is better calculated to foster the unbridled quest for money and the concentration of the entire money power in the hands of a few, than this dissolution of all of the legitimate associations which used to bind together and regulate the various lesser organisms of society. In the year 1863 liberalism made its ultimate proposals to bring about the clean slate from which it could proceed to re-structure society according to its norms. Grant them the full freedom of entry and the mobility, etc., which they ask for, and there will be no stopping the complete fulfillment of their pro-gram. Then even the last remaining natural social bonds that hold small communities together will be dissolved, to the extent that this is possible. In the process too, the socialist state proposes only one further step beyond what liberalism is trying to accomplish, the dissolution of marriage. The state would now begin to look like a parallel one in nature, where wheat and clover, etc. would all be pulverized into one gigantic mix and put into one sack. All of the alleged organization into provinces, etc., may be well-intentioned enough, but these do not offer a valid substitute for what is being destroyed. They have no real natural common bond, no separate soul, which is the true basis of individuality.

No one class of people has suffered more from this destruction of all natural social or-ganisms than the working class. No class needs the help and the protection which these natural intermediate organizations offer, more than the workers. By the protection and support which they provide, he is enabled to develop his full human personality. Without that he is shorn of the full utilization of the energies and capa-cities which are latent in his individual per-sonality. A man bereft of natural association is a man with a stunted personality. Other classes have ways of compensating in some degree

590

for the destruction of these natural social bonds.
They can do so because they enjoy a preferred
status in society, as well as money and wealth.
The possession of wealth opens up all sorts of
opportunities for a privileged status among one's
fellow men, which makes possible considerable
influence. All such avenues are not available
to the workingman. He who has money has the protection and security which money can provide. The
man who lacks money, on the other hand, and who
enjoys no special status among his fellow men,
must rely totally on the support and security
which can come from cooperation with others who
are in the same station in life, and whom he
bands together with a durable, vital association.
The state, by itself, cannot offer him the protection and the support that the various demands
of his every day existence make on him. It is
from the isolated condition that the worker now
finds himself in that all of the evils which now
beset the working class originated - a condition
that grows progressively worse day by day. From
it came the inhumane law on which the subsistence
of the greater part of our population supposedly
depends, which reduces labor to the status of a
commodity, the price of which is determined by
demand and supply. From it came the prevailing
competitive mentality where men have grown accustomed to pitting themselves against one another. From it came the drifting rootless
masses of workers who lack all ties to any
neighborhood or community. From it came the
condition where entire worker families are dependent for their livelihood upon means which
are undependable and vary from day to day.
From it, finally, comes the feeling of total
helplessness and desperation in the face of
misfortune, as when sickness or accidents befall a worker. We have these liberal principles to thank for the newest of all phenomena - that rootless, migrant band of workers
who, seduced by such principles, leave their
home towns to find work elsewhere, only to
suffer disillusionment. Then, unable to return
to the communities from which they came, they

591

are driven to desperation by the feeling of helplessness and become the easy prey for every movement which holds out the promise of aid. They
are ready to join forces with any fool or seducer
who offers them false hope.

*That is an abominable, pathetic state of
affairs which revolution and liberalism have
brought us. A large number of the demands which
the socialists make to remedy this state of affairs is justified to the extent that, if they
are not satisfied, the working class will never
be placated. There is therefore the same risk
of violent explosion as one would have if the
contents of a sealed kettle were subjected to
ever-increasing heat.   *

Associations are the answer to the great
problem - associations at all levels, but especially for the working class. We need associations that are natural to a man's station
in life, on other words, Divinely ordained
associations.

We are confronted by a difficult task.
I fear, in fact, that our age is not capable
of coming to grips with the problem. We may
have to settle for putting a few of the foundation stones in place on which some later generation may begin to build.

It is easier to tear down than to build up.
Recent centuries have demonstrated a real mastery
in the art of tearing down. There has, however,
been a lamentable impotence when it comes to re-
construction.

It appears to me that the first step toward
any successful attempt to restore to the working
class its natural bonds of organization would
have to include the acceptance of certain fundamental principles:

1. The desired organizations have to be
natural and spontaneous. That is how the ancient

592

trade and journeymen's association began. They
arose out of the nature of the situation, out
of the national characteristics and out of their
religious Faith. Since the guilds began in an
age when Roman law and institutions had not yet
had a decisive influence upon German customs,
the guilds have little in common with the Roman
workingmens' guilds. Instead, the Church with
her wisdom and grace, which are so eminently disposed toward uniting men for all good and worthwhile purposes, exercised the decisive influence.

The men of our age occupy themselves with
wiping out all traces of what is traditional,
all that comes from past history, so as to make
humanity into a kind of tabula rasa. On the
other hand, they expend all of their energies
trying to establish one, confused, ephemeral,
doctrinaire system after another. It is painfully apparent how impossible it is for such
men to establish anything that would conform
to the real nature of things. Yet, unless we
do just that, the miserable conditions that afflict our working classes cannot be eliminated.

2. The hoped for associations must once
again be associations designed for genuine
economic purposes and not for mere political
intrigues and utopian schemes.

That too poses real difficulties for our
time. Matters that are not remotely related to
politics are now politicalized, and we are not
speaking of "political" in the better sense of
the word. We mean political in the petty, narrow
partisan mold. Unfortunately, the people of our
time find such party shenanigans hard to resist,
but they fall into the same ruts time and again.

The socialists, it is true, have made a
real effort to rise above the level of interminable political rhetoric and phrase-making,
which the liberals have wallowed in. The former
have in fact proposed a few genuine issues in

place of the repetitive political sloganeering
that the liberals engage in. They have not succeeded entirely in escaping from the liberal rut,
however, as is evidenced by their animosity toward
religion. Such animosity is the stock-in-trade
of narrow-minded liberalism; in fact, liberals
impudently include it in their political program
even though it is a purely religious matter.

We need associations based on economic common
interests, not ones that are based on a half dozen
or so of the political interests that the liberals
make hollow political proclamations about - an
activity which seems to claim all of the energies
of our contemporaries.

3. Such associations must be established on
a firm moral basis which includes a keen awareness
of the dignity of one's station in life, a sense
of obligation, and a code of ethics.

That is still another consequence of the dissolution of all free associations among the working classes. It served not only to reduce human
labor to the level of a commodity, the value of
which was subject to the capricious behavior of
supply and demand, but it also demolished all
pride in one's vocation, codes of behavior, and
sense of responsibility. Solid associations nurture such codes of conduct and self-respect together with a reciprocal sense of responsibility.
The conduct of the individual members, whether
good or bad, reflects on the entire association.
This identity is one of the most vital kinds of
moral identification that is conceivable. Deception, shoddy work, lack of honor on the part of
the individual member reflects on the entire
corporate body. For that reason, the group exercises control over the members and penalizes
dishonest and dishonorable practices. That
serves as a check, and it is all lost now. The
individual answers only to himself. Every true
association must foster pride in one's calling,
along with a sense of duty to one's group and
to the rest of its members.

594

4. An association must embrace all who follow the same calling.

5. Finally, the association must have a proper measure of autonomous self-government and self-regulation.

Those are the indispensable prerequisites for a proper reorganization of the working classes. So long as liberalism reigns supreme, what with its hostility toward the Church, the institution which nurtures humanity's moral energies, we can expect nothing but misfortune. If, on the other hand, Church and State would complement and support each other, the outcome could be no other than a happy one.

We have yet to turn our attention to such attempts as have been made to date to set up associations of workers.

The so-called producers cooperatives and partnerships-in-enterprise that have appeared in isolated instances undoubtedly have a value. They serve to ameliorate the conditions of the workers, making them part owners of the enterprise rather than mere wage earners. So far, the results have unfortunately been minimal. But even if there had been greater success, only a small sector of the working class could benefit from such an approach.

The so-called Schulze-Delitzsch Societies, though not without certain dangers, also have some value. Nevertheless, it is painfully clear even now that they are not capable of making a significant contribution toward relieving the plight of the working class as a whole.

In labor unions, on the other hand, there is at least the nucleus of the kind of organization that could offer some promise. There is still some doubt as to whether unions could be transformed into true vocational associations (<u>Wirt=</u> <u>schaftsgenossenschaften</u>) and purged of their political-revolutionary character. They do

contain one valid element of truth, that organizations of workers must be formed on the basis
of their various crafts and occupations. Given
the present context, where the old bases for association have disappeared and new ones need to
be established, it would seem reasonable that a
worker ought to associate himself with an organization according to his craft or occupation. [3]

Other unions would have to be established on
a wider basis corresponding to the local organization. In the local unions individual crafts are
united and in the broader unit all crafts are
bound together. They are, of course, subject to
the risk of becoming mere pawns of revolutionary
movements. Yet, if their leadership were confined to its proper jurisdiction and forbidden
to engage in political activity, the worst could
be avoided.

So much for the first area where the state
may legitimately intervene: it may foster organization.

2. Appropriate support for workingmen's
associations by the State.

(What follows is taken from fragmentary
notes, many of them penciled which the original
publisher had great difficulty reading and organizing).

I include among these demands:

1. All that is necessary to unite them into
a vocational grouping or a grouping which is appropriate to the present industrial structure of
society.

2. Benevolent support by the state according to proper economic norms, not merely on the
basis of what seems opportune for the moment.
Avoid contrary positions. It would be a mistake
to try to obligate the state to support all workers,
as it would be to support principles....(?) [4]

3. Protection of the industrial workers against exploitation, cheating, mistreatment and tyranny.

4. A ban on female labor to protect the family and to assure the man of the services of a wife, and the children of the attention of a mother.

5. A ban on child labor.

6. Sunday rest.

7. Suppression of exploitative wages......

II. <u>Efforts That are Only Partly Justified</u>.[5]

The lack of solid organization, isolation, is just one part of the desperate plight facing the working class. The other part is the depreciated value of labor which is, to a degree,a consequence of that lack of organization. In this isolated condition, the value of a worker's labor is eventually reduced to the level of the cheapest bidders estimate. That, however, does not represent the true value of labor. It is much higher. 6

The situation becomes all the more desperate inasmuch as the worker has no other means of support than his labor. Therefore, if the value of his labor is reduced to this minimal level, it follows that his entire material standard of living is reduced to the minimum.

The so-called Workers' Party wants to restore the value of labor to a proper level - a value that is totally depreciated at present. But the Party is striving to accomplish this legitimate goal by illegitimate means. Since it has no proper conception of the nature of labor, the Party cannot find the proper norm for rewarding labor in the distribution process.

<u>Si Quis no vult operari, nec manducet</u> (Thess. 3:1)[7] This passage establishes labor as the proper basis for the satisfaction of man's temporal wants.

III <u>Endeavors That are Highly Questionable</u>.

The so-called Workers' Party has departed from these legitimate, practical endeavors to go chasing instead after solutions that are beyond reach, solutions which would require that the present mode of production be turned upside down and which could only be achieved by bloody insurrection. And after all is said and done, the outcome would still be, at best, highly dubious and, at worst, fraught with great danger.

The so-called Workers' Party pretends to concern itself with the various practical and useful measures whenever its agitators get up to address an assembly of workingmen, in order to hold the interest and attention of the rank and file of the workers. That is because workers, by and large, are only interested in practical measures. The leaders of the party, however, humor the workers, whereas they themselves are only interested in their own utopian schemes about which workers are kept in the dark.

This adds up to a massive injustice to the workers and to their cause. What is it that they are really after? What is their proposed system all about?

I want to express myself in plain language so that people can understand what I am saying. I find it deplorable that so many of the leaders of the social party explain this important part of their program in language that is so confusing and obscure that one cannot help but wonder whether they themselves know what they are talking about. The workers, to be sure, cannot figure out what they are trying to say.

Their basic principle: all goods are divisible into two categories, those which are destined for consumption, and those which are not meant to be consumed directly, but which serve as the means for producing consumer goods.

598

The former include, e.g., food and shelter; the latter include capital, land, and natural resources, factories and the means of transportation. Only labor is capable of producing real goods, i.e., useful goods; and only labor, therefore, confers legitimate title to private property.

The basic principle of contemporary socialism leads to the following conclusion: The private ownership of consumer goods only is legitimate. All other goods, namely, those which are used to produce consumer goods, are the common property of the state. (They do not clarify whether states, as they are now constituted, are capable of exercising this collective ownership of the means of production, or whether they have another kind of state in mind. On the face of it, it would seem to me that one form of state is as capable as any other of assuming such ownership).

Therefore, the state alone becomes the producer of all useful goods. The amount of labor input which each individual performs determines his share of the output that results from the effort of all labor combined. It matters not whether one performs manual labor or any other kind of labor, so long as it generates utility for society, i.e., the work of a judge, an official, a teacher, etc. One kind of labor is like every other kind. Those who now own capital, land, etc., will be paid off in consumer goods.

Where will such a system lead?

1. All property owners would have to surrender title to their property, and they would receive consumer goods or claims to such goods.... ⁸

If all fantasies were to become realities, and if everyone were well-fed in some such worker state, I would still rather eat my potatoes which I myself plant, and wear the skins of animals which I myself raise, and thereby enjoy freedom rather than the slavery of a worker state where I get

599

to eat everything I want.

Here is what is so objectionable about the
whole scheme. Do we want to live in bondage,
revert to a slave society without personal
freedom.......? ....Basic denial of concupiscence in all men! Only he can help who
can master the evil in himself and fight evil
outside. 9

NOTES

1

Elsewhere Ketteler had formulated his plan and outline for this text as follows: "Can a Catholic associate himself with the aims of the Social Democratic Party?   To answer this question, we have to
divide those aims into three classes:
1.   Those which are justified.
2.   Those whose justification is very questionable
     and whose results are definitely illusory.
3.   Those which are completely objectionable and
     absolutely pernicious."

2

Paragraphs set off by asterisks are taken from a
second version of the same portion of the text and
inserted into this one wherever they definitely
apply.   Otherwise the first version is given preference because it is more concise, complete, and
interesting overall.

3

In any case, Ketteler noted also four reservations
regarding such unions, but only the first of these
is presented with complete clarity: "One reservation is that they manifest a definite socialist
orientation.   Another would be, if they are regarded
as obligatory by the state...."   This entire passage
dealing with unions is so illegible that it is impossible to vouch for its accuracy.   However, what
is here appears to follow the author's train of
thought.

4

Translator's Note: At this point the text has
omissions and is unclear.

5

In the second version there were only two main
divisions: I.   Legitimate worker aspirations;
II. Aims which are not legitimate.   The three
divisions used in the first version are presented
here.   Pfülf notes that the thoughts contained in
the entire second division were found only in the
brief and fragmentary form that is presented here.

6
Translator's Note: The German word, Ausführung"
contained in parenthesis follows this sentence.
It may be translated: explain more fully; or,
support with arguments.
7
Translator's Note: "....the man who refuses to
work must be left to starve."
8
The section dealing with workers' aims breaks off
here.
9
This thought recurs in Ketteler's writings as, for
example, on a scrap of paper found among his belong-
ings, under the caption: "Two concepts are lacking
in modern man: 1) The presence of evil in all persons.
Contemporary man acknowledges only evil in individual
phenomena and, as a matter of fact, only in others;
he does not accept the fact that evil in all mankind is the legacy of original sin. Therefore,
all of his calculations end up being wrong; 2) A
recognition of God's help. He recognizes only self-
help.